CHILDREN'S ISSUES, LAWS AND PROGRAMS

CHILD PROTECTION, THE COURTS AND SOCIAL WORKERS

CHILDREN'S ISSUES, LAWS AND PROGRAMS

Child Development and Child Poverty
Anselm Fiedler and Isidor Kuester (Editors)
2010 ISBN: 978-1-60741-816-0

Child Labor in America
Ian C. Rivera and Natasha M. Howard (Editors)
2010 ISBN: 978-1-60876-769-4

Child Protection, the Courts and Social Workers
Terrance R. Langely (Editor)
2010 ISBN: 978-1-60741-279-3

Adam Walsh Child Protection and Safety Act: Analysis and Law
Terrell G. Sandoval (Editor)
2010 ISBN: 978-1-61668-808-0
2010 ISBN: 978-1-61668-878-3 (E-book)

When Abuse and Neglect Occur at Residential Treatment Facilities
Kirsten S. Madsen (Editor)
2010 ISBN: 978-1-60876-965-0
2010. ISBN: 978-1-61728-054-2 (E-book)

Child Abduction Resources
Melanie H. Wilson (Editor)
2010 ISBN: 978-1-61668-247-7

Working with the Courts in Child Protection
Raymond T. Devon (Editor)
2010 ISBN: 978-1-61668-303-0
2010 ISBN: 978-1-61668-426-6 (E-book)

Load Carriage in School Children: Epidemiology and Exercise Science
Youlian Hong (Editor)
2010. ISBN: 978-1-61668-622-2
2010. ISBN: 978-1-61728-081-8 (E-book)

Children's Social Competence: Theory and Intervention
Melissa L. Greene, Jo R. Hariton, Andrew L. Robins and Barbara L. Flye
2010. ISBN: 978-1-61668-861-5
2010. ISBN: 978-1-61728-640-7 (E-book)

CHILDREN'S ISSUES, LAWS AND PROGRAMS

CHILD PROTECTION, THE COURTS AND SOCIAL WORKERS

TERRANCE R. LANGELY
EDITOR

Nova Science Publishers, Inc.

New York

Copyright © 2010 by Nova Science Publishers, Inc.

For permission to use material from this book please contact us:
Telephone 631-231-7269; Fax 631-231-8175
Web Site: http://www.novapublishers.com

NOTICE TO THE READER

The Publisher has taken reasonable care in the preparation of this book, but makes no expressed or implied warranty of any kind and assumes no responsibility for any errors or omissions. No liability is assumed for incidental or consequential damages in connection with or arising out of information contained in this book. The Publisher shall not be liable for any special, consequential, or exemplary damages resulting, in whole or in part, from the readers' use of, or reliance upon, this material. Any parts of this book based on government reports are so indicated and copyright is claimed for those parts to the extent applicable to compilations of such works.

Independent verification should be sought for any data, advice or recommendations contained in this book. In addition, no responsibility is assumed by the publisher for any injury and/or damage to persons or property arising from any methods, products, instructions, ideas or otherwise contained in this publication.

This publication is designed to provide accurate and authoritative information with regard to the subject matter covered herein. It is sold with the clear understanding that the Publisher is not engaged in rendering legal or any other professional services. If legal or any other expert assistance is required, the services of a competent person should be sought. FROM A DECLARATION OF PARTICIPANTS JOINTLY ADOPTED BY A COMMITTEE OF THE AMERICAN BAR ASSOCIATION AND A COMMITTEE OF PUBLISHERS.

LIBRARY OF CONGRESS CATALOGING-IN-PUBLICATION DATA
Child protection, the courts and social workers / editor, Terrance R. Langely.
 p. cm.
Includes index.
ISBN 978-1-60741-279-3 (hbk)
1. Child welfare--United States. 2. Child welfare workers--United States.
3. Children--Legal status, laws, etc.--United States. I. Langely, Terrance R.
HV741.C48755 2009
362.70973--dc22
                            2009051578

Published by Nova Science Publishers, Inc. ✦ *New York*

CONTENTS

PREFACE

Each day the safety and well-being of children across the nation are threatened by child abuse and neglect. Intervening effectively in the lives of these children and their families is not the sole responsibility of a single agency or professional group, but a shared community concern. This book provides a foundation for understanding child maltreatment and the roles and responsibilities of various practitioners in its prevention, identification, assessment, and treatment. The courts play a central role in making decisions regarding the protection of children who have been maltreated. Understanding this process is crucial for any professional involved in child protection. By having a thorough knowledge of this legal process and by working in partnership with the courts, child protective services (CPS) caseworkers and other professionals can work toward the safety, permanency, and well-being of children more effectively.

Chapter 1 - Child abuse and neglect is a community concern. Each community has a legal and moral obligation to promote the safety, permanency, and well-being of children, which includes responding effectively to child maltreatment. At the state and local levels, professionals assume various roles and responsibilities ranging from prevention, identification, and reporting of child maltreatment to intervention, assessment, and treatment. Child protective services (CPS) agencies, along with law enforcement, play a central role in receiving and investigating reports of child maltreatment. To protect children from harm, CPS also relies on community members to identify and report suspected cases of child maltreatment, including physical abuse, sexual abuse, neglect, and psychological maltreatment. Many community professionals (including health care providers, mental health professionals, educators, and legal and court system personnel) are involved in responding to child abuse and neglect and providing needed services. In addition, community-based agency staff, substance abuse treatment providers, domestic violence victim advocates, clergy, extended family members, and concerned citizens also play important roles in supporting families and keeping children safe.

This manual—the first in the series—provides an overview of the problem of child abuse and neglect and the prevention and intervention processes. It describes not only the activities involved in child protection, but also the roles and responsibilities of various community members in conducting these activities and working collaboratively. It is intended to provide the basic information that professionals and the public need to become involved in, and enhance, their community's response to child maltreatment. While the manual is comprehensive in scope and touches on major issues, it cannot reflect all the detailed information related to this complex problem. It is intended, therefore, as a starting point.

This manual answers the following 10 questions:

- What are the philosophical tenets of child protection?
- What is child maltreatment?
- What is the scope of the problem?
- What factors contribute to abuse and neglect?
- What are the consequences of abuse and neglect?
- What can be done to prevent abuse and neglect?
- Which laws and policies guide public intervention in child maltreatment?
- What does the child protection process look like?
- Who should be involved in child protection at the community level?
- How can organizations work together to protect children?

Chapter 2 - Child protective services (CPS), a division within state and local social services, is at the center of every community's child protection efforts. In most jurisdictions, CPS is the agency mandated by law to conduct an initial assessment or investigation of reports of child abuse and neglect. It also offers services to families and children where maltreatment has occurred or is likely to occur.

CPS does not work alone. Many community professionals—including law enforcement officers, health care providers, mental health professionals, educators, legal and court system personnel, and substitute care providers—are involved in efforts to prevent, identify, investigate, and treat child abuse and neglect. In addition, community-based and faith-based organizations, substance abuse treatment facilities, advocates for victims of domestic violence, extended family members, and concerned citizens, among others, also play important roles in supporting families and keeping children safe from harm. Typically, CPS is the lead agency in coordinating the efforts of the various disciplines working to protect children and to educate the community about the problems of child abuse and neglect.

This manual, *Child Protective Services: A Guidefor Caseworkers*, provides the fundamental information that CPS professionals must know toperform essential casework functions. The manualdescribes:

- The philosophical basis on which CPS is founded;
- The responsibilities of CPS and its roles and relationships with other community agencies and professionals;
- The nature of the "helping relationship" and use of authority in working with children and families;
- The purposes, key decisions, and practice issuesfor the following stages of the CPS process:

- Intake
- Initial assessment or investigation
- Comprehensive family assessment
- Planning
- Service provision

- Evaluation of family progress
- Case closure
- The effective documentation of actions in case records and information systems;
- The strategies for casework supervision, training, consultation, and support.

Appendices to this manual include a glossary, sample casework tools, and references to additional publications and organizations with information on child protection.

Child abuse and neglect is a complex problem, and child protection is a challenging responsibility. No single publication can provide all the information needed to promote effective CPS practice, explore all of the relevant issues, or reflect the multitude of policy and practice variations in place across the country. This manual, however, provides a starting point and a solid foundation for casework practice that should be augmented through training, other professional development activities, and experience.

CPS workers are encouraged to read *A Coordinated Response to Child Abuse and Neglect: The Foundation for Practice*. That manual, the first in the series, answers the following 10 questions:

- What are the philosophical tenets of child protection?
- What is child maltreatment?
- What is the scope of the problem?
- What factors contribute to abuse and neglect?
- What are the consequences of abuse and neglect?
- What can be done to prevent abuse and neglect?
- Which laws and policies guide public intervention in child maltreatment?
- What does the child protection process look like?
- Who should be involved in child protection at the community level?
- How can organizations work together to protect children?

This manual, the second in the series, recapitulates some of the most important points of the first manual.

Chapter 3 - The courts play a central role in making decisions regarding the protection of children who have been maltreated. Understanding this process is crucial for any professional involved in child protection. By having a thorough knowledge of this legal process and by working in partnership with the courts, child protective services (CPS) caseworkers and other professionals can work toward the safety, permanency, and well-being of children more effectively.

Child maltreatment cases are handled in a variety of courts. Thus, the rules and procedures that govern these cases may differ depending on the *type* of proceeding within which an allegation of abuse is brought, the laws governing the court involved, and the local practice in a particular court.

In recent years, a number of reforms have addressed the unique nature of child maltreatment and the special needs of its victims. Both legislative and judicial efforts have improved the ability and flexibility of the courts to respond to allegations of abuse or neglect. Courts now have more alternatives and resources with which to work when faced with a case where abuse or neglect has been established by the required burden of proof under state law.

This manual provides the basic information needed by CPS caseworkers to work successfully with the courts. It introduces concepts and terminology associated with the courts, describes the key court processes, and presents practical information to help caseworkers prepare for what can be an overwhelming experience. The manual describes:

- The general or common court system;
- The powers of the court and the rights of parents and children in child maltreatment cases;
- The interplay between child maltreatment legislation and caseworker practice;
- The juvenile court process;
- The criminal court process;
- Domestic relations and other court proceedings;
- The issues involved in going to court;
- The relationship between CPS caseworkers and the court;
- Court improvement and best practices.

Appendices to this manual include a glossary, resource listings, and guidelines for CPS caseworkers for permanency and review hearings.

Various terms are used within the field and throughout communities to describe CPS agencies and caseworkers, including:

- CPS agency:

- Department of Social Services – Child welfare agency
- Social services
- Family services
- CPS caseworker:

- Caseworker
- Social worker
- Social caseworker
- Worker

In many settings, there is little or no distinction among these terms. For the sake of clarity and ease of understanding, this manual primarily uses "CPS" and "CPS caseworker."

One note of caution is necessary. On its own, this manual cannot adequately prepare any professional, legal or non legal, to practice in the area of child protection. Consultation with a skilled legal specialist is *critical*, as is comprehensive training on working with the courts, particularly with respect to unique state laws and local practices.

Information and suggestions incorporated throughout this manual do not necessarily imply endorsement by the U.S. Department of Health and Human Services or official interpretation of Federal requirements.

In: Child Protection, the Courts and Social Workers
Editor: Terrance R. Langely

ISBN: 978-1-60741-279-3
© 2010 Nova Science Publishers, Inc.

Chapter 1

A COORDINATED RESPONSE TO CHILD ABUSE AND NEGLECT: THE FOUNDATION FOR PRACTICE

Jill Goldman, Marsha K. Salus, Deborah Wolcott and Kristie Y. Kennedy

1. PURPOSE AND OVERVIEW

Child abuse and neglect is a community concern. Each community has a legal and moral obligation to promote the safety, permanency, and well-being of children, which includes responding effectively to child maltreatment. At the State and local levels, professionals assume various roles and responsibilities ranging from prevention, identification, and reporting of child maltreatment to intervention, assessment, and treatment. Child protective services (CPS) agencies, along with law enforcement, play a central role in receiving and investigating reports of child maltreatment. To protect children from harm, CPS also relies on community members to identify and report suspected cases of child maltreatment, including physical abuse, sexual abuse, neglect, and psychological maltreatment. Many community professionals (including health care providers, mental health professionals, educators, and legal and court system personnel) are involved in responding to child abuse and neglect and providing needed services. In addition, community-based agency staff, substance abuse treatment providers, domestic violence victim advocates, clergy, extended family members, and concerned citizens also play important roles in supporting families and keeping children safe.

This manual—the first in the series—provides an overview of the problem of child abuse and neglect and the prevention and intervention processes. It describes not only the activities involved in child protection, but also the roles and responsibilities of various community members in conducting these activities and working collaboratively. It is intended to provide the basic information that professionals and the public need to become involved in, and enhance, their community's response to child maltreatment. While the manual is comprehensive in scope and touches on major issues, it cannot reflect all the detailed information related to this complex problem. It is intended, therefore, as a starting point.

This manual answers the following 10 questions:

- What are the philosophical tenets of child protection?
- What is child maltreatment?
- What is the scope of the problem?
- What factors contribute to abuse and neglect?
- What are the consequences of abuse and neglect?
- What can be done to prevent abuse and neglect?
- Which laws and policies guide public intervention in child maltreatment?
- What does the child protection process look like?
- Who should be involved in child protection at the community level?
- How can organizations work together to protect children?

2. WHAT ARE THE PHILOSOPHICAL TENETS OF CHILD PROTECTION?

The importance of the family in U.S. society is central to the Nation's history and tradition. Parents have a fundamental right to raise their children as they see fit, and society presumes that parents will act in their children's best interest. When parents do not protect their children from harm and meet their basic needs—as with cases of child abuse and neglect—society has a responsibility to intervene to protect the health and welfare of these children. Any intervention into family life on behalf of children must be guided by State and Federal laws, sound professional standards for practice, and strong philosophical underpinnings. This chapter presents key principles underscored in Federal legislation and the philosophical tenets on which the community's responsibility for child protection is based.

Key Principles of Child Protection

The key principles guiding child protection are largely based on Federal statutes, primarily delineated in the Child Abuse Prevention and Treatment Act (CAPTA) and the Adoption and Safe Families Act (ASFA). CAPTA, in its original inception, was signed into law in 1974 (P.L. 93-247) and is reauthorized by Congress every 5 years. As of the publication of this manual, CAPTA is in the process of its latest reauthorization. ASFA was signed into law in 1997 (P.L. 105-89) and built upon earlier laws and reforms to promote the safety and well-being of maltreated children. These laws and other guiding legislation are referenced throughout this publication and are specifically discussed in "Federal Legislation and Programs" in Chapter 8. ASFA promotes three national goals for child protection:

- **Safety.** All children have the right to live in an environment free from abuse and neglect. The safety of children is the paramount concern that must guide child protection efforts.

- **Permanency.** Children need a family and a permanent place to call home. A sense of continuity and connectedness is central to a child's healthy development.
- **Child and family well-being.**Children deserve nurturing environments in which their physical, emotional, educational, and social needs are met. Child protection practices must take into account each child's needs and should promote healthy development.

In addition, ASFA underscored the importance of accountability of service delivery systems in achieving positive outcomes for children related to each of these goals.

Philosophical Tenets

The following philosophical tenets expand upon the principles set forth in ASFA and the values that underlie sound practices in community responses to child abuse and neglect:

- **Prevention programs are necessary to strengthen families and reduce the likelihood of child abuse and neglect.** Child maltreatment results from a combination of factors: psychological, social, situational, and societal. Factors that may contribute to an increased risk for child abuse and neglect include, for example, family structure, poverty, substance abuse, poor housing conditions, teenage pregnancy, domestic and community violence, mental illness, and lack of support from extended families and community members. To reduce the occurrence of maltreatment, communities should develop and implement prevention programs that support children and families.
- **The responsibility for addressing child maltreatment is shared among community professionals and citizens.** No single agency, individual, or discipline has all the necessary knowledge, skills, or resources to provide the assistance needed by abused and neglected children and their families. While public child protective services (CPS) agencies, law enforcement, and courts have legal mandates and primary responsibility for responding to child maltreatment, other service providers working with children and families—along with community members—play important roles in supporting families and protecting children. To be effective in addressing this complex problem, the combined expertise and resources of interdisciplinary agencies and professionals are needed.
- **A safe and permanent home is the best place for a child to grow up.** Most children are best cared for in their own families. Children naturally develop a strong attachment to their families and when removed from them, they typically experience loss, confusion, and other negative emotions. Maintaining the family as a unit preserves important relationships with parents, siblings, and extended family members and allows children to grow and develop within their own culture and environment.
- **When parents (or caregivers) are unable or unwilling to fulfill their responsibilities to provide adequate care and to keep their children safe, CPS has the mandate to intervene.** Both laws and good practice maintain that

interventions should be designed to help parents protect their children in the least intrusive manner possible. Interventions should build on the family's strengths and address the factors that contribute to the risk of maltreatment. Reasonable efforts must be made to maintain child safety and keep the children with their families except when there is significant risk to child safety. Referral to court and removal of children from their families should only be done when it is determined that children cannot be kept safely in their own homes.

- **Most parents want to be good parents and have the strength and capacity, when adequately supported, to care for their children and keep them safe.** Underlying CPS intervention is the belief that people have the strength and potential to change their lives. Professionals must search for and identify the strengths and the inner resiliencies in families that provide the foundation for change.

- **To help families protect their children and meet their basic needs, the community's response must demonstrate respect for every person involved.** All people deserve to be treated with respect and dignity. This means showing respect for a person, while not necessarily approving or condoning his or her actions. In addition to caregivers and children, service providers should demonstrate respect for mothers, fathers, grandparents, other family members, and the family's support network.

- **Services must be individualized and tailored.** While people may have similar problems, there are elements that will vary from family to family. In addition, each family's strengths and resources are different. The community's response, therefore, must be customized to reflect the particular circumstances, strengths, and needs of each family.

- **Child protection and service delivery approaches should be family centered.** Parents, children, their extended families, and support networks (e.g., the faith community, teachers, health care providers, substitute caregivers) should be actively involved as partners in developing and implementing appropriate plans and services to reduce or eliminate the risk of maltreatment. Tapping into the strengths and resources of a family's natural support network is fundamental to enhancing family functioning.

- **Interventions need to be sensitive to the cultures, beliefs, and customs of all families.** Professionals must acknowledge and show respect for the values and traditions of families from diverse cultural, ethnic, and religious backgrounds. To become culturally competent, professionals must first understand themselves and the effects of their own background on their values, behaviors, and judgments about others.[1] In working with children and families different from themselves, professionals need to be aware of the context of the family's culture and background in order to help provide access to culturally relevant services and solutions.

- **To best protect a child's overall well-being, agencies must assure that children move to permanency as quickly as possible.** Along with developing plans to facilitate reunification of children, agencies must develop alternative plans for permanence from the time the child enters care. For those children who cannot be safely reunified with their families, timely efforts must be made to ensure a stable, secure, and permanent home for the child through adoption or other permanent living arrangements.

3. WHAT IS CHILD MALTREATMENT?

To prevent and respond to child abuse and neglect effectively, there needs to be a common understanding of the definitions of those actions and omissions that constitute child maltreatment. Unfortunately, there is no single, universally applied definition of child abuse and neglect. Over the past several decades, different stakeholders—including State and Federal legislative bodies, agency officials, and researchers—have developed definitions of maltreatment for different purposes. Definitions vary across these groups and within them. For example, legal definitions describing the different forms of child maltreatment for reporting and criminal prosecution purposes are found mainly in State statutes, and definitions vary from State to State. Similarly, agency guidelines for accepting reports, conducting investigations, and providing interventions vary from State to State and sometimes from county to county. In addition, researchers use varying methods to measure and define abuse and neglect, making it difficult to compare findings across studies. Despite the differences, there are commonalities across definitions. This chapter describes sources of definitions in Federal and State laws and summarizes those elements commonly recognized as child maltreatment.

Definitions in Federal Law

The Child Abuse Prevention and Treatment Act (CAPTA) provides minimum standards for defining physical child abuse, child neglect, and sexual abuse that States must incorporate in their statutory definitions to receive Federal funds. Under CAPTA, child abuse and neglect means:

- Any recent act or failure to act on the part of a parent or caretaker that results in death, serious physical or emotional harm, sexual abuse, or exploitation;
- An act or failure to act that presents an imminent risk of serious harm.

The definition of child abuse and neglect refers specifically to parents and other caregivers. A "child" under this definition generally means a person who is under the age of 18 or who is not an emancipated minor. In cases of child sexual abuse, a "child" is one who has not attained the age of 18 or the age specified by the child protection law of the State in which the child resides, whichever is younger.

While CAPTA provides definitions for sexual abuse and the special cases related to withholding or failing to provide medically indicated treatment, it does not provide specific definitions for other types of maltreatment—physical abuse, neglect, or psychological maltreatment.

CAPTA DEFINITION OF SEXUAL ABUSE

CAPTA defines "sexual abuse" as:

"[T]he employment, use, persuasion, inducement, enticement, or coercion of any child to engage in, or assist any other person to engage in, any sexually explicit conduct or simulation of such conduct for the purpose of producing a visual depiction of such conduct;"

"[T]he rape, and in cases of caretaker or inter-familial relationships, statutory rape, molestation, prostitution, or other form of sexual exploitation of children, or incest with children."

CAPTA DEFINITION OF WITHHOLDING OF MEDICALLY INDICATED TREATMENT

CAPTA defines the "withholding of medically indicated treatment" as:

"[T]he failure to respond to the infant's life-threatening conditions by providing treatment...which, in the treating physician's reasonable medical judgment, will be most likely to be effective in ameliorating or correcting all such conditions."

The term "withholding of medically indicated treatment" does not include the failure to provide treatment (other than appropriate nutrition, hydration, and medication) to an infant when, in the treating physician's reasonable medical judgment:

- The infant is chronically and irreversibly comatose;
- The provision of such treatment would merely prolong dying;
- The provision of such treatment would not be effective in ameliorating or correcting all of the infant's life-threatening conditions;
- The provision of such treatment would otherwise be futile in terms of the survival of the infant;
- The provision of such treatment would be virtually futile in terms of the survival of the infant, and the treatment itself under such circumstances would be inhumane.[2]

Sources of Definitions in State Law

While the Federal legislation sets minimum definitional standards, each State is responsible for providing its own definition of maltreatment within civil and criminal contexts. The problem of child maltreatment is generally subject to State laws (both statutes and case law) and administrative regulations. Definitions of child abuse and neglect are located primarily in three places within each State's statutory code:

- **Mandatory child maltreatment reporting statutes (civil laws)** provide definitions of child maltreatment to guide those individuals mandated to identify and report suspected child abuse. These reports activate the child protection process. (See

Chapter 9, "What Does the Child Protection Process Look Like?," for more information on mandated reporters and reporting procedures.)

- **Criminal statutes** define those forms of child maltreatment that are criminally punishable. In most jurisdictions, child maltreatment is criminally punishable when one or more of the following statutory crimes have been committed: homicide, murder, manslaughter, false imprisonment, assault, battery, criminal neglect and abandonment, emotional and physical abuse, child pornography, child prostitution, computer crimes, rape, deviant sexual assault, indecent exposure, child endangerment, and reckless endangerment.
- **Juvenile court jurisdiction statutes** provide definitions of the circumstances necessary for the court to have jurisdiction over a child alleged to have been abused or neglected. When the child's safety cannot be ensured in the home, these statutes allow the court to take custody of a child and to order specific treatment services for the parents and child.

Together, these legal definitions of child abuse and neglect determine the minimum standards of care and protection for children and serve as important guidelines for professionals regarding those acts and omissions that constitute child maltreatment.

Child protective services (CPS) workers use statutory definitions of child maltreatment to determine whether maltreatment has occurred and when intervention into family life is necessary. For particular localities within a State, local CPS policies and procedures, based on statutes and regulations, further define different types of maltreatment and the conditions under which intervention and services are warranted.

STATE STATUTES

To review a summary of reporting laws, visit the State Statutes section of the National Clearinghouse on Child Abuse and Neglect's Web site at www.calib.com/nccanch/statutes

---

General Definitions by Type of Maltreatment

There are four commonly recognized forms of child abuse or maltreatment:

- Physical
- Sexual
- Neglect
- Psychological

There is great variation from State to State regarding the details and specificity of child abuse definitions, but it is still possible to identify commonalities among each different type of child maltreatment. These commonalities, in part, reflect societal views of parental actions that are seen as improper or unacceptable because they place children at a risk of physical and emotional harm.

Physical abuse

Generally, physical abuse is characterized by physical injury, such as bruises and fractures that result from:

- Punching
- Beating
- Kicking
- Biting
- Shaking
- Throwing
- Stabbing
- Choking
- Hitting with a hand, stick, strap, or other object
- Burning

Although an injury resulting from physical abuse is not accidental, the parent or caregiver may not have intended to hurt the child. The injury may have resulted from severe discipline, including injurious spanking, or physical punishment that is inappropriate to the child's age or condition. The injury may be the result of a single episode or of repeated episodes and can range in severity from minor marks and bruising to death.

Some cultural practices are generally not defined as physical abuse, but may result in physically hurting children. For example:

- "Coining" or *cao gio*—a practice to treat illness by rubbing the body forcefully with a coin or other hard object.
- *Moxabustion*—an Asian folkloric remedy that burns the skin.

As Howard Dubowitz, a leading researcher in the field, explains: "While cultural practices are generally respected, if the injury or harm is significant, professionals typically work with parents to discourage harmful behavior and suggest preferable alternatives."[3]

Sexual abuse

Child sexual abuse generally refers to sexual acts, sexually motivated behaviors involving children, or sexual exploitation of children.[4] Child sexual abuse includes a wide range of behaviors, such as:

- Oral, anal, or genital penile penetration;
- Anal or genital digital or other penetration;
- Genital contact with no intrusion;
- Fondling of a child's breasts or buttocks;
- Indecent exposure;
- Inadequate or inappropriate supervision of a child's voluntary sexual activities;
- Use of a child in prostitution, pornography, Internet crimes, or other sexually exploitative activities.

Sexual abuse includes both touching offenses (fondling or sexual intercourse) and nontouching offenses (exposing a child to pornographic materials) and can involve varying degrees of violence and emotional trauma. The most commonly reported cases involve incest—sexual abuse occurring among family members, including those in biological families, adoptive families, and step-families.[5] Incest most often occurs within a father-daughter relationship; however, mother-son, father-son, and sibling-sibling incest also occurs. Sexual abuse is also sometimes committed by other relatives or caretakers, such as aunts, uncles, grandparents, cousins, or the boyfriend or girlfriend of a parent.

Child neglect

Child neglect, the most common form of child maltreatment, is generally characterized by omissions in care resulting in significant harm or risk of significant harm. Neglect is frequently defined in terms of a failure to provide for the child's basic needs—deprivation of adequate food, clothing, shelter, supervision, or medical care. Neglect laws often exclude circumstances in which a child's needs are not met because of poverty or an inability to provide. In addition, many States establish religious exemptions for parents who choose not to seek medical care for their children due to religious beliefs that may prohibit medical intervention.

The Department of Health and Human Services' *Third National Incidence Study of Child Abuse and Neglect* (NIS-3)[6] is the single most comprehensive source of information about the current incidence of child maltreatment in the United States. NIS-3 worked with researchers and practitioners to define physical, educational, and emotional neglect in a succinct and clear manner, as described below.

Physical neglect

- **Refusal of health care**—the failure to provide or allow needed care in accordance with recommendations of a competent health care professional for a physical injury, illness, medical condition, or impairment.
- **Delay in health care**—the failure to seek timely and appropriate medical care for a serious health problem that any reasonable layman would have recognized as needing professional medical attention.
- **Abandonment**—the desertion of a child without arranging for reasonable care and supervision.
- **Expulsion**—other blatant refusals of custody, such as permanent or indefinite expulsion of a child from the home without adequate arrangement for care by others or refusal to accept custody of a returned runaway.
- **Inadequate supervision**—leaving a child unsupervised or inadequately supervised for extended periods of time or allowing the child to remain away from home overnight without the parent or caretaker knowing or attempting to determine the child's whereabouts.
- **Other physical neglect**—includes inadequate nutrition, clothing, or hygiene; conspicuous inattention to avoidable hazards in the home; and other forms of reckless disregard of the child's safety and welfare (e.g., driving with the child while intoxicated, leaving a young child in a car unattended).

Educational Neglect

- **Permitted chronic truancy**—habitual absenteeism from school averaging at least 5 days a month if the parent or guardian is informed of the problem and does not attempt to intervene.
- **Failure to enroll or other truancy**—failure to register or enroll a child of mandatory school age, causing the child to miss at least 1 month of school; or a pattern of keeping a school-aged child home without valid reasons.
- **Inattention to special education need**—refusal to allow or failure to obtain recommended remedial education services or neglect in obtaining or following through with treatment for a child's diagnosed learning disorder or other special education need without reasonable cause.

Emotional Neglect

- **Inadequate nurturing or affection**—marked inattention to the child's needs for affection, emotional support, or attention.
- **Chronic or extreme spouse abuse**—exposure to chronic or extreme spouse abuse or other domestic violence in the child's presence.
- **Permitted drug or alcohol abuse**— encouragement or permitting of drug or alcohol use by the child.
- **Permitted other maladaptive behavior**— encouragement or permitting of other maladaptive behavior (e.g., chronic delinquency, severe assault) under circumstances where the parent or caregiver has reason to be aware of the existence and seriousness of the problem but does not intervene.
- **Refusal of psychological care**—refusal to allow needed and available treatment for a child's emotional or behavioral impairment or problem in accordance with a competent professional recommendation.
- **Delay in psychological care**—failure to seek or provide needed treatment for a child's emotional or behavioral impairment or problem that any reasonable layman would have recognized as needing professional, psychological attention (e.g., suicide attempt).

SPOTLIGHT ON CHRONIC NEGLECT

One issue in defining child neglect involves consideration of "incidents" of neglect versus a pattern of behavior that indicates neglect. Susan J. Zuravin, from the University of Maryland at Baltimore School of Social Work, recommends that if some behaviors occur in a "chronic pattern," they should be considered neglectful.[7] Examples include lack of supervision, inadequate hygiene, and failure to meet a child's educational needs. This suggests that rather than focusing on individual incidents that may or may not be classified as "neglectful," one should look at an accumulation of incidents that may together constitute neglect. "If CPS focuses only on the immediate allegation before them and not the pattern reflected in multiple referrals, then many neglected children will continue to be inappropriately excluded from the CPS system."[8] For example, a family exhibiting a pattern of behavior that may constitute neglect might include frequent reports of not having enough food in the home or keeping older children home from school to watch younger children. In most CPS systems, however, the criteria for identifying neglect focuses on recent, discrete, verifiable incidents.

One study found that many children who had been referred to CPS for neglect did not receive services because their cases did not meet the criteria for "incidents" of neglect. It also found, however, that all of these children had, in fact, suffered severe developmental consequences. In recognition of this issue, the Missouri Division of Family Services (n.d.) has assigned one of its CPS staff as a "Chronic Neglect Specialist." This office defines chronic neglect as ". . . a persistent pattern of family functioning in which the caregiver has not sustained and/or met the basic needs of the children which results in harm to the child." The focus here is on the "accumulation of harm." CPS and community agencies across the country are recognizing the importance of early intervention and service provision to support families so that neglect does not become chronic or lead to other negative consequences.[9]

Psychological maltreatment

Psychological maltreatment—also known as emotional abuse and neglect—refers to "a repeated pattern of caregiver behavior or extreme incident(s) that convey to children that they are worthless, flawed, unloved, unwanted, endangered, or only of value in meeting another's needs."[10] Summarizing research and expert opinion, Stuart N. Hart, Ph.D., and Marla R. Brassard, Ph.D., present six categories of psychological maltreatment:

- Spurning (e.g., belittling, hostile rejecting, ridiculing);
- Terrorizing (e.g., threatening violence against a child, placing a child in a recognizably dangerous situation);
- Isolating (e.g., confining the child, placing unreasonable limitations on the child's freedom of movement, restricting the child from social interactions);
- Exploiting or corrupting (e.g., modeling antisocial behavior such as criminal activities, encouraging prostitution, permitting substance abuse);
- Denying emotional responsiveness (e.g., ignoring the child's attempts to interact, failing to express affection);
- Mental health, medical, and educational neglect (e.g., refusing to allow or failing to provide treatment for serious mental health or medical problems, ignoring the need for services for serious educational needs).[11]

To warrant intervention, psychological maltreatment must be sustained and repetitive. For less severe acts, such as habitual scapegoating or belittling, demonstrable harm to the child is often required for CPS to intervene.

Psychological maltreatment is the most difficult form of child maltreatment to identify. In part, the difficulty in detection occurs because the effects of psychological maltreatment, such as lags in development, learning problems, and speech disorders, are often evident in both children who have experienced and those who have *not* experienced maltreatment. Additionally, the effects of psychological maltreatment may only become evident in later developmental stages of the child's life.

Although any of the forms of child maltreatment may be found alone, they often occur in combination. Psychological maltreatment is almost always present when other forms are identified.

CASE EXAMPLES OF MALTREATMENT

Physical Abuse

During a violent fight between her mother and her mother's boyfriend, 8-year-old Kerry called 911. She told the operator that her mother's boyfriend always hit her mommy when he came home drunk. In addition, Kerry said she was worried about her 5-year-old brother, Aaron, because he tried to help their mom and the boyfriend punched him in the face. As a result, Aaron fell, hit his head on the coffee table, and had not moved since. The operator heard yelling in the background and the mother screaming, "Get off the phone!" When the police and paramedics arrived, Aaron was unconscious and the mother had numerous bruises on her face.

Child Neglect

Robert and Carlotta are the parents of a 9-month-old son named Ruiz. Robert and Carlotta used various drugs together until Robert was arrested and sent to prison for distributing cocaine. Since Robert's arrest, Carlotta has been living with different relatives and friends. Recently, she left her son with her sister who also has a history of drug use. Her sister then went to a local bar and left Ruiz unattended. After hearing the baby boy cry for over an hour, the neighbors called the police. When Carlotta arrived to pick up Ruiz, the police and the CPS worker were also there. It appeared that she had been using drugs.

Sexual Abuse

Jody, age 11, said that she was asleep in her bedroom and that her father came in and took off his robe and underwear. She stated that he got into bed with her and pulled up her nightgown and put his private part on her private part. She stated that he pushed hard and it hurt. Jody said that the same thing had happened before while her mother was at work. Jody stated that she told her mother, but her father insisted that she was telling a lie.

Psychological Abuse

Jackie is a 7-year-old girl who lives with her mother. Jackie's mother often screams at her, calls her degrading names, and threatens to kill her when Jackie misbehaves. Jackie doesn't talk in class anymore, doesn't have any friends in her neighborhood, and has lost a lot of weight.

4. WHAT IS THE SCOPE OF THE PROBLEM?

Each year, hundreds of thousands of children in the United States are victims of maltreatment. Knowledge of the scope of the problem is drawn primarily from data reported by State child protective service (CPS) agencies to the National Child Abuse and Neglect Data System (NCANDS). Not all maltreatment, however, is known by the authorities. This chapter summarizes the 2000 NCANDS findings related to the number and characteristics of child maltreatment victims and perpetrators reported to CPS and also discusses estimates of the actual incidence of abuse and neglect, including incidents that are not reported to CPS.

Reported Child Maltreatment Victims

The number of children actually maltreated is unknown. In 2000, there were an estimated 879,000 victims of maltreatment nationwide.[12] The term "victims" refers to those children who were found by CPS to have experienced abuse or neglect (i.e., substantiated cases).

During that same year, an estimated 3 million referrals were made to CPS regarding one or more children in a family, and nearly two-thirds of those referrals were "screened in" for investigation of potential maltreatment. "Screened in" indicates that the referral was deemed appropriate for investigation or assessment based on State statutes and agency guidelines. The CPS processes for screening referrals, conducting investigations, and substantiating maltreatment are described further in Chapter 9, "What Does the Child Protection Process Look Like?"

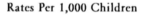

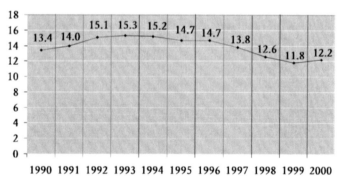

Reporting Year

Source: Child Maltreatment 2000

Exhibit 4-1. Trend of Reported Victimization 1990–2000

For every 1,000 children in the population in 2000, approximately 12 were victims of maltreatment.[13] Exhibit 4-1 presents NCANDS data on the reported annual victimization rates over the past 11 years.

Types of maltreatment

The following findings describe reported child victimization rates by major types of maltreatment as stated in NCANDS for 2000:

- **Neglect.** More than half of all reported victims (62.8 percent) suffered neglect (including medical neglect), an estimated rate of 7 per 1,000 children.
- **Physical abuse.** Approximately one-fifth of all known victims (19.3 percent) were physically abused, an estimated rate of 2 per 1,000 children.
- **Sexual abuse.** Of all reported maltreated children, just over one-tenth (10.1 percent) had been sexually abused, an estimated rate of 1 per 1,000 children.
- **Psychological maltreatment.** Less than one- tenth (7.7 percent) were identified as victims of psychological maltreatment, or less than 1 per 1,000 children.[14]

Keep in mind that some children are reported as victims of more than one type of maltreatment.

Characteristics of victims

Overall, in 2000, 52 percent of victims of child maltreatment were girls and 48 percent were boys. While rates of most types of maltreatment were similar for both sexes, more girls than boys were sexually abused.

The youngest and most vulnerable children—children under the age of 3—had the highest victimization rate, approximately 16 per 1,000.[15] Overall, rates of victimization declined as children's age increased. (Victimization patterns by age, however, differ by type of maltreatment.)

While children of every race and ethnicity were maltreated, victimization rates varied. Out of all children reported as maltreated in 2000:

- 50.6 percent of victims were White;
- 24.7 percent of victims were African American;
- 14.2 percent of victims were Hispanic;
- 1.6 percent of victims were American Indian- Alaska Native;
- 1.4 percent of victims were Asian-Pacific Islander.[16]

It is important to remember that these figures represent those children who have been referred to CPS, investigated, and found to have credible evidence of maltreatment. Other studies suggest that there are not significant differences in the actual incidence of maltreatment by race, but rather that certain races may receive different attention during the processes of referral, investigation, and service allocation.[17]

Fatalities

According to NCANDS, an estimated 1,200 children known to CPS died of abuse and neglect in 2000. Over two-fifths of these children (43.7 percent) were less than 1 year old. Child maltreatment fatalities were more frequently associated with neglect (34.9 percent) than with other types of maltreatment, including physical abuse.

Child Maltreatment Perpetrators

The majority of victims reported to NCANDS in 2000 (78.8 percent) were maltreated by a parent. This is not surprising given that child maltreatment is defined as the abuse or neglect of children by parents or caregivers. The definition of who is considered a caregiver (e.g., babysitter, daycare worker, residential facility staff, relatives, or household members) varies from State to State. Approximately three-fifths of perpetrators of maltreatment (59.9 percent) were women. Nearly 42 percent of that group of women perpetrators were younger than 30. While mothers were more frequently identified as perpetrators of neglect and physical abuse (the most common forms of maltreatment), fathers were more frequently identified as the perpetrators of sexual abuse.[18]

Nonreported Child Abuse and Neglect

Not all victims of abuse and neglect are reported to CPS and not all reports are verifiable. As such, the statistics presented above likely under- represent the true scope of child maltreatment. The *Third National Incidence Study of Child Abuse and Neglect* (NIS-3) surveyed community-level professionals (e.g., educators, medical professionals, and mental health care providers) who came into contact with children in 1993. The study estimated that less than one-third of the children who were identified as having experienced harm from abuse or neglect had been investigated by CPS.[19] General population surveys also suggest that maltreatment is higher than the official reports. For example, based on what parents say they did in disciplining their children, a 1995 Gallup Poll estimated the number of physical abuse victims to be 16 times the official reported number of victims for that time period.

KEY SOURCES OF CHILD ABUSE AND NEGLECT STATISTICS

The primary sources of national statistics on child abuse and neglect are two reports sponsored by the Children's Bureau of the U.S. Department of Health and Human Services:

- **Child Maltreatment: Reports from the States to the National Child Abuse and Neglect Data System (NCANDS).** NCANDS collects national information on maltreated children known to State CPS. The annual NCANDS report presents national and State level findings on the number and sources of child abuse and neglect reports, investigation dispositions, types of maltreatment, characteristics of children victimized, relationship of perpetrators to victims, and services provided for child maltreatment victims.

- **National Incidence Study of Child Abuse and Neglect (NIS).** NIS is designed to estimate the actual number of abused and neglected children nationwide including both cases reported and cases not reported to CPS. NIS bases estimates on information provided by a nationally representative sample of community professionals (e.g., educators, law enforcement personnel, medical professionals, and other service providers) who come into contact with maltreated children.

The most recent reports from these studies are available from the National Clearinghouse on Child Abuse and Neglect Information, 800-FYI-3366, nccanch@calib.com, or online at www.calib.com/nccanch.

5. WHAT FACTORS CONTRIBUTE TO CHILD ABUSE AND NEGLECT?

There is no single known cause of child maltreatment. Nor is there any single description that captures all families in which children are victims of abuse and neglect. Child maltreatment occurs across socio-economic, religious, cultural, racial, and ethnic groups. While no specific causes definitively have been identified that lead a parent or other caregiver to abuse or neglect a child, research has recognized a number of risk factors or attributes commonly associated with maltreatment. Children within families and environments in which these factors exist have a higher probability of experiencing maltreatment. It must be emphasized, however, that while certain factors often are present among families where maltreatment occurs, this does not mean that the presence of these factors will *always* result in child abuse and neglect. The factors that may contribute to maltreatment in one family may not result in child abuse and neglect in another family. For example, several researchers note the relation between poverty and maltreatment, yet it must be noted that most people living in poverty do not harm their children. Professionals who intervene in cases of child maltreatment must recognize the multiple, complex causes of the problem and must tailor their assessment and treatment of children and families to meet the specific needs and circumstances of the family.

Risk factors associated with child maltreatment can be grouped in four domains:

- Parent or caregiver factors
- Family factors
- Child factors
- Environmental factors

It is increasingly recognized that child maltreatment arises from the interaction of multiple factors across these four domains.[20] The sections that follow examine risk factors in each category. Available research suggests that different factors may play varying roles in accounting for different forms of child maltreatment (physical abuse, sexual abuse, neglect, and psychological or emotional abuse). Some of these differences are highlighted throughout the chapter.

A greater understanding of risk factors can help professionals working with children and families both to identify maltreatment and high- risk situations and to intervene appropriately. Assessment of the specific risk factors that affect a family may influence the prioritization of intervention services for that family (e.g., substance abuse treatment). Moreover, addressing risk and protective factors can help to prevent child abuse and neglect. For example, prevention programs may focus on increasing social supports for families (thereby reducing the risk of social isolation) or providing parent education to improve parent's age-appropriate expectations for their children. Prevention activities and their link to risk factors are discussed further in Chapter 7, "What Can Be Done to Prevent Child Abuse and Neglect?"

Parent or Caregiver Factors

Parent or caregiver factors potentially contributing to maltreatment relate to:

- Personality characteristics and psychological well-being
- History of maltreatment
- Substance abuse
- Attitudes and knowledge
- Age

Personality characteristics and psychological well-being

No consistent set of characteristics or personality traits has been associated with maltreating parents or caregivers. Some characteristics frequently identified in those who are physically abusive or neglectful include low self-esteem, an external locus of control (i.e., belief that events are determined by chance or outside forces beyond one's personal control), poor impulse control, depression, anxiety, and antisocial behavior.[21] While some maltreating parents or caregivers experience behavioral and emotional difficulties, severe mental disorders are not common.[22]

Parental histories and the cycle of abuse

A parent's childhood history plays a large part in how he or she may behave as a parent. Individuals with poor parental role models or those who did not have their own needs met may find it very difficult to meet the needs of their children.

While the estimated number varies, child maltreatment literature commonly supports the finding that some maltreating parents or caregivers were victims of abuse and neglect themselves as children.[23] One review of the relevant research suggested that about one-third of all individuals who were maltreated will subject their children to maltreatment.[24] Children who either experienced maltreatment or witnessed violence between their parents or caregivers may learn violent behavior and may also learn to justify violent behavior as appropriate.[25]

An incorrect conclusion from this finding, however, is that a maltreated child will always grow up to become a maltreating parent. There are individuals who have not been abused as children who become abusive, as well as individuals who have been abused as children and do not subsequently abuse their own children. In the research review noted above, approximately two-thirds of all individuals who were maltreated did not subject their children to abuse or neglect.[26]

It is not known why some parents or caregivers who were maltreated as children abuse or neglect their own children and others with a similar history do not.[27] While every individual is responsible for his or her actions, research suggests the presence of emotionally supportive relationships may help lessen the risk of the intergenerational cycle of abuse.[28]

Substance abuse

Parental substance abuse is reported to be a contributing factor for between one- and two-thirds of maltreated children in the child welfare system.[29] Research supports the association between substance abuse and child maltreatment.[30] For example:

- A retrospective study of maltreatment experience in Chicago found children whose parents abused alcohol and other drugs were almost three times likelier to be abused and more than four times likelier to be neglected than children of parents who were not substance abusers.[31]
- A Department of Health and Human Services study found all types of maltreatment, and particularly neglect, to be more likely in alcohol- abusing families than in nonalcohol-abusing families.[32]

Substance abuse can interfere with a parent's mental functioning, judgment, inhibitions, and protective capacity. Parents significantly affected by the use of drugs and alcohol may neglect the needs of their children, spend money on drugs instead of household expenses, or get involved in criminal activities that jeopardize their children's health or safety.[33] Also, studies suggest that substance abuse can influence parental discipline choices and child-rearing styles.[34]

Over the past decade, prenatal exposure of children to drugs and alcohol during their mother's pregnancy and its potentially negative, developmental consequences has been an issue of particular concern. The number of children born each year exposed to drugs or alcohol is estimated to be between 550,000 and 750,000.[35] While this issue has received much attention, children who are exposed prenatally represent only a small proportion of children negatively affected by parental substance abuse.[36]

The number and complexity of co-occurring family problems often makes it difficult to understand the full impact of substance abuse on child maltreatment.[37] Substance abuse and child maltreatment often co-occur with other problems, including mental illness, HIV/AIDS or other health problems, domestic violence, poverty, and prior child maltreatment. These co-occurring problems produce extremely complex situations that can be difficult to resolve.[38] Because many of the problems may be important and urgent, it can be difficult to prioritize what services to provide. Additionally, identifying and obtaining appropriate resources to address these needs is a challenge in many communities.

Attitudes and knowledge

Negative attitudes and attributions about a child's behavior and inaccurate knowledge about child development may play a contributing role in child maltreatment.[39] For example, some studies have found that mothers who physically abuse their children have both more negative and higher than normal expectations of their children, as well as less understanding of appropriate developmental norms.[40] Not all research, however, has found differences in parental expectations.[41]

A parent's lack of knowledge about normal child development may result in unrealistic expectations. Unmet expectations can culminate in inappropriate punishment (e.g., a parent hitting a one-year-old for soiling his pants). Other parents may become frustrated with not knowing how to manage a child's behavior and may lash out at the child. Still others may have attitudes that devalue children or view them as property.

Age

Caretaker age may be a risk factor for some forms of maltreatment, although research findings are inconsistent.[42] Some studies of physical abuse, in particular, have found that mothers who were younger at the birth of their child exhibited higher rates of child abuse than did older mothers.[43] Other contributing factors, such as lower economic status, lack of social support, and high stress levels may influence the link between younger childbirth—particularly teenage parenthood—and child abuse.[44]

Family Factors

Specific life situations of some families—such as marital conflict, domestic violence, single parenthood, unemployment, financial stress, and social isolation—may increase the likelihood of maltreatment. While these factors by themselves may not cause maltreatment, they frequently contribute to negative patterns of family functioning.

Family structure

Children living with single parents may be at higher risk of experiencing physical and sexual abuse and neglect than children living with two biological parents.[45] Single parent households are substantially more likely to have incomes below the poverty line. Lower income, the increased stress associated with the sole burden of family responsibilities, and fewer supports are thought to contribute to the risk of single parents maltreating their children. In 1998, 23 percent of children lived in households with a single mother, and 4 percent lived in households with a single father.[46] A strong, positive relationship between the child and the father, whether he resides in the home or not, contributes to the child's development and may lessen the risk of abuse.

In addition, studies have found that compared to similar non-neglecting families, neglectful families tend to have more children or greater numbers of people living in the household.[47] Chronically neglecting families often are characterized by a chaotic household with changing constellations of adult and child figures (e.g., a mother and her children who live on and off with various others, such as the mother's mother, the mother's sister, or a boyfriend).[48]

THE CHILD ABUSE AND FATHER ABSENCE CONNECTION

- The rate of child abuse in single parent households is 27.3 children per 1,000, which is nearly twice the rate of child abuse in two parent households (15.5 children per 1,000).
- An analysis of child abuse cases in a nationally representative sample of 42 counties found that children from single parent families are more likely to be victims of physical and sexual abuse than children who live with both biological parents. Compared to their peers living with both parents, children in single parent homes had:

- 77 percent greater risk of being physically abused;
- 87 percent greater risk of being harmed by physical neglect;
- 165 percent greater risk of experiencing notable physical neglect;
- 74 percent greater risk of suffering from emotional neglect;
- 80 percent greater risk of suffering serious injury as a result of abuse;
- 120 percent greater risk of experiencing some type of maltreatment overall.
- A national survey of nearly 1,000 parents found that 7.4 percent of children who lived with one parent had been sexually abused, compared to only 4.2 percent of children who lived with both biological parents.
- Using data from 1,000 students tracked from seventh or eighth grade in 1988 through high school in 1992, researchers determined that only 3.2 percent of the boys and girls who were raised with both biological parents had a history of maltreatment. However, a full 18.6 percent of those in other family situations had been maltreated.
- A study of 156 victims of child sexual abuse found that the majority of the children came from disrupted or single-parent homes; only 31 percent of the children lived with both biological parents. Although stepfamilies make up only about 10 percent of all families, 27 percent of the abused children in this study lived with either a stepfather or the mother's boyfriend.[49]

Marital conflict and domestic violence

According to published studies, in 30 to 60 percent of families where spouse abuse takes place, child maltreatment also occurs.[50] Children in violent homes may witness parental violence, may be victims of physical abuse themselves, and may be neglected by parents who are focused on their partners or unresponsive to their children due to their own fears.[51] A child who witnesses parental violence is at risk for also being maltreated, but, even if the child is not maltreated, he or she may experience harmful emotional consequences from witnessing the parental violence.[52]

Stress

Stress is also thought to play a significant role in family functioning, although its exact relationship with maltreatment is not fully understood.[53] Physical abuse has been associated with stressful life events, parenting stress, and emotional distress in various studies.[54] Similarly, some studies have found that neglectful families report more day-to-day stress than non-neglectful families.[55] It is not clear, however, whether maltreating parents actually *experience* **more** life stress or, rather, *perceive* **more events and life** experiences as being stressful.[56] In addition, specific stressful situations (e.g., losing a job, physical illness, marital problems, or the death of a family member) may exacerbate certain characteristics of the family members affected, such as hostility, anxiety, or depression, and that may also aggravate the level of family conflict and maltreatment.[57]

Parent-child interaction

Families involved in child maltreatment seldom recognize or reward their child's positive behaviors, while having strong responses to their child's negative behaviors.[58] Maltreating parents have been found to be less supportive, affectionate, playful, and responsive with their children than parents who do not abuse their children.[59] Research on maltreating parents, particularly physically abusive mothers, found that these parents were more likely to use harsh discipline strategies (e.g., hitting, prolonged isolation) and verbal aggression and less likely to use positive parenting strategies (e.g., using time outs, reasoning, and recognizing and encouraging the child's successes).[60]

Child Factors

Children are not responsible for being victims of maltreatment. Certain factors, however, can make some children more vulnerable to maltreating behavior. The child's age and development—physical, mental, emotional, and social—may increase the child's vulnerability to maltreatment, depending on the interactions of these characteristics with the parental factors previously discussed.

Age

The relationship between a child's age and maltreatment is not clear cut and may differ by type of maltreatment. In 2000, for example, the rate of documented maltreatment was highest for children between birth and 3 years of age (15.7 victims per 1,000 children of this age in the population) and declined as age increased.[61] The inverse relationship between age and maltreatment is particularly strong for neglect, but not as evident for other types of maltreatment (physical, emotional, or sexual abuse).

Infants and young children, due to their small physical size, early developmental status, and need for constant care, can be particularly vulnerable to child maltreatment. Very young children are more likely to experience certain forms of maltreatment, such as shaken baby syndrome and nonorganic failure to thrive. Teenagers, on the other hand, are at greater risk for sexual abuse.[62]

Disabilities

Children with physical, cognitive, and emotional disabilities appear to experience higher rates of maltreatment than do other children.[63] A national study, completed in 1993, found that children with disabilities were 1.7 times more likely to be maltreated than children without disabilities.[64] To date, the full degree to which disabilities precede or are a result of maltreatment is unclear.

In general, children who are perceived by their parents as "different" or who have special needs— including children with disabilities, as well as children with chronic illnesses or children with difficult temperaments—may be at greater risk of maltreatment.[65] The demands of caring for these children may overwhelm their parents. Disruptions may occur in the bonding or attachment processes, particularly if children are unresponsive to affection or if children are separated by frequent hospitalizations.[66] Children with disabilities also may be vulnerable to repeated maltreatment because they may not understand that the abusive behaviors are inappropriate, and they may be unable to escape or defend themselves in abusive situations.[67] Some researchers and advocates have suggested that some societal attitudes, practices, and beliefs that devalue and depersonalize children with disabilities sanction abusive behavior and contribute to their higher risk of maltreatment.[68] For instance, there may be greater tolerance of a caregiver verbally berating or physically responding to a disabled child's inability to accomplish a task or act in an expected way than there would be if similar behavior was directed at a normally abled child.

Other child characteristics

While some studies suggest that infants born prematurely or with low birth-weight may be at increased risk for maltreatment, other studies do not.[69] The relationship between low birth-weight and maltreatment may be attributable to higher maternal stress heightened by high caregiver demands, but it also may be related to poor parental education about low birth-weight, lack of accessible prenatal care, and other factors, such as substance abuse or domestic violence.[70]

Child factors such as aggression, attention deficits, difficult temperaments, and behavior problems—or the parental perceptions of such problems—have been associated with increased risk for all types of child maltreatment.[71] These factors may contribute indirectly to child maltreatment when interacting with certain parental characteristics, such as poor coping skills, poor ability to empathize with the child, or difficulty controlling emotions. In addition, these same child characteristics may be reinforced by the maltreatment (e.g., a physically abused child may develop aggressive behaviors that elicit harsh reactions from others) and create conditions that can lead to recurring maltreatment.[72]

Environmental Factors

Environmental factors are often found in combination with parent, family, and child factors, as highlighted in previous sections of this chapter. Environmental factors include poverty and unemployment, social isolation, and community characteristics. It is important to reiterate that most parents or caregivers who live in these types of environments are not abusive.

Poverty and Unemployment

Poverty and unemployment show strong associations with child maltreatment, particularly neglect.[73] The NIS-3 study, for example, found that children from families with annual incomes below $15,000 in 1993 were more than 22 times more likely to be harmed by child abuse and neglect as compared to children from families with annual incomes above $30,000.[74] It is important to underscore that most poor people do not maltreat their children. However, poverty—particularly when interacting with other risk factors such as depression, substance abuse, and social isolation—can increase the likelihood of maltreatment. In 1999, 85 percent of States identified poverty and substance abuse as the top two problems challenging families reported to child protective service (CPS) agencies.[75]

Rod Plotnik, emeritus professor, Department of Psychology, San Diego State University, describes several theories related to the association between poverty and maltreatment, all of which may hold some truth. One theory is that low income creates greater family stress, which, in turn, leads to higher chances of maltreatment. A second theory is that parents with low incomes, despite good intentions, may be unable to provide adequate care while raising children in high-risk neighborhoods with unsafe or crowded housing and inadequate daycare. A third theory is that some other characteristics may make parents more likely to be both poor and abusive. For example, a parent may have a substance abuse problem that impedes the parent's ability to obtain and maintain a job, which also may contribute to abusive behavior. A final theory is that poor families may experience maltreatment at rates similar to other families, but that maltreatment in poor families is reported to CPS more frequently, in part because they have more contact with and are under greater scrutiny from individuals who are legally mandated to report suspected child maltreatment.[76]

Social isolation and social support

Some studies indicate that compared to other parents, parents who maltreat their children report experiencing greater isolation, more loneliness, and less social support.[77] Social isolation may contribute to maltreatment because parents have less material and emotional support, do not have positive parenting role models, and feel less pressure to conform to conventional standards of parenting behaviors.[78] It is not clear, however, whether social isolation in some cases precedes and serves as a contributing factor to maltreatment or whether it is a consequence of the behavioral dynamics of maltreatment.[79]

Violent communities

Children living in dangerous neighborhoods have been found to be at higher risk than children from safer neighborhoods for severe neglect and physical abuse, as well as child sexual victimization.[80] Some risk may be associated with the poverty found in dangerous neighborhoods, however, concerns remain that violence may seem an acceptable response or behavior to individuals who witness it more frequently.

Societal attitudes and the promotion of violence in cultural norms and the media have been suggested as risk factors for physical abuse.[81] In addition, while the research is controversial, some studies show a positive relationship between televised violence and aggressive behaviors, particularly for individuals who watch substantial amounts of television.[82]

Protective Factors

Just as there are factors that place families at risk for maltreating their children, there are other factors that may protect them from vulnerabilities—factors that promote resilience. In general, research has found that supportive, emotionally satisfying relationships with a network of relatives or friends can help minimize the risk of parents maltreating children, especially during stressful life events.[83] For example, parents who were abused as children are less likely to abuse their own children if they have resolved internal conflicts and pain related to their history of abuse and if they have an intact, stable, supportive, and nonabusive relationship with their partner.[84] Additionally, programs on marriage education and enhancement may provide a roadmap of expected challenges such as the birth of the first child, parenting adolescents, and common gender differences which may act as a protective factor by strengthening families.[85]

6. WHAT ARE THE CONSEQUENCES OF CHILD ABUSE AND NEGLECT?

The consequences of child maltreatment can be profound and may endure long after the abuse or neglect occurs. The effects can appear in childhood, adolescence, or adulthood, and may affect various aspects of an individual's development (e.g., physical, cognitive, psychological, and behavioral). These effects range in consequence from minor physical injuries, low self-esteem, attention disorders, and poor peer relations to severe brain damage, extremely violent behavior, and death.[86]

While substantial evidence exists for the negative consequences of maltreatment, practitioners should be aware of the limitations of current research. First, many research efforts have studied the effects of child maltreatment among individuals from lower socio-economic backgrounds, prison populations, mental health patients, or other clinical populations who may exhibit the most serious behavior problems and whose families often have had many other problems (e.g., poverty, parental substance abuse, domestic violence). Further, many early studies examining consequences did not compare outcomes among maltreated individuals with outcomes among individuals who had not experienced maltreatment. In addition, studies often rely on official records or self-reporting of current or past child maltreatment, both of which may undercount the true prevalence of maltreatment. Finally, the nature and extent of maltreatment are different for each child and family, and these differences may influence the consequences.

Despite the above challenges, it is still possible to identify effects that have been more commonly associated with individuals who have experienced abuse and neglect. These effects are discussed in the sections that follow as they relate to three overlapping areas:

- Health and physical effects
- Intellectual and cognitive development
- Emotional, psychological, and behavioral consequences

While maltreated children have a higher risk of certain problems, it cannot be concluded that any given consequence will always occur. Not all children who have been maltreated will suffer severe consequences. A number of factors may influence the effects of maltreatment, including the child's age and developmental status at the time of the maltreatment, as well as the type, the frequency, the duration, and the severity of the maltreatment and co-occurring problems.[87] In addition, research has identified certain protective factors that mediate the effects of maltreatment. These protective factors and a child's resilience to negative consequences are addressed in the final section of this chapter.

Health and Physical Effects

Health and physical effects can include the immediate effects of bruises, burns, lacerations, and broken bones and also longer-term effects of brain damage, hemorrhages, and permanent disabilities. Negative effects on physical development can result from physical trauma (e.g., blows to the head or body, violent shaking, scalding with hot water, or asphyxiation) and from neglect (e.g., inadequate nutrition, lack of adequate motor stimulation, or withholding medical treatments). Specific physical effects as they relate to the early brain development of infants are highlighted in the following sections, along with some general health problems associated with maltreatment. The issue of child fatalities, the most tragic consequence of child maltreatment, is discussed in Chapter 4, "What Is the Scope of the Problem?"

Physical effects on infants

Infants and young children are particularly vulnerable to the physical effects of maltreatment. Shaking an infant may result in bruising, bleeding, and swelling in the brain. The health consequences of "shaken baby syndrome" can range from vomiting or irritability to more severe effects, such as concussions, respiratory distress, seizures, and death.[88] Other possible consequences include partial loss of vision or blindness, learning disabilities, mental retardation, cerebral palsy, or paralysis.[89]

Infants who have been neglected and malnourished may experience a condition known as "nonorganic failure to thrive." With this condition, the child's weight, height, and motor development fall significantly below age-appropriate ranges with no medical or organic cause. The death of the child is the end result in extreme cases. Nonorganic failure to thrive can result in continued growth retardation as well as cognitive and psychological problems.[90] Even with treatment, the long-term consequences can include continued growth problems, diminished cognitive abilities, retardation, and socio-emotional deficits such as poor impulse control.

Effects on brain development

Over the last decade, researchers have enhanced the field's understanding of the adverse effects of maltreatment on early brain development. Recent brain research has established a foundation for the neurobiological explanations for many of the physical, cognitive, social, and emotional difficulties exhibited by children who experienced maltreatment in their early years.

One explanation begins with the link between chronic physical abuse, sexual abuse, or neglect and the chronic stress it typically causes in a young child. In reaction to this persistent stress associated with ongoing maltreatment, the child's brain may strengthen the pathways among neurons that are involved in the fear response. As a result, the brain may become "wired" to experience the world as hostile and uncaring. This negative perspective may influence the child's later interactions, prompting the child to become anxious and overly aggressive or withdrawn.[91]

Research shows that maltreatment also may inhibit the appropriate development of certain regions of the brain. A neglected infant or young child, for example, may not be exposed to stimuli that would activate important regions of the brain and strengthen cognitive pathways. Consequently, the connections among neurons in these inactivated regions can literally whither away, hampering the individual's later functioning. If the regions responsible for emotional regulation are not activated, the child may have trouble controlling his or her emotions and behaving or interacting appropriately (e.g., impulsive behavior, difficulties in social interactions, or a lack of empathy).[92]

Other health-related problems

Maltreatment may affect an individual's health in a number of direct and indirect ways. Victims of sexual abuse, for example, may become infected with sexually transmitted diseases including syphilis and human immunodeficiency virus (HIV). Studies have found that women who had experienced sexual abuse were more likely to experience ongoing health problems such as chronic pelvic pain and other gynecologic problems, gastrointestinal problems, headaches, and obesity.[93] Recent research suggests that adults who were maltreated as children show higher levels of many health problems not typically associated with abuse and neglect—heart disease, cancer, chronic lung disease, and liver disease.[94] The link between maltreatment and these diseases may be depression, which can influence the immune system and may lead to higher risk behaviors such as smoking, alcohol and drug use, and overeating.[95]

Cognitive Development and Academic Achievement

Current research differs on findings related to the consequences of maltreatment on cognitive development, verbal abilities, and problem-solving skills. Some studies find evidence of lowered intellectual and cognitive functioning in abused children as compared to children who had not been abused,[96] and other studies find no differences.[97]

Research has consistently found that maltreatment increases the risk of lower academic achievement and problematic school performance.[98] Abused and neglected children in these studies received lower grades and test scores than did nonmaltreated children.

Emotional, Psychosocial and Behavioral Development

All types of maltreatment—physical abuse, sexual abuse, neglect, and psychological or emotional maltreatment—can affect a child's emotional and psychological well-being and lead to behavioral problems. These consequences may appear immediately after the maltreatment or years later.

Emotional and psychological consequences

While there is no single set of behaviors that is characteristic of all children who have been abused and neglected, the presence of emotional and psychological problems among many maltreated children is well documented. Clinicians and researchers report behaviors that range from passive and withdrawn to active and aggressive.[99] Physically and sexually abused children often exhibit both internalizing and externalizing problems.[100] Emotional and psychosocial problems identified among individuals who were maltreated as children include:

- Low self-esteem
- Depression and anxiety
- Post-traumatic stress disorder (PTSD)
- Attachment difficulties
- Eating disorders

- Poor peer relations
- Self-injurious behavior (e.g., suicide attempts)[101]

Maltreated children who developed insecure attachments to caregivers may become more mistrustful of others and less ready to learn from adults. They also may experience difficulties in understanding the emotions of others, regulating their own emotions, and in forming and maintaining relationships with peers.[102]

Violence, substance abuse and other problem behaviors

Individuals victimized by child maltreatment are more likely than people who were not maltreated to engage in juvenile delinquency, adult criminality, and violent behavior.[103] A study sponsored by the National Institute of Justice followed cases from childhood through adulthood and compared arrest records of a group of substantiated cases of maltreatment with a comparison group composed of individuals who were not officially recorded as maltreated. While most members of both groups had no juvenile or adult criminal records, being abused or neglected as a child increased the likelihood of arrest as a juvenile by 53 percent and as a young adult by 38 percent.[104] Physically abused children were the most likely of maltreated children to be arrested later for violent crime, followed closely by neglected children.

Other studies also have found maltreated children to be at increased risk (at least 25 percent more likely) for a variety of adolescent problem behaviors, including delinquency, teen pregnancy, drug use, low academic achievement, and mental health problems.[105] It must be underscored, however, that while the risk is higher, most abused and neglected children will not become delinquent, experience adolescent problem behaviors, or become involved in violent crime.

Research also suggests a relationship between child maltreatment and later substance abuse.[106] In addition to being a risk factor, child maltreatment, particularly sexual abuse, may be a precursor of substance abuse.[107]

Resilience

Not every child who is maltreated will experience the negative consequences discussed above. "Protective factors" that appear to mediate or serve as a "buffer" against the effects of the negative experiences may include:

- Personal characteristics, such as optimism, high self-esteem, high intelligence, or a sense of hopefulness.[108]
- Social support and relationships with a supportive adult(s).[109]

The finding that the seriousness of negative effects experienced by victims can be influenced by the availability of support from parents, relatives, professionals, and others has important implications for prevention and early intervention, discussed later in this manual.

Exhibit 6-1. The Estimated Costs of Child Maltreatment[110]

Source of Costs	Estimated Annual Cost
Direct Costs	
Hospitalization	$6,205,395,000
Chronic health problems	$2,987,957,400
Mental health care system	$425,110,400
Child welfare system	$14,400,000,000
Law enforcement	$24,709,800
Judicial system	$341,174,702
Total direct costs	$24,384,347,302
Indirect Costs	
Special education	$223,607,803
Mental health and health care	$4,627,636,025
Juvenile delinquency	$8,805,291,372
Lost productivity to society (due to unemployment)	$656,000,000
Adult criminality	$55,380,000,000
Total indirect costs	$69,692,535,227
Total Cost	**$94,076,882,529**

Studies have documented the link between abuse and neglect of children and a range of physical, emotional, psychological, and behavioral problems. In addition to the tragic consequences endured by the children who have been maltreated, society pays a high monetary cost for child maltreatment. The costs for child maltreatment include both direct costs (i.e., those associated with the immediate needs of abused and neglected children) and indirect costs (i.e., those associated with the longer term and secondary effects of child maltreatment). Since some maltreatment goes unrecognized and it is difficult to link costs to specific incidents, it is not possible to determine the actual cost of child abuse and neglect. As estimated by Prevent Child Abuse America, the total annual cost of child abuse and neglect in the United States may be as high as $94 billion, as shown in Exhibit 6-1.

7. WHAT CAN BE DONE TO PREVENT CHILD ABUSE AND NEGLECT?

The seriousness of the effects of maltreatment, presented in the previous chapter, underscore the importance for professionals, along with concerned community members, to help prevent child maltreatment. To break the cycle of maltreatment, communities across the country must continue to develop and implement strategies that prevent abuse or neglect from happening. While experts agree that the causes of child abuse and neglect are complex, it is possible to develop prevention initiatives that address known risk factors. This chapter provides an overview of prevention as a strategy, differentiates the various types of prevention activities, describes major prevention program models, and presents the roles of various sectors in prevention efforts.

Prevention as a Strategy

Prevention efforts most commonly occur before a problem develops so that the problem itself, or some manifestation of the problem, can be stopped or lessened.[111] Child abuse and neglect prevention covers a broad spectrum of services—such as public awareness, parent education, and home visitation— for audiences ranging from the general public to individuals who have abused or neglected a child. Community groups, social services agencies, schools, and other concerned citizens may provide these services. Typically, prevention activities attempt to deter predictable problems, protect existing states of health, and promote desired life objectives.[112] More specifically, family support services, a major component of child abuse prevention, are designed to strengthen and stabilize families, increase parental abilities, provide a safe and stable family environment, and enhance child development.[113]

To prevent child abuse and neglect, programs may focus on one or several risk factors discussed in Chapter 5, "What Factors Contribute to Child Abuse and Neglect?" For example, prevention programs may include:

- Substance abuse treatment programs for women with children;
- Respite care programs for families with children who have disabilities;
- Parent education programs and support groups for families affected by domestic violence.

Many prevention programs also focus efforts on strengthening child and family protective factors such as the knowledge and skills children need to help protect themselves from sexual abuse, the promotion of positive interactions between children and parents, and the knowledge and skills parents need to raise healthy, happy children.

Types of Prevention Activities

Child abuse and neglect prevention activities generally occur at three basic levels:

- Primary, or universal, prevention activities are directed at the general population with the goal of stopping the occurrence of maltreatment before it starts.
- Secondary, or selective, prevention activities focus on families at high risk of maltreatment to alleviate conditions associated with the problem.
- Tertiary, or indicated, prevention activities direct services to families where maltreatment has occurred to reduce the negative consequences of the maltreatment and to prevent its recurrence.

Primary or universal prevention

Primary prevention includes activities or services available to the general public. Frequently such activities aim to raise awareness among community members, the public, service providers, and decision- makers about the scope and problems associated with child maltreatment. For example:

- Public awareness campaigns informing citizens how and where to report suspected child abuse and neglect;
- Public service announcements on the radio or television encouraging parents to use nonviolent forms of discipline.

These types of programs are particularly popular during April, which is designated by presidential proclamation as Child Abuse Prevention Month. Other primary prevention efforts focus on support services available to the general population, such as pediatric care for all children, childcare, or parent education classes.

Secondary or selective prevention

Secondary prevention activities focus efforts and resources on children and families known to be at higher risk for maltreatment. Several risk factors such as substance abuse, young maternal age, developmental disabilities, and poverty are associated with child maltreatment. Programs may direct services to communities or neighborhoods that have a high incidence of one or several risk factors. Examples of secondary prevention programs include the following:

- Parent education programs located in high schools for teen mothers;
- Substance abuse treatment programs for parents with young children;
- Respite care for families who have children with special needs;
- Family resource centers offering information and referral services to families living in low- income neighborhoods.

Family support activities that are available to individuals identified as at risk or community members in a high-risk neighborhood also are considered secondary prevention. For example, local hospitals or community organizations may offer prenatal care and parenting classes to new or expectant parents. Local agencies may provide home visitation services for at risk families with infants and young children. Family support services are intended to assist parents in creating safe home environments and fostering healthy children.

Tertiary or Indicated Prevention

Tertiary prevention activities focus efforts on families in which maltreatment has already occurred. The goal of these programs is to prevent maltreatment from recurring and to reduce the negative consequences associated with maltreatment (e.g., social-emotional problems in children, lower academic achievement, decreased family functioning). These prevention programs may include services such as:

- Intensive family preservation services with trained mental health counselors available to families 24 hours per day for several weeks;
- Parent mentor programs with stable, nonabusive families acting as "role models" and providing support to families in crisis;
- Mental health services for children and families affected by maltreatment to improve family communication and functioning.

A combination of primary, secondary, and tertiary prevention services are necessary for any community to provide a full continuum of services to deter the devastating effects of child maltreatment.

Major Prevention Program Models

Many popular prevention programs are patterned after one of four models:

- Public awareness activities
- Parent education programs
- Skills-based curricula for children
- Home visitation programs

Public awareness activities

Public awareness activities are an important part of an overall approach to addressing child abuse and neglect. The purpose of public awareness activities is to raise community awareness of child abuse and neglect as a public issue and to provide the public with information about available resources and solutions. Such activities have the potential to reach diverse community audiences: parents and prospective parents, children, and community members, including professionals, who are critical to the identification and reporting of abuse.

In designing prevention education and public information activities, national, State, and local organizations use a variety of media to promote these activities, including:

- Public service announcements
- Press releases
- Posters
- Information kits and brochures
- Television or video documentaries and dramas

Through these media, communities are able to promote support for healthy parenting practices, child safety skills, and protocols for reporting suspected maltreatment.

ORGANIZATIONS SUPPORTING PUBLIC AWARENESS ACTIVITIES

State Children's Trust Funds

State Children's Trust Funds (CTFs) exist in all 50 States and the District of Columbia with the specific goal of preventing child maltreatment. CTFs coordinate prevention activities throughout their State by promoting and funding a variety of community-based programs including public awareness campaigns, home visitation programs, skills-based curricula for children, and parent education and support activities. In addition, many CTFs develop and distribute posters for community groups, schools, and many other professionals working with children. The poster may encourage parents to use positive discipline techniques or encourage children to say "no" to touching that makes them uncomfortable.

Don't Shake the Baby Campaign

One of the largest public awareness initiatives focuses on the prevention of Shaken Baby Syndrome. A national network of *Don't Shake the Baby* State contacts was established to ensure that all professionals involved in the care of children (e.g., teachers, physicians, nurses, home visitors, parent educators) become aware of the dangers associated with shaking infants. In addition to professionals, this campaign targets parents to alert them to the dangers of shaking their baby as well as playing with the baby in certain ways (e.g., throwing the baby in the air, bouncing the baby on a knee, twisting the baby in the air).

Prevent Child Abuse America

Prevent Child Abuse America, formerly the National Committee to Prevent Child Abuse (NCPCA), is a leading national organization actively engaged in public awareness activities. Prevent Child Abuse America, together with Marvel Comics, developed Spider-Man comic books that address child sexual abuse and child safety issues. This organization also distributes an information packet each year to assist community groups planning Child Abuse Prevention Month activities. Both the national office and Prevent Child Abuse America State Chapters throughout the country provide public awareness and other activities to prevent child abuse and neglect.

Blue Ribbon Campaign

The Blue Ribbon Campaign began as a tribute from a Virginia grandmother to a grandchild whose battered body was found at the bottom of a canal. By tying a blue ribbon—signifying the pain and bruises suffered by abused children—around the antennae of her van, Bonnie Finney sought to raise awareness of the devastating effects of child abuse and neglect. Since those early days in the 1 980s, the Blue Ribbon Campaign has grown into a national effort to raise awareness of the scope and problem of child maltreatment. The blue ribbon, often worn during April for Child Abuse Prevention Month, serves as the most recognized symbol for child abuse prevention.

Parent education programs

Parent education programs focus on enhancing parental competencies and promoting healthy parenting practices and typically target teen and highly stressed parents. Some of these programs are led by professionals or paraprofessionals, while others are facilitated by parents who provide mutual support and discuss personal experiences. These programs address issues such as:

- Developing and practicing positive discipline techniques;
- Learning age-appropriate child development skills and milestones;
- Promoting positive play between parents and children;
- Locating and accessing community services and supports.

Parent education programs are designed and structured differently, usually depending on the curriculum being used and the target audience. Programs may be short-term (i.e., those offering classes once a week for 6 to 12 weeks) or they may be more intensive (i.e., those offering services more than once a week and for up to 1 year). Popular parent education programs include:

- Parents as Teachers—visit www.patnc.org for more information;
- Every Person Influences Children (EPIC)— visit www.epicforchildren.org for more information;
- The Nurturing Parenting Program—visit www.nurturingparenting.com for more information.

In addition to parent education programs, mutual support groups also may strengthen families and help prevent child maltreatment. For example, *Parents Anonymous* affiliates work within their communities and States to provide support and resources to overwhelmed families struggling to cope with everyday stresses and strains.

Skills-based curricula for children

Many schools and local community social service organizations offer skills-based curricula to teach children safety and protection skills. Most of these programs focus efforts on preventing child sexual abuse and teaching children to distinguish appropriate touching from inappropriate touching. Many curricula have a parent education component to give parents and other caregivers the knowledge and skills necessary to recognize and discuss sexual abuse with their children. Curricula may use various methods to teach children skills including:

- Workshops and school lessons
- Puppet shows and role-playing activities
- Films and videos
- Workbooks, storybooks, and comics

Examples of skills-based curricula include programs such as *Talk About Touching, Safe Child,* Reach, Recovery, Challenge, Good Touch/Bad Touch, Kids *on the Block, and Illusion Theater.*

Home visitation programs

Home visitation programs that emphasize the health and well-being of children and families have existed in the United States since the late 19th century. Organizations and agencies in fields as varied as education, maternal and child health, and health and human services, use home visitation programs to help strengthen families. Home visitation programs offer a variety of family-focused services to pregnant mothers and families with newborns. Activities encompass structured visits in the family's home, informal visits, and telephone calls. Topics addressed through these programs often include:

- Positive parenting practices and nonviolent discipline techniques;
- Child development;
- Maternal and child health issues;
- Accessing available social services;
- Establishing social supports and networks;
- Learning to advocate for oneself, one's child, and one's family;
- Preventing accidental childhood injuries through the development of a safe home environment.

Recent evaluations suggest that both short- and long-term positive outcomes may occur for mothers and children receiving home visitation services. During a two-year period, nurses provided home visitation services to a group of poor, unmarried, teen mothers in Elmira, New York. Only 4 percent of the nurse-visited families had verified reports of child abuse and neglect compared to 19 percent of the families who did not receive home visits by nurses.[114] A follow-up study further supported these positive results: the number of verified reports of child maltreatment for the nurse-visited group of mothers was nearly half that of mothers who did not receive home visitation services during the next 15 years.[115] Additional positive outcomes among nurse-visited mothers included lower levels of smoking, fewer and better-spaced subsequent pregnancies, and more months working, as well as fewer emergency room visits by children for injuries. Several studies of home visitation programs using nonmedical professionals also showed a significantly lower number of verified maltreatment reports for home- visited mothers.[116]

HOME VISITATION PROGRAMS

- **Home Visitation 2000** provides services to first-time mothers in Denver, Colorado. This program focuses efforts on improving maternal health, environmental health (home safety), quality of caregiving for infants and toddlers, maternal life course development (education and employment), and social support. For more information, visit www.unitedwaydenver.org/IRIS/aa0g6f81.htm.

- **Hawaii's Healthy Start** is a statewide, multisite program that screens, identifies, and provides services to families at high risk for child abuse and neglect. Most families are enrolled after the birth of a child, but some enroll during the prenatal period. For more information, visit www.state.hi.us/doh/legrpts2002/mchs_healthystart.pdf.

- **Healthy Families America** (HFA) is a national initiative launched by Prevent Child Abuse America and Ronald McDonald House Charities in 1992. Modeled after Hawaii's Healthy Start, HFA currently has home visitation programs in more than 3,000 sites across the country. For more information, visit www.healthyfamiliesamerica.org.

Role of Various Entities in Prevention Efforts

Prevention programs typically are administered through specific entities, based on an area of interest or professional expertise. Increasingly, health care providers, community organizations, social services agencies, schools, the faith community, and employers are becoming involved in the wellbeing of children and families. All members of the community are working together to prevent child maltreatment and ensure the health and safety of children and families. The following sections describe how these organizations are providing prevention services to strengthen and support families.

Health care providers

Health care providers are in a unique position to assist in the prevention of child maltreatment. These professionals have routine access to children and families by providing regular appointments, immunizations, and interventions to common illnesses. Activities that promote the health of children and their parents and contribute to the prevention of child maltreatment include:

- Prenatal health care that improves pregnancy outcomes and health among new mothers and infants;
- Early childhood health care that supports normal development and the health of young children;
- Family-centered birthing and perinatal coaching that strengthens early attachment between parents and their children;
- Home health visitation that provides support, education, and community linkages for new parents;
- Support programs that assist parents of children with special health and developmental problems.

Primary care providers emphasize the prevention of disease and the promotion of health and well-being. With this foundation, they have a natural role in the prevention of child abuse and neglect.

Community-based organizations

Many community organizations offer a wide range of services for children and families. Boys and Girls Clubs, scouting troops, and local YMCA/YWCAs provide social and recreational opportunities for children and families. Community centers, food banks, emergency assistance programs, and shelters offer various family support services to increase family resources and decrease stress. Exchange Clubs, fraternal organizations, advocacy groups, and ethnic, cultural, and religious organizations also support child maltreatment prevention activities.

Specific examples of prevention activities found within community-based organizations include:

- Self-help and mutual aid groups that provide nonjudgmental support and assistance to troubled families;

- Natural support networks that provide families with informal helpers and community resources;
- Child and respite care programs that reduce the stress parents experience and provide positive modeling for parents and children.

Many grassroots efforts develop dynamic partnerships of professionals, businesses, faith-based organizations, concerned citizens, and other groups interested in creating prevention efforts that address the needs of their community.

Social services agencies

Increasingly, social service agencies and professionals are expanding their focus to include programs that prevent family problems from escalating to abuse or neglect. Effective social service initiatives for strengthening families and preventing child maltreatment include:

- Parent education services, which help parents to develop adequate child-rearing knowledge and skills;
- Parent aide programs, which provide supportive, one-on-one relationships for parents;
- Crisis and emergency services, which support parents and children at times of exceptional stress or crisis;
- Treatment for abused children, which prevents an intergenerational repetition of family violence.

As State and local social service agencies examine new ways of "doing business," many are pooling resources to provide more prevention services.

Schools

With increased public and professional attention on the serious social problems affecting children and adolescents, schools have become the focus for many new prevention efforts including:

- Comprehensive, integrated prevention curricula to provide children with the skills, knowledge, and information necessary to cope successfully with the challenges of childhood and adolescence;
- Personal safety programs;
- Support programs for children with special needs to help reduce the stress on families with a child with disabilities.

Since most children attend public or private schools, school-based prevention activities have the potential to reach the majority of U.S. children.

Faith community

Religious institutions are among the most influential organizations in many communities. Churches, temples, synagogues, mosques, and other faith-based groups play an important role in reaching out to and helping families at risk. Spiritual leaders can use their religious messages as a positive force in preventing child abuse and neglect and advocating nonabusive parenting practices. Faith communities frequently foster and offer important social supports to families.[117] Empirical studies suggest a significant relationship between an individual's participation in faith practices and physical and mental well-being.[118] Improved social supports and enhanced well-being can help strengthen families and act as protective factors. Faith communities can participate in prevention efforts through activities such as:

- Training religious and lay leaders to recognize the signs and symptoms of child maltreatment;
- Sponsoring or allowing self-help, parent education, and support groups to meet at their facilities;
- Offering respite care for congregation members in need of short-term relief from caregiving responsibilities;
- Collecting clothes and baby care products (e.g., diapers, car seats) for new parents;
- Sponsoring after school programs and safety training for latchkey children;
- Organizing mentoring programs that pair responsible adults with children;
- Disseminating information on child development, parental stress, and community resources for parents;
- Offering special outreach and education programs for parents and students associated with parochial schools.

Employers

As the number of parents working outside the home continues to grow, the need increases for workplace policies that support family functioning and promote the prevention of child maltreatment. Family-focused initiatives for the workplace include:

- Flexible work schedules and other "family friendly" policies that help employees to balance the demands of their work and parental commitments;
- Parental leave policies that reduce stress on new parents and help facilitate positive attachments between parents and their infants;
- Employer-supported child care;
- Family-oriented policies that support healthy and humane working conditions and ensure adequate family income;
- Employee assistance programs that can provide information on reducing stress.

For all working parents, a supportive work environment can help ease the stress of the dual responsibilities of work and family. For some already vulnerable parents, a supportive work climate may prevent family dysfunction, breakdown, abuse, and neglect.[119]

Working together, the various sectors of the community—health care providers, community-based organizations, social services agencies, schools, the faith community, employers, other community practitioners and concerned citizens—can help strengthen families, foster healthy child development, and reduce child maltreatment.

For more information on child abuse and neglect prevention, contact one of the organizations listed in Appendix B.

8. WHICH LAWS AND POLICIES GUIDE PUBLIC INTERVENTION IN CHILD MALTREATMENT?

Most Americans believe, and professionals agree, that parents are in the best position to nurture, protect, and care for the needs of their children. Although most parents are usually capable of meeting these needs, the State has the authority to intervene in the parent-child relationship if a parent is unable or fails to protect his or her child from preventable and significant harm. The purpose of this chapter is to present basic information about the Federal and State governments' power and authority to intervene into the private lives of families when child maltreatment is alleged. The first section reviews the Federal role in addressing child maltreatment, while the second section discusses the basis for State intervention in family life, highlights State child maltreatment reporting statutes, and describes the functions of civil and criminal courts.

The Federal Role in Addressing Child Abuse and Neglect

States initiated mechanisms to assist and protect children prior to any Federal-level activity. In 1912, the Federal government established the Children's Bureau to address these issues. Federal programs designed to support child welfare services and to direct Federal aid to families date from 1935, with the passage of the Social Security Act (SSA). Since State-supervised and State-administered programs were already in place, the child welfare policy of the SSA layered Federal funds over existing State-level foundations. These child welfare programs, thus, were new only to the extent that they established a uniform framework for administration.[120] Congress has amended the Act several times and changed the Act significantly with the passage of the Personal Responsibility and Work Opportunity Reconciliation Act of 1996. Within the Federal government, the Children's Bureau and its Office on Child Abuse and Neglect (OCAN) serve as a focal point for efforts to respond to the problem of child maltreatment.

Parens patriae

The basis for intervention in child maltreatment is grounded in the concept of *parens patriae*—a legal term that asserts the government's role in protecting the interests of children and intervening when parents fail to provide proper care. The legal framework regarding the parent-child relationship balances the rights and responsibilities among parent, child, and State, as guided by Federal statutes. It has long been recognized that parents have a fundamental liberty interest, protected by the Constitution, to raise their children as they choose. This parent- child relationship grants certain rights, duties, and obligations to both parent and child, including the responsibility of the parent to protect the child's safety and well-being. If a parent, however, is unable or unwilling to meet this responsibility, the State has the power and authority to take action to protect a child from significant harm.

A series of U.S. Supreme Court cases have defined when it is constitutional for the State to intervene in family life.[121] Although the Court has given parents great latitude in the upbringing and education of their children, it has held that the rights of parenthood and the family have limits and can be regulated in the interest of the public. The Court has further concluded that the State, as *parens patriae*, may restrict the parent's control by regulating or prohibiting the child's labor, requiring school attendance, and intervening in other ways to promote the child's well-being.[122] This doctrine has evolved into the principle that the community, in addition to the parent, has a strong interest in the care and nurturing of children, who represent the future of the community. When basic needs of children are not met or when their rights have been violated, as with cases of child maltreatment, the State has an obligation to intervene to assist the affected individuals.

Federal legislation and programs

Over the past several decades, Congress also has passed significant pieces of child welfare legislation that support the States' duty and power to act on behalf of a child when parents are unable or unwilling. Key Federal legislation that addresses the protection of maltreated children are highlighted below:

- **The Child Abuse Prevention and Treatment Act** (CAPTA) of 1974 (P.L. 93-247) was established to ensure that victimized children are identified and reported to appropriate authorities. The Act was most recently amended in 1996 (P.L. 104-235) and continues to provide minimum standards for definitions and reports of child maltreatment.
- **The Adoption Assistance and Child Welfare Act** of 1980 (P.L. 96-272) requires States to establish programs and implement procedures to support maltreated children and their families, in their own homes, and facilitate family reunification following out-of-home placements.
- **Family Preservation and Support Services Program** enacted as part of the **Omnibus Budget Reconciliation Act** of 1993 (P.L. 103- 66) provides funding for prevention and support services for families at risk of maltreatment and family preservation services for families experiencing crises that might lead to out-ofhome placement.
- **The Adoption and Safe Families Act** (ASFA) of 1997 (P.L. 105-89) was built on earlier laws and reforms in the field to promote the safety, permanency, and well-being of maltreated children. A component of ASFA is the Promoting Safe and Stable Families (PSSF) Program, which was developed from and expanded upon the Family Preservation and Support Services Program mentioned above. While the legislation reaffirms the importance of making reasonable efforts to preserve and reunify families, it also specifies instances where reunification efforts do not have to be made (e.g., when a child is not safe with his or her family), establishes tighter time frames for termination of parental rights, and promotes adoption initiatives.
- **Child Abuse Prevention and Enforcement Act** of 2000 (P.L. 106-177) focuses on improving the criminal justice system's ability to provide timely, accurate criminal-record information to agencies engaged in child protection, and enhancing prevention and law enforcement activities.
- **Strengthening Abuse and Neglect Courts Act** of 2000 (P.L.106-314) was designed to improve the administrative efficiency and effectiveness of the courts' handling of abuse and neglect cases.

- **Promoting Safe and Stable Families Program Reauthorization** of 2002 (P.L.107-133) continued to build upon ASFA by extending the PSSF for an additional 5 years and increasing discretionary funding. It also created several new programs including a new state grant program that provides education and training vouchers for youth aging out of foster care and a mentoring program for children with incarcerated parents.

These and other pieces of legislation also provide for a variety of funding streams—particularly State grant and discretionary grant programs—which support prevention and treatment services for children and families.

Federal agencies

The Children's Bureau, an agency within the Administration for Children and Families (ACF), Administration on Children, Youth and Families, U.S. Department of Health and Human Services, is the focal point for Federal efforts to address the problem of child abuse and neglect. The Children's Bureau's mission is to provide for the safety, permanency, and well-being of children and families through leadership, support for necessary services, and productive partnerships with States, Tribes, and communities. The Children's Bureau fulfills this mission through its Office on Child Abuse and Neglect (OCAN) and its five divisions:

- OCAN provides leadership and direction on the issues of child maltreatment and the prevention of abuse and neglect as directed by CAPTA and the Children's Justice Act. Also, OCAN is the focal point for interagency collaborative efforts, national conferences, and special initiatives related to child abuse and neglect.
- The Division of Child Welfare Capacity Building provides leadership and direction in the areas of training, technical assistance, and information dissemination as directed by Titles IV-B and IV- E of the Social Security Act (SSA) and CAPTA.
- The Division of Policy provides leadership and direction in policy development and interpretation as directed by Titles IV-B and IV-E of SSA, the Basic State Grant (BSG), and CAPTA.
- The Division of Program Implementation provides leadership and direction in the operation and review of programs as directed by Titles IV-B and IV-E of SSA, CAPTA, and BSG.
- The Division of Data, Research, and Innovation provides leadership and direction in program development, innovation, research, and management of the Bureau's information systems as directed by Titles IV-B and IV-E of SSA and CAPTA.
- The Division of State Systems provides leadership and direction to States in the development and operation of automated systems, including all Statewide Automated Child Welfare Information System (SACWIS), to support welfare programs under Titles IV-B and IV-E of SSA.

While this discussion focuses primarily on activities related to child protection and the "front end" of the child welfare system (e.g., prevention, investigation, assessment, and service planning), the Children's Bureau also oversees activities and programs related to foster care, permanency planning, adoption, and other "back end" child welfare issues.

The Office on Child Abuse and Neglect convenes a Federal Interagency Work Group (FEDIAWG) on Child Abuse and Neglect that provides a forum for collaboration among Federal agencies with an interest in child maltreatment. The FEDIAWG shares information, makes policy and programmatic recommendations, implements joint activities, and works toward establishing complementary agendas in the areas of training, research, legislation, information dissemination, and delivery of services as they relate to the prevention, intervention, and treatment of child abuse and neglect.

SELECTED CHILD MALTREATMENT STATE GRANT PROGRAMS

The following are selected, legislatively mandated child maltreatment or child welfare grant programs available to State entities that meet certain eligibility requirements:

- **Basic State Grants** provide funds for States to enhance their child protective services (CPS) systems and to develop and strengthen child maltreatment prevention, treatment, and research programs.

- **The Community-based Family Resource and Support (CBFRS) Program** supports the development of comprehensive networks of community-based, prevention-focused family resource and support programs.

- **Children's Justice Act (CJA) Grants** help States to develop, establish, and operate programs designed to improve the investigation and prosecution of child abuse and neglect cases, particularly cases of child sexual abuse and exploitation, and fatality cases.

- **Child Welfare Services** assist State public welfare agencies in delivering child welfare services (including preventive interventions, alternative placements, and reunification services) with the goal of keeping families together.

- **Promoting Safe and Stable Families Program** (formerly called the Family Preservation and Support Services Program) supplies funds to States to provide family support, family preservation, time-limited family reunification services, and services to promote and support adoptions. These services are aimed at preventing the risk of abuse as well as promoting nurturing families, assisting families at risk of having a child removed from the home, promoting the timely return of a child to his or her home, and, if returning home is not an option, placing a child in a permanent setting with services that support the family.

In addition to the Children's Bureau, several other Federal agencies support programs and research and demonstration initiatives related to child maltreatment and child protection. For example, the Child Protection Division within the Office on Juvenile Justice and Delinquency Prevention (OJJDP), U.S. Department of Justice, conducts research, provides training and technical assistance, and supports demonstration programs that address child victimization and missing and exploited children. Several agencies within the U.S.

Department of Health and Human Services— including the National Institutes for Health (NIH), Centers for Disease Control and Prevention, Maternal and Child Health Bureau (MCHB), Health Resources and Services Administration (HRSA), and the Substance Abuse and Mental Health Service Administration (SAMHSA), to name a few—conduct research and support service delivery on the identification, prevention, and treatment of child maltreatment as well as risk factors and consequences.

Basis for State Intervention

States must comply with the child abuse and neglect guidelines mandated under CAPTA in order to receive Federal funds. Beyond that, however, States generally have autonomy in how services are provided to maltreated children and their families. All States have enacted child maltreatment laws that play a significant role in reporting and intervening in cases of child abuse and neglect. In order to enforce these laws, civil and criminal courts often must intervene in the lives of families when parents are unable or unwilling to provide for the safety and well-being of their children.

State reporting statutes

Many States define the parent-child legal relationship in their State statutes. These statutes define who is considered a "parent" (birth or adoptive parent) or other caregiver and indicate that the law imposes rights, privileges, duties, and obligations on this relationship. As noted above, the State has the authority to intervene in this relationship if the parent fails to provide for or protect the child. The State's intervention into family life is often triggered by a report of child maltreatment by a voluntary or mandated reporter as defined by State law under the CAPTA requirements.

Through mandated reporting statutes, the State requires certain individuals, typically defined by profession (e.g., health care professionals), to identify and help protect children from harm. These statutes also include definitions of the acts and omissions considered abuse and neglect in a particular State. Reports of suspected maltreatment, which are required under such laws, activate the child protection process. Currently, all States, the District of Columbia, and U.S. territories have enacted statutes requiring that the maltreatment of children be reported to a designated agency or official. Reporting laws generally specify the conditions under which the State may intervene in family life. (See Chapter 9, "What Does the Child Protection Process Look Like?", for more information about reporting of maltreatment and child protection procedures after a report has been made.)

Child protective service agency

State legislation mandates that CPS agencies respond to reports of alleged child maltreatment and children at risk of maltreatment, determine the safety of the children who are the subject of the report, and decide what initial response is needed. Intervention into family life on behalf of children must be guided by the legal basis for action and sound family-centered practice.[123] While CPS agencies are at the center of the child protection system, an array of service providers and community professionals collaborate to protect children and support families. (See Chapter 10, "Who Should Be Involved in Child Protection at the Community Level?", for further information about the roles and responsibilities of various community practitioners in child protection.)

Civil court intervention

Family and juvenile courts have the authority to make decisions about what happens to a child after he or she has been identified as needing the court's protection. The courts' involvement is initiated by the filing of a petition, usually by CPS, containing the allegations of abuse or neglect. The primary purpose of these courts is to resolve conflict and otherwise intervene in the lives of families in a manner that promotes the best interest of the child. The court is responsible for making the final determination about whether a child ought to be removed from his or her home, where a child is to be placed, or whether to terminate parental rights.

In cases of child maltreatment, family and juvenile court intervention may be required when:

- Families refuse to cooperate after an initial assessment has determined that an incident of abuse or neglect has occurred;
- The child is determined to be in imminent danger of harm and the child's safety cannot be assured in the home through services provided to the family;
- Families are unwilling to accept needed services, yet maltreatment exists and the safety of the child is a concern.

There are four types of court hearings held in family or juvenile courts when abused and neglected children are involved:

- Emergency hearings are convened to determine the need for intervention on behalf of, or emergency protection of, a child who may have been a victim of maltreatment.
- Adjudicatory hearings are held to determine whether a child has been maltreated or whether some other legal basis exists for the State to intervene to protect the child.
- Dispositional hearings are convened to determine the action to be taken on the case after adjudication, for example, whether State custody and out-of-home placement is necessary and what services the children and family will need to reduce the risk of maltreatment and to address the effects of maltreatment.
- Review hearings are held to review the dispositions and to determine the need to continue out-of-home placement, services, or court jurisdiction of a child.

One of the most drastic options available to a juvenile or family court judge is the termination of parental rights. Parental behaviors that may lead to such action are usually defined in State statutes. The parent-child relationship may be limited or ended, thus making the child eligible for temporary or permanent placement or adoption, when a parent:

- Abandons the child;
- Has a long-term mental illness or deficiency;
- Severely or chronically abuses or neglects the child or other children in the household;

- Has a long-term alcohol or drug abuse problem;
- Fails to support or maintain contact with the child.

Parental rights are not terminated simply because a person is not a model parent. In all States, parental rights can be terminated only if the State can prove by clear and convincing evidence that a parent has failed to provide for or protect the child in one of the ways defined in a State's statutes. Most State statutes also contain provisions for parents to voluntarily relinquish their rights. In addition to temporarily placing children in out-of-home care, the State has the authority to return a child to his or her parents. Children may return home once a determination is made that they will be safe and that their parents will be able to provide the appropriate care.

Criminal court intervention

Depending on State law, behavior that constitutes child abuse and neglect in the civil court process may also be considered a crime. Each State has enacted criminal statutes that define those forms of child abuse and neglect that are criminally punishable. In most jurisdictions, child maltreatment is criminally punishable when one or more of the following statutory crimes have been committed:

- Homicide, murder, or manslaughter
- False imprisonment
- Assault or battery
- Criminal neglect and abandonment
- Emotional, physical, or sexual abuse
- Pornography or child prostitution
- Rape or deviant sexual assault
- Indecent exposure
- Child endangerment or reckless endangerment

The same family may be simultaneously involved in both a criminal and civil case. Criminal prosecution, however, is directed at deterring future incidents and rehabilitating the defendant rather than ensuring the safety of the child. In a criminal case, the burden of proof—beyond a reasonable doubt—is higher than in a civil case and the rules of evidence are more stringent.

Responsibility for investigation of crimes related to child abuse and neglect rests with law enforcement agencies and the district attorney or local prosecutor. They are vested with the responsibility for deciding under what circumstances prosecution of perpetrators of child abuse and neglect will occur. Criminal courts serve to protect victims and the public from offenders and to rehabilitate those who break the law.

The defendant in a criminal case is entitled to full protection guaranteed by the Fourth, Fifth, and Sixth amendments to the U.S. Constitution. These protections include the right to a jury, the right to cross-examination, the right to appointed counsel, and the right to a public and speedy trial. Criminal prosecution may result in such penalties as probation or incarceration.

9. WHAT DOES THE CHILD PROTECTION PROCESS LOOK LIKE?

This chapter traces the child protection process beginning with the identification and reporting of suspected child maltreatment. As previously discussed, every State has enacted reporting laws. These laws provide guidance to individuals required to identify and report suspected maltreatment, require investigations by specified agencies to determine if a child was abused, and provide for the delivery of protective services and treatment to maltreated children and their families. Reports of maltreatment required under such laws activate the child protection process, which includes:

- Intake
- Initial assessment and investigation
- Family assessment
- Case planning
- Service provision
- Evaluation of family progress
- Case closure

Exhibit 9-1 presents an overview of the typical child protection process for most locales and is described further below.

Identification

The first step in any child protection response system is the identification of possible incidents of child maltreatment. Medical personnel, educators, child care providers, mental health professionals, law enforcement personnel, the clergy, and other professionals are often in a position to observe families and children on an ongoing basis and identify abuse or neglect when they occur. Private citizens, such as family members, friends, and neighbors, also may identify suspected incidents of child maltreatment.

To ensure that community professionals working with children and families recognize possible indicators of child maltreatment, preservice and inservice training must be provided on an ongoing basis. In addition, public awareness campaigns should be planned and implemented to promote understanding of the problem in the community.

Reporting

The next step in responding to child maltreatment is to report the suspected incident. Although there is tremendous variation in the requirements described in State reporting laws, they typically:

- Specify selected individuals mandated to report suspected child maltreatment;
- Define reportable conditions;

- Explain how, when, and to whom reports are to be filed and the information to be contained in the report;
- Describe the agencies designated to receive and investigate reports;
- Describe the abrogation of certain privileged ommunication rights (e.g., doctor–patient);
- Provide immunity from legal liability for reporters;
- Provide penalties for failure to report and false reporting.

Key aspects of reporting laws are described in the sections that follow.

Reporting procedures

Every State has reporting laws specifying procedures that a mandatory reporter must follow when making a report of suspected child abuse and neglect. Generally, these procedures specify how, where, when, and what to report.

How and when to report

The majority of States require that reports of child maltreatment be made orally—either by telephone or in person—to the specified authorities. Some States require that a written report follow the oral report, while in other States written reports are filed only upon request, and still other States require written reports only from mandated reporters.

Reports of suspected maltreatment are required by statute to be made immediately to protect children from potentially serious consequences that may be caused by a delay in reporting. While an individual may want to collect additional information before reporting, waiting for proof may place the child in danger.

Who receives the reports

Each State designates specific agencies to receive reports of child abuse and neglect. In most States, child protective services (CPS) has the primary responsibility for receiving reports. Other States allow reports to be made to either CPS or law enforcement. Some State laws require that certain forms of maltreatment—such as sexual abuse, child pornography, or severe physical abuse—be reported to law enforcement in addition to CPS. The nature of the relationship of the alleged perpetrator may also affect where reports are made. Most alleged cases of child maltreatment within the family are reportable to CPS. Depending on the State, reports of allegations of abuse or neglect by other caregivers, such as foster parents, daycare providers, teachers or residential care providers, may need to be filed with a law enforcement office. Additionally, in some States, allegations of abuse in out-of-home care are reported to a centralized investigative body within CPS at the State or regional level.

In most States, statutes also include requirements for ross-system reporting procedures or information sharing among professional entities. Typically, reports are shared among social services agencies, law enforcement, and prosecutors' offices.

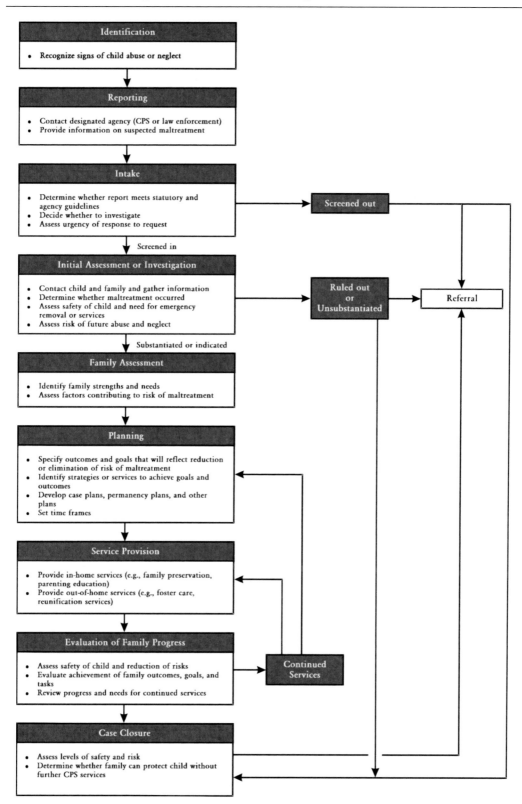

Exhibit 9-1 Overview of Child Protection Process

Mandatory reporters

Every State has statutes identifying mandatory reporters of child maltreatment and the circumstances under which they are required to report. This designation creates a legal responsibility to report, which can result in criminal and civil liability for failure to report as required. In approximately 18 States, *any person* who suspects child abuse or neglect is required to report.[124] Most States, however, limit mandatory reporting to professionals working with children. Individuals typically designated as mandatory reporters include:

- Physicians, nurses, hospital personnel, and dentists
- Medical examiners
- Coroners
- Mental health professionals
- Social workers
- School personnel
- Child care providers
- Law enforcement officers

In addition, any person in any State *may* report incidents of suspected abuse or neglect.

The legal standards used to determine when a mandatory reporter is required to notify authorities of abuse or neglect also vary slightly from State to State. Typically, a report must be made when a reporter has reasonable cause to know, suspect, or believe that a child has been abused or neglected.

STATE STATUTES

To review a summary of reporting laws, visit the State Statutes section of the National Clearinghouse on Child Abuse and Neglect Web site at www.calib.com/nccanch/statutes

---

Exhibit 9-2. Sources of Child Abuse and Neglect Reports in 2000[125]

Reporter	Percent
Education personnel	16.1
Legal, law enforcement, criminal justice personnel	15.2
Social services and mental health personnel	14.4
Medical personnel	8.3
Child daycare and substitute care providers	2.0
Anonymous or unknown reporters	13.6
Other relatives	8.3
Friends and neighbors	5.9
Parents	5.9
Alleged victims	0.9
Alleged perpetrators	0.1
Other	9.2

Source: Based only on sources of "screened-in" referrals in 2000

REPORTING CHILD ABUSE AND NEGLECT

See Appendix C for a list of State toll-free telephone numbers for reporting suspected child abuse or call the Childhelp USA National Child Abuse Hotline at 1-800-4-A-CHILD. This hotline is available 24 hours a day, 7 days a week.

Contents of the Report

Reporting laws also describe the information that must be contained in the report. Typically, reports contain the following information:

- The name, age, sex, and address of the child;
- The nature and extent of the child's injuries or condition;
- The name and address of the parent or other person(s) responsible for the child's care;
- Any other information relevant to the investigation.

It is essential that reporters provide as much detailed information as possible about:

- The child, the child's condition, and the child's whereabouts;
- The parents and their whereabouts;
- The person alleged to have caused the child's condition and his or her current location;
- The family, including other children in the home;
- The type and nature of the maltreatment, such as the length of time it has been occurring, whether the maltreatment has increased in severity or frequency, and whether objects or weapons were used.

If the alleged maltreatment occurred in an outof-home care setting, reporters should provide information about the setting, such as hours of operation; number of other children in the facility, if known; and identification of any others in the facility who may have information about the alleged maltreatment. The more comprehensive the information provided by the reporter, the better able CPS staff will be to evaluate the appropriateness of the report for CPS intervention, determine the urgency of the response needed, and prepare for an initial assessment and investigation, if warranted.

While most States allow anonymous reporting, it is preferred that reporters provide their name and contact information. This information will enable a caseworker to ask follow-up questions or obtain clarification. At intake, caseworkers should discuss immunity for reporters, issues of confidentiality, and the extent and nature of follow up with the reporter upon completion of the initial assessment or investigation.

Special issues, exceptions, and penalties related to reporting

To encourage reporting of child maltreatment and provide protection for reporters, State statutes include provisions related to privileged communications, immunity for reporters, and penalties for failure to report. The laws also discourage intentionally false reporting through specified penalties.

Privileged communications

The law provides special protection to communications in certain relationships. For example, the content of communications between an attorney and client, physician and patient, and clergy and congregant often is protected by a privilege. This means that professionals in such relationships are prohibited from disclosing confidential information communicated to them by their client, patient, or penitent to any unauthorized person. Mandatory child abuse reporting statutes specify when communications are confidential. The attorney-client privilege is most frequently maintained by States. The privilege pertaining to clergy-congregant also is frequently recognized by States. Most States, however, void the physician- patient, mental health professional-patient, and husband-wife privileges in instances of child maltreatment. When a privileged communication is voided, a mandated reporter must report instances of child maltreatment and cooperate in the ensuing investigation.

Immunity to reporters

Every State provides immunity from civil or criminal liability for individuals making reports of suspected or known instances of child abuse or neglect. Immunity provisions typically apply both to mandatory reporters and permissive reporters (i.e., individuals not required under law to report). These provisions may not prevent the filing of civil lawsuits, but they help prevent, within limitations, an outcome unfavorable to the reporter. Immunity provisions, like other aspects of reporting statutes, vary from State to State. The majority of jurisdictions require that reports be made in good faith. A number of States include a presumption in their statutes that the reporter is acting in good faith. Immunity, therefore, does not extend to reports made maliciously or in bad faith.

Penalties for failure to report

To encourage reporting, the majority of States now provide in their reporting statutes a specific penalty for failure to report suspected cases of abuse. Most of these jurisdictions impose penalties on mandatory reporters who knowingly or willfully fail to report suspected abuse. Failure to report is typically classified as a misdemeanor. Sanctions specified in the statutes are generally in the form of a fine or imprisonment.

Penalties for False Reporting

In order to prevent malicious or intentional false reporting, the majority of States impose penalties for false reporting of abuse. Most of these jurisdictions impose penalties on mandatory reporters who knowingly or willfully file a false report of abuse or neglect. False reporting is typically classified as a misdemeanor. Sanctions specified in the statutes are generally in the form of a fine or imprisonment.

Problems in reporting

Paradoxically, both underreporting and overreporting have been cited as problems in the identification of child abuse and neglect.

Underreporting

Numerous professionals admit that during their careers, they have failed to report suspected maltreatment to the appropriate agencies.[126] One possible reason is that professionals still lack training and knowledge about legal obligations and procedures for reporting. The issue of subjectivity also may account for some of the underreporting of abuse. Many laws defining child maltreatment are broadly written with ambiguous requirements, which may result in professionals lacking guidance and clarity regarding when intervention is required.

One of the biggest obstacles to reporting is personal feelings. Some people do not want to get involved. Others have difficulty reporting a person they suspect is an abuser, especially if they know that person well. Still others may think they can help the family more by working with the child or family themselves. Mandated reporters may believe that their professional relationship with the child will be strained if they report their suspicions of abuse. When a professional has established a relationship with a parent or family prior to recognizing maltreatment, reporting becomes a delicate issue.

Some reporters also may be reluctant to report because they have had negative experiences with CPS or they view social services agencies as overburdened, understaffed, or incompetent. At times, professionals become concerned that nothing will be done if they report or that the investigation and service provision will do more harm than good. Consequently, they choose not to report. This reluctance to report, which can have serious consequences for a child in an unsafe situation, underscores the critical need for ongoing communication and feedback between CPS and mandated reporters. It also underscores the need for CPS to function sensitively and competently in the best interests of the child while creating as little disruption as possible.

Professionals must report regardless of their concerns or previous experiences. The law requires it, and no exemptions are granted to those who have had a bad experience. In addition, while reporting does not guarantee that the situation will improve, not reporting guarantees that, if abuse and neglect exists, the child will continue to be at risk of further and perhaps more serious harm.

Overreporting

Only a portion of reports received and investigated by CPS reflect children who are found to be victims of, or at risk for, maltreatment. While the children and families in these reports may be in need of help or services, they frequently do not meet the legal definition of maltreatment in that family's jurisdiction. This apparent pattern of over-reporting raises several concerns. First, children and families who will not receive child welfare services may be subjected to an intrusive public agency investigation. Second, these reports may divert CPS resources from higher risk cases.

Overreporting may occur in a community following a serious case of child maltreatment that receives a lot of media attention. There is often a significant increase in the number of reports of suspected child maltreatment made during such times, in part because the community's awareness has been heightened.

Intake

Intake is the point at which reports of suspected child maltreatment are received by the agency designated by the State (typically the CPS agency and sometimes the police department). The agency receiving the report must make two primary decisions at intake:

- Does the reported information meet the statutory and agency guidelines for child maltreatment?
- How urgent is the required response?

The first decision consists of three essential steps:

1. Gathering sufficient information from the reporter to allow accurate decision-making;
2. Evaluating the information to determine if it meets the statutory and agency guidelines for child maltreatment;
3. Assessing the credibility of the reporter based on the relationship of the alleged victim and family, knowledge of the family and circumstances, and apparent motives for reporting.

There will be a check of agency records and State central registries to determine if the family is currently involved in an open case or has a history of involvement in a maltreatment case. (A central registry is a database containing information on all previously substantiated reports of child maltreatment.)

When the agency determines that an initial assessment or investigation is warranted, the report is "screened in"; cases closed without further investigation are referred to as "screened out." While screening rates vary substantially across States, CPS agencies screened in and investigated approximately 62 percent of the nearly 3 million report referrals received nationwide in 2000.[127] In some instances, screened out cases will receive referrals to other community services (e.g., substance abuse treatment, mental health services, child care, domestic violence shelters, or income support agencies).

Once the CPS agency determines that an initial assessment is warranted, the immediacy of the response is evaluated. The decision regarding the urgency of the response is based on an analysis of the information gathered to determine if the child is at imminent risk of serious harm. This decision will be based upon a number of factors including:

- The nature of the act or omission;
- The severity of harm to the child;
- The relationship of the child to the person responsible for the maltreatment;
- The access of the perpetrator to the child;
- The child's vulnerability (e.g., due to age, illness, or disability);
- The other known cases of maltreatment by the parent or caregiver;
- The availability of persons who can protect the child.

Exhibit 9-3. Primary Decisions Considered During Initial Assessment or Investigation

CPS	Law Enforcement	CPS and Law Enforcement
Is the child safe? If not, whatmeasures are necessary to ensure the child's safety?	Did a crime occur?	Do sources of corroboration or witnesses exist?
Did the child suffer maltreatment or is he or she threatened by harm as defined by the State reporting law?	Who is the alleged offender?	Has all physical evidence been obtained or preserved?
Is maltreatment likely to occur in the future? If so, what is the level of risk of maltreatment?	Is there evidence to arrest the alleged offender?	Are there any other victims (e.g., siblings)?
Are there emergency needs in the family that must be met?	Has all physical evidence been obtained, preserved, and/or photographed?	Should the child be taken into protective custody?
Are continuing agency services necessary to protect the child and reduce the risk of maltreatment occurring in the future?	Have all witnesses been interviewed?	

Some CPS agencies provide guidelines for initial assessment response times, although it is difficult to generalize. Caseworkers are required to respond to reports within a specified time, typically ranging from 24 to 72 hours on more serious cases. If it is determined that the child in a report may not be safe, caseworkers must respond immediately.

Initial Assessment or Investigation

The initial assessment or investigation follows the intake process for those reports that are screened in.

Primary initial assessment or investigation decisions
The purpose of the initial assessment or investigation of cases of child abuse and neglect is to determine the following:

- Is child maltreatment substantiated as defined by State statute?
- Is the child at risk of maltreatment and what is the level of risk?
- Is the child safe, and if not, what type of agency or community response will ensure the child's safety in the least intrusive manner?
- If the child's safety cannot be assured within the family, what type and level of care does the child need?
- Does the family have emergency needs that must be met?
- Should ongoing agency services be offered to the family to reduce the risk or address the treatment needs of the child?

CPS agencies and law enforcement are each responsible for conducting initial assessments or investigations in cases of child abuse and neglect. Exhibit 9-3 presents the primary decisions or issues considered at this stage according to the agency that typically considers the decision.

Involvement of other professionals

In addition to CPS and law enforcement, other disciplines have a role to play in the initial assessment process:

- **Medical personnel** may be involved in assessing and responding to the medical needs of a child or parent and perhaps in documenting the nature and extent of maltreatment. It is helpful to have medical practitioners in each community who have had specific training in child maltreatment because they will provide a more complete and accurate evaluation than will an examiner without specific training.

- **Mental health personnel** may be involved in assessing the effects of any alleged maltreatment and in determining the validity of specific allegations. At this stage of the CPS process, referrals to mental health providers are primarily for help in determining whether abuse occurred, whether there is sufficient information to file charges related to child maltreatment, and whether the child is capable of providing valid and reliable information. In addition, referrals to mental health practitioners may be made for assistance in assessing the safety of the child. For example, parents or caregivers may be referred for an evaluation of their mental status, the presence of psychiatric problems, personality disorders, or substance abuse.

- **Teachers and child care providers** may be involved in providing direct information about the effects of maltreatment and in describing information pertinent to risk assessment. In addition, during the investigative stage, educators provide support for the efforts of CPS and law enforcement. For example, if the CPS caseworker or law enforcement needs to interview the child in the school, the school should provide a private place for the interview.

- **Foster care, residential, or child care licensing personnel** may participate in the initial assessment if abuse is allegedly committed by an out-of-home caregiver. Each State differs with respect to who is responsible for initially assessing or investigating allegations of child abuse and neglect in out-of-home care. In some States, local CPS staffs have responsibility for investigating certain types of allegations, for example, those in foster care and daycare. Frequently, the investigation of alleged maltreatment in institutional settings is handled by central or regional CPS or licensing staff, rather than by local CPS agencies. Depending on the nature of the allegations, law enforcement agencies also will assume a primary role in investigating these types of cases.

Other community service providers also may have past experience with the child or family and may be used as a resource in addressing any emergency needs that the child or family may have.

MAJOR TYPES OF INVESTIGATION DISPOSITIONS

- **Substantiated** is an investigation disposition that concludes that the allegation of maltreatment or risk of maltreatment was supported or founded by State law or State policy. This is the highest level of finding by a State Agency.

- **Indicated** or **Reason to Suspect** is an investigation disposition that concludes that maltreatment cannot be substantiated under State law or policy, but there is reason to suspect that the child may have been maltreated or was at risk of maltreatment. This is applicable only to States that distinguish between substantiated and indicated dispositions.

- **Not Substantiated** is an investigation disposition that determines that there is not sufficient evidence under State law or policy to conclude that the child has been maltreated or is at risk of being maltreated.[128]

Investigation in out-of-home care settings

In cases of child maltreatment in out-of-home care (e.g., residential facilities, foster homes), an investigation must be completed by an independent authority designated by the State. For cases involving out-of-home care abuse, there are other decisions and issues to consider:

- Did the reported event occur?
- Are personnel actions indicated and, if so, are they being initiated appropriately by the child care facility?
- What responsibility do others in the facility have for any incident of maltreatment, and is a corrective action plan needed to prevent the likelihood of future incidents?
- Can the problem, if validated, be addressed administratively?
- Is the administrative authority responsible and, if so, in what manner?
- Should the facility's or foster care or other child care provider's license be revoked?

These decisions are made by thoroughly gathering and analyzing information from and about the child, family, or in some cases, the out-of-home provider. Typically, a protocol is employed for interviewing the child victim, family members, the person alleged to have maltreated the child, and others possessing information about the child and the family.

DIFFERENTIAL RESPONSE SYSTEMS

Over the past decade, States have begun to enhance CPS practice and build community partnerships in responding to cases of child maltreatment. One area of CPS reform emphasizes greater flexibility in responding to allegations of abuse and neglect. A "dual track" or "multiple track" response permits CPS agencies to respond differentially according to the children's safety, the degree of risk present, and the family's needs for support services. Implementation models vary across States piloting differential response systems. Typically, in cases where abuse and neglect are severe or serious criminal offenses against children have occurred, an investigation will commence. The investigation focuses on evidence gathering and may include a referral to law enforcement. In less serious cases of child maltreatment, where the family may benefit from community services, an assessment will be conducted. In these cases the facts regarding what happened will be obtained, but the intervention will emphasize the comprehensive assessment of family strengths and needs and an appropriate match with community services.

The assessment is designed to be a process where parents or caregivers are partners with CPS, and that partnership begins with the very first contact. In addition, the family's support network is frequently brought into the process. States that have implemented the differential response strategy have shown that a majority of cases now coming to CPS can be handled safely through an approach that emphasizes service delivery and voluntary family participation as well as the fact finding of "traditional" CPS investigations.[129]

Family Assessment

The family assessment is a comprehensive process for identifying, considering, and weighing factors that affect the child's safety, permanency, and well-being. The family assessment is a process designed to gain a greater understanding about the strengths, needs, and resources of the family so that children can be safe and the risk of maltreatment can be reduced. The family assessment is initiated immediately after the decision is made that ongoing services are needed. The following are the key decisions made as a result of the family assessment:

- What are the risks and needs of this family that affect safety, permanency, or well-being?
- What are the effects of maltreatment that affect safety, permanency, and well-being?
- What are the individual and family strengths?
- How do the family members perceive their conditions, problems, and strengths?
- What must change in order for the effects of maltreatment to be addressed and for the risk of maltreatment to be reduced or eliminated?
- What is the parent's or caregiver's level of readiness for change? What is their motivation and capacity to assure safety, permanency, and well-being?

Family assessment should be strengths-based, culturally sensitive, and developed with the family. In addition to gathering information regarding problems, risks, and needs, strengths should be identified that may mitigate the identified concern(s) and the family's stated goals as they relate to each problem. The strengths identified will provide the foundation upon which the family can change.

Assessments should be conducted in a partnership with the family to help parents or caregivers recognize and remedy conditions so children can safely remain in their own home. Family assessments must be individualized and tailored to the unique strengths and needs of each family. When possible, this assessment also should be undertaken in conjunction with the extended family and support network through family decision-making meetings and other processes designed to involve this network in the process.[130]

CONCURRENT PLANNING

The passage of the Adoption and Safe Families Act (ASFA) in 1997 has resulted in time limits for permanency for children and termination of parental rights so that children are provided safe, stable, and permanent placements more quickly. Concurrent planning works toward reunification of children in care with their birth families while at the same time establishing a "back-up" permanency plan that will be implemented if the children cannot be reunified with their birth family. The concurrent plan provides a safeguard to assure secure childhood attachments by developing a stronger bond to the birth families and simultaneously supporting ties between the child and other possible permanent families, for example, kin or foster parents. Concurrent permanency plans provide a structured approach to move children quickly from temporary foster care to the stability of a safe and continuous family home.[131]

Planning

The comprehensive assessment of the family's circumstances and conditions is the foundation on which the case plan is built. Armed with this knowledge, CPS caseworkers, other service providers or community professionals, and the family and its support network will determine the best possible strategies for reducing or eliminating the behaviors and conditions contributing to the risk of maltreatment of the child. The purposes of case planning are to identify the strategies with clients that will help address the effects of maltreatment and lessen the risk of further abuse and neglect; to provide a clear and specific guide for the professional and the family for changing the behaviors and conditions that impact risk; to provide a benchmark for measuring client progress toward achieving outcomes; and to provide a framework for case decision-making.

The key decisions made at the case planning stage are:

- What are the client outcomes that, when achieved, will indicate that risk has been reduced and the effects of maltreatment have been successfully addressed?
- What goals must be accomplished to achieve the outcomes?
- What intervention approaches or services will facilitate the successful goal achievement and the accomplishment of outcomes?
- How and when will progress toward achievement of these outcomes and goals be evaluated?

In order to achieve the client outcomes, the case plan must be developed with, not for, the family. Involving the family in planning serves several purposes. It facilitates the family's investment in and commitment to the plan, it empowers parents or caregivers to take the necessary action to change behavior, and ensures that the agency and the family are working toward the same end. Some CPS agencies use models that optimize family strengths in the planning process. These models bring together the family, the extended family, and others important in the family's life—for example, friends, clergy, neighbors—to make decisions regarding how best to ensure the safety of the family members.

Service Provision

Once the case plan has been developed, the CPS caseworker must provide or arrange for services identified in the plan to help family members achieve the outcomes, goals, and tasks outlined in the case plan. Selecting and matching interventions that will support the family in achieving outcomes and goals is a major responsibility in child protection.

The needs of families are often complex. As discussed in Chapter 5, child abuse and neglect is caused by multiple and interacting intrapersonal, interpersonal, and environmental factors. Interventions need to address as many of these contributing issues as possible.[132] Research on the effectiveness of child abuse and neglect treatment suggests that successful intervention with maltreating families requires addressing both the interpersonal and concrete needs (e.g., housing, child care) of all family members. Evaluation projects found that programs that rely solely upon professional therapy, without augmenting the service strategies with other supportive or remedial services to children and families, will offer less opportunity for maximizing client gains.[133]

Therefore, each community must provide a broad range of services to meet the multidimensional needs of abused and neglected children and their families. These may include:

- Services provided to the entire family (e.g., family preservation services, multisystemic therapy for children and families, or family strengthening programs);
- Services provided specifically to parents or caregivers (e.g., sex offender treatment, parent education, substance abuse treatment, or mutual support programs);
- Services provided to children (e.g., counseling, therapeutic preschool, peer-based training, or mentoring programs).

Depending on the assessed needs, strengths, and safety issues, services may be provided either in or out of the family's home. When a child is unsafe because the risk of imminent harm is great or when the child's behavioral and emotional needs cannot be addressed at home, out-of-home placement services, such as foster care, should be considered.

Selection of services in a particular case is based on:

- Assessing factors that contribute to the risk of maltreatment;
- Identifying family strengths;
- Targeting outcomes for change;
- Identifying treatment approaches best suited to the desired outcome, based on any available research evidence;
- Listing resources available and accessible in the community.

The CPS caseworker serves as the case manager, articulating the needs of the family, coordinating services provided to them, and advocating on their behalf.[134] The case management functions include: collecting and analyzing information, reaching decisions at all stages of the case process, coordinating services provided by others, and directly providing supportive services. This critical case-management function requires open and continuous communication among CPS, the family, and other service providers; developing a teamwork relationship; clarifying roles and responsibilities in delivering and monitoring services; and reaching consensus on goals and methods for monitoring progress toward goal achievement.

Evaluation of Family Progress

Evaluating whether risk behaviors and conditions have changed is central to case decisions. Monitoring change should begin as soon as an intervention is implemented and should continue throughout the life of a case until appropriate outcomes have been achieved.[135]

The importance of evaluating family progress is to help answer the following questions:

- Is the child safe? Have the protective factors, strengths, or the safety factors changed, warranting a change or elimination of the safety plan or the development of a safety plan?
- What changes, if any, have occurred with respect to the conditions and behaviors contributing to the risk of maltreatment?
- What outcomes have been accomplished and how does the caseworker know that they have been accomplished?
- What progress has been made toward achieving case goals?
- Have the services been effective in helping clients achieve outcomes and goals and, if not, what adjustments need to be made to improve outcomes?
- What is the current level of risk in the family?
- Have the risk factors been reduced sufficiently so that parents or caregivers can protect their children and meet their developmental needs so the case can be closed?
- Has it been determined that reunification is not likely in the ASFA-required time frames and there is no significant progress toward outcomes? If so, is an alternative permanent plan goal needed?

Since intervention and service provision to families at risk of maltreatment is a collaborative effort between CPS and other agencies or individual providers, the evaluation of family progress must be a collaborative venture. It is the CPS caseworker's responsibility to manage the comparison of client progress based on information reported from all service providers. In some cases, it may be appropriate to convene a team meeting to review the progress in relation to the family assessment and the case plan.

The process of evaluating family progress is a continual case management function. Once the case plan is established, each client contact will be focused on assessing the progress being made to achieve established outcomes, goals, and tasks, and to reassess safety. Formal case evaluations should occur at regular intervals. Good practice suggests evaluation of progress at least every 3 months.

Case Closure

Closure is the point at which the agency no longer maintains an active relationship with the family. The decision to end the agency's involvement must be based on the monitoring and evaluation of the case. ASFA requires decisions regarding case closure to be made in conjunction with the family and individuals important to the family. The preeminent concerns that inform case closure decisions are based on safety and permanency outcomes. The agency should support the family's right to self- determination by ending services when the risks to child safety have been reduced significantly and the family believes they no longer need services.[136]

> For more detailed information on the child protection process, check other manuals in the series at www.calib.com/nccanch/pubs/usermanual.cfm.

10. WHO SHOULD BE INVOLVED IN CHILD PROTECTION AT THE COMMUNITY LEVEL?

Child protective services (CPS) is typically the central agency in each community's child protection system. It usually plays the lead role in coordinating communication and services among the various disciplines responsible for addressing child maltreatment. In addition to CPS, law enforcement, educators, child care providers, health care providers, mental health care providers, legal and judicial system professionals, substitute care providers, support service providers, domestic violence victim advocates, substance abuse treatment providers, and concerned community members all play important roles in keeping children safe. All relevant professionals must be aware of their role in child protection and the unique knowledge and skills they bring to their community's prevention and intervention efforts. They must also understand the roles, responsibilities, and expertise of other professionals.

Child Protective Services

CPS is the agency mandated in most States to respond to reports of child abuse and neglect.

CPS is responsible for:

- Receiving reports of child abuse and neglect;
- Conducting initial assessments and investigations regarding suspected maltreatment;
- Conducting assessments of family strengths, resources, and needs;
- Developing individualized case plans;

- Providing direct services to support families in addressing the problems that led to maltreatment and reducing the risk of subsequent maltreatment;
- Coordinating services provided by other professionals;
- Completing case management functions such as maintaining case records, systematically reviewing case plans, and developing court reports.

CPS also helps educate the community about child abuse and neglect and seeks to enhance community prevention and treatment resources.

Law Enforcement

In the initial stages of the child protection response, law enforcement and CPS often have similar responsibilities. Law enforcement's involvement in the initial assessment and investigation of child abuse and neglect varies across States and communities. For example, in many States, sexual abuse or severe physical abuse must be investigated by law enforcement. In a few States, abuse allegations are reported initially to law enforcement rather than to CPS.[137] Whether the community has a protocol for joint or separate initial assessments and investigations, a high degree of coordination between CPS and law enforcement is necessary to minimize the confusion and trauma to the child as a result of system intervention.

The primary responsibilities of law enforcement include:

- Identifying and reporting suspected child maltreatment;
- Receiving reports of child abuse and neglect;
- Conducting investigations of reports of child maltreatment when there is a suspicion that a crime has been committed;
- Gathering physical evidence;
- Determining whether sufficient evidence exists to prosecute alleged offenders;
- Assisting with any need to secure the protection of the child;
- Providing protection to CPS staff when a caseworker's personal safety may be in jeopardy if confrontation occurs with alleged offenders;
- Supporting the victim through the criminal court process.

In several States, law enforcement plays a key role in multidisciplinary teams or Child Advocacy Centers (CACs). These teams and centers aim to reduce the trauma to the child caused by multiple interviewing. They also work to improve the prosecution of cases, particularly in sexual abuse cases.[138] (For more information on multidisciplinary teams and CACs, see Chapter 11, "How Can Organizations Work Together to Protect Children?")

Educators and Early Child Care Providers

Principals, teachers, school social workers, and counselors, as well as early childhood education and child care providers, play a critical role in the community child protection system. Key functions of educators include:

- Developing and implementing prevention programs for children and parents;
- Identifying and reporting suspected child abuse and neglect;
- Recognizing and reporting child abuse and neglect occurring in the school system or child care program;
- Developing a school or program policy for reporting instances of child abuse and neglect and cooperating with CPS investigations;
- Keeping CPS informed of the changes or improvements in the child's behavior and condition following the investigation;
- Providing input in diagnostic and treatment services for the child;
- Supporting the child through potentially traumatic events, for example, court hearings and out-of-home placement;
- Providing support services for parents such as school-sponsored self-help groups;
- Serving on child maltreatment multidisciplinary teams.

Health Care Providers

Physicians, nurses, emergency medical technicians, and other medical personnel play a major role in the child protection system in every community. Key functions of health care providers include:

- Identifying and reporting suspected cases of child abuse and neglect;
- Providing diagnostic and treatment services (medical and psychiatric) for maltreated children and their families;
- Providing consultation to CPS regarding medical aspects of child abuse and neglect;
- Participating on the multidisciplinary case- consultation team;
- Providing expert testimony in child protection judicial proceedings;
- Providing information to parents regarding the needs, care, and treatment of children;
- Identifying and providing support for families at risk of child maltreatment;
- Developing and conducting primary prevention programs;
- Providing training for medical and nonmedical professionals regarding the medical aspects of child abuse and neglect;
- Participating on community multidisciplinary teams.

Mental Health Professionals

Mental health services are a prerequisite for any community system designed to prevent and treat child abuse and neglect. Key functions of psychiatrists, psychologists, social workers, and other mental health professionals include:

- Identifying and reporting suspected cases of child abuse and neglect;
- Conducting necessary evaluations of abused and neglected children and their families;
- Providing treatment for abused and neglected children and their families;
- Providing clinical consultation to CPS;
- Providing expert testimony in child protection judicial proceedings;
- Providing self-help groups for parents who have maltreated or are at risk of maltreating their children;
- Developing and implementing prevention programs;
- Participating on community multidisciplinary teams.

Legal and Judicial System Professionals

Responsibilities of legal professionals vary depending upon who the attorney's client is and the stage of a judicial proceeding.

Attorneys representing the CPS agency who are responsible for presenting child maltreatment cases in court:

- Assure that CPS personnel are given appropriate legal advice and consultation, for example, on decisions regarding emergency removal of children;
- Prepare necessary legal pleadings when court intervention becomes necessary;
- Participate in multidisciplinary team meetings when potential legal actions on behalf of the child may be explored;
- Prepare CPS caseworkers, expert witnesses, and other witnesses, especially children, for testifying in court.

Criminal prosecutors:

- Assure that any criminal action is coordinated with a civil child protection proceeding involving the same child;
- Assure that the child is adequately prepared for testifying;
- Provide the child with victim advocacy services when necessary;
- Assist the court in arriving at a sentence that serves the interest of justice and assures that proper treatment is provided;
- Participate in multidisciplinary team meetings when potential legal actions on behalf of the child may be explored.

Guardians ad Litem, legal counsel for children, and court-appointed special advocates (CASAs):

- Assure that the needs and interests of a child in child protection judicial proceedings are fully protected;
- Conduct an independent investigation into background and facts of the case;
- Determine the child's educational, psychological, and other treatment needs and help assure that the judicial intervention leads to appropriate treatment;
- Facilitate a speedy, nonadversarial resolution of the case whenever possible and appropriate.

Defense attorneys for the parents or other maltreating caregiver:

- Assure that the parents' or caregivers' statutory and constitutional rights are fully protected in any judicial proceeding;
- Assure that the parents or caregivers understand the judicial process and the potential impact of the process.

Juvenile or family court judges:

- Provide emergency protective orders when necessary, 24 hours a day, 7 days a week;
- Resolve speedily all court cases of alleged child maltreatment;
- Apply relevant case law and adjust the court process, as appropriate, to deal sensitively with child victims;
- Encourage the development of greater community resources for maltreated children and their families.

Court personnel help assure that children and families are dealt with sensitively throughout the judicial process. It is important for all family members to feel respected by the legal system as they go through a process that may feel intimidating and overwhelming. They also identify possible child maltreatment in cases before the court for other reasons, for example, delinquency.

KINSHIP CARE

In recent decades, increasing numbers of substitute care providers are relatives of the maltreated children. "Kinship care" often involves formal child placement by the child welfare agency and juvenile court in the home of a child's relative—most frequently the child's grandmother.[139] Kinship care offers several benefits including greater familiarity between the caregiver and the child, potentially less traumatic placements, more visitation and contact with birth parents, and fewer placement changes.[140]

Substitute Care Providers

When children are removed from their parents' care and placed in foster care or residential care to ensure their safety, foster parents and residential care providers become part of the treatment team, which is focused on the objective of family reunification. Substitute care providers help ensure that the basic needs of maltreated children are met in safe, stable, and nurturing environments. Foster families typically become a part of their child's extended family and help negotiate relationships that support the birth parents and case plan goals.

Faith Community

Clergy and spiritual leaders can play important roles in supporting families and protecting children by:

- Providing counseling, support, and spiritual leadership to their congregation;
- Developing and implementing prevention programs to help stop child maltreatment;
- Identifying and reporting suspected child abuse and neglect;
- Supporting the child and family through potentially traumatic events, for example, court hearings and out-of-home placement;
- Attending family team meetings to help make decisions about case plans;
- Organizing self-help or mutual support groups at their facilities for parents who have maltreated a child or are at risk for doing so;
- Participating in community multidisciplinary teams.

Community Organizations and Support Services Providers

There are many other individuals who support the community intervention efforts, including youth service workers, community-based organizations, housing and job assistance agencies, civic groups, volunteers, and parent aides. These individuals offer prevention, support, and treatment services to abused and neglected children and their families. Support services frequently address the reduction of risk factors and enhancement of protective factors discussed in Chapter 5, "What Factors Contribute to Child Abuse and Neglect?" Involvement may occur prior to CPS involvement (e.g., supporting families at risk), concurrent with CPS involvement (e.g., attending family team meetings to help make decisions about case plans), or following CPS involvement (e.g., providing ongoing support and services).

Some examples of the diverse community support provided to maltreated children and their families include:

- Home visitors supporting new parents and modeling appropriate parenting practices;
- Substance abuse treatment providers offering services to parents who are addicted to drugs;

- Big Brother/Big Sister Organizations providing mentoring and social opportunities for maltreated children;
- Domestic violence shelters offering safe housing arrangements for abused spouses and their children;
- Neighborhood centers helping to build family skills and providing networking opportunities;
- Homeless shelter staff providing homemaking and advocacy services for families in a shelter;
- Child care programs offering respite care to stressed parents;
- Family service agencies lending support to teen parents.

As part of ongoing CPS reform movements across the country, community organizations and support service providers increasingly are playing more active roles in collaborative child protection efforts.

Concerned Citizens

In addition to the various practitioners described above, concerned citizens, particularly friends and neighbors, play an important role in responding to child maltreatment. All individuals in the community can contribute to the protection of children by providing social and emotional support to fellow community members, reporting suspected maltreatment, modeling good parenting behaviors, advocating for needed resources, and helping educate others about the problems of maltreatment.

11. How Can Organizations Work Together to Protect Children?

National, State, and local movements to integrate services and improve collaboration have been among the most significant trends in human services over the last decade.[141] Catalysts supporting this trend toward increased collaboration include changes in Federal funding programs that now encourage collaborative efforts and the desire to enhance service delivery to clients who exhibit multifaceted problems.[142] Likewise, many communities are experimenting with a new approach to child protection and family well-being by broadening the commitment and responsibility from a single public agency to the community.[143]

This chapter examines the essential elements of a well-coordinated child protection system. Other manuals in the series include more detailed information regarding community collaboration and integrated service systems.

Principles to Guide Collaboration

Collaboration is grounded in interdependent relationships. There are several basic guidelines to foster collaborative efforts:

- **Build and maintain trust.** Trust enables people to share information, perceptions, and feedback. Professionals and nonprofessionals working together must trust each other, respect each other, view each other as an important contributor, and value the uniqueness of their colleagues. Collaborators can build trust by:
    - Reaching agreement regarding norms for behavior for working together;
    - Developing mutual respect, which enables them to be creative, take risks, and openly explore difficult issues;
    - Correcting common misconceptions and learning up-to-date information regarding other agencies;
    - Developing an informal, relaxed atmosphere, for example, by getting to know team members outside of the work setting;
    - Viewing all participants as equal members in designing and implementing the collaborative efforts.[144]

- **Reach agreement on core values.** All the parties must reach consensus on a core set of values for the collaborative effort. Each of the parties must honor the importance of the values and their implementation in practice.

- **Reach agreement and stay focused on common goals.** A well-coordinated system is based on agreement between all of the parties on common goals, such as the prevention of child abuse, the safety of children, and the permanency for children. In spite of the fact that the professionals or agencies involved in child welfare have differences in philosophy, focus, mission, and perceptions, which may sometimes come into conflict with one another, it is possible to agree on common goals. This requires that all parties:
    - Set aside or merge their vested interests;
    - Believe that by developing and maintaining common goals children and families will attain more positive outcomes.

- **Develop a common language.** Each profession and agency has its own terminology, jargon, and acronyms. It is important to help the parties overcome language barriers. Each of the parties should:
    - Explain the technical language, words, and phrases they use;
    - Refrain from using acronyms and professional jargon;
    - Achieve a common understanding of what terms mean, for example, "strengths-based" or "family involvement."

- **Demonstrate respect for the knowledge and experience of each person.** Respect is a fundamental starting point for understanding and action. Effective collaboration requires the expertise and knowledge of all parties, who should listen to and be respectful of each person's opinions and ideas. Any misunderstandings, unreasonable expectations, myths, previous problems, or other issues must be worked through.

- **Assume positive intentions of the parties.** When a variety of professionals, as well as nonprofessionals, comes together to develop and implement a collaborative effort, they bring with them different ideas, perspectives, and approaches. It is important to believe that each of the parties is genuinely interested in working toward the agreed upon goals and positive outcomes for children and families.

- **Recognize the strengths, needs, and limitations of all of the parties.** Each person and agency comes to the collaborative process with strengths, needs, and limitations. For example, community agencies bring with them specific resources needed to build an effective community response to child maltreatment. They also bring with them limitations, such as differing missions, goals, policies, and procedures. Capitalizing on the strengths and being aware of and addressing any barriers to participation are essential. It may require being open to and exploring alternative ways individuals can contribute to the collaborative effort.

- **Work through conflict.** Conflict is healthy and inevitable when people work together collaboratively. The extent to which people feel comfortable with conflict and airing differences affects reaching consensus or an acceptable conclusion. Since communication is a significant part of one's culture, great care must be taken to encourage the equal participation of all members.

- **Share decision-making, risk taking, and accountability.** A true collaborative effort means that decisions are made and risks are taken as a team. Members participate in planning and decision- making and openly collaborate with others. All members feel a professional responsibility for the performance of the partnership. This means the entire team is accountable for achieving the outcomes and goals.[145]

Effective Leadership— An Essential Component Of Successful Collaboration

Leadership is key to successful collaboration. The leader:

- Assures that all of the stakeholders are represented on the team;
- Is able to search for and discover opportunities, benefits, and resources;
- Can build trust across agencies, professionals, and nonprofessionals;
- Is responsive to the needs of the group;
- Is flexible and can flow with the dynamics of the group;
- Understands the dynamics of power, authority, and influence and uses this knowledge to facilitate collaboration;
- Is able to manage conflict effectively;
- Does not promote his or her own agenda to the exclusion of others;
- Understands and responds appropriately to people from diverse cultures;
- Treats all members with respect;
- Facilitates group discussions effectively;
- Frames needs, problems, and opportunities for the group.[146]

Collaborative Models

The following models demonstrate the effectiveness of collaboration.

Fatality review team

In the event of a child's death due to abuse or neglect, a child fatality review team provides a systemic and multidisciplinary means to identify discrepancies between policy and practice and gaps in communication systems. Child fatality review teams typically consist of representatives from pertinent agencies or offices, such as CPS, law enforcement, and the coroner or medical examiner.

The outcomes achieved through child fatality review teams include: the improvement of child protection through better coordination and collection of information; the protection of siblings in at-risk families; a decrease in the number of child deaths; and an enhanced collection of evidence, which improves the prosecution of abusers.[147]

Child advocacy centers

Child advocacy centers (CAC) are community-based facilities designed to coordinate services to victims of nonfatal abuse and neglect, especially in cases of child sexual abuse and severe physical abuse. The key goal of these centers is to reduce the trauma to victims that may result from agency intervention. CACs seek to improve the handling of cases at key points in the child protection process—investigation, prosecution, and treatment—by assuring the collaboration of the key professionals and agencies involved.[148]

The Child Advocacy Center is a child-friendly facility where all of the key professionals—child protective services (CPS), law enforcement, prosecutors, mental health professionals, and child advocates—are co-located. Also, CACs typically work closely with medical personnel who specialize in child sexual abuse. CACs enhance coordination and achievement of positive outcomes by the close proximity of professionals, the assignment of a child advocate who monitors the case through the various systems, and the case review, which promotes formal and informal discussion of cases.

INTEGRATED SERVICE DELIVERY SYSTEMS

Many communities throughout the United States are attempting to create integrated service delivery systems that honor the unique strengths, needs, and culture of each child and family. One example is the six sites implementing "Partnerships in Action," which brings together families and child welfare, mental health, and other related systems.

- The program in Branch County, Michigan, assessed and redesigned community-based services to develop a seamless, integrated system of care for pregnant women and their families with newborn children (up to 6 years of age).
- The program in the Pueblo of Zuni, New Mexico, created a single point of entry among tribal agencies for families experiencing domestic violence and child abuse. Also, the program strengthened domestic violence codes and created a state-of-the-art shelter for female victims of domestic violence and their children.

- The program in Lorain County, Ohio, developed an infrastructure to provide the strongest possible community safety net for adolescents who "fell through the cracks" because their needs were not severe enough to require immediate, crisis, or intensive services from child welfare or mental health agencies. An essential part of the program was the development of a written operational interagency agreement.
- The Rhode Island program provided seed money to communities to develop a specialized team approach for transition planning for youth with multiple agency needs who are incarcerated in a training school.
- The program in Sedgwick County, Kansas, collaborated with a private contractor providing foster care to develop individualized plans of care for children diagnosed with serious emotional disturbances in need of mental health services. They also provided training to staff regarding family involvement.
- The program in Maryland identified the individual and collective effects of multiple reform efforts in the State and identified ways the efforts could reinforce each other.[149]

Conclusion

Every child deserves to grow up in a safe and nurturing environment. Unfortunately, hundreds of thousands of children are reported to be victims of child abuse and neglect each year.[150] An untold number of other children are maltreated but not reported to responding agencies. As outlined in this manual, a number of practitioners and professionals assume different roles and responsibilities in identifying and responding to reported cases of child abuse and neglect. Child maltreatment, however, is so widespread and, thus, such a significant issue that every citizen and organization shares in the responsibility for responding to this problem.

Interventions are designed to strengthen families as an integral part of ensuring child safety, permanency, and well-being. This includes promoting responsible parenting, fostering families' support networks, and providing comprehensive services customized to meet the circumstances, strengths, and needs of each family.

This manual is intended as a foundation for understanding child maltreatment issues and responses. Interested parties are encouraged to read the accompanying profession-specific and special- issue publications contained in the *User Manual Series*.

APPENDIX A. GLOSSARY OF TERMS

Adjudicatory Hearings – held by the juvenile and family court to determine whether a child has been maltreated or whether another legal basis exists for the State to intervene to protect the child.

Adoption and Safe Families Act (ASFA) – signed into law November 1997 and designed to improve the safety of children, to promote adoption and other permanent homes for children who need them, and to support families. The law requires CPS agencies to provide more timely and focused assessment and intervention services to the children and families that are served within the CPS system.

CASA – court-appointed special advocates (usually volunteers) who serve to ensure that the needs and interests of a child in child protection judicial proceedings are fully protected.

Case Closure – the process of ending the relationship between the CPS worker and the family that often involves a mutual assessment of progress. Optimally, cases are closed when families have achieved their goals and the risk of maltreatment has been reduced or eliminated.

Case Plan – the casework document that outlines the outcomes, goals, and tasks necessary to be achieved in order to reduce the risk of maltreatment.

Case Planning – the stage of the CPS case process where the CPS caseworker develops a case plan with the family members.

Caseworker Competency – **demonstrated** professional behaviors based on the knowledge, skills, personal qualities, and values a person holds.

Central Registry – a centralized database containing information on all substantiated/founded reports of child maltreatment in a selected area (typically a State).

Child Abuse Prevention and Treatment Act (CAPTA) – the law (P.L. 93-247) that provides a foundation for a national definition of child abuse and neglect. Reauthorized in October 1996 (P.L. 104-235), it was up for reauthorization at the time of publication. CAPTA defines child abuse and neglect as "at a minimum, any recent act or failure to act on the part of a parent or caretaker, which results in death, serious physical or emotional harm, sexual abuse or exploitation, or an act or failure to act which presents an imminent risk of serious harm."

Child Protective Services (CPS) – the designated social services agency (in most States) to receive reports, investigate, and provide intervention and treatment services to children and families in which child maltreatment has occurred. Frequently, this agency is located within larger public social service agencies, such as Departments of Social Services.

Concurrent Planning – identifies alternative forms of permanency by addressing both reunification or legal permanency with a new parent or caregiver if reunification efforts fail.

Cultural Competence – a set of attitudes, behaviors, and policies that integrates knowledge about groups of people into practices and standards to enhance the quality of services to all cultural groups being served.

Differential Response – an area of CPS reform that offers greater flexibility in responding to allegations of abuse and neglect. Also referred to as "dual track" or "multi-track" response, it permits CPS agencies to respond differentially to children's needs for safety, the degree of risk present, and the family's needs for services and support. See "dual track."

Dispositional Hearings – held by the juvenile and family court to determine the disposition of children after cases have been adjudicated, such as whether placement of the child in out-of-home care is necessary and what services the children and family will need to reduce the risk of maltreatment and to address the effects of maltreatment.

Dual Track – term reflecting new CPS response systems that typically combine a nonadversarial service-based assessment track for cases where children are not at immediate risk with a traditional CPS investigative track for cases where children are unsafe or at greater risk for maltreatment. See "differential response."

Evaluation of Family Progress – the stage of the CPS case process where the CPS caseworker measures changes in family behaviors and conditions (risk factors), monitors risk elimination or reduction, assesses strengths, and determines case closure.

Family Assessment – the stage of the child protection process when the CPS caseworker, community treatment provider, and the family reach a mutual understanding regarding the behaviors and conditions that must change to reduce or eliminate the risk of maltreatment, the most critical treatment needs that must be addressed, and the strengths on which to build.

Family Group Conferencing – a family meeting model used by CPS agencies to optimize family strengths in the planning process. This model brings the family, extended family, and others important in the family's life (e.g., friends, clergy, neighbors) together to make decisions regarding how best to ensure safety of the family members.

Family Unity Model – a family meeting model used by CPS agencies to optimize family strengths in the planning process. This model is similar to the Family Group Conferencing model.

Full Disclosure – CPS information to the family regarding the steps in the intervention process, the requirements of CPS, the expectations of the family, the consequences if the family does not fulfill the expectations, and the rights of the parents to ensure that the family completely understands the process.

Guardian ad Litem – a lawyer or lay person who represents a child in juvenile or family court. Usually this person considers the "best interest" of the child and may perform a variety of roles, including those of independent investigator, advocate, advisor, and guardian for the child. A lay person who serves in this role is sometimes known as a court-appointed special advocate or CASA.

Home Visitation Programs – prevention programs that offer a variety of family-focused services to pregnant mothers and families with new babies. Activities frequently encompass structured visits to the family's home and may address positive parenting practices, nonviolent discipline techniques, child development, maternal and child health, available services, and advocacy.

Immunity – established in all child abuse laws to protect reporters from civil law suits and criminal prosecution resulting from filing a report of child abuse and neglect.

Initial Assessment or Investigation – the stage of the CPS case process where the CPS caseworker determines the validity of the child maltreatment report, assesses the risk of maltreatment, determines if the child is safe, develops a safety plan if needed to assure the child's protection, and determines services needed.

Intake – the stage of the CPS case process where the CPS caseworker screens and accepts reports of child maltreatment.

Interview Protocol – a structured format to ensure that all family members are seen in a planned strategy, that community providers collaborate, and that information gathering is thorough.

Juvenile and Family Courts – established in most States to resolve conflict and to otherwise intervene in the lives of families in a manner that promotes the best interest of children. These courts specialize in areas such as child maltreatment, domestic violence, juvenile delinquency, divorce, child custody, and child support.

Kinship Care – formal child placement by the juvenile court and child welfare agency in the home of a child's relative.

Liaison – the designation of a person within an organization who has responsibility for facilitating communication, collaboration, and coordination between agencies involved in the child protection system.

Mandated Reporter – groups of professionals required by State statutes to report suspected child abuse and neglect to the proper authorities (usually CPS or law enforcement agencies). Mandated reporters typically include: educators and other school personnel, health care and mental health professionals, social workers, childcare providers, and law enforcement officers.

Multidisciplinary Team – established between agencies and professionals within the child protection system to discuss cases of child abuse and neglect and to aid in decisions at various stages of the CPS case process. These terms may also be designated by different names, including child protection teams, interdisciplinary teams, or case consultation teams.

Neglect – the failure to provide for the child's basic needs. Neglect can be physical, educational, or emotional. *Physical neglect* can include not providing adequate food or clothing, appropriate medical care, supervision, or proper weather protection (heat or coats). *Educational neglect* includes failure to provide appropriate schooling, special educational needs, or allowing excessive truancies. *Psychological neglect* includes the lack of any emotional support and love, chronic inattention to the child, exposure to spouse abuse, or drug and alcohol abuse.

Out-of-Home Care – child care, foster care, or residential care provided by persons, organizations, and institutions to children who are placed outside their families, usually under the jurisdiction of juvenile or family court.

Parent or caretaker – person responsible for the care of the child.

***Parens Patriae* Doctrine** - originating in feudal England, a doctrine that vests in the State a right of guardianship of minors. This concept has gradually evolved into the principle that the community, in addition to the parent, has a strong interest in the care and nurturing of children. Schools, juvenile courts, and social service agencies all derive their authority from the State's power to ensure the protection and rights of children as a unique class.

Physical Abuse – the inflicting of a nonaccidental physical injury upon a child. This may include, burning, hitting, punching, shaking, kicking, beating, or otherwise harming a child. It may, however, have been the result of over-discipline or physical punishment that is inappropriate to the child's age.

Primary Prevention – activities geared to a sample of the general population to prevent child abuse and neglect from occurring. Also referred to as "universal prevention."

Protocol – an interagency agreement that delineates joint roles and responsibilities by establishing criteria and procedures for working together on cases of child abuse and neglect.

Protective Factors – strengths and resources that appear to mediate or serve as a "buffer" against risk factors that contribute to vulnerability to maltreatment or against the negative effects of maltreatment experiences.

Psychological Maltreatment – a pattern of caregiver behavior or extreme incidents that convey to children that they are worthless, flawed, unloved, unwanted, endangered, or only of value to meeting another's needs. This can include parents or caretakers using extreme or bizarre forms of punishment or threatening or terrorizing a child. The term "psychological maltreatment" is also known as emotional abuse or neglect, verbal abuse, or mental abuse.

Response Time – a determination made by CPS and law enforcement regarding the immediacy of the response needed to a report of child abuse or neglect.

Review Hearings – held by the juvenile and family court to review dispositions (usually every 6 months) and to determine the need to maintain placement in out-of-home care or court jurisdiction of a child.

Risk – the likelihood that a child will be maltreated in the future.

Risk Assessment – to assess and measure the likelihood that a child will be maltreated in the future, frequently through the use of checklists, matrices, scales, and other methods of measurement.

Risk Factors – behaviors and conditions present in the child, parent, or family that will likely contribute to child maltreatment occurring in the future.

Safety – absence of an imminent or immediate threat of moderate-to-serious harm to the child.

Safety Assessment – a part of the CPS case process in which available information is analyzed to identify whether a child is in immediate danger of moderate or serious harm.

Safety Plan – a casework document developed when it is determined that the child is in imminent risk of serious harm. In the safety plan, the caseworker targets the factors that are causing or contributing to the risk of imminent serious harm to the child, and identifies, along with the family, the interventions that will control the safety factors and assure the child's protection.

Secondary Prevention – activities targeted to prevent breakdowns and dysfunctions among families who have been identified as at risk for abuse and neglect.

Service Agreement – the casework document developed between the CPS caseworker and the family that outlines the tasks necessary to achieve goals and outcomes necessary for risk reduction.

Service Provision – the stage of the CPS casework process when CPS and other service providers provide specific services geared toward the reduction of risk of maltreatment.

Sexual Abuse – inappropriate adolescent or adult sexual behavior with a child. It includes fondling a child's genitals, making the child fondle the adult's genitals, intercourse, incest, rape, sodomy, exhibitionism, sexual exploitation, or exposure to pornography. To be considered child abuse, these acts have to be committed by a person responsible for the care of a child (for example a baby-sitter, a parent, or a daycare provider) or related to the child. If a stranger commits these acts, it would be considered sexual assault and handled solely be the police and criminal courts.

Substantiated – an investigation disposition concluding that the allegation of maltreatment or risk of maltreatment was supported or founded by State law or State policy. A CPS determination means that credible evidence exists that child abuse or neglect has occurred.

Tertiary Prevention – treatment efforts geared to address situations where child maltreatment has already occurred with the goals of preventing child maltreatment from occurring in the future and of avoiding the harmful effects of child maltreatment.

Treatment – the stage of the child protection case process when specific services are provided by CPS and other providers to reduce the risk of maltreatment, support families in meeting case goals, and address the effects of maltreatment.

Universal Prevention – activities and services directed at the general public with the goal of stopping the occurrence of maltreatment before it starts. Also referred to as "primary prevention."

Unsubstantiated (not substantiated) – an investigation disposition that determines that there is not sufficient evidence under State law or policy to conclude that the child has been maltreated or at risk of maltreatment. A CPS determination means that credible evidence does not exist that child abuse or neglect has occurred.

APPENDIX B. RESOURCE LISTINGS OF SELECTED NATIONAL ORGANIZATIONS CONCERNED WITH CHILD MALTREATMENT

Listed below are several representatives of the many national organizations and groups that deal with various aspects of child maltreatment. Please visit www.calib.com/nccanch to view a more comprehensive list of resources and visit www.calib.com/nccanch/database to view an organization database. Inclusion on this list is for information purposes and does not constitute an endorsement by the Office on Child Abuse and Neglect or the Children's Bureau.

For the General Public

American Bar Association Center on Children and the Law
    address: 740 15th St., NW Washington, DC 20005
    phone: (202) 662-1720
    fax: (202) 662-1755
    e-mail: ctrchildlaw@abanet.org
    Web site: www.abanet.org/child
Promotes improvement of laws and policies affecting children and provides education in child-related law topics.

Childhelp USA
    address: 15757 North 78th St.
                  Scottsdale, AZ 85260
    phone: (800) 4-A-CHILD
                  (800) 2-A-CHILD (TDD line)
                  (480) 922-8212
    fax: (480) 922-7061
    e-mail: help@childhelpusa.org
    Web site: www.childhelpusa.org

Provides crisis counseling to adult survivors and child victims of child abuse, offenders, and parents and operates a national hotline.

National Center for Missing and Exploited Children (NCMEC)
address: Charles B. Wang International
             Children's Building 699 Prince St.
             Alexandria, VA 22314-3175
phone: (800) 843-5678
             (703) 274-3900
fax: (703) 274-2220
Web site: www.missingkids.com

Provides assistance to parents, children, law enforcement, schools, and the community in recovering missing children and raising public awareness about ways to help prevent child abduction, molestation, and sexual exploitation.

Parents Anonymous
address: 675 West Foothill Blvd., Suite 220 Claremont, CA 91711
phone: (909) 621-6184
fax: (909) 625-6304
e-mail: parentsanon@msn.com
Web site: www.parentsanonymous.org

Leads mutual support groups to help parents provide nurturing environments for their families.

Community Partners

The Center for Faith-based and Community Initiatives
e-mail: CFBCI@hhs.gov
Web site: www.hhs.gov/faith

Welcomes the participation of faith-based and community-based organizations as valued and essential partners with the U.S. Department of Health and Human Services. Funding goes to faith-based organizations through Head Start and to programs for refugee resettlement, runaway and homeless youth, independent living, child care, child support enforcement, and child welfare.

Family Support America
(formerly Family Resource Coalition of America)
address: 20 N. Wacker Dr., Suite 1100 Chicago, IL 60606
phone: (312) 338-0900
fax: (312) 338-1522
e-mail: info@familysupportamerica.org
Web site: www.familysupportamerica.org

Works to strengthen and empower families and communities so that they can foster the optimal development of children, youth, and adult family members.

National Children's Alliance

address:	1612 K St., NW, Suite 500 Washington, DC 20006
phone:	(800) 239-9950
	(202) 452-6001
fax:	(202) 452-6002
e-mail:	info@nca-online
Web site:	www.nca-online

Provides training, technical assistance, and networking opportunities to communities seeking to plan, establish, and improve Children's Advocacy Centers.

National Exchange Club Foundation for the Prevention of Child Abuse

address:	3050 Central Ave. Toledo, OH 43606-1700
phone:	(800) 924-2643
	(419) 535-3232
fax:	(419) 535-1989
e-mail:	info@preventchildabuse.com
Web site:	www.nationalexchangeclub.com

Conducts local campaigns in the fight against child abuse by providing education, intervention, and support to families affected by child maltreatment.

National Fatherhood Initiative

address:	101 Lake Forest Blvd., Suite 360 Gaithersburg, MD 20877
phone:	(301) 948-0599
fax:	(301) 948-4325
Web site:	www.fatherhood

Works to improve the well-being of children by increasing the proportion of children growing up with involved, responsible, and committed fathers.

Prevention Organizations

National Alliance of Children's Trust and Prevention Funds (ACT)

address:	Michigan State University Department of Psychology
	East Lansing, MI 48824-1117
phone:	(517) 432-5096
fax:	(517) 432-2476
e-mail:	millsda@msu.edu
Web site:	www.ctfalliance.org

Assists State children's trust and prevention funds to strengthen families and protect children from harm.

Prevent Child Abuse America

address:	200 South Michigan Ave., 17th Floor Chicago, IL 60604-2404
phone:	(800) 835-2671 (orders)
	(312) 663-3520

fax: (312) 939-8962
e-mail: mailbox@preventchildabuse.org
Web site: www.preventchildabuse.org
Conducts prevention activities such as public awareness campaigns, advocacy, networking, research, and publishing. Also, provides information and statistics on child abuse.

Shaken Baby Syndrome Prevention Plus
address: 649 Main St., Suite B Groveport, OH 43125
phone: (800) 858-5222
                (614) 836-8360
fax: (614) 836-8359
e-mail: sbspp@aol.com
Web site: www.sbsplus.com
Develops, studies, and disseminates information and materials designed to prevent shaken baby syndrome and other forms of physical child abuse and to increase positive parenting and child care.

Child Welfare Organizations

American Humane Association Children's Division
address: 63 Inverness Dr., East Englewood, CO 80112-5117
phone: (800) 227-4645
                (303) 792-9900
fax: (303) 792-5333
e-mail: children@americanhumane.org
Web site: www.americanhumane.org
Conducts research, analysis, and training to help public and private agencies respond to child maltreatment.

American Public Human Services Association
address: 810 First St., NE, Suite 500 Washington, DC 20002-4267
phone: (202) 682-0100
fax: (202) 289-6555
Web site: www.aphsa.org
Addresses program and policy issues related to the administration and delivery of publicly funded human services. Professional membership organization.

American Professional Society on the Abuse of Children
address: 940 N.E. 13th St. CHO 3B-3406 Oklahoma City, OK 73104
phone: (405) 271-8202
fax: (405) 271-2931
e-mail: tricia-williams@ouhsc.edu
Web site: www.apsac.org

Provides professional education, promotes research to inform effective practice, and addresses public policy issues. Professional membership organization.

AVANCE Family Support and Education Program
    address: 301 South Frio, Suite 380 San Antonio, TX 78207
    phone: (210) 270-4630
    fax: (210) 270-4612
    Web site: www.avance.org
Operates a national training center to share and disseminate information, material, and curricula to service providers and policy makers interested in supporting high-risk Hispanic families.

Child Welfare League of America
    address: 440 First St., NW, Third Floor Washington, DC 20001-2085
    phone: (202) 638-2952
    fax: (202) 638-4004
    Web site: www.cwla.org
Provides training, consultation, and technical assistance to child welfare professionals and agencies while also educating the public about emerging issues affecting children.

Children's Defense Fund
    address: 25 E St., NW Washington, DC 20001
    phone: (202) 628-8787
    fax: (202) 662-3540
    e-mail: cdfinfo@childrensdefense.org
    Web site: www.childrensdefense.org
Provides technical assistance to State and local child advocates, gathers and disseminates data on children, and advocates for children's issues.

National Black Child Development Institute
    address: 1023 15th St., NW, Suite 600 Washington, DC 20005
    phone: (202) 387-1281
    fax: (202) 234-1738
    e-mail: moreinfo@nbcdi.org
    Web site: www.nbcdi.org
Operates programs and sponsors a national training conference through Howard University to improve and protect the well-being of African-American children.

National Children's Advocacy Center
    address: 200 Westside Sq., Suite 700 Huntsville AL 35801
    phone: (256) 533-0531
    fax: (256) 534-6883
    e-mail: webmaster@ncac-hsv.org
    Web site: www.ncac-hsv.org

Provides prevention, intervention, and treatment services to physically and sexually abused children and their families within a child-focused team approach.

National Indian Child Welfare Association
address: 5100 SW Macadam Ave., Suite 300 Portland, OR 97201
phone: (503) 222-4044
fax: (503) 222-4007
e-mail: info@nicwa.org
Web site: www.nicwa.org

Disseminates information and provides technical assistance on Indian child welfare issues. Supports community development and advocacy efforts to facilitate tribal responses to the needs of families and children.

National Resource Center on Child Maltreatment
address: Child Welfare Institute 3950 Shackleford Rd., Suite 175 Duluth, GA 30096
phone: (770) 935-8484
fax: (770) 935-0344
e-mail: tsmith@gocwi.org
Web site: www.gocwi.org

Helps States, local agencies, and Tribes develop effective and efficient child protective services systems. Jointly operated by the Child Welfare Institute and ACTION for Child Protection, it responds to needs related to prevention, identification, intervention, and treatment of child abuse and neglect.

For More Information

National Clearinghouse on Child Abuse and Neglect Information
address: 330 C St., SW Washington, DC 20447
phone: (800) 394-3366 (703) 385-7565
fax: (703) 385-3206
e-mail: nccanch@calib.com
Web site: www.calib.com/nccanch

Collects, stores, catalogs, and disseminates information on all aspects of child maltreatment and child welfare to help build the capacity of professionals in the field. A service of the Children's Bureau.

APPENDIX C. STATE TOLL-FREE TELEPHONE NUMBERS FOR REPORTING CHILD ABUSE

Each State designates specific agencies to receive and investigate reports of suspected child abuse and neglect. Typically, this responsibility is carried out by child protective services (CPS) within a Department of Social Services, Department of Human Resources, or Division of Family and Children Services. In some States, police departments also may receive reports of child abuse or neglect.

Many States have an in-State toll-free telephone number, listed below, for reporting suspected abuse. **The reporting party must be calling from the same State where the child is allegedly being abused for most of the following numbers to be valid.**

For States not listed or when the reporting party resides in a different State than the child, please call **Childhelp, 800-4-A-Child** (800-422-4453), or your local CPS agency.

Alaska (AK) 800-478-4444	**Kentucky (KY)** 800-752-6200	**New Hampshire (NH)** 800-894-5533 800-852-3388 (after hours)	**Rhode Island (RI)** 800-RI-CHILD (800-742-4453)
Arizona (AZ) 888-SOS-CHILD (888-767-2445)	**Maine (ME)** 800-452-1999		
Arkansas (AR) 800-482-5964	**Maryland (MD)** 800-332-6347	**New Jersey (NJ)** 800-792-8610 800-835-5510 (TDD)	**Texas (TX)** 800-252-5400
Connecticut (CT) 800-842-2288 800-624-5518 (TDD)	**Massachusetts (MA)** 800-792-5200	**New Mexico (NM)** 800-797-3260	**Utah (UT)** 800-678-9399
Delaware (DE) 800-292-9582	**Michigan (MI)** 800-942-4357	**New York (NY)** 800-342-3720	**Vermont (VT)** 800-649-5285
Florida (FL) 800-96-ABUSE (800-962-2873)	**Mississippi (MS)** 800-222-8000	**North Dakota (ND)** 800-245-3736	**Virginia (VA)** 800-552-7096
Illinois (IL) 800-252-2873	**Missouri (MO)** 800-392-3738	**Oklahoma (OK)** 800-522-3511	**Washington (WA)** 866-END-HARM (866-363-4276)
Indiana (IN) 800-800-5556	**Montana (MT)** 800-332-6100	**Oregon (OR)** 800-854-3508, ext. 2402	**West Virginia (WV)** 800-352-6513
Iowa (IA) 800-362-2178	**Nebraska (NE)** 800-652-1999	**Pennsylvania (PA)** 800-932-0313	**Wyoming (WY)** 800-457-3659
Kansas (KS) 800-922-5330	**Nevada (NV)** 800-992-5757		

End Notes

[1] Rycus, J. S., & Hughes, R. C. (1998). Family-centered child protection: An integrated model of child welfare practice *assuring children's rights to protection and permanence*. Columbus, OH: Institute for Human Services.

[2] Child Abuse and Prevention Act (1996), 42 U.S.C. 5 106g, SEC.111 (6).

[3] Dubowitz, H. (2000). What is physical abuse? In H. Dubowitz & D. DePanfilis (Eds.), Handbook for *child protection practice (pp. 16-17). Thousand Oaks, CA:* Sage.

[4] Berliner, L. (2000). What is sexual abuse? In H. Dubowitz & D. DePanfilis (Eds.), *Handbook for child protection practice* (pp. 18-22). Thousand Oaks, CA: Sage.

[5] U.S. Department of Health and Human Services, Administration on Children, Youth and Families. (2002). *Child maltreatment* 2000. Washington, DC: U.S. Government Printing Office.

[6] Sedlak, A. J., & Broadhurst, D. D. (1996). *Third national incidence study of child abuse and neglect (NIS-3).* Washington, DC: U.S. Department of Health and Human Services, National Center on Child Abuse and Neglect.

[7] Zuravin, S. J. (1991). Research definitions of child physical abuse and neglect: Current problems. In R. H. Starr & D. A. Wolfe (Eds.), *The effects of child abuse and neglect* (pp. 100-128). New York, NY: The Guildford Press.

[8] English, D. (1999). Evaluation and risk assessment of child neglect in public child protection services. In H. Dubowitz (Ed.), *Neglected children: Research, practice, and policy (*pp. 19 1-210). Thousand Oaks, CA: Sage.

[9] Egeland, B. (1988). The consequences of physical and emotional neglect on the development of young children. In *Child neglect monograph: Proceedings from a symposium* (pp. 7-19). Washington, DC: U.S. Department of Health and Human Services, National Center on Child Abuse and Neglect.

[10] Hart, S., & Brassard, M. (1995). *Psychosocial evaluation of suspected psychological maltreatment in children and adolescents: APSAC practice guidelines (p. 2).* Chicago, IL: American Professional Society on the Abuse of Children (APSAC).

[11] Hart, S., & Brassard, M. (1991). Psychological maltreatment: Progress achieved. *Development and Psychology, 3*, 61-70; Hart, S., Brassard, M., & Karlson, H. (1996). Psychological maltreatment. In J. Briere, L. Berliner, J. Bulkley, C. Jenny, & T. Reid (Eds.), *The APSAC* handbook on child maltreatment (pp. 72-89). Thousand Oaks, CA: Sage.

[12] U.S. Department of Health and Human Services. (2002).

[13] U.S. Department of Health and Human Services. (2002).

[14] U.S. Department of Health and Human Services. (2002).

[15] U.S. Department of Health and Human Services. (2002).

[16] U.S. Department of Health and Human Services. (2002).

[17] Sedlak, A. J., & Broadhurst, D. D. (1996).

[18] U.S. Department of Health and Human Services. (2002).

[19] Sedlak, A. J., & Broadhurst, D. D. (1996).

[20] Chalk, R., & King, R. A. (Eds.). (1998). Family violence and family violence interventions. *In Violence in families: Assessing prevention and treatment programs* (pp. 3 1-58). Washington, DC: National Academy Press; National Research Council. (1993). *Understanding child abuse and neglect.* Washington, DC: National Academy Press; Belsky, J. (1993). Etiology of child maltreatment: A developmental-ecological analysis. Psychological Bulletin, 114, 413-434.

[21] National Research Council. (1993); Black, D. A., Heyman, R. E., & Smith Slep, A. M. (2001a). Risk factors for child physical abuse. *Aggression and Violent Behavior, 6,* 121-188. Schumacher, J., Smith Slep, A. M., & Heyman, R. E. (2001). Risk factors for child neglect. *Aggression and Violent Behavior*, 6, 231-254; Polansky, N. A., Gaudin, J. M., Jr., & Kilpatrick, A. C. (1992). The maternal characteristics scale: A cross validation. *Child Welfare League of America, 71,* 271-280; Christensen, M. J., Brayden, R. M., Dietrich, M. S., McLaughlin, F. J., Sherrod, K. B., & Altemeier, W. A. (1994). The prospective assessment of self-concept in neglectful and physically abusive low-income mothers. *Child Abuse and Neglect, 18(3),* 225-232; Rohrbeck, C. A., & Twentyman, C. T. (1986). Multimodal assessment of impulsiveness in abusing, neglectful, and nonmaltreating mothers and their preschool children. *Journal of Consulting and Clinical Psychology, 54(2),* 231-236. Dinwiddie, S. H., & Bucholz, K. K. (1993). Psychiatric diagnoses of self-reported child abusers. *ChildAbuse and Neglect, 17(4),* 465-476; Dubowitz, H. (1995). *Child neglect: Child, mother, and family functioning.* Baltimore, MD: University of Maryland, School of Medicine; Paradise, J. E., Rose, L., Sleeper, L. A., & Nathanson, M. (1994). Behavior, family function, school performance and predictors of persistent disturbance in sexually abused children. *Pediatrics 93,* 452-459; Chaffin, M., Kelleher, K., & Hollenberg, J. (1996). Onset of physical abuse and neglect: Psychiatric, substance abuse, and social risk factors from prospective community data. *Child Abuse and Neglect, 20(3),* 191-203; Pianta, R., Egeland, B., & Erickson, M. F. (1989). The antecedents of maltreatment: Results of the mother-child interaction research project. In D. Cicchetti & V. Carlson (Eds.), *Child maltreatment: Theory and research on the causes and consequences of child abuse and neglect* (pp. 203-253). New York, NY: Cambridge University Press.

[22] Chalk, R., & King, R. A. (Eds.). (1998); Melnick, B., & Hurley, J .R. (1969). Distinctive personality attributes of child-abusing mothers. Journal of Consulting and Clinical *Psychology, 33(6), 746-749.*

[23] Kaufman, J., & Zigler, E. (1993). The intergenerational transmission of abuse is overstated. In R. J. Gelles & D. Loseke (Eds.), *Current controversies on family violence (pp.* 209-221). Newbury Park, CA: Sage; Widom, C. S. (1992). *The cycle of violence. Washington, DC: U.S. Department* of Justice, National Institute of Justice; National Research Council, (1993); Finkelhor, D., Moore, D., Hamby, S. L., & Strauss, M. A. (1997). Sexually abused children in a national survey of parents: Methodological issues. Child Abuse and Neglect, 21(1), 1-9; Hemenway, D., Solnick, S., & Carter, J. (1994). Child-rearing violence. Child Abuse and Neglect, *18(12), 1011-1020; Whipple, E. E., & Webster-Stratton, C.* (1991). The role of parental stress in physically abusive families. *Child Abuse and Neglect, 15(3),* 279-291.

[24] Kaufman, J., & Zigler, E. (1993).

[25] Gelles, R. J. (1998). The youngest victims: Violence toward children. In R. K. Bergen (Ed.), Issues in intimate violence (pp. 5-24). Thousand Oaks, CA: Sage.

[26] Kaufman, J., & Zigler, E. (1993).

[27] National Research Council. (1993).

[28] Egeland, B., Jacobvitz, D., & Papatola, K. (1987). Intergenerational continuity of abuse. In R. J. Gelles & J. B. Lancaster (Eds.), Child abuse and neglect: Biosocial *dimensions (pp. 255-276). Hawthorne, NY: Aldine de Gruyter;* Zuravin, S. J., McMillen, C., DePanfilis, D., & Risley-Curtiss, C. (1996). The intergenerational cycle of maltreatment: Continuity versus discontinuity. Journal of Interpersonal *Violence,* 11(3), 315-334.

[29] U.S. Department of Health and Human Services, Office of the Assistant Secretary for Planning and Evaluation. (1999). *Blending perspectives and building common ground: A report to congress on substance abuse and child protection* (p. 41). Washington, DC: U.S. Government Printing Office; Young, N. K., Gardner, S. L., & Dennis, K. (1998). Facing the problem. In Responding to alcohol and other drug problems *in child welfare: Weaving together practice and policy (pp.* 1-26). Washington, DC: Child Welfare League of America (CWLA) Press.

[30] Jaudes, P. K., Ekwo, E., & Van Voorhis, J. (1995). Association of drug abuse and child abuse. *Child Abuse and Neglect, 19(9),* 1065-1075; U.S. Department of Health and Human Services, National Center on Child Abuse and Neglect. (1993). Study of child maltreatment in alcohol abusing families. Washington, DC: U.S. Government Printing Office; Famularo, R., Kinsheriff, R., & Fenton, T. (1992). Parental substance abuse and the nature of child maltreatment. Child *Abuse and Neglect, 16(4), 475-483;* Kelleher, K., Chaffin, M., Hollenberg, J., & Fischer, E. (1994). Alcohol and drug disorders among physically abusive and neglectful parents in a community-based sample. American Journal of Public *Health, 84(10), 1586-1590.*

[31] Jaudes, P. K., Ekwo, E., & Van Voorhis, J. (1995). Association of drug abuse and child abuse. *Child Abuse and Neglect, 19(9),* 1065-1075.

[32] U.S. Department of Health and Human Services. (1993).

[33] Zuckerman, B. (1994). Effects on parents and children. In D. J. Besharov (Ed.), When drug addicts have children: Reorienting child welfare's response (pp. 49-63). Washington, DC: CWLA Press.

[34] U.S. Department of Health and Human Services. (1999); Hans, S. (1995). Diagnosis in etiologic and epidemiologic studies. In C. Jones & M. De La Rosa (Eds.), *Methodological issues: etiology and consequences of drug abuse among women.* Washington, DC: National Institute on Drug Abuse; Tarter, R., Blackson, T., Martin, C., Loeber, R., & Moss, H. (1993). Characteristics and correlates of child discipline practices in substance abuse and normal families. *American Journal on Addictions, 2(1), 18-25;* Kumpfer, K. L., & Bayes, J. (1995). Child abuse and drugs. In J. H. Jaffe (Ed.), *The encyclopedia of drugs and alcohol (Vol. 1, pp.* 2 17-222). New York, NY: Simon & Shuster.

[35] Landdeck-Sisco, J. (1997, April). *Children with prenatal drug and/or alcohol exposure.* Retrieved May 9, 2002, from http://www.chtop.com/ARCH/archfs49.htm.

[36] U.S. Department of Health and Human Services. (1999).

[37] National Research Council. (1993).

[38] U.S. Department of Health and Human Services. (1999).

[39] National Research Council. (1993); Black, D. A. et al. (2001a); Larrance, D. T., & Twentyman, C. T. (1983). Maternal attributions and child abuse. *Journal of Abnormal Psychology,* 92, 449-457; Zuravin, S. J., & Taylor, R. (1987). The ecology of child maltreatment: Identifying and characterizing high-risk neighborhoods. Child Welfare, 66, 497-506.

[40] Black, D. A. et al. (2001a); Larrance, D. T., & Twentyman, C. T. (1983); Williamson, J. M., Bordin, C. M., & Howe, B. A.. (1991). The ecology of adolescent maltreatment: A multilevel examination of adolescent physical abuse, sexual abuse, and neglect. *Journal of Consulting and Clinical Psychology, 59(3) 449-457; Twentyman, C. T., & Plotkin, R. C.* (1982). Unrealistic expectations of parents who maltreat their children: An educational deficit that pertains to child development. *Journal of Clinical Psychology, 38, 407-503.*

[41] Milner, J. S., & Dopke, C. (1997). Child physical abuse: Review of offender characteristics. In D. A. Wolfe, R. J. McMahon, & R. D. Peters, (Eds.), Child abuse: New *directions in prevention and treatment across the lifespan (pp.* 27-53). Thousand Oaks, CA: Sage.

[42] National Research Council. (1993); Schumacher, J. A. et al. (2000).

[43] Black, D. A. et al. (2001a); Straus, M. A., Hamby, S. L., Finkelhor, D., Moore, D. W., & Runyan, D. (1998). Identification of child maltreatment with the parent-child conflict tactics scales: Development and psychometric data for a national sample of American parents. *Child Abuse and Neglect 22, 249-270; Connelly, C. D., & Straus, M. A. (1992).* Mother's age and risk for physical abuse. Child Abuse and Neglect *16(5), 709-718.*

[44] Buchholz, E. S,. & Korn-Bursztyn, C. (1993). Children of adolescent mothers: Are they at risk for abuse? *Adolescence,* 28, 361-382; Kinard, E. M., & Klerman, L. V. (1980). Teenage parenting and child abuse: Are they related? *American Journal of Orthopsychiatry, 50(3), 481-488.*

[45] Sedlak, A. J., & Broadhurst, D. D. (1996); Finkelhor, D. et al. (1997); Boney-McCoy, S., & Finkelhor, D. (1995). Prior victimization: A risk factor for child sexual abuse and for PTSD-related symptomatology among sexually abused youth. *Child Abuse and Neglect, 19, 1401-1421*

[46] Federal Interagency Forum on Child and Family Statistics. (1999). America's children: *Key national indicators of wellbeing.* Washington, DC: U.S. Government Printing Office.

[47] Sedlak, A. J., & Broadhurst, D. D. (1996); Chaffin, M. et al. (1996); Polansky, N. A., Guadin, J. M., Ammons, P. W., & Davis, K. B. (1985). The psychological ecology of the neglectful mother. *Child Abuse and Neglect, 9,* 265-275; Zuravin, S. J., & Taylor, R. (1987).

[48] Polansky, N. A., Gaudin, J. M., & Kilpatrick, A. C. (1992). Family radicals. *Children and Youth Services Review,* 14, 19- 26.

[49] Horn, W. F., & Sylvester, T. (2001). Father facts.

[50] Edelson, J. L. (1999). The overlap between child maltreatment and woman battering. *Violence Against Women, 5(2), 134-154;* Appel, A. E., & Holden, G. W. (1998). The co-occurrence of spouse and physical child abuse: A review and appraisal. *Journal of Family Psychology, 12(4), 578-599.*

[51] National Clearinghouse on Child Abuse and Neglect Information. (1999). In harm's way: Domestic violence and child maltreatment. Washington, DC: Author.

[52] Margolin, G,. & John, R.S. (1997). Children's exposure to marital aggression. In G. K. Kantor & J. L. Jasinski (Eds.), *Out of darkness: Contemporary perspectives on family violence* (pp. 90-104). Thousand Oaks, CA: Sage; Kolbo, J. R. (1996). Risk and resilience among children exposed to family violence, *Violence and Victims,* 11, 113-128.

[53] National Research Council. (1993).

[54] Whipple, E. E., & Webster-Stratton, C. (1991); Coohey, C., & Braun, N. (1997). Toward an integrated framework for understanding child physical abuse. *Child Abuse and Neglect,* 21(11), 108 1-1094; Rosenberg, M. S., & Reppucci, N. D. (1983). Abusive mothers: Perceptions of their own and their children's behavior. *Journal of Consulting and Clinical Psychology, 51,* 674-682; Mash, E. J., Johnston, C., & Kovitz, K. (1983). A comparison of the mother-child interactions of physically abused and non-abused children during play and task situations. *Journal of Clinical Child Psychology,* 12, 8-29.

[55] Williamson, J. M. et al. (1991); Gaines, R., Sandgrund, A., Green, A. H., & Power, E. (1978). Etiological factors in child maltreatment: A multivariate study of abusing, neglectful, and normal mothers. *Journal of Abnormal Psychology,* 87, 53 1-540.

[56] Milner, J. S., & Dopke, C. (1997).

[57] Rycus, J. S., & Hughes, R.C. (1998). *Field guide to child welfare: Volume I. Foundations of child protective services.* Washington, DC: CWLA Press.

[58] Garbarino, J. (1984). What have we learned about child maltreatment? In *Perspectives on child maltreatment in the mid '80s.* (pp. 6-8). Washington, DC: U.S. Department of Health and Human Services, National Center on Child Abuse and Neglect.

[59] National Research Council. (1993); Bousha, D. M., & Twentyman, C. T. (1984). Mother-child interactional style in abuse, neglect, and control groups: Naturalistic observations in the home. *Journal of Abnormal Psychology,* 93, 106-114.

[60] Black, D. A. et al. (2001a); Bousha, D. M., & Twentyman, C. T. (1984); Whipple, E. E., & Webster-Stratton, C. (1991); Trickett, P. K., & Kucynski, L. (1986). Children's misbehaviors and parental discipline strategies in abusive and non-abusive families. *Developmental Psychology, 22, 115-123.*

[61] U.S. Department of Health and Human Services. (2002).

[62] Finkelhor, D. et al. (1997); Boney-McCoy, S., & Finkelhor, D. (1995).

[63] Crosse, S. B., Kaye, E., & Ratnofsky, A. C. (n.d.). *A report on the maltreatment of children with disabilities.* Washington, DC: Department of Health and Human Services, National Center on Child Abuse and Neglect; Sullivan, P. M., & Knutson, J. F. (2000). Maltreatment and disabilities: A population-based epidemiological study. *Child Abuse and Neglect, 24(10), 1257-1273.*

[64] Crosse, S. B. et al. (n.d.).

[65] Rycus, J. S., & Hughes, R. C. (1998).

[66] Ammerman, R. T., & Patz, R. J. (1996). Determinants of child abuse potential: Contribution of parent and child factors. *Journal of Clinical Child Psychology, 25(3), 300-3 07;* Sobsey, D. (1994). Violence and abuse in the lives of people *with disabilities: The end of silent acceptance? Baltimore,* MD: Paul H. Brookes.

[67] Steinberg, M. A., & Hylton, J. R., & Wheeler, C. E. (Ed.). (1998). Responding to maltreatment of children with *disabilities: A trainer's guide. Portland, OR: Oregon Health* Sciences University, Oregon Institute on Disability and Development.

[68] Steinberg, M. A., & Hylton, J. R. (1998).

[69] Chalk, R., & King, P. (Eds.). (1998); Zuravin, S. J., Masnyk, K., DiBlasio, F. (1992). Predicting child abuse and neglect by adolescent mothers. In F. L. Parker, R. Robinson, S. Sambrano et al. (Eds.), *New directions in child and family research: Shaping Head Start in the 90's: First national working conference on early childhood and family research* (pp. 246-247). Washington, DC: Department of Health and Human Services, Administration on Children, Youth and Families; Parker, R. D., & Collmer, C. W. (1975). Child abuse: An interdisciplinary analysis. In E. M. Hetherington (Ed.), *Review of child development research* (Vol. 5, pp. 1-102). Chicago, IL: University of Chicago Press; Starr, R. H., Jr. (1982). A research-based approach to the predictions of child abuse. In R. H. Starr (Ed.), *Child abuse prediction: Policy implications* (pp. 105-134). Cambridge, MA: Ballinger; Egeland, B., & Vaughn, B. (1981). Failure of "bond formation" as a cause of abuse, neglect, and maltreatment. *American Journal of Orthopsychiatry, 51(1)*, 78-84.

[70] National Research Council. (1993).

[71] Black, D. A. et al. (2001); Schumacher, J. A. et al. (2001); Black, D., Smith Slep, A. M., & Heyman, R. (2001b). Risk factors for child psychological abuse. *Aggression and Violent Behavior, 6,* 189-201; Vissing, Y. M., Straus, M. A., Gelles, R. J., & Harrop, J. W. (1991). Verbal aggression by parents and psychosocial problems of children. *Child Abuse and Neglect, 15, 223-238;* Paradise, J. E. et al. (1994); Williamson, J. M. et al. (1991); Whipple, E. E., & Webster-Stratton, C. (1991).

[72] National Research Council. (1993).

[73] Drake, B., & Pandy, S. (1996). Understanding the relationship between neighborhood poverty and specific types of child maltreatment. *Child Abuse and Neglect, 20(11), 1003-1018;* Sedlak, A. J., & Broadhurst, D. D. (1996); Whipple, E. E., & Webster-Stratton, C. (1991); Pelton, L. H., & Milner, J. S. (1994). Is poverty a key contributor to child maltreatment? In E. Gambrill & T. J. Stein (Eds.), Controversial issues in *child welfare (pp. 16-28). Needham Heights, MA: Allyn and* Bacon; Coulton, C., Korbin, J., Su, M., & Chow, J. (1995). Community level factors and child maltreatment rates. *Child Development, 66(5), 1262-1276; Jones, L. (1990).* Unemployment and child abuse. Families in Society (71)10, 579-587.

[74] Sedlak, A. J., & Broadhurst, D. D. (1996).

[75] National Clearinghouse on Child Abuse and Neglect Information. (2002). *National child abuse and neglect data system (NCANDS) summary of key findings for calendar year 2000.* Washington, DC: Author.

[76] Plotnik, R. (2000). Economic security for families with children. In P. J. Pecora, J. K. Whittaker, A. N. Maluccio, & R. P. Barth (Eds.), *The child welfare challenge: Policy, practice, and research* (2nd ed., pp. 95-127). New York, NY: Aldine de Gruyter.

[77] Williamson, J. M. et al. (1991); Chan, Y. C. (1994). Parenting stress and social support of mothers who physically abuse their children in Hong Kong. *Child Abuse and Neglect,* 18, 26 1-269; Polansky, N. A., Guadin, J. M., Ammons, P. W.,& Davis, K. B. (1985). The psychological ecology of the neglectful mother. *Child Abuse and Neglect, 9(2),* 265-275; Pianta, R. et al. (1989); Blacker, D. M., Whitney, L. M., Morello, A., Reed, K., & Urquiza, J. (1999, June). Depression, Distress and Social Isolation in Physical Abusive and Nonabusive Parents. Paper presented at the American Professional Society on the Abuse of Children 7th Annual Colloquium, San Antonio, TX.

[78] Harrington, D., & Dubowitz, H. (1999). Preventing child maltreatment. In R. L. Hampton (Ed.), *Family violence: Prevention and treatment* (2nd ed., pp. 122-147). Thousand Oaks, CA: Sage.

[79] Chalk, R., & King, P. (Eds.) (1998).

[80] Cicchetti, D., Lynch, M., & Manly, J. T. (1997). *An ecological developmental perspective on the consequences of child maltreatment.* Washington, DC: U.S. Department of Health and Human Services, National Center on Child Abuse and Neglect. Boney-McCoy, S., & Finkelhor, D. (1995).

[81] Garbarino, J. (1980). What kind of society permits child abuse? *Infant Mental Health Journal,* 1(4), 270-280.

[82] Jason, L., Hanaway, L. K., & Brackshaw, E. (1999). In T. P. Gullotta & S. J. McElhaney (Eds.), *Violence in homes and communities: Prevention, intervention, and treatment.* Thousand Oaks, CA: Sage.

[83] Quinton, D., & Rutter, M. (1988). Parenting breakdown: The making and breaking of intergenerational links. Brookfield, VT: Gower; Moncher, F. J. (1995). Social isolation and child- abuse risk. *Families in Society, 76(7),* 421-433. Kotch, J. B., Browne, D. C., Ringwalt, C. L., Stewart, P. W., Ruina, E., Holt, K., Lowman, B., & Jung, J. W. (1995). Risk of child abuse or neglect in a cohort of low-income children. *Child Abuse and Neglect, 19(9), 1115-1130.*

[84] Egeland, B., Jacobvita, D., & Sroufe, L. A. (1988). Breaking the cycle of abuse. *Child Development, 59,* 1080-1088.

[85] Stanley, S. M., Markman, H. J., & Jenkins, N. H. (2002). *Marriage education and government policy: Helping couples who choose marriage achieve success.* Bethesda, MD: National Institute of Mental Health.

[86] National Research Council. (1993).

[87] Gelles, R. J. (1998). The youngest victims: Violence toward children. In R. K. Bergen (Ed.), *Issues in intimate violence* (pp. 5-24). Thousand Oaks, CA: Sage. National Research Council. (1993).

[88] Conway, E. E. (1998). Nonaccidental head injury in infants: The shaken baby syndrome revisited. *Pediatric Annals, 27(10), 677-690.*

[89] Conway, E. E. (1998); Alexander, R. C., & Smith, W. L. (1998). Shaken baby syndrome. *Infants and Young Children, 10(3),* 1-9.

[90] Wallace, H. (1996). *Family violence: Legal, medical, and social perspectives.* Needham Heights, MA: Allyn & Bacon.

[91] Perry, B. D., Pollard, R., Blakely, T., Baker, W., & Vigilante, D. (1995). Childhood trauma, the neurobiology of adaptation and "use-dependent" development of the brain: How "states" become "traits." *Infant Mental Health Journal, 16(4), 271-291.*

[92] Greenough, W. T., Black, J. E., & Wallace, C. S. (1987). Experience and brain development. *Child Development,* 58, 539-559; Shore, R. (1997). *Rethinking the brain.* New York, NY: Families and Work Institute.

[93] Moeller, T. P., Bachman, G. A., & Moeller, J. R. (1993). The combined effects of physical, sexual, and emotional abuse during childhood: Long-term health consequences for women. *Child Abuse and Neglect. 17(5), 623-340; Felitti, V. J.* (1991). Long-term medical consequences of incest, rape, and molestation. *Southern Medical Journal, 84(3), 328-33 1.*

[94] Felitti, V. J., Anda, R. F., Nordenberg, D., Williamson, D. F., Spitz, A. M., Edwards, V., Koss, M. P., & Marks, J. S. (1998). Relationship of childhood abuse and household dysfunction to many of the leading causes of death in adults. *American Journal of Preventative Medicine, 14(4), 245-258.*

[95] Felitti, V. J. et al. (1998).

[96] Perry, M. A., Doran, L. D., & Wells, E. A. (1983). Developmental and behavioral characteristics of the physically abused child. *Journal of* Clinical Child *Psychology, 12(3), 320-324; Hoffman-Plotkin, D.,* & Twentyman, C. (1984). A multimodal assessment of behavioral and cognitive deficits in abused and neglected preschoolers. *Child Development, 55,* 794-802; Veltman, M. W., & Browne, K. D. (2001). Three decades of child maltreatment research: Implications for the school years. *Trauma, Violence, and Abuse, 2(3),* 215-239.

[97] Allen, R. E., & Oliver, J. M. (1982). The effects of child maltreatment on language development. *Child Abuse and Neglect, 6*(3), 299-305; Lynch, M. A., & Roberts, J. (1982). *Consequences of child abuse.* New York, NY: Academic Press.

[98] Kelley, B. T., Thornberry, T. P., & Smith, C. (1997). *In the wake of childhood maltreatment.* Washington, DC: U.S. Department of Justice, Office of Juvenile Justice and Delinquency Prevention; Trickett, P. K., McBride-Chang, C.; & Putnam, F. W. (1994). The classroom performance and behavior of sexually abused females. *Developmentand Psychopathology, 6*(1), 183-194; Eckenrode, J., Laird, M., & Doris, J. (1991). *Maltreatment and social adjustment of school children.* Washington, DC: U.S. Department of Health and Human Services, National Center on Child Abuse and Neglect; Wodarski, J. S., Kurtz, P. D., Gaudin, J. M., & Howing, P. T. (1990). Maltreatment and the school-age child: Major academic, socioemotional, and adaptive outcomes. *Social Work, 35*(6), 506-513; Egeland, B. (1991). A longitudinal study of high-risk families: Issues and findings. In R. H. Starr & D. A. Wolfe (Eds.), *The effects of child abuse and neglect: Issues and research* (pp. 33-56). New York, NY: Guilford.

[99] Egeland, B. (1993). A history of abuse is a major risk factor for abusing the next generation. In R. J. Gelles & D. R. Loseke (Eds.), *Current controversies on family violence.* Newbury Park, CA: Sage.

[100] Trickett, P. K., & McBride-Chang, C. (1995). The developmental impact of different forms of child abuse and neglect. *Developmental Review,* 15, 311-337; Wodarski, J. S. et al. (1990); Kaplan, S. J., Labruna, V., Pecovitz, D., & Salzinger, S. (1999). Physically abused adolescents: Behavior problems, functional impairment, and comparison of informants. *Pediatrics, 104(1), 43-49.*

[101] Trickett, P. K., & Putnam, F. W. (1993). Impact of child sexual abuse on females: Toward a developmental, psychobiological integration. *Psychological Science, 4*(2),81-87; Kazdin, A. E., Moser, J., Colbus, D., & Bell, R.(1985). Depressive symptoms among physically abused andpsychiatrically disturbed children. *Journal of AbnormalPsychology, 94*(3), 298-307; Jumper, S. A. (1995). A metaanalysisof the relationship of child sexual abuse to adultpsychological adjustment. *Child Abuse and Neglect, 19*(6),715-728; Oates, R. K., Forrest, D., & Peacock, A. (1985). Selfesteemof abused children. *Child Abuse and Neglect, 9*(2),159-163; Brown, J., Cohen, P., Johnson, J. G., & Smailes,E. M. (1999). Childhood abuse and neglect: Specificityof effects on adolescent and young adult depression andsuicidality. *Journal of the American Academy of Child andAdolescent Psychiatry, 38*(12), 1490-1496; Zuravin, S. J.,& Fontanella, C. (1999). The relationship between childsexual abuse and major depression among low-incomewomen: A function of growing up experiences? *ChildMaltreatment, 4*(1), 3-12; Wozencraft, T., Wagner, W., &Pellegrin, A. (1991). Depression and suicidal ideation insexually abused children. *Child Abuse and Neglect, 15*(4),505-511; Toth, S. L., Manly, J.T., & Cicchetti, D. (1992). Childmaltreatment and vulnerability to depression. *Developmentand Psychopathology, 4*(1), 97-112; Kazdin, A. E. et al.(1985); Allen, D. M., & Tarnowski, K. J. (1989). Depressivecharacteristics of physically abused children. *Journal ofAbnormal Child Psychology, 17*(1), 1-11; Silva, R. R.,Alpert, M., Munoz, D. M., & Singh, S. (2000). Stress andvulnerability to Post Traumatic Stress Disorder in childrenand adolescents. *American Journal of Psychiatry, 157*(8),1229-1235; Ackerman, P. T., Newton, J. E., McPherson,W. B., Jones, J. G., & Dykman, R. A. (1998). Prevalenceof Post Traumatic Stress Disorder and other psychiatricdiagnoses in three groups of abused children (sexual,physical, and both). *Child Abuse and*

Neglect, 22(8), 759-774; Lindberg, F. H., & Distad, L. J. (1985). Post TraumaticStress Disorders in women who experienced childhoodincest. *Child Abuse and Neglect, 9*(3), 329-334; Crittenden,P. M., & Ainsworth, M. D. S. (1989). Child maltreatmentand attachment theory. In D. Cicchetti & V. Carlson (Eds.),*Child maltreatment: Theory and research on the causesand consequences of child abuse and neglect* (pp. 432-463).New York, NY: Cambridge University Press; Egeland, B., &Sroufe, L. A. (1981). Attachment and early maltreatment.*Child Development, 52*(1), 44-52; Carlson, V., Cicchetti,D., Barnett, D., & Braunwald, K. (1989). Disorganized anddisoriented attachment relationships in maltreated infants.*Developmental Psychology, 25*(4), 525-531; Hernandez, J.(1995). The concurrence of eating disorders with histories ofchild abuse among adolescents. *Journal of Child Sexual Abuse,4*(3), 73-85; Wonderlich, S., Donaldson, M. A., Carson, D. K.,& Staton, D. (1996). Eating disturbance and incest. *Journal ofInterpersonal Violence, 11*(2), 195-207; Rogosch, F. A., Cicchetti,D., & Aber, J. L. (1995). The role of child maltreatmentin early deviations in cognitive and affective processingabilities and later peer relationship problems. *Developmentand Psychopathology, 7,* 591-609; Shields, A. M., Cicchetti,D., & Ryan, R. M. (1994). The development of emotionaland behavioral self-regulation and social competenceamong maltreated school-age children. *Development andPsychology, 6*(1), 57-75; Haskett, M. E., & Kistner, J. A.(1991). Social interactions and peer perceptions of youngphysically abused children. *Child Development, 62*(5), 979-990; Widom, C. S. (2000, January). Childhood victimization:Early adversity, later psychopathology. *National Institute ofJustice Journal,* 1-9; Boudewyn, A. C., & Liem, J. H. (1995).Childhood sexual abuse as a precursor to depression andself-destructive behavior in adulthood. *Journal of TraumaticStress, 8*(3), 445-459; Riggs, S., Alario, A. J., & McHorney,C. (1990). Health risk behaviors and attempted suicidein adolescents who report prior maltreatment. *Journal ofPediatrics, 116*(5), 815-821.

[102] Morrison, J. A., Frank, S. J., Holland, C. C., & Kates, W. R. (1999). Emotional development and disorders in young children in the child welfare system. In J. A. Silver, B. J. Amster, & T. Haecker (Eds.), *Young children and foster care: A guide for professionals* (pp. 33-64). Baltimore, MD: Paul H. Brookes; Rogosch, F. A. et al. (1995).

[103] Widom, C. S. (1992); Maxfield, M., & Widom, C. S. (1996). The cycle of violence: Revisited 6 years later. *Archives of Pediatrics & Adolescent Medicine, 150*(4), 390-395; Kelley, B. T., Thornberry T. P., & Smith, C. (1997). *In the wake of child maltreatment.* Washington, DC: U.S. Department of Justice, Office of Juvenile Justice and Delinquency Prevention.

[104] Widom, C. S. (1992).

[105] Kelley, B. T. et al. (1997).

[106] Dembo, R., Dertke, M., LaVoie, L., Borders, S., Washburn,M., & Schmeidler, J. (1997). Physical abuse, sexualvictimization and illicit drug use: A structural analysisamong high risk adolescents. Journal of Adolescence,10, 13; McCauley, J., Kern, D., Kolodner, K., Dill, L.,Schroeder, A., DeChant, H., Ryden, J., Derogatis, L., &Bass, E. (1997). Clinical characteristics of women with ahistory of childhood abuse. Journal of the American MedicalAssociation, 277, 1362-1368; Riggs, S., Alario, A. J., &McHorney, C. (1990); National Research Council. (1993);U.S. Department of Health and Human Services. (1999).

[107] U.S. Department of Health and Human Services. (1999).

[108] Heller, S. S., Larrieu, J. A., D'Imperiod, R., & Boris, N. W. (1999). Research on resilience to child maltreatment: Empirical considerations. *Child Abuse and Neglect, 23*(4), 321-338; National Research Council. (1993).

[109] Egeland, B. (1993); Masten, A. S., & Wright, M. O. (1998). Cumulative risk and protection models of child maltreatment. *Journal of Aggression, Maltreatment & Trauma, 2(1),*7-30; Muller, R. T., Goebel-Fabbri, A. E., Diamond, T., & Dinklage, D. (2000). Social support and the relationship between family and community violence exposure and psychopathology among high risk adolescents. Child Abuse *and Neglect, 24*(4), 449-464.

[110] Prevent Child Abuse America. (2001). *Total estimated cost of child abuse and neglect in the United States: Statistical evidence.* Retrieved August 1, 2001, from http://preventchildabuse.org/learn_more/research_docs/cost_analysis.pdf.

[111] Willis, D. J., Holden, E. W., & Rosenberg, M. (Eds.). (1992). *Prevention of child maltreatment: Developmental and ecological perspectives (pp. 1-16). New York, NY: John Wiley* & Sons.

[112] Bloom, M. (1996). *Primary prevention practices.* Thousand Oaks, CA: Sage.

[113] Child Welfare League of America. (1989). *Standards for services to strengthen and preserve families with children.* Washington, DC: Author; Family Resource Coalition of America. (1996). *Making the case for family support.* Chicago, IL: Author.

[114] Olds, D., Henderson, C. R., Tatelbaum, R., & Chamberlin, R. (1986). Improving the delivery of prenatal care and outcomes of pregnancy: A randomized trial of nurse home visitation. *Pediatrics, 78, 65-78.*

[115] Eckenrode, J. (2000). What works in nurse home visiting programs. In M. P. Kluger, G. Alexander, and P. A. Curtis (Eds.), *What works in child welfare (pp. 35-43). Washington,* DC: CWLA Press.

[116] McCurdy, K. (2000). What works in nonmedical home visiting: Healthy Families America. In M. P. Kluger, G. Alexander, and P. A. Curtis (Eds.), *What works in child welfare* (pp. 45-55). Washington, DC: CWLA Press.

[117] National Clearing House on Child Abuse and Neglect Information. (2002). *Actions for faith communities for child abuse prevention.* Washington, DC: Author.

[118] Aldridge, D. (1991). Spirituality, healing and medicine. *British Journal of General Practice,* 41 ,425-427; Friedman, R., & Benson, H. (1997). Spirituality and medicine. *Mind/ BodyMedicine,* 2, 1-2; Larson, D. B., Sherrill, K. A., Lyons, J. S., Craigie, F. C., Theilman, S. B., Greenwold, M. A., et al. (1992). Associations between dimensions of religious commitment and mental health reported *in the American Journal of Psychiatry and Archives of General Psychiatry:* 1978 –1989. American Journal of Psychiatry, 149, 557-559; Matthews, D. A. (1997). Religion and spirituality in primary care. Mind/Body Medicine, 2, 9-19; Koenig, H. G., Meador, K. G., & Parkerson, G. (1997). Religion index for psychiatric research: A 5-item for use in health outcome studies. *American Journal of Psychiatry,* 154, 885-886.

[119] National Clearinghouse on Child Abuse and Neglect Information. (n.d.) *Actions for the business community for child abuse prevention.* Washington, DC: Author.

[120] Doblestein, A. W. (1996). Child welfare. In *Social welfare: Policy and analysis (2* nd *ed.)* (pp. 212-243). Chicago, IL: Nelson-Hall.

[121] *Meyer v. Nebraska,* 262 U.S. 390 (1923); Pierce v. Society *of Sisters, 268 U.S. 510 (1925); Prince v. Massachusetts, 321* U.S. 158 (1944).

[122] *Prince, 321 U.S. at 166.*

[123] National Association of Public Child Welfare Administrators. (1999). *Guidelines for a model system of protective services for abused and neglected children and their families.* Washington, DC: American Public Human Services Association.

[124] National Clearinghouse on Child Abuse and Neglect Information. (2001). *Child abuse and neglect State statutes series: Reporting laws, number 2: Mandated reporters of child abuse and neglect.* Washington, DC: Author.

[125] U.S. Department of Health and Human Services. (2001a).

[126] Sedlak, A., & Broadhurst, D. (1996); Besharov, D., & Laumann, L. A. (1996). Child abuse reporting. Society, *33(4), 40-46; Kalichman, S. C., & Law, C. L. (1993).* Practicing psychologists' interpretations of and compliance with child abuse reporting laws. *Law and Human Behavior, 17(1), 83-93.*

[127] U.S. Department of Health and Human Services. (2002).

[128] U.S. Department of Health and Human Services. (2002).

[129] Farrow, F. (1997). *Child protection: Building community partnerships. Getting from here to there.* Boston, MA: Harvard University, John F. Kennedy School of Government.

[130] Hudson, J., Morris, A., Maxwell, G., & Galaway, B. (1996). *Family group conferences: Perspectives on policy and practice.* Monsey, NY: Willow Tree Press; Merkel-Holguin, L. (2000). How do I use family meetings to develop optimal service plans? In H. Dubowitz & D. DePanfilis (Eds.), Handbook for child protection practice (pp. 373-378). Thousand Oaks: CA: Sage; Merkel-Holguin, L. (1998). Implementation of family group decision-making in the U.S.: Policies and practices in transition. *Protecting Children, 14(4), 4-10; U.S. Department of Health* and Human Services, Children's Bureau. (2000). Rethinking child welfare practice under the Adoption and Safe Families Act of 1997. Washington, DC: U.S. Government Printing Office.

[131] Lutz, L. (2000). *Concurrent planning: Tool for permanency survey of selected sites.* New York, NY: City University of New York, Hunter College School of Social Work, National Resource Center for Foster Care and Permanency Planning.

[132] National Research Council. (1993).

[133] Cohn, A., & Daro, D. (1987). Is treatment too late? What 10 years of evaluative research tell us. *Child Abuse and Neglect,* 11, 433-442; Dubowitz, H. (1990). Costs and effectiveness of interventions in child maltreatment. *Child Abuse and Neglect,* 14, 177-186; Daro, D., & Cohn, A. (1998). Child maltreatment evaluation efforts: What have we learned? In G. T. Hotaling, D. Finkelhor, J. T. Kirkpatrick, & M.A. Straus (Eds.), C*oping with family violence: Research and policy perspectives (pp. 275-287). Newbury Park, CA: Sage.*

[134] *Johnson, H. W. (1990). The social services: An introduction* (3rd ed.). Itasca, IL: Peacock.

[135] Ivanoff, A., Blythe, B., & Tripodi, T. (1994). *Involuntary clients in social work practice.* New York, NY: Aldine de Guyter.

[136] U.S. Department of Health and Human Services. (2000).

[137] U.S. Department of Health and Human Services, Administration on Children, Youth and Families. (2001a). *National survey of child and adolescent well-being:State child welfare agency survey. Washington, DC: U.S.* Government Printing Office.

[138] U.S. Department of Health and Human Services, Children's Bureau. (2001b). National study of child protective services *systems and reform efforts. Literature review. Washington,* DC: U.S. Government Printing Office.

[139] Hardin, A. W., Clark, R. L., & Maguire, K. (1997). *Informal and formal kinship care.* Washington, DC: Department of Health and Human Services, Office of the Assistant Secretary for Planning and Evaluation.

[140] Berrick, J. (2000). What works in kinship care. In M. Kluger, G. Alexander, & P. Curtis (Eds.), *What works in child welfare* (pp. 127-137). Washington, DC: CWLA Press.

[141] Lawson, H., & Barkdull, C. (2001). Gaining the collaborative advantage and promoting systems and cross-systems change. In A. Sallee, H. Lawson, & K. Briar-Lawson (Eds.), *Innovative practices with vulnerable children and families* (pp. 245-269). Dubuque, IA: Eddie Bowers.

[142] Waldfogel, J. (2000). Reforming child protective services. *Child Welfare, 79(1), 43-57.*

[143] National Child Welfare Resource Center for Family- Centered Practice. (2000). *Best practice - next practice: Family-centered child welfare. Washington, DC: Author.*

[144] Lawson, H., & Barkdull, C. (2001).

[145] Stark, D. R. (1999). *Collaboration basics: Strategies from six communities engaged in collaborative efforts among families, child welfare and children's mental health: A partnership for action.* Washington, DC: Georgetown University, Child Development Center, National Technical Assistance Center for Children's Mental Health.

[146] Lawson, H., & Barkdull, C. (2001).

[147] Chalk, R., & King, P. (Eds.). (1998).

[148] Chalk, R., & King, P. (Eds.). (1998).

[149] Dark, D. R. (1999). *Collaboration basics: Strategies from 6 communities engaged in collaborative efforts among families, child welfare and children's mental health. A partnership for action.* Washington, DC: Georgetown University, Child Development Center, National Technical Assistance Center for Child Mental Health.

[150] U.S. Department of Health and Human Services. (2002).

In: Child Protection, the Courts and Social Workers
Editor: Terrance R. Langely

ISBN: 978-1-60741-279-3
© 2010 Nova Science Publishers, Inc.

Chapter 2

CHILD PROTECTIVE SERVICES: A GUIDE FOR CASEWORKERS

Diane De Panfilis and Marsha K. Salus

1. PURPOSE AND OVERVIEW

Child protective services (CPS), a division within State and local social services, is at the center of every community's child protection efforts. In most jurisdictions, CPS is the agency mandated by law to conduct an initial assessment or investigation of reports of child abuse and neglect. It also offers services to families and children where maltreatment has occurred or is likely to occur.

CPS does not work alone. Many community professionals—including law enforcement officers, health care providers, mental health professionals, educators, legal and court system personnel, and substitute care providers—are involved in efforts to prevent, identify, investigate, and treat child abuse and neglect. In addition, community-based and faith-based organizations, substance abuse treatment facilities, advocates for victims of domestic violence, extended family members, and concerned citizens, among others, also play important roles in supporting families and keeping children safe from harm. Typically, CPS is the lead agency in coordinating the efforts of the various disciplines working to protect children and to educate the community about the problems of child abuse and neglect.

This manual, *Child Protective Services: A Guidefor Caseworkers*, provides the fundamental information that CPS professionals must know toperform essential casework functions. The manualdescribes:

- The philosophical basis on which CPS is founded;
- The responsibilities of CPS and its roles and relationships with other community agencies and professionals;
- The nature of the "helping relationship" and use of authority in working with children and families;

- The purposes, key decisions, and practice issuesfor the following stages of the CPS process:
  - Intake
  - Initial assessment or investigation
  - Comprehensive family assessment
  - Planning
  - Service provision
  - Evaluation of family progress
  - Case closure
- The effective documentation of actions in case records and information systems;
- The strategies for casework supervision, training, consultation, and support.

Appendices to this manual include a glossary, sample casework tools, and references to additional publications and organizations with information on child protection.

Child abuse and neglect is a complex problem, and child protection is a challenging responsibility. No single publication can provide all the information needed to promote effective CPS practice, explore all of the relevant issues, or reflect the multitude of policy and practice variations in place across the country. This manual, however, provides a starting point and a solid foundation for casework practice that should be augmented through training, other professional development activities, and experience.

CPS workers are encouraged to read *A Coordinated Response to Child Abuse and Neglect: The Foundation for Practice*. That manual, the first in the series, answers the following 10 questions:

- What are the philosophical tenets of child protection?
- What is child maltreatment?
- What is the scope of the problem?
- What factors contribute to abuse and neglect?
- What are the consequences of abuse and neglect?
- What can be done to prevent abuse and neglect?
- Which laws and policies guide public intervention in child maltreatment?
- What does the child protection process look like?
- Who should be involved in child protection at the community level?
- How can organizations work together to protect children?

This manual, the second in the series, recapitulates some of the most important points of the first manual.

2. CHILD PROTECTIVE SERVICES THEORY AND PRACTICE

The basis for child protective services (CPS) is a concern for the care of children, which is expressed through laws established in every State. The legal authority and the mandates that evolved from child abuse laws are described in *A Coordinated Response to Child Abuse and Neglect: The Foundation for Practice*. These laws do not specify all that must be done to assist families and children, but they do provide a framework within which action can be taken.

This chapter further explores how CPS staff fulfill their responsibilities of protecting children at risk of child maltreatment. It begins with an expanded discussion of the philosophical tenets of child protection that are described in *A Coordinated Response to Child Abuse and Neglect: The Foundation for Practice*. The chapter continues with a discussion of the theoretical and practical framework for CPS practice. Finally, there is an examination of the competencies required of CPS workers.

Philosophy of Child Protective Services

The basic philosophical tenets of CPS include the following:

A safe and permanent home and family is the best place for children to grow up. Every child has a right to adequate care and supervision and to be free from abuse, neglect, and exploitation. It is the responsibility of parents to see that the physical, mental, emotional, educational, and medical needs of their children are adequately met. CPS should intervene only when parents request assistance or fail, by their acts or omissions, to meet their children's basic needs and keep them safe.

Most parents want to be good parents and, when adequately supported, they have the strength and capacity to care for their children and keep them safe. Most children are best cared for in their own family. Therefore, CPS focuses on building family strengths and provides parents with the assistance needed to keep their children safe so that the family may stay together.

Families who need assistance from CPS agencies are diverse in terms of structure, culture, race, religion, economic status, beliefs, values, and lifestyles. CPS agencies and practitioners must be responsive to and respectful of these differences. Further, CPS caseworkers should build on the strengths and protective factors within families and communities. They should advocate for families and help families gain access to the services they need. Often, securing access means helping families overcome barriers rooted in poverty or discrimination, such as readily accessible transportation to services.

CPS agencies are held accountable for achieving outcomes of child safety, permanence, and family well-being. To achieve safety and permanence for children, CPS must engage families in identifying and achieving family-level outcomes that reduce the risk of further maltreatment and ameliorate the effects of maltreatment that has already occurred.

CPS efforts are most likely to succeed when clients are involved and actively participate in the process. Whatever a caseworker's role, he or she must have the ability to develop helping alliances with family members. CPS caseworkers need to work in ways that encourage clients to fully participate in assessment, case planning, and other critical decisions in CPS intervention.

When parents cannot or will not fulfill their responsibilities to protect their children, CPS has the right and obligation to intervene directly on the children's behalf. Both laws and good practice maintain that interventions should be designed to help parents protect their children and should be as unobtrusive as possible. CPS must make reasonable efforts to develop safety plans to keep children with their families whenever possible, although they may refer for juvenile or family court intervention and placement when children cannot be kept safely within their own homes. To read more about the working relationship between CPS and the court system, please refer to the user manual on working with the courts.

When children are placed in out-of-home care because their safety cannot be assured, CPS should develop a permanency plan as soon as possible. In most cases, the preferred permanency plan is to reunify children with their families. All children need continuity in their lives, so if the goal is family reunification, the plan should include frequent visits between children and their families as well as other efforts to sustain the parent-child relationship while children are in foster care. In addition, the CPS agency must immediately work with the family to change the behaviors and conditions that led to the maltreatment and necessitated placement in out-of-home care.

To best protect a child's overall well-being, agencies want to assure that children move to permanency as quickly as possible. Therefore, along with developing plans to support reunification, agencies should develop alternative plans for permanence once a child enters the CPS system. As soon as it has been determined that a child cannot be safely reunited with his or her family, CPS must implement the alternative permanency plan.

PHILOSOPHICAL UNDERPINNINGS OF CPS

Additional sources of information on the philosophical underpinnings of CPS and other child welfare service programs include:

- Pecora, P. J., Whittaker, J. K., Maluccio, A. N., Barth, R. P., & Plotnick, R. D. (2000). *The child welfare challenge* (2nd ed.). New York, NY: Aldine de Gruyter.
- National Association of Public Child Welfare Administrators. (1999). *Guidelines for a model system of protective services for abused and neglected children and their families.* Washington, DC: American Public Human Services Association.
- Child Welfare League of America. (1999). CWLA standards of excellence for services for abused and neglected children and their families (revised edition). Washington, DC: Author.
- Waldfogel, J. (1998). The future of child protection: How to break the cycle of abuse and neglect. Cambridge, MA: Harvard University Press.
- Horejsi, C. (1996). *Assessment and case planning in child protection and foster care services.* Englewood, CO: American Humane Association, Children's Division.

Framework for Practice

This section explains how practitioners apply the philosophical tenets described above to practice. Practitioners generally agree that a "child-centered, family-focused, and culturally responsive" framework for child welfare practice will promote the best outcomes for children.[1] This integrative framework for practice builds on five main perspectives described below:

- **Ecological perspective.** This perspective conceptualizes human behavior and social functioning within an environmental context. Personal, family, and environmental factors interact with each other to influence the family. Child maltreatment is viewed as the consequence of the interplay between a complex set of risk and protective factors at the individual, family, community, and society levels.

- **Strength-based perspective.** This perspective refers to practice methods and strategies that draw upon the strengths of children, families, and communities. Strength-based practice involves a shift from a deficit approach, which emphasizes problems and pathology, to a positive partnership with the family. The assessments focus on the complex interplay of risks and strengths related to individual family members, the family as a unit, and the broader neighborhood and environment.

- **Developmental perspective.** This perspective refers to understanding individual growth and development and family development from a lifespan perspective, and examines individuals and families interacting with their environments over the course of time. Effective case planning takes into account which interventions are effective with a specific child or family problem, in a specific environmental setting, and at a particular developmental stage.[2]

- **Permanency planning orientation.** This orientation holds that all children have a right to a permanent home. Child welfare service delivery should focus on safely maintaining children in their own homes or, if necessary, placing them permanently with other families. Interventions include a set of goal-directed activities designed to help children live in safe families who offer a sense of belonging and legal, lifetime family ties.

- **Cultural competence perspective.** This perspective requires CPS practitioners to understand the perspective of clients or peers who may come from culturally diverse backgrounds and to adapt their practice accordingly. Basic cultural competence is achieved when organizations and practitioners accept and respect differences, engage in ongoing cultural self-assessment, expand their diversity knowledge and skills, and adapt service models to fit the target populations, culture, situation, and perceived needs.[3]

EXHIBIT 2-1. CPS WORKER VALUES, KNOWLEDGE, AND SKILLS

Core Values

Belief that:

- All people have a reservoir of untapped, renewable, and expandable abilities (mental, physical, emotional, social, and spiritual) that can be used to facilitate change.
- Each child has a right to a permanent family.
- Each child and family member should be empowered to work toward his or her own needs and goals.

Commitment to:

- Using a strength-based, child-centered, family-focused practice.
- Assuring the safety of children in the context of their family.
- Practicing complete confidentiality.
- Ensuring accountability and an end-results orientation.
- Implementing quality professional practice.
- Continuing pursuit of knowledge and skills to effectively accomplish the mission of CPS.

Respect for:

- Persons of diverse racial, religious, ethnic, and cultural backgrounds, and a belief that there is strength in diversity.
- Each person's dignity, individuality, and right to self-determination.

Core Knowledge

Understanding of:

- Family systems, the family's environment, the family in a historical context, diverse family structures, and concepts of family empowerment.
- Individual growth and development with particular attention to attachment and bonding, separation, loss, and identity development.
- Child abuse and neglect dynamics.
- Cultural diversity, the characteristics of special populations, and the implications for assessment and intervention.
- Continuum of placement services including the foster care system, the residential care system, kinship care, placement prevention, familial ties maintenance, family reunification, and adoption.

- Services including crisis intervention, parenting skills training, family counseling, conflict resolution, and individual and group counseling.

Command of:

- Case management issues and responsibilities.
- Child welfare and child protection programs and models.
- Principles of permanency planning for children and the role of out-of-home care.

Familiarity with:

- Special problems of poverty, oppression, and deprivation.
- Substance abuse issues and their effect on children and families.
- Dynamics of community and family violence, including partner abuse and the impact of trauma.
- Direct services available to children and families in the mental health, health care, substance abuse treatment, education, juvenile justice, and community systems.
- Wraparound services available for families through the economic security, housing, transportation, and job training systems.
- Legal systems related to child welfare practice.
- Political and advocacy processes and how they relate to funding and acquiring services.

Core Skills

Ability to:

- Identify strengths and needs and engage the family in a strength-based assessment process.
- Take decisive and appropriate action when a child needs protection.
- Analyze complex information.
- Be persistent in approach to CPS work.
- Employ crisis intervention and early intervention services and strategies.
- Assess a family's readiness to change and employ appropriate strategies for increasing motivation and
- building the helping alliance.
- Function as a case manager and a team member, and collaborate with other service providers.
- Assess for substance abuse, domestic violence, sexual abuse, and mental illness.
- Work with birth families to create a permanent plan for a child in foster care, kinship care, or group care.
-

Aptitude for:

- Developing and maintaining professional relationships with families.
- Listening.
- Remaining flexible.
- Working with involuntary clients, including those who are hostile or resistant.
- Working with legal systems, including documentation and court testimony.
- Empowering the child and family to sustain gains and use family and community supports.

Expertise in:

- Assessing for abuse, neglect, and the safety of the child and others in the family setting.
- Negotiating, implementing, and evaluating the case plan with the family.
- Working with the family and key supports to accomplish the service agreement goals.
- Applying knowledge of human behavior and successful intervention methods with children and adolescents at various developmental stages.[4]

Caseworker Competence

Developing CPS caseworker competence is an ongoing process. Caseworkers build competence through education, training, experience, and supervision. Examples of the core qualities, values, knowledge, and skills associated with competency in CPS are included in Exhibit 2-1.

Since the 1990s, the need for competent workers has increased. This reflects concerns about the quality of the delivery of services; the increasing complexity of child welfare cases; and the need for inter- and intrasystem collaboration and coordination with the courts as well as mental health, juvenile justice, education, domestic violence, health care, and substance abuse services. It also stems from the legislative mandates of the Adoption and Safe Families Act (ASFA) of 1997, which requires the provision of timely assessment and intervention services to the children and families served within the CPS system.[5]

In response to ongoing staffing crises, some child welfare agencies are trying to address organizational problems and overburdened staff by setting standards for worker educational background and licensure—an effort toward "re-professionalization" of child welfare.[6] To increase the competency of CPS staff, many States have developed and implemented competency-based training and certification programs. Some of these programs include readiness assessments and competency exams.

There is research that strongly suggests that higher education is essential for developing caseworker competencies. Both the National Association of Public Child Welfare Administrators (NAPCWA) and the Child Welfare League of America (CWLA) suggest that CPS staff should have a bachelor's or master's degree in social work (B.S.W. or M.S.W.) or a degree in a closely related field. Social work education appears to be related to job retention and staff stability, which helps produce better child welfare practice.[7]

THE LINK BETWEEN HIGHER EDUCATION AND IMPROVED CHILD WELFARE PRACTICE

Research findings support the efficacy of social work education for public-sector child welfare practice. The following are highlights of several key studies:

- A national study of job requirements for child welfare workers found that turnover was consistently higher in States that do not require any academic social work preparation for child welfare positions and is consistently lower in States that require an M.S.W.[8]
- A Florida study suggested that workers without education in child welfare work were most likely to leave before 1 year.[9]
- A study by Hess, Folaron, and Jefferson found that caseworker turnover was a major factor in failed reunification efforts.[10]
- A Maryland study found that having an M.S.W. degree appeared to be the best predictor of overall performance in social service work.[11]
- A study of social service workers in Kentucky found that staff members with social work degrees were better prepared for their work than those without them.[12]
- Abers, Reilly, and Rittner found that child welfare staff with B.S.W. and M.S.W. degrees were more effective in developing successful permanency plans for children who had been in foster care for more than 2 years than were staff without these degrees.[13]

An important strategy for increasing the preparedness of CPS workers is to direct Federal funding toward the education and recruitment of social work students into public child welfare work. The Title IV-E Public Child Welfare Education Program represents a shift in Federally funded education and training of public child welfare workers from an emphasis on traditional inservice training through workshops, conferences, consultation, and staff development, to an emphasis on university and public agency collaboration and partnership.[14] B.S.W. students report that financial support opportunities (such as loan forgiveness or stipends) and exposure to child welfare practice during their social work education program are important factors in helping them choose child welfare as a future career.[15]

For examples of State and Federal initiatives focused on increasing the competency of child welfare personnel, see *Partnerships for Child Welfare* newsletters published by the Council on Social Work Education. Available at: www.cswe.org.

Child welfare training information and materials can be found on the Online Network of Child Welfare Training Resources: www.childwelfaretraining.org.

3. THE HELPING RELATIONSHIP

Developing a helping relationship with abused and neglected children and their families is critical to changing the conditions or patterns of behavior that contributed to the risk of maltreatment. Experience has demonstrated that successful intervention and treatment depend heavily on the quality of the caseworker's relationship with the children and family.

Developing helping alliances with families and children at risk for child maltreatment is challenging because they may have a history of difficulties in forming and sustaining mutually supportive, interpersonal relationships, and they may not have had positive relationships with formal systems, such as schools, social services, or counseling services.[16] Whether one's role is interviewing family members as part of the initial assessment or investigation, or determining what must change to reduce the risk of maltreatment and improve outcomes for risk reduction, the quality of the caseworker's effort is directly dependent on his or her ability to develop a collaborative relationship.[17]

This relationship begins with the very first contact and continues to develop with ongoing caseworker and client communication and interaction. By definition, relationships have a strong emotional component. Good relationships do not just happen; they must be built. The relationship does not result from a caseworker's charismatic personality or a mystical connection between people. Rather, it is a product of the caseworker's commitment to helping the children and family, his or her ability to relate effectively on an interpersonal level, and the children and the family's willingness to be open and risk "relating" to the caseworker. Caseworkers' behavior can significantly increase the chances that a positive relationship will develop.[18]

Core Conditions of the Helping Relationship

Researchers have defined three core conditions that are essential to the helping relationship:

- Empathy
- Respect
- Genuineness[19]

A caseworker's ability to communicate these three core conditions will strongly influence whether they will build a relationship with the children and family that is characterized by cooperation or a relationship that is hostile and distrustful. Each of the conditions is described below.

Empathy

Empathy is the ability to perceive and communicate with sensitivity the feelings and experiences of another person by being an active responder rather than a passive listener. Empathy is a process of attempting to experience another person's world and then communicating an understanding of, and compassion for, the other's experience. The caseworker should focus on the verbal and nonverbal cues, such as smiling or eye-rolling, presented by the children and family and frequently share his or her understanding of what the client has communicated. The content of the message is never ignored, but empathy goes beyond the facts, circumstances, and events of the children's and family's life and conveys an understanding of how those circumstances uniquely affect them.

Empathy builds trust and openness and helps to establish rapport between the children and family and the caseworker. Caseworkers can demonstrate empathy by:

- Paying attention to verbal and nonverbal cues;
- Communicating an understanding of the children's and family's message;
- Showing a desire to understand;
- Discussing what is important to the children and family;
- Referring to the children's and family's feelings.

In their effort to be empathetic, some new caseworkers may lose their objectivity and "over- identify" with the children's perspective or, in other cases, be so family-centered as to ignore some risk factors. It also should be recognized that some in the helping profession have been abused and may over-identify with either the child or the parent. Some signs of over-identification may include a difficulty or inability seeing a parent's strengths or being unable to see any possible positive intention behind the parent's behavior. This may make it difficult to be empathetic to other family members, which may lead to counterproductive outcomes for the family as a whole.[20]

Respect

Respect refers to the caseworker's communication of acceptance, caring, and concern for the children and family. It involves valuing the individual family members as people, separate from any evaluation of their behavior or thoughts, although this does not mean that caseworkers sanction or approve thoughts or behaviors that society may disapprove.

All human beings need to feel accepted and respected; it is especially important for abused and neglected children and their families to feel accepted and respected by their caseworker. Many abused and neglected children and their families fear or mistrust caseworkers and the social service system. The helping relationship will not be established unless the caseworker communicates respect for each person's potential. Caseworkers should believe that all people have the strength, internal resiliency, and capacity to become more competent.

Respect also means using culturally competent practice. Culturally competent practice entails:

- **Cultural awareness.** Caseworkers should understand and identify the critical cultural values important to the children and family as well as to themselves.

- **Knowledge acquisition.** Caseworkers should understand how these cultural values function as strengths in the children and family.

- **Skill development.** Caseworkers should be able to match services that support the identified cultural values and then incorporate them in the appropriate interventions.

- **Inductive learning.** Caseworkers should continue to seek solutions that include considering indigenous interventions and matching cultural values to Western interventions.[21]

Genuineness

Genuineness refers to caseworkers being themselves. This means simply that caseworkers are consistent in what they say and do, nondefensive, and authentic. They must have clear knowledge and an acceptance of the agency's authority, procedures, and policies, and of their professional role—both in its meaning to the worker and the meaning to abused and neglected children and their families. Genuineness means integrating who we are and our role in the agency with acceptance of children and families and a commitment to their welfare. If this occurs, then what caseworkers say will match their attitudes and beliefs.

However, a worker must use discretion. For example, if a caseworker feels shock, horror, or anger over a parent's abusive behavior, expressing these feelings would not be productive. In fact, it may alienate parents, causing them to be angry, defensive, or resistant. Rather, caseworkers need to be aware of their feelings and at the same time respond in a respectful manner that opens rather than closes communication.

Genuineness contributes to the helping relationship by reducing the emotional distance between the caseworker and the children and family and by helping them to identify the caseworker as another human being similar to himself or herself. Caseworkers can demonstrate genuineness by:

- Being themselves and not taking on a role or acting contrary to how they believe or feel;
- Making sure that their nonverbal and verbal responses match;
- Using nonverbal behaviors—such as eye contact, smiles, or sitting forward in the chair—to communicate trustworthiness and acceptance;
- Being able to express themselves naturally without artificial behaviors;
- Being nondefensive.[22]

Another means by which caseworkers can demonstrate genuineness is through the use of self-disclosure. When used carefully, this can be an effective method for establishing a connection between the caseworker and the client. It is important, however, that self-disclosure is used judiciously to prevent a shift in the focus from the client to the caseworker.

Techniques for Building Rapport

In addition to the core conditions and guiding principles for developing a helping relationship, there are specific techniques caseworkers can use to build rapport. The following list provides some examples:

- Approach each individual involved with an open mind.
- Find out what is important to the child and to the family. For example, do not press the issue of staying sober as the priority if that is not important to the parent or caretaker, but do explain that staying sober will speed up getting the children back if that is their priority.

- Use mirroring. Take note of words used by the child or family and try to incorporate them into your conversations.
- Listen to the child or parent's explanation of the situation without correcting or arguing.
- Ask questions rather than issuing threats or commands.
- Clarify expectations and purposes. Clearly explain the helping process and the caseworker's role in working together toward solutions.
- Help the child and parent or caretaker retain a sense of control; for example, involve them in scheduling appointments and ask how they would like to be addressed.
- Clarify commitment and obligations to the working relationship.
- Acknowledge difficult feelings and encourage open and honest discussion of feelings.
- Be consistent, persistent, and follow through.
- Promote participatory decision-making for meeting needs and solving problems.[23]

These are only a few key techniques; there are many other methods that will help build rapport.

Use of Authority in Child Protective Services

Child protective services (CPS) is an expression of a community's concern for the welfare of its citizens. Child protective services are provided because the community recognizes that children have the right to safety and that parents have obligations and responsibilities. The authority to provide these services is vested in the CPS agency and staff through laws and government policies. Competent CPS practice involves using this authority effectively. The use of CPS authority has special relevance at the initial assessment or investigation stage of the casework process, but is applicable at all other stages as well. In fact, effective use of authority is an essential ingredient in establishing helping relationships with all involuntary clients.

Authority, whatever its source, can impede or enable the development of trust between the CPS caseworker and the children and family. The constructive and positive use of authority involves (1) stating one's purpose and function clearly at all times, (2) supporting and challenging the children and family, and (3) expressing feelings. This approach provides the children and family with a feeling of confidence that the caseworker:

- Knows what he or she is doing;
- Is secure in his or her position;
- Intends the best for the child, parents, family, and society.[24]

Difficulties in Using Authority Effectively

The caseworker's effective use of authority reduces opposition and assists in engaging children and families. There are several factors in CPS work that may make this difficult:

- Even though CPS caseworkers have the legally mandated authority to investigate abuse and neglect, if they lack the children's and family's respect, they may experience difficulty influencing the change process.
- There may not be agreement between CPS, the children, and the family about what constitutes appropriate and effective intervention.
- If the caseworker is not able to overcome any negative perceptions he or she has of the children and family, it may influence engagement.
- Caseworkers may not be adequately prepared to engage families of different cultural backgrounds. As a result, families may feel "invaded" by casework ers.[25]

Engaging the resistant client

Due to the involuntary nature of the majority of CPS cases, it is not unusual for families to resist offers of help. Resistance is a normal and predictable response when people feel forced to change. Caseworkers should not personalize resistance. To deal with resistance effectively, caseworkers should first change their perspective of resistance and try to see the behavior as a potential strength. How the caseworker responds to the resistance is crucial in avoiding continued abuse or escalation of inappropriate behavior. To assist in engaging resistant clients:

- Be clear, honest, and direct. Caseworkers should maintain a nondefensive stance.
- Acknowledge the involuntary nature of the arrangement. Caseworkers should explain the structure and content of intervention to the children and family.
- Be matter-of-fact and nondefensive in explaining the legal authority that permits intervention. Caseworkers should not get into a debate about authority; instead caseworkers should state what their authority is and what legal recourse the children and family may have to challenge it.
- Contact children and families in a manner that is courteous and respectful, and assess strengths as well as risks.
- Elicit the parent's concerns and wishes for assistance and convey understanding of the parent's viewpoint, including reservations about CPS involvement.
- Reduce the children's and family's opposition to contact by clarifying available choices, even when choices are constrained, by emphasizing freedoms still available and by avoiding labeling.
- Earn the respect of the children and family (and gain psychological influence) by being a good listener who strives to understand their point of view.
- Respect the right of the children and family to express values and preferences different from those of the caseworker.
- Establish feasible, small steps to help build in early success in order to recognize client efforts and progress.
- Acknowledge difficult feelings and encourage open and honest discussion of feelings.

- Reframe the family's situation. This is particularly useful when the children and family are making arguments that deny a problem or risk; it acknowledges their statements, but offers a new meaning or interpretation for them. The children's and family's information is recast into a new form and viewed in a new light that is more likely to be helpful and support change.

TECHNIQUES FOR HANDLING HOSTILE AND ANGRY SITUATIONS

One form of client resistance that is particularly difficult for CPS caseworkers to manage is anger and hostility. The following are techniques for deescalating anger:

- Remain calm; try not to show fear or anxiety.
- Be firm without raising one's voice.
- Make statements simple and direct.
- Recognize and address feelings and do not take hostile statements personally.
- Offer the person a choice between positive alternatives.
- Be alert for the possibility of aggression.
- Attempt to have the person sit down, and distract him or her from the source of anger.
- Give the person lots of space; do not touch them.
- If the person attacks, use only enough force to protect yourself or restrain him or her.
- Remember it takes a person 30-40 minutes to calm down physiologically.
- After the visit, do not sit in front of the house to write notes.
- Carry a cell phone, whistle, or personal alarm and use it, if appropriate.
- Pay attention to intuition or "gut instinct," and leave if warranted.[26]

Stages of Change

All human beings are motivated to meet basic needs. Individuals frequently differ in their state of readiness to change. In addition, client readiness to change may fluctuate over time. Motivation is clearly linked to the degree of hope that change is possible. The degree to which clients are ready to change varies over time and is described in the pattern presented in Exhibit 3- (i.e., precontemplation, contemplation, determination, action, and maintenance).

Since most children and families are involved with CPS involuntarily, they enter the CPS system at the precontemplation stage. By the end of the initial assessment or investigation phase, it is hoped that caseworkers will have moved children and families to the contemplation stage or, even better, to the determination stage. It is essential for children and families to be at the determination stage when developing the intervention plan. If children and families have not moved to that point, the likelihood of change is compromised.

Exhibit 3-1. Stages of Change

Stage	Description	Caseworker Actions
Precontemplation	*Sees no need to change.* At this stage, the person has not even contemplated having a problem or needing to make a change. This is the stage where denial, minimization, blaming, and resistance are most commonly present.	Provide information and feedback to raise the client's awareness of the problem and the possibility of change. Do not give prescriptive advice.
Contemplation	*Considers change but also rejects it.* At this stage, there is some awareness that a problem exists. This stage is characterized by ambivalence; the person wants to change, but also does not want to. They will go back and forth between reasons for concern and justification for unconcern. This is the stage where clients feel stuck.	Help the client tip the balance in favor of change. Help the client see the benefits of changing and the consequences of not changing.
Determination	*Wants to do something about the problem.* At this stage, there is a window of opportunity for change: the person has decided to change and needs realistic and achievable steps to change.	Help the client find a change strategy that is realistic, acceptable, accessible, appropriate, and effective.
Action	*Takes steps to change.* At this stage, the person engages in specific actions to bring about change. The goal during this stage is to produce change in a particular area or areas.	Support and be an advocate for the client. Help accomplish the steps for change.
Maintenance	*Maintains goal achievement.* Making the change does not guarantee that the change will be maintained. The challenge during this stage is to sustain the change accomplished by previous action and to prevent relapse. Maintaining change may often require a different set of skills than making the change.	Help the client identify the possibility of relapse. Then, help the client identify and use strategies to prevent relapse.[27]

4. RESPONSIBILITIES OF CHILD PROTECTIVE SERVICES

According to the National Association of Public Child Welfare Administrators (NAPCWA), the mission of the child protective services (CPS) agency is to:

- Assess the safety of children;
- Intervene to protect children from harm;
- Strengthen the ability of families to protect their children;
- Provide either a reunification or an alternative, safe family for the child.[28]

CPS is the central agency in each community that receives reports of suspected child abuse and neglect; assesses the risk to and safety of children; and provides or arranges for services to achieve safe, permanent families for children who have been abused or neglected or who are at risk of abuse or neglect. The CPS agency also facilitates community collaborations and engages formal and informal community partners to support families and protect children from abuse and neglect. To fulfill its mission, CPS must provide services, either directly or through other agencies, which are child-centered, family-focused, and culturally responsive to achieve safety, well-being, and permanency for children.[29] When families are unable or unwilling to keep children safe, CPS petitions juvenile or family court on the child's behalf either to recommend strategies to keep children safe at home or to be placed in outof-home care. This chapter provides an overview of the seven stages of the CPS process, which are described in more detail throughout the manual.

Intake

CPS is responsible for receiving and evaluating reports of suspected child abuse and neglect, determines if the reported information meets the statutory and agency guidelines for child maltreatment, and judges the urgency with which the agency must respond to the report. In addition, CPS educates individuals who report allegations of child abuse or neglect (frequently referred to as "reporters") about State statutes, agency guidelines, and the roles and responsibilities of CPS.

Initial Assessment or Investigation

After receiving a report, CPS conducts an initial assessment or investigation to determine:

- If child maltreatment occurred;
- If the child's immediate safety is a concern and, if it is, the interventions that will ensure the child's protection while keeping the child
- within the family or with family members (e.g., kinship care or subsidized guardianship), if at all possible;
- If there is a risk of future maltreatment and the level of that risk;
- If continuing agency services are needed to address any effects of child maltreatment and to reduce the risk of future maltreatment.

The terms "assessment" and "investigation" are used interchangeably in many States and territories, but they are not synonymous. Investigation encompasses the efforts of the CPS agency to determine if abuse or neglect has occurred. Assessment goes beyond this concept to evaluate a child's safety and risk, and to determine whether and what services are needed to ameliorate or prevent child abuse and neglect.[30]

The initial assessment or investigation is not just a fact-finding process; it establishes the tone for all future work that may take place with a particular family. During the initial assessment or investigation, CPS must determine whether child abuse and neglect occurred and can be substantiated and whether to conduct an evaluation to determine the risk of maltreatment occurring in the future. CPS also must establish rapport with family members and engage them in the intervention process.

Family Assessment

Once a determination of child abuse or neglect has been made and the child's immediate safety has been ensured, the next step is to conduct a family assessment. During this step, the caseworker engages family members in a process to understand their strengths and needs. In particular, the caseworker works with the family to:

- Identify family strengths that can provide a foundation for change;
- Reduce the risk of maltreatment by identifying and addressing factors that place children at risk;
- Help children cope with the effects of maltreatment.

Since the impact of child maltreatment depends on the interaction of risk and protective factors, using an ecological developmental framework for this assessment is often appropriate.[31]

Case Planning

In order to achieve the desired programmatic outcomes of CPS (i.e., child safety, child permanency, child and family well-being), interventions must be well planned and purposeful. These outcomes are achieved through three types of plans:

- A safety plan, which is developed whenever it is determined that the child is at risk of imminent harm;
- A case plan, which follows the family assessment and sets forth goals and outcomes and describes how the family will work toward these outcomes;
- A concurrent permanency plan, which identifies alternative forms of permanency and addresses both how reunification can be achieved and how legal permanency with a new family might be achieved if reunification efforts fail.

All three plans should be developed collaboratively, when possible, among the CPS caseworker, the family, and community professionals who will provide services to the family.

Service Provision

This is the stage during which the case plan is implemented. It is CPS's role to arrange, provide, and coordinate the delivery of services to children and families. When possible, the services that are selected to help families achieve goals and outcomes should be based on an appropriate match of services to goals and should use best practice principles.

When needed services are not readily available or accessible, an interim or alternative plan must be made with families.

Family Progress

Assessment is an ongoing process that begins with the first client contact, continues throughout the life of the case, and should incorporate reports from other service providers. When evaluating family progress, caseworkers focus on:

- Ensuring the child's safety;
- Reducing the risk of maltreatment;
- Addressing successfully any of the effects of maltreatment on the child and family;
- Achieving the goals and tasks in the case plan;
- Achieving family-level outcomes.

Case Closure

The process of ending the relationship between the CPS worker and the family involves a mutual review of the progress made throughout the helping relationship. Optimally, cases are closed when families have achieved their goals and the risk of maltreatment has been reduced or eliminated.

Some closings occur because the client discontinues services, and the agency does not have a sufficient basis to refer the situation to juvenile or family court. Other cases are closed, however, when families still need assistance. When this happens, the caseworker should carefully document what risks may still be present so this information is available should the family be referred to the agency at a later time. At the time of closure, workers should involve the family in a discussion about what has changed over time and what goals they may still have. When family needs are still apparent and are outside the scope of the CPS system, every effort should be made to help the family receive services through appropriate community agencies.

5. INTAKE

Intake is the first stage of the child protective services (CPS) process and is one of the most important decision-making points in the child protection system. It is the point at which reports of suspected child abuse and neglect are received. Information gathered by caseworkers is used to make decisions regarding safety (e.g., Is the child at risk of imminent harm?), risk (e.g., What is the likelihood that maltreatment will occur sometime in the future?), and the type of CPS response required. At intake, caseworkers also perform a critical public relations function by responding professionally and sensitively to the concerns raised by community professionals and citizens, and by clarifying the role of the agency regarding referrals of suspected abuse or neglect. Referrals are accepted from all sources, and each report is treated as a potential case of child maltreatment.[32]

Intake Process

Specific guidelines for conducting the intake process vary from State to State and community to community. In general, caseworkers must:

- Gather sufficient information from the reporter and agency records to be able to:
  - Identify and locate the children and the parents or primary caregiver;
  - Determine if the report meets the statutory and agency guidelines for child maltreatment;
  - Assess whether the child is safe;
  - Evaluate the motives of the reporter.
- Provide support and encouragement to the reporter by:
  - Explaining that the purpose of CPS is to protect children and strengthen families;
  - Emphasizing the importance of reporting and explaining the process in which the report will be tracked;
  - Describing the types of cases accepted by CPS as well as the types of information needed from the reporter;
  - Responding sensitively to the fears and concerns of the reporter;
  - Discussing the State's regulations regarding confidentiality, including the circumstances under which a reporter's identity may be revealed (e.g., if required by court action in a particular case).
- Handle emergency situations such as:
  - Calming the caller;
  - Determining how to meet the immediate needs of the child and family being reported.
- Check agency records and the State's central registry (if appropriate) to determine if the family or child is known or has been reported to the agency previously.

Gathering Information from Reporters

The more comprehensive the information provided by the reporter, the more experienced caseworkers are able to determine the appropriateness of the report for CPS intervention; whether the child is safe; and the urgency of the response needed. State and local child protection agencies have guidelines for information-gathering at intake. In general, caseworkers should obtain information on:

- **The contact information for the child and family,** which helps to locate the child and family and determine if the child is at immediate risk of harm;

- **The alleged maltreatment,** including type, nature, severity, chronicity, and where it occurred;

- **The child,** including the child's condition and behavior, which helps in evaluating whether the child is in immediate risk of harm or danger and determining the urgency and type of the response;

- **The parent or caregiver,** including their emotional and physical condition, behavior, history, view of the child, child-rearing practices, and relationships outside the family;

- **The family,** including family characteristics, dynamics, and supports.

Exhibit 5-1 presents more detailed information that should be collected from the reporter within each of these areas. Although not every reporter will have all the information described, it is important to attempt to gather it to guide the investigation and ensure the appropriate decisions at intake. This may be the only opportunity the agency has to talk with the reporter.

Exhibit 5-1. Sample Information to Obtain from Reporter during Intake

Demographic Information			
Child: • Name • Age (date of birth) • Sex • Race • Permanent address • Current location • School or daycare attending	**Parents or Caregivers:*** • Name • Age (date of birth) • Race • Relationship to the child • Permanent address • Current location • Place of employment • Telephone number(s) * If the person alleged to have maltreated the child is a caregiver other than the child's parents, the above information should be gathered about both the parents and caregiver.	**Family Composition:** • Names • Ages (dates of birth) • Sex • Race • Location of all children in the family • Names, ages, and location(s) of other children in the alleged maltreater's care • Names of other relatives and nonrelatives living in the home, if the maltreater is not the birth parent (e.g., a babysitter, boyfriend, stepparent) • Names, addresses, and telephone numbers of other relatives and their relationship to the child • Names, addresses, telephone numbers, and other sources of information about the family	**Reporter:** • Name • Address • Telephone number • Relationship to the child or family • How they learned of alleged maltreatment
Information Regarding the Alleged Maltreatment			
Type(s): • Physical abuse • Sexual abuse • Neglect • Emotional maltreatment	**Nature of Maltreatment:** (Specific characteristics and parental acts or omissions) • Physical abuse: burning, beating, kicking, biting, and other physical abuse • Neglect: abandonment, withholding of needed medical care, lack of supervision, lack of adequate food or shelter, emotional deprivation, failure to register or send to school, and the effects of exposure to partner abuse	**Severity:** • Extent of the physical injury (e.g., second- and third-degree burns on half of the child's body) • Location of the injury on the child's body • Extent of the emotional injury to the child (e.g., suicidal behavior,excessive fear of the parents or caregivers) **Chronicity:** • Prior incidents of abuse or neglect	**Location:** • Setting where abuse or neglect occurred (e.g., home, school, supermarket)

(Continued)

Information Regarding the Alleged Maltreatment		
	• Sexual abuse or exploitation: fondling, masturbation, oral or anal sex, sexual intercourse, viewing or involved in pornography or forced prostitution • Emotional maltreatment: constant berating or rejecting treatment, scapegoating, and bizarre/cruel/ritualistic forms of punishment	• How long the abuse or neglect has been occurring Whether abuse or neglect has increased in frequency or remained relatively constant	

Examples of Information Regarding the Parents or Caregivers		
Emotional and Physical Condition: • Expresses feelings in positive and healthy ways • Misuses drugs or alcohol • Suffers from physical illness • Suffers from mental illness **Behavior:** • Good impulse control • Awareness of triggers that cause them to be angry • Engagement in violent outbursts • Engagement in bizarre or irrational behavior • Possession of weapons in the home • Abuse of pets	**View of the Child:** • Empathizes with the child • Views the child as bad or evil • Blames the child for the child's condition **Relationships Outside the Home:** • Friends and the quality of those friendships • Social and emotional isolation	**Child-rearing Practices:** • Realistic and age-appropriate expectations of the child • Extent to which use of inappropriate verbal or physical punishment as the first response to misbehavior • Knowledge of different disciplinary techniques appropriate for the child's age and developmental status

Examples of Information Regarding the Child	
Child's Condition: • Physical condition • Emotional condition • Disabilities or impairments • Strengths	**Child's Behavior:** • Extremes in behavior • Appropriateness of behavior given child's age and developmental level

Examples of Information Regarding the Family		
Family Characteristics: • Single parent or blended family • Adequate family income • Parents employed • Flow of strangers in and out of home • Evidence of drug dealing in the home	**Family Dynamics:** • Serious marital conflict • Partner abuse • Disorganization and chaos	**Family Supports:** • Extended family members who are accessible and available • Relationships with others outside the family • Connections in the community, such as houses of worship

Gathering this detailed information is essential to determine if the child is safe and how quickly contact with the family must be made to assure safety. It also enables caseworkers to identify the victim, the parent or caregiver, and the maltreater (if different from the parent or caregiver), and to determine how to locate them so that the initial assessment or investigation can be conducted. In addition, information from the reporter may identify other possible sources of information about the family and the possibility of past, current, or future abuse or neglect. Finally, it will assist the caseworker responsible for the initial assessment or investigation in planning the approach to the investigation in an accurate and effective manner.

Providing support to reporters

Reports of child abuse and neglect are most often initiated by telephone and may come from any number of sources. Each reporter should be given support and encouragement for making the decision to report. In addition, the reporter's fears and concerns should be elicited and addressed. These can range from fear that the family will retaliate to fear of having to testify in court.

It is often very difficult for the reporter to make the call. The telephone call usually comes after much thought has been given to the possible consequences to the child and family. More than likely, the reporter has considered that it would be easier just to do nothing or that the CPS system may not be able to help the family. It may be difficult for a reporter to think that this call will actually help the family rather than hurt it. Simple verbal reassurances or a follow-up letter that expresses the agency's gratitude to the reporter for taking the initiative to call can make the difference in the reporter's future willingness to cooperate.

Intake Information Analysis

Upon receiving a referral, the intake worker or caseworker attempts to gather as much information as possible about each family member; the family as a whole; and the nature, extent, severity, and chronicity of the alleged child maltreatment. Once the initial intake information is collected, the caseworker conducts a check of agency records or, in some States, a central registry to determine any past reports or contact with the family. Then the caseworkers must collect and analyze the information and determine if it meets the following criteria.

Statutory and agency guidelines

This determination is made by comparing the data collected to State law regarding the definition of child abuse and neglect and the requirements for State or county response; agency policies interpreting the laws and practice standards; agency or office customs regarding further refinement of definitions; required response times; and practical issues, such as jurisdictional authority or caseload management.[33]

Credibility

An essential step in the intake process is determining the consistency and accuracy of the information being reported. In some locations, the intake workers take all reports and the investigator determines the credibility of the report; in other locations, the intake workers determine the credibility of the report. Sometimes caseworkers question the validity of the report suspecting it may be influenced by a contentious divorce, custody battle, or bad neighbor relationships. Regardless of suspicions about the motives of the reporter, if the allegations meet the statutory and agency guidelines, the case must be accepted.

A number of questions will help caseworkers evaluate the credibility of the report:

- Is the reporter willing to give his or her name, address, and telephone number?
- What is the reporter's relationship to the victim and family?
- How well does the reporter know the family?

- Does the reporter know of previous abuse or neglect? What has led him or her to report now?
- How does the reporter know about the case?
- Does the reporter stand to gain anything from reporting?
- Has the reporter made previous unfounded reports on this family?
- Is the reporter willing to meet with a caseworker in person if needed?
- Does the reporter appear to be intoxicated, extremely bitter, angry, or exhibiting behavior that makes the caseworker question his or her competency?
- Can or will the reporter refer CPS to others who know about the situation?
- What does the reporter hope will happen as a result of the report?
- Does the reporter fear reprisal from family?
- Does the reporter fear self-incrimination? For example, due to substance-abusing behavior or participation in physically abusive behavior.

When an initial assessment or investigation is warranted

One of the primary decisions in the intake process is whether or not to accept a report for a CPS investigation. This decision is based on the law, agency policy, and information about the characteristics of the case that are likely to indicate, or result in, harm to the child. The appropriateness of this decision depends on the ability of the caseworker to gather critical and accurate information about the family and the alleged maltreatment and to apply law and policy to the information gathered.[34]

States have different criteria and tools for acceptance of the report. Some of the steps caseworkers should take in making this decision include:

- **Referring to State law.** The law defines what is considered child maltreatment under State statutes. These definitions are the caseworkers' ultimate source of guidance.

- **Reviewing agency policies.** Agency policies include State and local guidelines. They may have additional information regarding definitions and how to respond to different types of reports.

- **Discussing with the supervisor how these guidelines are implemented in the office.** Sometimes customs develop among caseworkers or units that may not reflect agency guidelines. This often occurs as a result of many years of practice and improvisation over time. Unfortunately, these adaptations to circumstances may lead caseworkers away from carrying out their mandated responsibilities.

Whether to accept a case for initial assessment or investigation or to refer it to other community agencies depends on the following:

- If the child appears to be at risk of harm due to circumstances other than direct parental or caregiver maltreatment, are there other agencies that can intervene quickly enough to guard the safety of the child? For example, in cases of partner abuse with the child in the home, the police are often the most appropriate first responders. CPS also may need to be involved if it is determined that there is potential for harm to the child.

- Problems that may be more appropriately served by other agencies include parental substance abuse, parental or child physical or mental illness, developmental disability, lack of resources to meet basic needs, lack of information about appropriate parenting, lack of sufficient support systems during a crisis, lack of daycare, the child's constant truancy, or severe learning problems that do not endanger the child.

- The circumstances that could result in imminent danger to the child should be determined, as well as whether a referral to an appropriate agency will ensure service delivery; whether the connection between appropriate services and the family is so tenuous that the child may not receive the needed intervention, thereby requiring protective intervention; or whether an initial report focused on the need for other services is masking other, more serious, dangers to the child.

This decision is based on having accurate and comprehensive information as well as the ability of the worker to assess and use the information to develop a clear picture of the situation and to apply the law and policy to the case. Agency screening tools can be helpful in making this decision.[35]

Immediate risk

Determining the urgency of the response to the report is essential to the safety assessment. CPS's primary concern should be to establish whether the child is safe, pending a face-to-face contact by the agency or another professional trained in assessing safety.[36] Many States have their own criteria for response times based on the nature of the report. The criteria considered are the level of severity of the incident or the harm to the child, the person responsible for the alleged abuse or neglect, and the family's situation.[37]

Response Time

Once it has been determined that an initial assessment or investigation is warranted, the next step is to determine the safety of the child and how quickly CPS must respond to the case. Many States have their own criteria for response times based on the nature of the maltreatment and the family situation.

The following factors generally are used by CPS agencies to distinguish between reports that require an immediate response, reports requiring a response within 24 hours, and reports that require a CPS response but do not involve immediate or continuing danger of serious harm to the child. CPS should respond immediately when:

- The child's injury is severe or the alleged maltreatment could have resulted in serious harm—for example, shooting a gun, pushing a child down the stairs, locking a child in a small enclosed space, not providing enough food to eat over an extended period of time, or locking a toddler out of the house without supervision.

- The child is particularly vulnerable because of age, illness, disability, or proximity to the alleged perpetrator, or the child is a danger to himself or herself, or others.
- The behavior of the parent or caregiver, including an inability to take care of the child, is known to have caused harm or endangered the child or others. Or the behavior of the parent or caregiver is unpredictable and could result in serious harm to the child.
- There is no person who is able and willing to act on the child's behalf in the time that is required to keep the child safe long enough for CPS to intervene within normal time frames.
- The family is likely to flee the area with the child or abandon the child.
- The report involves child sexual abuse, and the child continues to have contact with the alleged perpetrator.
- The child has current physical injuries that need to be documented, such as photographing injuries or measuring bruises.[38]

CASE EXAMPLES

A Case Requiring an Immediate CPS Response

A single mother who has been diagnosed as having paranoid schizophrenia is having delusions of killing her 6-month-old infant. The mother stopped taking her medication (often required when pregnant) and has been drinking heavily. The community psychiatric nurse who has been visiting the home weekly was told by the mother never to come back.

A Case Requiring a CPS Response within 24 Hours

A daycare provider reports a 3 1/2-year-old child because he has bruises and welts on his buttocks. The child provides three different stories of how they occurred, none of which seem plausible. There are no previous reports of maltreatment and the daycare provider who has been caring for this child for 18 months has never seen bruises before. The daycare provider reports that the mother drops off and picks up the son. The child is very active, difficult to manage, and has attempted to hurt other children.

A Case Not Requiring a CPS Reponse within 24 Hours

During the first 3 months of school, the children of a single mother were absent over one-half of the days. When the 7-year-old girl and 10-year-old boy do come to school, they have severe body odor and dirty clothes. The school nurse treated the children for lice and scabies, and the 7-year-old falls asleep in class. The school has contacted the mother, who has not followed through with any of her commitments regarding the children.

Case Examples

The caseworker must examine the total picture to evaluate if there is a clear opportunity for the child to be seriously harmed if there is no immediate intervention. To determine how quickly the agency must respond to a particular case, caseworkers must consider the factors that individually present a risk to the child, as well as any factors (such as domestic violence or substance abuse) that in combination present an even greater risk to the child. The presence of several factors and one or more combinations of factors requires an immediate response by CPS.

Importance of Community Education in Reporting

CPS is dependent on the general public and community professionals to report suspected child abuse and neglect. CPS is responsible for educating the community on how to identify suspected child maltreatment and what types of referrals are appropriate. Intake provides an important opportunity to educate the public regarding the types of cases that should be reported to CPS, the type of information needed in a report, and CPS's initial assessment or investigation and intervention efforts. In addition, it is essential to treat reporters professionally and with respect and sensitivity. Communication and interaction at the intake stage affect how the community views CPS and influence the community's willingness to report cases in the future.

COMMUNITY PARTNERS IN CHILD PROTECTION

Because child abuse and neglect is complex and multidimensional, CPS alone cannot effectively intervene in the lives of maltreated children and their families. A coordinated effort that involves a broad range of community agencies and professionals is essential for effective child protection. (These roles and responsibilities are outlined in more detail in the user manual, *A Coordinated Response to Child Abuse and Neglect: The Foundation for Practice*.) CPS must take a lead role in developing and maintaining collaborative relationships with potential referral sources, law enforcement officials, and other professionals who investigate the presence of maltreatment, and with professionals and agencies that provide medical and mental health evaluation and treatment.

Over the past 10 years, promising, community-based child protection initiatives have been implemented that broadened the base of responsibility for supporting families and protecting children. Initially, model programs evolved from targeting intervention activities in high-risk neighborhoods and rebuilding a sense of community toward empowering individual families by teaching and mentoring, building on strengths, and respecting cultural diversity.[39] More recent child welfare reforms have focused on a more flexible and differential response for investigating reports of child abuse and neglect, including the diversion of low- and moderate-risk families to community-based services.[40]

For more information on developing partnerships, check other manuals in the series by visiting www.calib.com/nccanch/pubs/usermanual.cfm.

---

6. Initial Assessment or Investigation

Caseworkers feel pressure from many different directions—children, families, statutory and agency expectations, and themselves. Family members who are reported to child protective services (CPS) typically feel embarrassed, defensive, angry, confused, threatened, and helpless. As families experience these feelings, they need the CPS caseworker to provide them with information to understand what they are accused of, what may happen, what the next steps are, what they can expect from the agency, and what they are expected to do. The agency expects the caseworker to meet the statutory deadlines by quickly gathering information about the children and family and determining if maltreatment occurred, the likelihood that it will occur again, and the threat of immediate serious harm to the child. At the same time caseworkers should manage their own fears and doubts—Is the child really safe? What else could I have done?[41]

This chapter describes the purposes of the initial assessment or investigation—to gather and analyze information in response to CPS reports, to interpret the agency's role to the children and families, and to determine which families will benefit from further agency intervention. After interviewing all parties and gathering all relevant information, CPS caseworkers must determine whether maltreatment has occurred and can be substantiated. In most States, CPS staff are mandated by law to determine whether the report is substantiated or founded (meaning that credible evidence indicates that abuse or neglect has occurred) or whether the report is unsubstantiated or unfounded (meaning that there is a lack of credible evidence to substantiate child maltreatment—but does not mean it did not necessarily occur). Depending on State law, CPS agencies usually have up to 30, 60, or 90 days after receiving the report to complete the initial assessment or investigation. A major part of the initial assessment or investigation includes determining whether there is a risk or likelihood of maltreatment occurring in the future and whether the child is safe (not at risk of imminent, serious harm). In addition, CPS caseworkers must decide whether ongoing services to reduce risk and assure child safety should be provided by the CPS agency or other community partners. This chapter addresses the following:

- Effective initial assessment or investigation characteristics
- Initial assessment or investigation decisions
- Initial assessment or investigation processes
- Interviewing techniques
- Community involvement
- Special practice issues

Effective Initial Assessment or Investigation Characteristics

In cooperative investigations, CPS workers form an alliance with both the children and family. In a well-handled investigation, the worker:

- Involves the children and family during the exploration of the allegations to gain their perceptions of the allegations;

- Focuses on the children's, the parent's, and the family's strengths and resources; their plans for building protective factors; and past and present actions to protect the children;
- Listens carefully to the family's experience to make sure they know they have been heard and understood;
- Demonstrates sensitivity and empathy regarding the anxiety experienced by the children and family;
- Communicates clearly and openly CPS's statutory role;
- Focuses on small steps, making sure the children and family understand each one;
- Involves the children and family in the decisions that affect them by providing choices and opportunities for input;
- Demonstrates flexibility in the interview;
- Focuses on gathering comprehensive information rather than trying to identify solutions, which is best left for later in the casework process.[42]

Initial Assessment or Investigation Decisions

To make effective decisions during the initial assessment or investigation process, the CPS caseworker must have competent interviewing skills; be able to gather, organize, and analyze information; and arrive at accurate conclusions. Critical decisions that must be made at this stage of the CPS process include the following:

- Is child maltreatment substantiated as defined by State statute or agency policy?
- Is the child at risk of maltreatment, and what is the level of risk?
- Is the child safe and, if not, what type of agency or community response will ensure the child's safety in the least intrusive manner?
- If the child's safety cannot be assured within the family, what type and level of care does the child need?
- Does the family have emergency needs that must be met?
- Should ongoing agency services be offered to the family?

Decision Point One: Substantiating Maltreatment

The substantiation decision depends on the answers to two questions: "Is the harm to the child severe enough to constitute child maltreatment?" and "Is there sufficient evidence to support this being a case of child maltreatment?"[43] Even in those cases lacking evidence, CPS caseworkers should still document information since unsubstantiated reports may eventually show a pattern that can be substantiated. Due to varying State regulations regarding the expungement of records, this may not be possible for all agencies.

Upon completion of the initial assessment, the caseworker must determine the disposition of the report based on State laws, agency guidelines, and the information gathered. CPS agencies use different terms for this decision—substantiated, confirmed, unsubstantiated, founded, or unfounded. To guide caseworker judgment in making the substantiation decision, each State has developed policies that outline what constitutes credible evidence that abuse or neglect has occurred. Most States have a two-tiered system: substantiated-unsubstantiated or founded- unfounded. Some States have a three-tiered system of substantiated, indicated, or unsubstantiated. The indicated classification means the caseworker has some evidence that maltreatment occurred, but not enough to substantiate the case.

At this point in the decision-making process, caseworkers should ask themselves:

- Have I obtained enough information from the children, family, and collateral contacts to adequately reach a determination about the alleged abuse or neglect?
- Is my decision on substantiation based upon a clear understanding of State laws and agency policies?
- Have I assessed the need for other agency or community services when CPS intervention is not warranted?[44]

The following sections discuss substantiation decisions for different types of maltreatment— child neglect, physical abuse, sexual abuse, and psychological maltreatment.

Determining Child Neglect

Determining child neglect is based on the answers to two questions: "Do the conditions or circumstances indicate that a child's basic needs are unmet?" and "What harm or threat of harm may have resulted?"[45] Answering these questions requires sufficient information to assess the degree to which omissions in care have resulted in significant harm or significant risk of harm. Unlike the other forms of maltreatment, this determination may not be reached by looking at one incident; the decision often requires looking at patterns of care over time. The analysis should focus on examining how the child's basic needs are met and identifying situations that may indicate specific omissions in care that have resulted in harm or the risk of harm to the child.[46]

Affirmative answers to the following questions may indicate that a child's physical and medical needs are unmet:

- Have the parents or caregivers failed to provide the child with needed care for a physical injury, acute illness, physical disability, or chronic condition?
- Have the parents or caregivers failed to provide the child with regular and ample meals that meet basic nutritional requirements, or have the parents or caregivers failed to provide the necessary rehabilitative diet to the child with particular health problems?
- Have the parents or caregivers failed to attend to the cleanliness of the child's hair, skin, teeth, and clothes? It is difficult to determine the difference between marginal hygiene and neglect. Caseworkers should consider the chronicity, extent, and nature of the condition, as well as the impact on the child.
- Does the child have inappropriate clothing for the weather and conditions? Caseworkers must consider the nature and extent of the conditions and the potential consequences to the child.
- Does the home have obvious hazardous physical conditions? For example, homes with exposed wiring or easily accessible toxic substances.
- Does the home have obvious hazardous unsanitary conditions? For example, homes with feces- or trash-covered flooring or furniture.

- Does the child experience unstable living conditions? For example, frequent changes of residence or evictions due to the caretaker's mental illness, substance abuse, or extreme poverty?
- Do the parents or caregivers fail to arrange for a safe substitute caregiver for the child?
- Have the parents or caregivers abandoned the child without arranging for reasonable care and supervision? For example, have caregivers left children without information regarding their whereabouts?[47]

While State statutes vary, most CPS professionals agree that children under the age of 8 who are left alone are being neglected. It is also agreed that children older than 12 are able to spend 1 to 2 hours alone each day. In determining whether neglect has occurred, the following issues should be considered, particularly when children are between the ages of 8 and 12:

- The child's physical condition and mental abilities, coping capacity, maturity, competence, knowledge regarding how to respond to an emergency, and feelings about being alone.
- Type and degree of indirect adult supervision. For example, is there an adult who is checking in on the child?
- The length of time and frequency with which the child is left alone. Is the child being left alone all day, every day? Is he or she left alone all night?
- The safety of the child's environment. For example, the safety of the neighborhood, access to a telephone, and safety of the home.

Determining Physical Abuse

In determining whether physical abuse occurred, the key questions to answer are "Could the injury to the child have occurred in a nonabusive manner?" and "Does the explanation given plausibly explain the physical findings?"[48] The caseworker must gather information separately from the child, the parents, and other possible witnesses regarding the injuries. The following questions may help determine if abuse occurred:

- **Does the explanation fit the injury?** For example, the explanation of a baby falling out of a crib is not consistent with the child having a spiral fracture. It is important to know the child's age and developmental capabilities to assess the plausibility of some explanations. It is also crucial to receive input from medical personnel and exams.

- **Is an explanation offered?** Some caregivers may not offer an explanation, possibly due to denial or an attempt to hide abuse.

- **Is there a delay in obtaining medical care?** Abusive caregivers may not immediately seek medical care for the child when it is clearly needed, possibly to deny the seriousness of the child's condition, to try to cover up the abuse, or in hope that the injury will heal on its own.

Caseworkers must also examine the nature of the injury, such as bruises or burns in the shape of an implement, e.g., a welt in the shape of a belt buckle or a cigarette burn.

Determining Sexual Abuse

In addition to the factors mentioned in determining physical abuse, the caseworker should ask the following questions to determine whether sexual abuse has occurred:

- Who has reported that the child alleges sexual abuse? For example, caseworkers should be alert to separated or divorced parents making allegations against each other.
- What are the qualifications of the professional reporting the physical findings? For example, if the health care providers do not routinely examine the genitalia of young children, they may mistake normal conditions for abuse or vice versa.
- What did the child say? Did the child describe the sexual abuse in terms that are consistent with their developmental level? Can the child give details regarding the time and place of the incident?
- When did the child make a statement or begin demonstrating behaviors suspicious of sexual abuse and symptoms causing concern? Was the child's statement spontaneous? Has the child been exposed to adult sexual acts?
- Where does the child say the abuse took place? Is it possible for it to have occurred in that setting? Is it possible that the child is describing genital touching that is not sexual in nature? For example, bathing the child.[49]

Determining Psychological Maltreatment

Psychological maltreatment has been given relatively little serious attention in research and practice until recently. There are many reasons for this, including problems with inadequate definitions, failure to establish cause-and-effect relationships, and the difficulty of clarifying the cumulative impact of psychological maltreatment.[50] In order to determine if psychological maltreatment or emotional abuse occurred, caseworkers must have information on the caregiver's behavior over time and the child's behavior and condition. Caseworkers must determine whether there is a chronic behavioral pattern of psychological maltreatment, such as caregivers who place expectations on the child that are unrealistic for the child's developmental level, threaten to abandon the child, or direct continually critical and derogatory comments toward the child. There also must be indicators in the child's behavior suggestive of psychological maltreatment; however, the child's behavior alone is often insufficient to substantiate a case. Caseworkers must determine whether the child has suffered emotional abuse. The following questions may help determine if psychological maltreatment has occurred:

- Is there an inability to learn not explained by intellectual, sensory, or health factors?
- Is there an inability to build or maintain satisfactory interpersonal relationships with peers or adults?
- Are there developmentally inappropriate behaviors or feelings in normal circumstances?
- Is there a general pervasive mode of unhappiness, depression, or suicidal feelings?

- Are there physical symptoms or fears associated with personal or school functioning, such as bedwetting or a marked lack of interest in school activities?[51]

Demonstrating a causal connection between the caregiver's behavior and the child's behavior is often difficult to substantiate. This minimally necessitates that the caseworker observe caregiver- child interaction on several occasions, as well as be informed from other sources' observations (e.g., school personnel, relatives, and neighbors).

Decision Point Two: Assessing Risk

Risk factors are influences present in the child, the parents, the family, and the environment that may increase the likelihood that a child will be maltreated. Risk assessment involves evaluating the child and family's situation to identify and weigh the risk factors, family strengths and resources, and agency and community services.[52] While risk assessment has been an integral part of CPS since the field's inception, the formalization of the process and decision-making, through the development of risk assessment instruments, has taken place just within the last 12 to 15 years.[53]

This section describes risk assessment models and its key elements, the analysis of risk assessment information, special cases of risk assessment (when substance abuse or domestic violence coexist with maltreatment), and cultural factors for consideration.

Risk Assessment Models

The majority of States use risk assessment models or systems that are designed to:

- Guide and structure decision-making;
- Predict future harm and classify cases;
- Aid in resource management by identifying service needs for children and families served;
- Facilitate communication within the agency and with other community stakeholders.[54]

Exhibit 6-1 presents additional detail of the types of risk assessment information in each area.

Analysis of Risk Assessment Information

Caseworkers analyze the information collected to determine what information is significant as it relates to the risk of maltreatment. The following are suggested steps for assessing risk:

- Organize the information by defined category (e.g., education level, stressors);
- Determine if there is sufficient and believable information to confirm the risk factors, strengths and resources, and their interaction;
- Use the risk model to assign significance to each of the risk factors and strengths.[56]

The caseworker groups this information into an overall picture of the family and its dynamics and analyzes it to assess the current level of risk of maltreatment. This dictates the next steps in service provision and interaction with the family.

Exhibit 6-1. Risk Assessment Information

Maltreatment
- Caregiver actions and behaviors responsible for the maltreatment
- Duration and frequency of the maltreatment
- Physical and emotional manifestations in the child
- Caregiver's attitude toward the child's condition and the assessment process
- Caregiver's explanation of the events and effects of the maltreatment

Child
- Age
- Developmental level
- Physical and psychological health
- Temperament
- Behavior
- Current functioning
- Child's explanation of events and effects, if possible and appropriate

Caregiver(s)
- Physical and mental health
- History
- Current functioning
- Coping and problem-solving capacity
- Relationships outside of the home
- Financial situation

Family Functioning
- Power and issues of control within the family
- Interactions and communications among family members
- Interactions and connections with others outside the family
- Quality of relationships
- Problem-solving ability[55]

Risk Assessment in cases of substance-abusing families

Risk assessment in these cases also examines the extent of substance use, its impact on lifestyle, and its impact on parenting. The following scales are often used to assess risk in families where there is substance abuse:

- **Parent's commitment to recovery.** This scale assesses a parent's stage of recovery, willingness to change behavior, and desire to live a life free from alcohol and other drugs.
- **Patterns of substance use.** This scale assesses the parent's pattern of alcohol and other drug use—ranging from active use without regard to consequences to significant periods of abstinence.

- **Effects of substance use on child caring.** This scale assesses the parent's ability to care for his or her children and meet their emotional and physical needs.
- **Effects of substance use on lifestyle.** This scale assesses a parent's ability to carry out his or her everyday responsibilities and any consequences that may have for the family.
- **Support for recovery.** This scale assesses parent's social network and how that network may support or interfere with recovery.[57]

The Child Welfare League of America (CWLA) suggests some questions caseworkers can ask regarding alcohol and other drug abuse to facilitate risk assessment in these cases:

- Do you use any drugs other than those prescribed by a physician?
- Have you ever felt you should cut down on your drinking or drug use?
- Has a physician ever told you to cut down or quit the use of alcohol or drugs?
- Have people annoyed you by criticizing or complaining about your drinking or drug use?
- Have you ever felt bad or guilty about your drinking or drug use?
- Have you ever had a drink or drug in the morning ("eye opener") to steady your nerves or to get rid of a hangover?
- Has your drinking or drug use caused a family, job, or legal problem?
- When drinking or using drugs, have you had a memory loss or blackout?[58]

Risk Assessment in cases in which partner abuse and child maltreatment coexist
The following factors should be considered to assess risk in cases where partner abuse and child abuse and neglect coexist:

- An abuser's access to the child or adult victim
- The abuser's pattern of abuse
  - Frequency or severity of the abuse in current and past relationships
  - Use and presence of weapons
  - Threats to kill the victim or other family members
  - Stalking or abduction
  - Past criminal record
  - Abuse of pets
  - Child's exposure to violence
- The abuser's state of mind
  - Obsession with the victim
  - Jealousy
  - Ignoring the negative consequences of the violence
  - Depression or desperation
- Individual factors that reduce the behavioral controls of either the victim or abuser
  - Abuses alcohol or other substances
  - Uses certain medications
  - Suffers from psychosis or other major mental illnesses
  - Suffers from brain damage

- A victim, child, or abuser thinking about or planning suicide
- An adult victim's use of physical force or emotional abuse
- A child's use of violence
- Situational factors
  - Presence of other major stresses, such as poverty, loss of a job, or chronic illness
  - Increased threat of violence when victim leaves or attempts to leave abuser
  - Increased risk when abuser has ongoing or easy access to victims
  - Physical inability of nonabusing parent to protect child due to assault
  - Nonabusing parent's fear of leaving or inability to leave due to economic status or lack of place to go
- Past failures of response systems (e.g., courts, law enforcement) to react appropriately.[59]

The following are areas to assess with a child regarding partner abuse and child maltreatment:

- **Pattern of the abusive conduct.** What happens when your parents (the adults) fight? Does anyone hit, shove, or push? Are serious threats made? Does anyone throw things or damage property? Has anyone used a gun or knife? When was the last big fight between your parents?

- **Impact of domestic violence on the adult victim.** Has anyone been hurt or injured? Is your mom or dad afraid? How do your parents act after a bad fight? Have you ever seen the police or anyone come over because of their fights? Have you seen injuries or damaged property?

- **Impact of domestic violence on the child.** Have you ever been hurt by any of their fights? What do your brothers or sisters do during fights? Are you ever afraid when your parents fight? How do you feel during a fight? After the fight? Do you worry about the violence? Do you talk to anyone about the fights? Do you feel safe at home? Have you ever felt like hurting yourself or someone else?

- **Child's protection.** Where do you go during their fights? Have you tried to stop a fight? Have you ever had to take sides? In an emergency for your parent or yourself, what would you do? Who would you call? Have you ever called for help? What happened?

- **Child's knowledge of danger.** Has anyone needed to go to a doctor after a fight? Do the adults use guns or knives? Do you know where the gun is? Has anyone threatened to hurt someone? What did the person say?[60]

Cultural Factors in Risk Assessment
Caseworkers should integrate cultural sensitivity into the risk assessment process by:
- Considering the family's cultural identification and perception of the dominant culture;

- Inquiring about the family's experience with mainstream institutions, including CPS and other service providers in the community;
- Assuring clarity regarding language and meanings in verbal and nonverbal communication;
- Understanding the family's cultural values, principles of child development, child caring norms, and parenting strategies;
- Gaining clarity regarding the family's perceptions of the responsibilities of adults and children in the extended family and community network;
- Determining the family's perceptions of the impact of child abuse or neglect;
- Assessing each risk factor with consideration to characteristics of the cultural or ethnic group;
- Considering the child and family's perceptions of their response to acute and chronic stressors;
- Explaining why a culturally accepted behavior in the family's homeland may be illegal here.[61]

Decision Point Three: Determining Child Safety

A child is considered unsafe when he or she is at imminent risk of serious harm. Safety is an issue throughout the life of a case. The Adoption and Safe Families Act (ASFA) requires that States assess and assure a safe environment for children in birth families, out-of-home placements, and adoptive homes. It is important to remember that determining the risk of maltreatment and the child's safety are two separate decisions. Children may be at risk of harm some time in the future (risk assessment) and they may currently be safe (no threat of imminent serious harm). The following sections describe the key safety decision points, the steps for arriving at the safety decision, and the development of a safety plan.

Safety Decision Points

There are two key decision points during the initial assessment or investigation in which the child's safety is evaluated. During the first contact with the child and family, the caseworker must decide whether the child will be safe during the initial assessment or investigation. The question caseworkers must ask themselves is, "Is the child in danger right now?" Caseworkers assess current danger by searching for factors in the family situation and caregiver behavior or condition, including emotions, physical circumstances, and social contexts. Examples include: young children with serious injuries that are inconsistent with the caregiver's explanation; children in the care of people who are out of control or violent; and premeditated maltreatment or cruelty.

The second critical time for evaluating safety is at the conclusion of the initial assessment. This safety assessment follows the determination of the validity of the report and the level of risk. Caseworkers must determine:

- Whether the child will be safe in his or her home with or without continuing CPS services;
- Under what circumstances a case can be diverted to community partners;
- Under what circumstances intensive, home-based services are necessary to protect a child;

- Whether the child needs to be placed in out-ofhome care.

To determine safety at this point, the caseworker uses the findings of the risk assessment. The caseworker identifies the risk factors that directly affect the safety to the child; the risk factors that are operating at a more intense, explosive, immediate, or dangerous level; or those risk factors that in combination present a more dangerous mix. The caseworker weighs the risk factors directly affecting the child's safety against the family protective factors (i.e., strengths, resiliencies, resources) to determine if the child is safe.[62]

Steps for arriving at the safety decision
The sequential steps for arriving at the safety decision include:

1. Identifying the behaviors and conditions that increase concern for the child's safety, and considering how they affect each child in the family.
2. Identifying the behaviors or conditions (i.e., strengths, resiliencies, resources) that may protect the child.
3. Examining the relationship among the risk factors. When combined, do they increase concern for safety?
4. Determining whether family members or other community partners are able to address safety concerns without CPS intervention.
5. Considering what in-home services are needed to address the specific behaviors or conditions for each risk factor directly affecting the child's safety.
6. Identifying who is available (CPS or other community partners) to provide the needed service or intervention in the frequency, timeframe, and duration the family needs to protect the child.[63]
7. Evaluating the family's willingness to accept and ability to use the intervention or service at the level needed to protect the child.

If the services or interventions are not available or accessible at the level necessary to protect the child, or if the caregivers are unable or unwilling to accept the services, the caseworker should consider whether the abusive caregiver can leave home and the nonoffending caregiver can protect the child. If not, the caseworker should consider whether out-ofhome care and court intervention is needed to assure the child's protection.

Development of a safety plan
The safety plan and the case plan have two different purposes. The interventions in the safety plan are designed to control the risk factors posing a safety threat to the child. Interventions in the case plan, however, are designed to facilitate change in the underlying conditions or contributing factors resulting in maltreatment. To control the risk factors directly affecting child safety, the safety interventions must:
- Have a direct and immediate impact on one or more of the risk factors;
- Be accessible and available in time and place;
- Be in place for the duration of the threat of harm;
- Fill the gaps in caregiver protective factors.

In identifying safety interventions and developing a safety plan, CPS caseworkers are required to make reasonable efforts to preserve or reunify families. Child safety is the most important consideration in these efforts. ASFA also states that when certain factors are present (e.g., abandonment, torture, chronic abuse, some forms of sexual abuse, killing of another person or the child's sibling, or termination of parental rights for another child), they constitute enough threat to a child's safety that reasonable efforts are not required to prevent placement or to reunify the family. The sequence of least intrusive to most intrusive safety interventions include:

- In-home services, perhaps combined with partial out-of-home services (e.g., daycare services);
- Removal of abusive caregiver;
- Relative or kinship care;
- Out-of-home-placement.

When possible, the safety assessment should be conducted jointly with the family; it may not, however, be safe to include the perpetrator. The safety plan also should be negotiated with the family. This accomplishes the following:

- Caseworker and caregiver can assess the feasibility of the caregiver following the safety plan.
- Caseworker can be assured that the caregiver understands the consequences of his or her choices.
- Caregiver is provided with a sense of control over what happens.
- Caregiver is able to salvage a sense of dignity.[64]

Decision Point Four: Determining Emergency Needs

Child maltreatment is often not an isolated problem; many families referred to CPS experience multiple and complex problems, often at crisis levels. Due to any number of these problems that may be identified during the initial assessment or investigation, the CPS caseworker is often in the position of determining whether a family has emergency needs and of arranging for emergency services for the child and family. Examples of emergency services can include:

- Medical attention
- Food, clothing, and shelter
- Mental health care
- Crisis counseling

Decision Point Five: Offering Services

The decision that a caseworker makes at the end of the initial assessment or investigation is whether a family should be offered ongoing child protective services or other agency services. Who is offered services and on what basis that decision is made depend on the guidelines and availability of services that vary from State to State and sometimes county to county. In some cases, the decision is made based on whether a report is substantiated. In other instances, the decision to offer services is based on the level of perceived risk of maltreatment in the future since substantiation alone is not the best predictor of future maltreatment.

NONINVESTIGATIVE OR ALTERNATIVE RESPONSES

Traditionally, CPS agencies are required to respond to all reports of child maltreatment with a standard investigation that is narrowly focused on determining whether a specific incident of abuse actually occurred.[65] States are attempting to enhance CPS practice and build community partnerships in responding to cases of child maltreatment. One changing area of CPS practice is greater flexibility in responding to allegations of abuse and neglect. A "dual track" or "multi-track" response permits CPS agencies to respond differentially to children's needs for safety, the degree of risk present, and the family's need for support or services. Typically, in cases where abuse and neglect are serious or serious criminal offenses against children have occurred, an investigation will commence. An investigation focuses on evidence gathering and will include a referral to law enforcement. In less serious cases of child maltreatment where the family may benefit from services, an assessment will be conducted. In these cases, the facts regarding what happened will be obtained, but the intervention will emphasize a comprehensive assessment of family strengths and needs. The assessment is designed to be a process where parents or caregivers are partners with the CPS agency, and that partnership begins with the very first contact. States that have implemented the "dual track" approach have shown that a majority of cases now coming to CPS can be safely handled through an approach that emphasizes service delivery and voluntary family participation in addition to the fact finding of usual CPS investigations.[66] CPS can switch a family to the investigative track at any point if new evidence is uncovered to indicate that the case is appropriate for investigation rather than assessment.[67]

Initial Assessment or Investigation Process

To make accurate decisions during the initial assessment or investigation, caseworkers must:

- Employ a protocol for interviewing the identified child, the siblings, all of the adults in the home, and the alleged maltreating parent or caregiver;
- Observe the child, the siblings, and the parent or caregiver's interaction among family members, as well as the home, the neighborhood, and the general climate of the environment;
- Gather information from any other sources who may have information about the alleged maltreatment or the risk to and safety of the children;
- Analyze the information gathered in order to make necessary decisions.

Using Interview Protocols

The initial assessment or investigation of alleged maltreatment of children requires that CPS respond in an orderly, structured manner to gather sufficient information to determine if maltreatment took place and to assess the risk to and safety of the child. Employing a structured interview protocol ensures that all family members are involved and that information-gathering is thorough; increases staff control over the process; improves the capacity of CPS staff to collaborate with other disciplines; and increases staff confidence in the initial assessment or investigation conclusions. If at all possible, family members should be interviewed separately in the following order:

- Identified child
- Any siblings or other children in the home
- Alleged perpetrator
- All other adults in the home separately
- Family as a whole

Depending on the circumstances of the report, it must be determined whether it is in the child's best interest for the CPS worker to initiate an unannounced visit to interview the parent or to contact the parent to schedule an interview.[68] If the child is out of the home at the time (e.g., the child is at school), the process should begin with an introduction to the parent(s) to explain the purposes of the initial assessment or investigation and, if required by law, request permission to interview all family members individually, beginning with the identified child. It is important to remember that the safety of the child is of paramount importance in every case. If there is concern that talking with the parents first or obtaining their permission to interview the child places the child at risk of imminent harm, then the CPS caseworker should proceed in a manner that assures the child's safety. All family members should be interviewed alone to establish rapport and a climate of trust and openness with the caseworker, which is designed to increase the accuracy of the information gathered. A benefit noted across professional boundaries regarding the use of individual interviewing protocols is that it enables the caseworker to utilize information gathered from one interview to assist in the next interview.

Planning the Interview Process

Based on the information gathered at intake, each initial assessment or investigation should be planned with consideration given to:

- Where the interviews will take place;
- When the interviews will be conducted;
- How many interviews will likely be needed;
- How long each interview will likely last;
- Whether other agencies should be notified to participate in the interviews.

During the initial assessment or investigation process, caseworkers should conduct interviews with the following individuals:

- **Identified child victim.** The purpose of the initial interview with the identified child is to gather information regarding the alleged maltreatment and any risk of future maltreatment, and to assess the child's immediate safety. Because CPS's purpose is beyond just finding out what happened with respect to any allegations of maltreatment, the interview with the child addresses the strengths, risks, and needs regarding the child, his or her parents, and his or her family.

- **Siblings.** Following the interview with the identified child, the next step in the protocol is to interview siblings. The purpose of these interviews is to determine if siblings have experienced maltreatment, to assess the siblings' level of vulnerability, to gather corroborating information about the nature and extent of any maltreatment of the identified child, and to gather further information about the family that may assist in assessing risk to the identified child and any siblings.

- **All of the nonoffending adults in the home.** The primary purpose of these interviews is to find out what adults know about the alleged maltreatment, to gather information related to the risk of maltreatment and the safety of the child, to gather information regarding family strengths or protective factors, and to determine the adults' capacity to protect the child, if indicated.

- **Alleged maltreating parent or caregiver.** The purpose of this interview is to evaluate the alleged maltreating caregiver's reaction to allegations of maltreatment as well as to the child and his or her condition, and to gather further information about

Examples of the types of information that a caseworker should gather from each of these sources are presented in Exhibit 6-2.

Obtaining Information from Other Sources

Other sources may have information that will help in understanding the nature and extent of the alleged maltreatment and in assessing the risk to and safety of the child. According to CWLA's *Standards for Service for Abused or Neglected Children and Their Families*, other potential sources include, but are not limited to, professionals such as teachers, law enforcement officers, and physicians. Other community agencies, institutions, caretakers, or individuals known to the child and the family, such as relatives and neighbors, also may be consulted.[69] It also may be advisable to run a criminal background check on all adults in the

Exhibit 6-2. Examples of Information to Obtain during Initial Interviews

Topic Area	Interview with the Identified Child	Interview with the Siblings	Interview with All Non-offending Adults in the Home	Interview with Alleged Maltreating Parent or Caretaker
The Alleged Maltreatment	• Description of what happened with respect to the alleged altreatment, when and where it occurred, and who was present • Child's current condition • Type, severity, and chronicity of the maltreatment • Effects of maltreatment (e.g, extreme withdrawal, fear of parents) • Identity of others who have information about the child's condition and the family situation	• Information about alleged maltreatment • Maltreatment they have experienced and, if so, how, when, where, how often, and for how long	• What the adults know about the alleged maltreatment • • Feelings regarding the maltreatment and about CPS • Acceptance or rejection of the child's version of what might have happened and who the adult deems responsible • Capacity to protect the child (if indicated) and his or her opinion about the vulnerability of the child	• Description of what happened in relation to alleged maltreatment • Response to the incident(s) and to CPS • Access to the child
The Child	• Child's characteristics (e.g., age, developmental level, physical or mental handicaps, health, mental health status) • Child's behavior and feelings • Child's relationship with peers, family, and others • Child's daily routine (e.g., school, home life)	• Information that could not be obtained from the identified child or confirmation of information gathered during the initial interview	• Feelings, expectations, and perspective about the identified child and siblings • Empathy for the child's condition and experience • Description of the child's feelings and behaviors	• View of the child and the child's characteristics and condition • Relationship with the child and others in the family
The Family	• Asking who resides in the home • Child's relationship with and feelings toward the	• Siblings' characteristics, behaviors, and feelings • Further information about the parents (e.g., feelings	• Relationship to the child and to the alleged maltreating caretaker • Approach to and view of parenting	• Approach to parenting, expectations, and sensitivity to children • Roles and functioning in the family

Topic Area	Interview with the Identified Child	Interview with the Siblings	Interview with All Non-offending Adults in the Home	Interview with Alleged Maltreating Parent or Caretaker
	• parents or caregivers and siblings • Child's perception of the relationships among others in the household • Child's perception of how family problems are addressed and how the family communicates • Description of who's involved in child care responsibilities (e.g., extended family, informal kin) • Child's perception of the family's identification with a tribe, race, or larger cultural group • Child's perception of the family's rituals, traditions, and behaviors • Child's description and perception of what happens when parents or caregivers fight	and behaviors frequently exhibited, problems, child rearing easures, and parents' relation-ships outside the home) • Further information about the family's functioning, dynamics, demographics, and characteristics	• How decisions are made in the family, and who usually makes decisions about the children • Types of discipline they considered appropriate • Who is involved in child care responsibilities in the family • How cultural beliefs are incorporated in family functioning • Role religion plays in the family, and how it affects child-rearing practices • Family's rituals, traditions, and behaviors • Roles in the family and family functioning • Communication and expressions of affection • Demographics about the family, including financial status and other factors that may be stress producing • Presence of domestic violence or partner abuse	• Methods of communication and level of affection • Who usually makes decisions about the children in the family • Discipline the family considers to be appropriate • Responsibility for child care • Cultural beliefs incorporated in family functioning • Role religion plays in the family and how it affects child rearing • Family's rituals, traditions, and behaviors • Description of demographics about the family, including financial status and other factors that may be stress producing • Presence of domestic violence or partner abuse
The Environment	• Child's description of where they go during parent or caregiver fights, whether they have tried to stop a fight, and who they would call for help	• Child's description of where they go during parent or caregiver fights, whether they have tried to stop a fight, and who they would call for help	• Description of the neighborhood, available resources, and the degree of crime or violence	• A description of the neighborhood, available resources, and the degree of crime or violence

(Continued)

Topic Area	Interview with the Identified Child	Interview with the Siblings	Interview with All Non-offending Adults in the Home	Interview with Alleged Maltreating Parent or Caretaker
	• Description of the neighborhood, available resources, and the degree of crime or violence	• Description of the neighborhood, available resources, and the degree of crime or violence		
The Adult or Caretaker			• Approach to solving problems, ability to deal with stress, use of drugs or alcohol • History as a child (positive and negative memories), educational and employment history, any criminal activity, or history of physical or mental health problems • Relationships with others, memberships in clubs, or other activities • View of support network in his or her life, relationships with extended family, and the climate of the neighborhood and community	• Present emotional state, particularly in terms of the possibility of further harm to the child • Approach to solving problems, dealing with stress, using drugs or alcohol, coping • View of self • History as a child and an adult, including any mental health or health problems, criminal history, etc. • Relationships outside the home, supports, memberships, and affiliations • Willingness to accept help (if needed)

Exhibit 6-3. Principles Underlying Motivational Interviewing

Principle	Description	Guiding Beliefs
Expressing Empathy	**Expressing empathy** involves communicating warmth and using reflective listening during every contact with the family members. The caseworker should use reflective listening to understand the family member's feelings and perspectives without judging, criticizing, or blaming. Acceptance is not the same thing as agreement or approval of the abusive or neglectful behavior. The crucial attitude is respectful listening to the family member with a desire to understand. Through the expression of respect and acceptance, caseworkers engage the client and embrace the child or adult's self-esteem.	• Acceptance facilitates change • Skillful, reflective listening is fundamental • Ambivalence is normal
Developing Discrepancy	**Developing discrepancy** is creating and amplifying in the family member's mind a discrepancy between present behavior and broader goals. This means helping the family member to see the discrepancy between where they are and where they want to be. This can be triggered by the family member's awareness of the costs of the present behavior. When a person sees that a behavior conflicts with important personal goals, change is likely to occur.	• Awareness of consequences • Disconnect between present behavior and important goals will motivate change
Avoiding Arguments	**Avoiding argumentation** is important in lessening resistance. What caseworkers want to do is increase the family member's awareness of problems and the need to do something about them. When caseworkers encounter resistance, they may need to stop their current approach because they are likely to be "fighting against the resistance" and may therefore need to take another approach. Caseworkers also need to avoid labeling the children and family.	• Arguments are counterproductive • Defending breeds defensiveness • Resistance is a signal to change strategies • Labeling is unnecessary
Rolling with Resistance	**Rolling with resistance** requires the caseworker to acknowledge that reluctance and ambivalence are both natural and understandable. Caseworkers need to help the children and family consider new information and new perspectives. To do this, caseworkers turn a question or problem back to the children and family to help them discover their own solutions. This is based on the assumption that the person is capable of insight and that he or she can solve his or her own problems. This may not be possible, however, in all circumstances because of a variety of factors including cognitive impairment, mental illness, or substance abuse.	• Momentum can be used to good advantage • Perceptions can be shifted • New perspectives are invited, not imposed • The child and family are a valuable resource in finding solutions to problems
Supporting Self-Efficacy	**Supporting self-efficacy** means supporting the child or adult's belief in his or her ability to carry out and succeed with a specific task. The caseworker's task is to help increase the person's perceptions of his or her capability to cope with obstacles and succeed in changing their behavior.	• Hope and faith are important elements of change • Children and families can be helped to discover solutions • Personal responsibility is the cornerstone for change
Asking for the Client's Perspective	**Asking for the client's perspective** means letting the client know that the caseworker wants to understand their view of the problems, conditions, and behaviors. When the caseworker seeks to understand the client's view of their situation, the client becomes more invested in the process and will view the caseworker as desiring to help them change.	• Children and families become more invested when they feel heard[70]

home to ascertain prior abuse or other illegal activity. To protect the family's confidentiality, however, interviews or contacts with others should not be initiated without cause. The family also may disclose other persons who may have information about the alleged maltreatment or about the family in general. These contacts should be pursued within the constraints of the State law that mandates the scope of the initial assessment or investigation or, if indicated, clients may give permission for others to be contacted.

Following up with the children and family

Following the completion of the interviews, the caseworker should reconvene the child and family, as appropriate, to:

- Share with them a summary of the findings and impressions;
- Seek individual responses concerning perceptions and feelings;
- Indicate interest in the children and family;
- Provide information about next steps, including whether ongoing services will be offered and whether court intervention will occur;
- Demonstrate appreciation for their participation in the process.

Interviewing Techniques

Part of the caseworker's responsibility is to increase the likelihood that the family will engage with the agency and follow a recommended course of action. This section describes techniques for interviewing and observing children and families. Exhibit 6-3 delineates principles underlying motivational interviewing.

Interviewing young children

The primary goals of interviewing young children are increasing the accuracy and reliability of information, decreasing potential suggestibility, and minimizing trauma. Very young children are often more compliant, suggestible, and easily confused than older children. In addition to various emotions such as fear and anxiety, the accuracy of the interview is influenced by the child's age, understanding of events, interviewer style and demand for details, as well as by the structure and nature of questions.[71] Interviewing young children involves special considerations that include the use of age-appropriate interviewing techniques and tools to minimize the trauma of the initial assessment or investigation process. Use of these tools also increases the reliability of the information obtained. In addition, the child may have already had to go through numerous earlier interviews, which will affect the caseworker's interview. Since investigatory interviews determine the need for protection and can influence the legal viability and the outcome of court cases, only caseworkers trained in interviewing young children should conduct these interviews.

Basic Interviewing Principles

Regardless of what methods the caseworker uses to interview children, there are some basic principles to consider in all such interviews:

- Establish credibility and attempt to develop rapport with the child.
- Help the child relax by playing with available toys, sit with the child at his or her eye-level, and wait patiently until the child is relatively comfortable.
- Assess the child's understanding of key concepts that will help to establish credibility as the interview proceeds into sensitive areas.
- Reduce vocabulary problems by using the child's language and clarify any areas of confusion.

- Be attuned to the capacities and limitations of a young child as the interview progresses.

It is important to be aware of the child's level of comfort, and, if he or she becomes distracted or fidgety, take a break and continue the interview at a later time. The caseworker should directly address any fears that the child may have.

Developmental considerations

Children go through a series of normal developmental stages and changes. Therefore, it is important to consider the following stages when interviewing young children:

- Preschool children's thinking is very concrete, and their ability to think abstractly is still developing. Since irony, metaphor, and analogy are beyond their grasp, it is very important not to assume that children understand concepts presented.
- Preschool children do not organize their thinking or speech logically. Instead, they say whatever enters their mind at the moment, with little censoring or consideration. Therefore, their narratives tend to be disjointed and rambling, resulting in the need for the interviewer to sort out relevant from irrelevant data; it is beyond the children's cognitive capacities to do this alone. It is important not to ask them leading questions, however.
- Preschool children's understanding of space, distance, and time is not logical or linear, generally. Their memory will not work chronologically, since they have not learned units of measurement. To help place the time of an incident, use reference points such as birthdays, holidays, summer, night or day, lunchtime, or bedtime.
- Issues of truth versus lying are particularly complex in the preschool years. Children in this age group may tell lies under two circumstances: to avoid a problem or punishment, or to impress adults or get attention. Research varies, however, on whether children can manufacture stories based on information that they have not learned or experienced. Despite their occasional tendency to tell false stories, children in the preschool years usually do know the difference between fact and fantasy and between the truth and a lie. Gentle probing and nonleading questions from the interviewer will usually help children reveal what is true and what is false.
- Preschool children are generally egocentric. They think the world revolves around them and they relate all that happens to personal issues. These children do not usually think of what effect their actions will have on others, nor do they usually worry about what others think. As a result, interviewers of young children must be aware that children may be emotionally spontaneous in ways that are occasionally disconcerting to adults.
- The attention span of preschool children is limited. Long interviews are often not possible because the child simply cannot concentrate or sit in one place for long periods of time. The interviewer should be flexible, conducting several short sessions over a period of time.
- Many 2- and 3-year-olds are afraid to talk with an unfamiliar person without a parent present. The interviewer should work slowly to help children separate from the parent, when possible. If this process is difficult, the interview may need to begin

with a parent present, working toward separate interviews at a later time once the child feels more comfortable. Interviewers should be flexible and follow a child's lead, as long as it is within the protocol and policies established by their agency.[72]

Techniques and tools for interviewing young children

The most important tool in any interview is individualizing the approach based on the circumstances and the child's developmental status and level of comfort with the interviewer. Planning for the interview should take the setting into consideration. The ideal interview setting is a comfortable room where stress is minimized for the child. The following should be employed in creating the setting:

- A neutral setting where the child does not feel pressured or intimidated. The alleged maltreating person should not be in the vicinity.
- A room with a one-way mirror. This enables one person to be with the child while other professionals who need information can observe.
- A small table and chairs or pillows or rugs for sitting on the floor.
- Availability of anatomical dolls, felt-tipped markers or crayons and paper, toy telephones, doll house with dolls, Playdough, puppets, etc.

ANATOMICALLY CORRECT DOLLS

The use of anatomically correct dolls can be useful when interviewing children regarding alleged sexual abuse. Anatomical dolls have genitalia and breasts proportional to body size and appropriate to the gender and age of the child. The clothes the dolls wear can be easily removed and are appropriate to the child's age and gender. The uses of dolls include:

- **Icebreaker.** The dolls can be used to begin the conversation, cueing the child that the interviewer wants to talk about body parts. It can enhance the child's comfort level.

- **Anatomical model.** This is one of the most common uses of the dolls. The interviewer can use the dolls to determine the child's labels for different body parts. They can also be used to help the child show where any touching occurred.

- **Demonstration aid.** This is the most common function of the dolls. It enables the child to show behaviors that he or she has described to confirm the interviewer's understanding and help reduce any miscommunication. The dolls may be used with children who have limited verbal skills to help them show, rather than tell, what happened.

- **Memory stimulus and screening tool.** The dolls may trigger a child's recall of specific events of a sexual nature. The child may either demonstrate a specific sexual act while interacting with the dolls or have a strong negative reaction[73]

Observing young children

Part of the process of gathering adequate information includes the caseworker's responsibility to observe the identified child, other family members, and the environment. Specific areas for observation are:

- Physical condition of the child, including any observable effects of maltreatment;
- Emotional status of the child, including mannerisms, signs of fear, and developmental status;
- Reactions of the parents or caregivers to the agency's concerns;
- Emotional and behavioral status of the parents or caregivers during the interviewing process;
- Interactions between family members, including verbal and body language;
- Physical status of the home, including cleanliness, structure, hazards or dangerous living conditions, signs of excessive alcohol use, and use of illicit drugs;
- Climate of the neighborhood, including level of violence or support, and accessibility of transportation, telephones, or other methods of communication.

Community Involvement

While CPS agencies have the primary responsibility for conducting initial assessment or investigation, other agencies or professionals may be integrally involved in the process.

Coordinating with law enforcement

Since CPS and law enforcement often work together in responding to child abuse and neglect (in some States, all abuse and neglect reports go initially to the police), it is vital for them to establish strong working relationships and collaborate effectively. A memorandum of understanding (MOU) and protocols should be established between CPS and law enforcement agencies to identify roles and responsibilities as well as the circumstances that dictate when:

- Reports should be initiated and shared between agencies;
- Joint initial assessment or investigation should be initiated;
- Cases necessitate immediate notification to other agencies;
- Oral and written reports should be initiated and shared.

For more information on reporting laws, see the State Statute series published by the National Clearinghouse on Child Abuse and Neglect Information available at: www.calib.com/nccanch/statutes

After an MOU or protocol is established, training should provide caseworkers with familiarity of the defined roles and responsibilities.

In addition, parameters should be established for cases where law enforcement assistance may be needed to remove a child or an alleged offender from the home, or when there is a concern for the caseworker's safety.

Involving other professionals

In addition to law enforcement, other disciplines often have a role in the initial assessment or investigation process:

- **Medical personnel** may be involved in assessing and responding to medical needs of a child or parent and perhaps in documenting the nature and extent of maltreatment.

- **Mental health** personnel may be involved in assessing the effects of any alleged maltreatment and in helping to determine the validity of specific allegations. They may also be involved in evaluating the parent's or caregiver's mental health status and its effect on the safety to the child.

- **Alcohol and other drug specialists** may be involved in evaluating parental or caregiver substance abuse and its impact on the safety of the child.

- **Partner abuse experts may** be asked to assist in examining the safety of the child in cases where partner abuse and child maltreatment co-exist. These professionals may also be involved in the safety planning process.

- **Educators** may be involved in providing direct information about the effects of maltreatment and other information pertinent to the risk assessment.

- **Other community service providers** who have had past experience with the child or family may be a resource in helping to address any emergency needs that the child or family may have.

- **Multidisciplinary teams** may be used to help the CPS agency analyze the information related to the substantiation of maltreatment and the assessment of risk and safety.

- **Other community partners** such as intensive, home-based service workers; parent aides; daycare providers; afterschool care providers; foster parents; volunteers; or relatives may be used to help the agency implement a plan to keep the child safe within his or her own home.

- **Juvenile court** may be involved in helping to assure the safety of the child and to provide continuing protective services to the child and family when the child's safety cannot be protected, and the parents or caregivers have refused agency intervention.

> For additional information on community collaboration, check other Manuals in the series at: www.calib.com/nccanch/pubs/usermanual.cfm.

Special Practice Issues

There are several special issues related to the initial assessment or investigation phase—the effects of removal, caseworker safety, substantiation appeal hearings or reviews, investigation in institutional settings, and the safety of children in foster care.

Effects of removal

In order to assure protection, CPS may have to remove the child or reach agreement with family members that the alleged offender will leave the family and have no unsupervised contact with the alleged victim. Removal of the alleged offender is a less intrusive intervention but it should only be used if the caseworker is certain that there will be no contact with the victim. The removal of a family member has a dramatic affect on the feelings, behaviors, and functioning of individual family members and the family as a whole.

When CPS has to remove children from their families to protect them, they set in motion numerous issues and problems for the child. Placement outside the family often negatively affects the child's emotional well-being. Being uprooted from the only family one has known, from one's routines and familiar surroundings, is emotionally debilitating to children. Parents who abuse or neglect their children may also demonstrate love and attention to their children. This may be the only adult to whom the child has bonded. It is important to remember that the child suffers a devastating loss—the loss of being taken away from his or her birth family.

Placement away from the birth family therefore means more than the physical loss of living with the family; it also means having to deal with the loss of relationships and the loss of control over one's life. Children coming into substitute care suffer a significant loss to their self-esteem and are under a great deal of stress. Therefore, it is important to remember that when placing children, caseworkers should always maintain a focus on reducing the uncertainty and anxiety for children. Some strategies for helping children better manage the placement include:

- Involving the family and children in the safety plan and the placement process, when appropriate;
- Providing contact with the family after placement as soon as possible—ideally, within the first week;
- Reassuring children that there is nothing wrong with them and that they are not to blame for the placement;
- Providing children with information about the reasons for the placement, where they are going, and how long they may remain there;
- Allowing children to take as many personal favorite items as possible, such as photos of the family or home, toys or stuffed animals, and clothing;
- Finding out as much about the children as possible—their likes and dislikes, routines, medical issues—and informing the substitute care provider;
- Encouraging children to express their feelings and normalize those feelings, possibly through starting a journal or notebook;
- Giving children a phone number to contact the caseworker.

Family members are also traumatized by the placement. They, too, need immediate contact with their children; concern and empathy from the caseworker; and involvement in the placement process.

Caseworker safety

Every CPS case has the potential for unexpected confrontation due to the involuntary nature of investigations and assessments. It is important for caseworkers to acknowledge the nature of CPS intervention and the client's view of their role. While difficulties may occur at any point in the process, threats and volatile situations are more likely to occur during the initial assessment or investigation, during crisis situations, and when dramatic action is taken (e.g., removal of a child or the decision to take a case to court). The first step in ensuring caseworker safety is to assess the risk of the situation before the initial contact. Questions caseworkers should consider include the following:

- Are the subjects violent or hostile?
- Does the situation involve family violence, including partner, elder, or child abuse?
- Does the situation involve physical or sexual abuse or a fatality?
- Are the family members exhibiting behaviors that indicate mental illness?
- Are the family members presently abusing or selling substances?
- Are the parents or caregivers involved in ritualistic abuse or cult practices?
- Does the information note life-threatening or serious injuries to the children?
- Will the children be removed from the family situation on this visit?
- Is the family's geographic location potentially dangerous?
- Will the caseworker go into an area with limited available supports?
- Is the area known for high crime or drug activity?
- Does the housing situation or neighborhood increase concerns for staff personal safety?
- Does anyone in the home have a previous history of violence or multiple referrals? Have there been previous involuntary removals of family members?[74]

PREVENTIVE MEASURES FOR MAKING HOME VISITS

- Always be sure that the supervisor or other agency personnel are informed of the caseworker's schedule.
- Observe each person in and around the area closely and watch for signs that may indicate any potential for personal violence.
- Follow one's instincts. Anytime the caseworker feels frightened or unsafe, he or she should assess the immediate situation and take whatever action is necessary to obtain protection.
- Learn the layout of the immediate area around the home and the usual types of activities that occur there to provide a baseline from which to judge potential danger.
- Avoid dangerous or unfamiliar areas at night.
- Learn the safest route to the family's home.
- Be sure the car is in good working order, and park in a way for quick escape, if necessary.

- Carry a cell phone.
- Assess whether it is safe to accept refreshments.
- Learn how to decline offers of food or other refreshments tactfully.[75]

Substantiation appeal hearings or reviews

Every State has a mechanism to appeal an agency's decision to substantiate abuse or neglect. Some States have a formal or administrative hearing process where the parent or caregiver substantiated as a perpetrator of child maltreatment can request a hearing to review the decision. In these hearings, the burden of proof rests with the CPS agency. If the review reverses or modifies the substantiation decision, then the CPS agency will have to revise the records.

Initial assessment or investigation in institutional settings

States differs with respect to who is responsible for initially assessing or investigating allegations of child abuse and neglect in out-of-home care. In some States, local CPS staff have responsibility for investigating certain types of allegations (e.g., in daycare settings). The investigation of alleged maltreatment in institutional settings is often handled by central or regional CPS or licensing staff rather than by local CPS agencies. Depending on the nature of the allegations, law enforcement agencies also will assume a primary role in investigating these types of cases. A coordinated approach helps minimize the trauma to children and childcare staff.

INTERVIEWS IN INSTITUTIONAL SETTINGS

Investigation of alleged maltreatment in institutional settings includes interviewing:

- Alleged victim(s)
- Staff witness(es)
- Child witness(es)
- Administrator or supervisor of the alleged perpetrator
- Alleged perpetrator.

The primary questions to be asked in these cases include:

- Did the reported event occur independent of extenuating circumstances?
- Is the administrative authority culpable and, if so, in what manner?
- Is the problem, if validated, administratively redressable?
- Are personnel actions indicated and, if so, are they being initiated appropriately by the residential facility?
- What responsibility do others in the facility have for any incident of maltreatment, and is a corrective action plan needed to prevent the likelihood of future incidents?
- How can the victim be interviewed and still be protected from repercussions?

Safety in foster care placements

Caseworkers should continually assess the risk to and safety of children once placed in foster or kinship care settings. Considerations include:

- What is the level of acceptance of the placed child into the family? Notice whether the placed child is included in family routines and life. Is the child appropriately physically incorporated into the home, for example, does the child have a place for his or her belongings and a seat at the table? Examine family interaction. Is the child fully or selectively involved? Is the child included appropriately in family communications? Does the family share equally with the child?
- Are the kinship or foster parents' expectations for the placement and the child being met?
- Are the kinship or foster parents satisfied with the arrangement?
- How do the kinship or foster parents explain their parenting expectations, style, and responses to the placed child?
- What specific perceptions of and attitudes toward the placed child do the kinship or foster parents hold?
- What are the kinship or foster parents' attitudes about, opinions of, and relationship to the placed child's parents and family?
- What methods of discipline does the foster or kinship family use?
- Have circumstances or composition of the family changed in any way since the placement?
- What does the child report? Listen for acceptance into and involvement with the family or exceptions or differences between how the family deals with its own children and the placed child.
- How is the child physically, emotionally, socially, and behaviorally? Is the child's condition a result of the care received in the child's own home, the adjustment to the new home or family setting, or the possible mistreatment by the kinship or foster parents?
- What are the attitudes and perceptions that the placed child has about the care situation?
- What expectations does the child have for this family situation? Are they realistic? Do they stimulate positive or negative reactions from family members (and caregivers specifically)? Do they result in the child behaving in challenging and difficult ways?
- What are the similarities and difference between the placed child and other children in the family?
- How has the family functioning been affected since the placement?[76]

7. Family Assessment

During the initial assessment, the child protective services (CPS) caseworker has identified behaviors and conditions about the child, parent, and family that contribute to the risk of maltreatment. During the family assessment, the CPS caseworker engages the family in a process designed to gain a greater understanding about family strengths, needs, and resources so that children are safe and the risk of maltreatment is reduced. The family assessment is initiated immediately after the decision is made that ongoing services are needed.

This chapter explores principles for conducting family assessments, key decisions made during family assessments, the family assessment process, community collaboration, and special practice issues related to cultural sensitivity and cultural competence.

Family Assessment Principles

Family assessments, in order to be most effective, should be culturally sensitive, strength-based, and developed with the family. They should be designed to help parents or caretakers recognize and remedy conditions so children can safely remain in their own home.[77] Given the emphasis on timeliness built into the Adoption and Safe Families Act (ASFA), the assessment of the family's strengths and needs should be considered in the context of the length of time it will take for the family to provide a safe, stable home environment.

A culturally sensitive assessment recognizes that parenting practices and family structures vary as a result of ethnic, community, and familial differences, and that this wide range can result in different but safe and adequate care for children within the parameters of the law. Each family has its own structure, roles, values, beliefs, and coping styles. Respect for and acceptance of this diversity is a cornerstone of family-centered assessments. The assessment process must acknowledge, respect, and honor the diversity of families.[78]

A strength-based assessment "recognizes that people, regardless of their difficulties, can change and grow, that healing occurs when a family's strengths, not its weaknesses, are engaged, and that the family is the agent of its own change."[79] While an outline for the family assessment process increases the likelihood that all assessment areas are covered, family assessments must be individualized and tailored to the unique strengths and needs of each family.[80] An individualized assessment is undertaken in conjunction with other service providers to form a comprehensive picture of the individual, interpersonal, and societal pressures on the family members—individually and as a group. This holistic approach takes both client competencies and environment into consideration and views the environment as both a source of and solution to families' problems.[81] When possible, the assessment process also should be conducted in conjunction with the families' extended family and support network through the use of family decision- making meetings and other formats.[82]

For both practice accountability and empirical usefulness, CPS caseworkers should consider using assessment tools and standardized clinical measures to evaluate risk and protective factors. Tools that support the assessment of specific family strengths, needs, and resources include:

- Genogram—diagram resembling a family tree completed with the family's assistance;
- Ecomap—diagram linking the family tree with outside systems and resources;
- Self-report instruments—questionnaire or survey measuring beliefs, strengths, risks, and behaviors;

- Observational tools—devices enabling professionals to examine personal and family dynamics.[83]

Using such tools, identified needs are translated into specific intervention outcomes that form the basis of time-limited, individualized case plans.

In summary, while the initial assessment identifies the risk factors of concern in the family, the family assessment considers the relationship between strengths and risks and identifies what must change in order to keep children safe, reduce the risk of future maltreatment, increase permanency, and enhance child and family well-being. Consequently, where the initial assessment identifies problems, the family assessment promotes an understanding of the problems and becomes the basis for an intervention plan.

Family Assessment Decisions

Based on the additional information gathered and analyzed, the caseworker must ask the following questions to inform the assessment:

- What are the risk factors and needs of the family that affect safety, permanency, and well-being?
- What are the effects of maltreatment that affect safety, permanency, and well-being?
- What are the individual and family strengths?
- What do the family members perceive as their problems and strengths?
- What must change in order for the effects of maltreatment to be addressed and for the risk of maltreatment to be reduced or eliminated?
- What are the parent's or caregiver's level of readiness for change and motivation and capacity to assure safety, permanency, and wellbeing?

To arrive at effective decisions during the family assessment process, the CPS caseworker should use competent interviewing skills to engage the family in a partnership; gather and organize information; analyze and interpret the meaning of the information; and draw accurate conclusions based on the assessment.

Family Assessment Process

To accomplish the purposes of the family assessment, caseworkers should:

- Review the initial assessment or investigation information;
- Develop a family assessment plan;
- Conduct the family assessment by interviewing all members of the household and other individuals the family identifies as having an interest in the safety and well-being of the child;
- Consult with other professionals as appropriate;
- Analyze information and make decisions.

Review the initial assessment or investigation information

To provide focus for the family assessment, the caseworker should begin by reviewing the information previously gathered and analyzed during the initial assessment or investigation. Based on an analysis of this information, the caseworker should develop a list of questions that need to be answered during the family assessment process. The following questions are examples of areas that the caseworker may want to examine:

- What was the nature of the maltreatment (type, severity, chronicity)?
- What was the family's understanding of the maltreatment?
- Which risk factors identified during the initial assessment or investigation are most concerning?
- What is the child's current living situation with regard to safety and stability?
- Was a safety plan developed? What has been the family's response to this plan?
- What is currently known about the parent or caregiver's history? Are there clues that suggest that further information about the past will help to explain the parent or caregiver's current functioning?
- What is known about the family's social support network? Who else is supporting the family and who will be available on an ongoing basis for the family to rely on?
- Are there any behavioral symptoms observed in the child? How has the child functioned in school and in social relationships? Who else may have information about any behavioral or emotional concerns?
- Have problems been identified that may need further examination or evaluation (e.g., drug or alcohol problems, psychiatric or psychological problems, and health needs)?
- What further information about the family will help provide an understanding of the risks and protective factors related to the potential of continued maltreatment?

Develop a family assessment plan

Based on the areas identified through the review, the caseworker should develop a plan for how the assessment process will occur. In general, it takes an average of 4 to 6 weeks to "get to know" the family enough to draw accurate conclusions, although laws may vary from state to state regarding the time before an assessment is required. The following issues need to be considered in developing the plan for the assessment:

- When will the first meeting be held with the family?
- How often will meetings with the family occur?
- Where will meetings be held and how will the setting be controlled?
- Who will be involved in each meeting? Are there other persons (e.g., friends, extended family, other professionals) who have critical information about the needs of this family? How will they be involved in the process?
- Will the services of other professionals be needed (e.g., for psychological tests, or alcohol or other drug abuse assessments)?
- What reports may be available to provide information about a particular family member or the family as a system (e.g., from school or health care providers)?
- When will the information be analyzed and a family assessment summary completed?

- How will the caseworker share this information with the family?

Conduct the family assessment

Once the plan for the assessment has been established, the caseworker should conduct interviews with the child and family to determine the treatment needs of the family. Four types of meetings are held:

Meeting with the family

If possible and if it is safe for all family members, the caseworker should meet with the entire family to begin the family assessment. This ensures that each family member knows the expectations from the beginning; everyone's participation is judged important; and communication is open and shared among family members.

During this initial contact, the caseworker should provide an opportunity for the family to discuss the initial assessment, share the plan for conducting the family assessment, and seek agreement on scheduling and participation. The caseworker should be specific with the family about the purposes of the family assessment and should avoid technical or professional terminology. It also is important to affirm that the intention of CPS is to help the family keep the child safe and address mutually identified problems to reduce the risk of child maltreatment in the future. The caseworker should attempt to gain an initial understanding of the family's perception of CPS and its current situation.

To gain a better understanding of family dynamics, at least one assessment meeting beyond the introductory session should be conducted with the entire family to observe and assess the roles and interactions. Caseworkers should consider communication patterns, alliances, roles and relationships, habitual patterns of interaction, and other family-related concepts.

Meeting with the individual family members

Meetings with individual family members, including the children, should be held. At the beginning of each meeting, the caseworker should clarify the primary purpose of the interview and attempt to build rapport by identifying areas of common interest. It is important to demonstrate appreciation of the person and his or her situation and worth. This is not an interrogation; the caseworker is trying to better understand the person and the situation.

In each individual meeting, the caseworker should carefully explore the areas that have been identified previously for study. In interviews with the children, the emphasis will likely be on understanding more about any effects of maltreatment. In interviews with the parents, the emphasis is on trying to uncover the causes for the behaviors and conditions that present risk and obtain the parents' perceptions of their problems. As part of meetings with the parents, it is important that the caseworker examines the influence that family history and culture may have on current behavior and functioning. In meetings with both children and parents, the caseworker should also attempt to obtain family members' perceptions about the strengths in their family and how these strengths can be maximized to reduce the risk of maltreatment.

Meeting with the parent or caregiver

In families with more than one adult caregiver, the caseworker should arrange to hold at least one of the meetings with the adults together, if it is possible and safe for both adults. During this interview, the caseworker should observe and evaluate the nature of the relationship and how the two communicate and relate. The caseworker should also consider and discuss parenting issues and the health and quality of the marital relationship as well as seek the parent or caregiver's perception of problems, the current situation, and the family. The worker should be alert to signs that could indicate the possibility of partner abuse and avoid placing either adult in a situation that could increase risk, such as referring to sensitive information that may have been disclosed in individual meetings. As appropriate or if requested, the caseworker may also provide referrals for resources or services to clients experiencing difficulties that are not risk factors.

Consulting with other professionals

While the CPS caseworker has primary responsibility for conducting the family assessment, frequently other community providers may be called upon to assist with the assessment. Other providers should be consulted when there is a specific client condition or behavior that requires additional professional assessment. For example:

- The child or parent exhibits undiagnosed physical health concerns or the child's behaviors or emotions do not appear to be age-appropriate (e.g., hyperactivity, excessive sadness and withdrawal, chronic nightmares, bed wetting, or aggressive behavior at home or at school);
- The parent exhibits behaviors or emotions that do not appear to be controlled, such as violent outbursts, extreme lethargy, depression, or frequent mood swings;
- The child or parent has a chemical dependency.

A good way to judge whether outside referrals are needed is to review the gathered information and assess whether significant questions still exist about the risks and strengths in this family. If the caseworker is having difficulty writing the tentative assessment, he or she should consult the supervisor to determine whether consultation with an interdisciplinary team or an evaluation of presenting problems by others in the community may be appropriate.

If the assessment identifies the need for specificevaluation, the referral should specify the following:

- The reason for referral, including specific areas for assessment as they relate to the risk of maltreatment;
- The parent's knowledge regarding the referral and their response;
- The time frames for assessment, and when the agency will need a report back from the provider;
- The type of report requested regarding the results of the evaluation;
- The purpose and objectives of the evaluation (e.g., the parents' level of alcohol use and its effects on their ability to parent);
- The specific questions the caseworker wants answered to assist in decision-making;
- The need for a confidentiality release.

In addition, sometimes other providers contribute to the assessment process because of their role as advocates for the child. For example, if juvenile or family court is involved, the child may have a Guardian ad Litem (GAL) or court-appointed special advocate (CASA) who advises the court on needed services based on interviews conducted with the child and other family members.

Analyze information and make decisions

Once adequate information has been gathered, the caseworker must analyze the information with regard to the key decisions. The CPS caseworker must identify which risk factors are most critical and what is causing them. This is determined by examining the information in terms of cause, nature, and extent; effects; strengths; and the family's perception of the maltreatment in order to individualize the CPS response to each child and family.

At the conclusion of the family assessment, the caseworker and family have identified changes necessary to keep children safe and reduce the risk of child maltreatment. These conclusions are then translated into desired outcomes and matched with the correct intervention response that will increase safety, well-being, and permanency for children. While the specific areas studied in the assessment are unique to each family circumstance, the following guide identifies areas for gathering essential information needed to draw necessary assessment conclusions.

FAMILY ASSESSMENT GUIDE

Reasons for Referral. Briefly summarize the primary reasons this family is receiving continuing child welfare services and define the terms of any safety plan that was developed with the family.

Sources of Information. Identify all sources of information used to frame this assessment and refer to the specific dates of contact with the family and other persons or systems that relate to assessment information.

Identifying Information. Describe the family system, as defined by the family. Include members' names, ages, and relationship to the primary caregiver; sources of economic support and whether it is perceived as adequate; and current school or vocational training status. Describe the current household situation, including sleeping arrangements, and the client's perception of their neighborhood, especially as it pertains to safety.

Presenting Problems, Needs, and Strengths. Describe family members' perceptions of the presenting needs as they relate to each individual member, the family system, and its environment. As appropriate, include a history of the problem development and previous attempts to address it, as well as an explanation of family members' readiness and motivation to engage in help for the problem at this particular time. Also, identify the family's stated goals as they relate to each problem.

Family Background and History. Write a social history. Ideally, the primary caregiver(s) should be described first. Begin with his or her birth, and describe the family of origin—its members, their relationships with each other, and significant descriptive characteristics of each member. Follow that member's development into adulthood and up to but not including the present time. Genograms are particularly helpful in understanding life events over time. Identify important personal relationships, including those characterized by maltreatment, substance abuse, or violence; identify positive life events as well as stressful ones; and describe relationships with systems, including educational, vocational, legal, religious, medical, mental health, and employment. The history of other adults and children in the household should be summarized, addressing the preceding points, as appropriate and available. Complete this history in chronological order, if possible.

Present Status. Describe the present life situation of the family, particularly information about risks and strengths related to each child in the family, each caregiver's functioning, the family system, and the environment and community. Standardized assessment measures may be helpful to better understand the family and identify areas to be recorded in the casefile.

Tentative Assessment. Summarize risks and strengths related to each family member. This is the opportunity for the worker to analyze the collected information and to draw conclusions about the most important strengths and needs of individual family members and the family as a system. Knowledge of human development, personality theory and psychopathology, family systems, ecological theory, and psychosocial theory should be drawn on to form these conclusions. The worker should make informed judgments about the objective and observational information that has been collected and recorded. In this section, the caseworker specifically summarizes what must change to reduce the risk of child maltreatment.

Special Practice Issue—Cultural Sensitivity

Cultural sensitivity is a critical element in obtaining a comprehensive understanding of a family's situation. For a thorough analysis, it is also a necessary component of the family assessment process. There are three important principles to consider when working with families from different cultures:

- Believe that diversity is a good thing and that having different ideals, customs, attitudes, practices, and beliefs does not, in and of itself, constitute deviance or pathology. If a worker approaches culturally different clients from this perspective, the client is more likely to perceive that the worker has communicated respect for them as persons, and the assessment will be more accurate.
- Accept that everyone has biases and prejudices. This helps to increase objectivity and guard against judgments affected by unconscious biases.

- Understand that the nature of the CPS caseworker and client relationship represents a power imbalance. If there are cultural differences between the caseworker and the client, the client may have difficulty trusting that the caseworker truly intends to empower the client to be an equal partner in the helping relationship.[84]

For example, to develop rapport with clients during the family assessment effectively, the caseworker should be sensitive to cultural similarities and differences with the client. In order to be empathetic, the caseworker should be aware of both the individual uniqueness and the cultural or historical roots of the client.[85] In all assessments, the client is the most important source of information about the family, including providing information about cultural aspects and lifestyles unique to that family. Effective cultural competence requires that caseworkers:

- Respect how clients differ from them;
- Be open to learning about cultural differences when assessing strengths and needs of families;
- Avoid judgments and decision-making resulting from biases, myths, or stereotypes;
- Ask the client about a practice's history and meaning if unfamiliar with it;
- Explain the law that regards a particular cultural practice as abuse;
- Elicit information from the client regarding strongly held family traditions, values, and beliefs, especially child rearing practices.

GUIDE TO UNDERSTANDING CULTURAL DIFFERENCES

With every family assessment, there are certain areas that may be affected by a person's history and culture. The following questions may be used as a guide to understand cultural difference as part of the assessment. According to the client:

- What is the purpose and function of the nuclear family?
- What roles do males and females play in the family?
- What is the role of religion for the family? How do these beliefs influence child-rearing practices?
- What is the meaning, identity, and involvement of the larger homogenous group (e.g., tribe, race, nationality)?
- What family rituals, traditions, or behaviors exist?
- What is the usual role of children in the family?
- What is the perception of the role of children in society?
- What types of discipline does the family consider to be appropriate?
- Who is usually responsible for childcare?
- What are the family's attitudes or beliefs regarding health care?
- What are the family's sexual attitudes and values?
- How are cultural beliefs incorporated into family functioning?
- How does the family maintain its cultural beliefs?
- Who is assigned authority and power for decision-making?
- What tasks are assigned based on traditional roles in the family?

- How do family members express and receive affection? How do they relate to closeness and distance?
- What are the communication styles of the family?
- How does the family solve problems?
- How do family members usually deal with conflict? Is anger an acceptable emotion? Do members yell and scream or withdraw from conflict situations?[86]

8. CASE PLANNING

Intervention with abused and neglected children and their families must be planned, purposeful, and directed toward the achievement of safety, permanency, and well-being. One of the essential elements of planned and purposeful intervention is a complete understanding of the factors contributing to maltreatment. The case plan identifies risks and problematic behaviors, as well as the strategies and interventions to facilitate the changes needed, by laying out tasks, goals, and outcomes. Safety plans and concurrent permanency plans are often incorporated into the case planning process, as needed.

Flexibility also is critical in developing and implementing case plans. The use of creativity helps in developing new approaches to tackle difficult problems. The children and family's needs and resources may change, and flexibility allows the plan to follow suit. Planning is a dynamic process; no plan should be static.

Since safety plan considerations are incorporated throughout this manual, this chapter focuses on the case plan process. This entails developing the case plan, involving the family, targeting outcomes, determining goals and tasks, and developing concurrent case plans.

Developing the Case Plan

The case plan that a child protective services (CPS) caseworker develops with a family is their road map to successful intervention. The outcomes identify the destination, the goals provide the direction, and the tasks outline the specific steps necessary to reach the final destination. The purposes of case planning are to:

- Identify strategies with the family that address the effects of maltreatment and change the behaviors or conditions contributing to its risk;
- Provide a clear and specific guide for the caseworker and the family for changing the behaviors and conditions that influence risk;
- Establish a benchmark to measure client progress for achieving outcomes;
- Develop an essential framework for case decision-making.

The primary decisions during this stage are guided by the following questions:

- What are the outcomes that, when achieved, will indicate that risk is reduced and that the effects of maltreatment have been successfully addressed?
- What goals and tasks must be accomplished to achieve these outcomes?

- What are the priorities among the outcomes, goals, and tasks?
- What interventions or services will best facilitate successful outcomes? Are the appropriate services available?
- How and when will progress be evaluated?

Involving the Family

Families who believe that their feelings and concerns are heard are more likely to engage in the case-planning process. Therefore, decisions regarding outcomes, goals, and tasks should be a collaborative process between the caseworker, family, family network, and other providers. Caseworkers should help the family maintain a realistic perspective on what can be accomplished and how long it will take to do so. Involving the family accomplishes the following:

- Enhances the essential helping relationship because the family's feelings and concerns have been heard, respected, and considered;
- Facilitates the family's investment in and commitment to the outcomes, goals, and tasks;
- Empowers parents or caregivers to take the necessary action to change the behaviors and conditions that contribute to the risk of maltreatment;
- Ensures that the agency and the family are working toward the same end.

FAMILY MEETINGS

Since the early 1990s, CPS agencies have primarily been using two models—the Family Unity Model and the Family Group Conferencing Model (also known as the Family Group Decision-making Model)—to optimize family strengths in the planning process. These models bring the family, extended family, and others in the family's social support network together to make decisions regarding how to ensure safety and well-being. The demonstrated benefits of these models include:

- Increased willingness of family members to accept the services suggested in the plan because they were integrally involved in the planning process;
- Enhanced relationships between professionals and families resulting in increased job satisfaction of professionals;
- Maintained family continuity and connection through kinship rather than foster care placements.

Family meetings can be powerful events. During the meetings, families often experience caring and concern from family members, relatives, and professionals. Since meetings are based on the strengths perspective, families may develop a sense of hope and vision for the future. The meetings also can show families how they should function by modeling openness in communication and appropriate problem- solving skills.[87]

Targeting Outcomes

One of the decisions resulting from the assessment is what changes must the family make to reduce or eliminate the risk of maltreatment. Achieving positive client outcomes indicates that the specific risks of maltreatment have been adequately reduced and that the effects of maltreatment are satisfactorily addressed.

Agency outcomes

With the passage of the Adoption and Safe Families Act (ASFA) in 1997, child welfare agencies have been directed to design their intervention systems to measure the achievement of outcomes. There has been consensus that child welfare outcomes, at the program level, can be organized around four domains: child safety, child permanence, child well-being, and family well-being (functioning). Although all four are important, Federal and State laws emphasize child safety and permanence, so these two outcomes are often used to evaluate agency performance. The agency outcomes are defined as:

- **Child safety.** The safety of children is the paramount concern that guides CPS practice. In many States, the evaluation of child safety is equivalent to the determination that the child is at imminent risk of serious harm.[88]

- **Child permanence.** Although maintaining a constant focus on child safety is critical, casework interventions also must be aimed at maintaining or creating permanent living arrangements and emotional attachments for children. This is based on the belief that stable, caring relationships in a family setting are essential for the healthy growth and development of the child. This stresses providing reasonable efforts to prevent removal and to reunify families, when safe and appropriate to do so and as specified under ASFA. This also promotes the timely adoption or other permanent placement of children who cannot return safely to their own homes.[89]

- **Child well-being.** The general well-being of children who come in contact with the CPS system also must be addressed, especially for children placed in substitute care. This requires that children's physical and mental health, educational, and other needs will be assessed, and that preventive or treatment services are provided when warranted.[90]

- **Family well-being.** Families must be able to function at a basic level in order to provide a safe and permanent environment for raising their children. Caseworkers are not expected to create optimal family functioning, but rather facilitate change so that the family can meet the basic needs of its members and assure their protection.

Child and family-level outcomes

Positive outcomes indicate that both the risks and the effects of maltreatment have been reduced due to changes in the behaviors or conditions that contributed to the maltreatment. The outcomes should address issues related to four domains—the child, the parents or other caregivers, the family system, and the envronment—and be designed to contribute to the achievement of the CPS agency outcomes for child safety, child permanence, child well-being, and family well-being.[91]

- **Child-level outcomes.** Outcomes for children focus on changes in behavior, development, mental health, physical health, peer relationships, and education. Sample desired outcomes are improved behavior control (as evidenced by managing angry impulses) or developmental appropriateness and adjustment in all areas of functioning (as evidenced by the child's physical development within range of the chronological age).

- **Parent or caregiver outcomes.** Outcomes for parents or caregivers focus on many areas, such as mental health functioning, problem solving ability, impulse control, substance abuse treatment, and parenting skills. A sample desired outcome is improved child management skills (as evidenced by establishing and consistently following through with rules and limits for children).

- **Family outcomes.** Outcomes for the family focus on such issues as roles and boundaries, communication patterns, and social support. A sample desired outcome is enhanced family maintenance and safety (as evidenced by the ability to meet members' basic needs for food, clothing, shelter, and supervision).

- **Environmental outcomes.** Sometimes outcomes focus on the environmental factors contributing to the maltreatment, such as social isolation, housing issues, or neighborhood safety. A sample desired outcome is utilizing social support (as evidenced by a family being adopted by a church that provides child care respite, support group, and family activities).

Determining Goals

Caseworkers should work with families to develop goals that indicate the specific changes needed to accomplish the outcomes. The objective is not to create a perfect family or a family that matches a caseworker's own values and beliefs. Rather, the goal is to reduce or eliminate the risk of maltreatment so that children are safe and have their developmental needs met. Goals should be **SMART**; in others words, they should be:

- *Specific.* The family should know exactly what has to be done and why.

- *Measurable.* Everyone should know when the goals have been achieved. Goals will be measurable to the extent that they are behaviorally based and written in clear and understandable language.

- *Achievable.* The family should be able to accomplish the goals in a designated time period, given the resources that are accessible and available to support change.

- **_Realistic._** The family should have input and agreement in developing feasible goals.

- **_Time limited._** Time frames for goal accomplishment should be determined based on an understanding of the family's risks, strengths, and ability and motivation to change. Availability and level of services also may affect time frames.

Goals should indicate the positive behaviors or conditions that will result from the change and not highlight the negative behaviors.

TARGETING OUTCOMES FOR A FAMILY: CASE EXAMPLE

The Dawn family consists of the father, Mr. Dawn, age 34; mother, Mrs. Dawn, age 32; daughter, Tina, age 6; and son, Scott, age 3 1/2. The family was reported to CPS by the daycare center. Scott had lateral bruises and welts on his buttocks and on the back of his thighs. The daycare center reported that Scott was an aggressive child; he throws things when he is angry, hits other children, and runs from the teacher. The center also has threatened not to readmit him.

Through investigation and family assessment, the caseworker learned that Mr. and Mrs. Dawn have been married for 10 years. Mr. Dawn completed high school and is employed as a clerk in a convenience store. He works the evening shift, 4 to 11 p.m., and was recently turned down for a promotion. Mrs. Dawn also completed high school, went on to become a paralegal, and is employed as a legal assistant. Tina was a planned child, but Scott was not. The parents described Tina as a quiet and easy child. They described Scott as a difficult child and as having a temper and not minding adults. Recently, he threw a truck at his sister, causing her to need stitches above her eye, and tore his curtains down in his bedroom. His parents described Scott as unwilling to be held and loved. Both parents are at their wits' end and do not know what to do with Scott. Mrs. Dawn reported that all of the discipline falls on her, and she cannot control Scott.

The home appeared chaotic with newspapers, toys, and magazines strewn all over the living room. There was no evidence of structure or consistent rules. Scott misbehaved during the interview. Sometimes the parents ignored his behavior, and other times they addressed his behavior only when it had escalated to the point that he was out of control. It also appeared that Tina had a lot of age-inappropriate responsibility, for example, making Scott's breakfast every morning.

Mr. Dawn said his mother used severe forms of punishment when he misbehaved. He feels it taught him right from wrong, believing that children need strong discipline to grow up into healthy, functioning adults. He said he often "sees red" when Scott misbehaves and that he yells at Scott or hits Scott with a nearby object.

The family is socially isolated. Mr. Dawn's mother is alive, but they are estranged. Mrs. Dawn's parents are deceased, and her two brothers live hundreds of miles away. Mrs. Dawn has a friend at work, but they do not communicate outside of work. The parents described being very much in love when they met. However, because of work schedules, they have very little time to spend together. Mrs. Dawn describes her husband as often yelling at her and the children rather than just talking.

The behaviors and conditions contributing to the risk include:

- Father's poor impulse control
- Father's childhood history of abuse
- Father's aggressive behavior
- Lack of structure, rules, and limits
- Inconsistent and inappropriate discipline
- Family isolation
- Inappropriate role expectations
- Poor family communication
- Scott's poor impulse control
- Scott's aggressive and dangerous behavior

Sample parent outcomes may be improved impulse control, child management skills, and coping skills. Sample family outcomes may be improved communication and family functioning. Sample child outcomes may be improved and age-appropriate behavioral control.

Determining Tasks

Goals should be broken down into small, meaningful, and incremental tasks. These tasks incorporate the specific services and interventions needed to help the family achieve the goals and outcomes. They describe what the children, family, caseworker, and other service providers will do and identify time frames for accomplishing each task. Families should understand what is expected of them, and what they can expect from the caseworker and other service providers. Matching services to client strengths and needs is discussed in Chapter 9, "Service Provision."

In developing tasks, caseworkers should also be aware of services provided by community agencies and professionals, target populations served, specializations, eligibility criteria, availability, waiting lists, and fees for services. With this knowledge, CPS caseworkers can determine the most appropriate services to help the family achieve its tasks. The following text box illustrates a sample outcome, the goals, and the tasks using the case example from earlier in this chapter.

Developing Concurrent Plans

Concurrent planning seeks to reunify children with their birth families while at the same time establishing an alternative permanency plan that can be implemented if reunification cannot take place. In cases such as these, the caseworker needs to develop two separate case plans, although it may seem confusing to work in two directions simultaneously. Concurrent permanency plans provide workers with a structured approach to move children quickly from foster care to the stability of a safe and continuous family home.[92]

SAMPLE OUTCOME, GOALS, AND TASKS FOR THE DAWN FAMILY

Outcome: Effective child management skills.

Goal: Mr. and Mrs. Dawn will establish, consistently follow, and provide positive reinforcement for rules and limits.

Task: Mr. and Mrs. Dawn will set consistent mealtimes, bedtimes, and wake-up times for the children.

Task: Mr. and Mrs. Dawn will work with the caseworker to set specific, age-appropriate expectations for their children.

Goal: Mr. and Mrs. Dawn will use disciplinary techniques that are appropriate to Scott and Tina's age, development, and type of misbehavior.

Task: Mr. and Mrs. Dawn will identify those components of Scott's behavior that are most difficult for them to manage and the disciplinary techniques they can use to help him control his behavior.

---

9. SERVICE PROVISION

Once the case plan has been developed, the caseworker provides or arranges for services identified in the plan to help family members achieve tasks, desired outcomes, and case plan goals. Selecting and matching interventions is a critical step in the casework process. To the extent possible, interventions that have demonstrated success in addressing the issues that brought the family to child protective services (CPS) should be selected.

An important consideration in selecting interventions is an assessment of the readiness to change. For further information, see Chapter 3, "The Helping Relationship," Chapter 7, "Family Assessment," and Chapter 8, "Case Planning." For example, if a family member is at the precontemplation stage, it is important to select initial interventions that will increase their motivation to change, rather than selecting interventions that assume the individual is at the action stage. However, there is significant variation in readiness or eagerness to change among clients, and an individual's readiness to change may fluctuate from time to time. The role of the caseworker is to collaborate with the individual or family in developing plans and selecting services that will best facilitate change.

Richard Gelles, a leading researcher in the field of family violence, suggests that some families with maltreatment problems are treatment-resistant. He proposes making early decisions about permanence because the risk of maltreatment is high and the readiness for change is low.[93] Since the principles and provisions of the Adoption and Safe Families Act (ASFA) are designed to ensure child safety and decrease the time necessary to reach permanency, it is critical to evaluate a family's readiness to change and select interventions that will help families ultimately achieve child safety and permanence.

This chapter introduces a conceptual framework for services based on levels of risk in a family and discusses case management and service coordination issues. The chapter also presents an overview of the various types of treatment and intervention services available for abused and neglected children and their families.

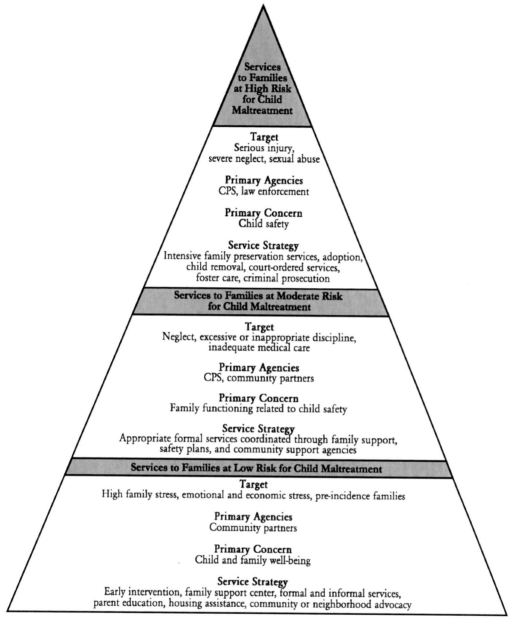

Exhibit 9-1. Child Protection Service Pyramid[94]

Service Framework Based on Levels of Risk

A conceptual framework developed by the National Association of Public Child Welfare Administrators (NAPCWA), presented in Exhibit 9-1, is helpful in thinking about the levels of services appropriate to the level of risk presented by the family. The top third of the pyramid represents reports of child abuse and neglect that pose the highest risk for children, are concerned primarily with child safety, and often involve child removal and court-ordered services. The primary role for the CPS caseworker is to help families understand and acknowledge the risk factors that contributed or could lead to serious maltreatment, and to engage them in developing safety, case, and concurrent permanency plans. Since services are often court-ordered, the likelihood of success will be dependent on both the caseworker's ability to communicate the potential benefits of specific intervention strategies effectively and the family's response. Family members served in this category are likely to be in the precontemplation stage of change.

The middle third of the pyramid represents family conditions that pose moderate risk to children, warrant services by CPS, focus on child safety and family well-being, and often involve collaboration with other service providers. The success of intervention is directly related to the CPS worker's ability to develop a partnership with the family. When referred, some families may be at the precontemplation stage of change, while others may be at the contemplation or determination stages of change. The role of the CPS worker is to help family members prepare for change and to collaborate on safety and case plans that will lead to improvements in family well-being and child safety.

The bottom third of the pyramid represents families that are identified as low risk for immediate maltreatment, but who experience high family stress. These families can often be served by early intervention, family support centers, and informal helping systems. The primary outcomes for these families are enhanced child and family well-being.

Case Management

Case management emphasizes decision-making, coordination, and provision of services.[95] Caseworkers collect and analyze information, arrive at decisions at all stages of the casework process, coordinate services provided by others, and directly provide supportive services. Three primary objectives for case management practice are relevant to the case management role of CPS caseworkers: (1) continuity of care, (2) accessibility and accountability of service systems, and (3) service system efficiency.[96] These objectives are best achieved when caseworkers know the resources available, have expertise in a particular area of practice, use interpersonal and group skills to interact with other professionals, and lead and coordinate the service delivery process by developing case plans that are clear to all parties. It is the caseworker's responsibility to:

- Select, provide, and arrange for the most appropriate services;
- Communicate and collaborate with identified service providers;
- Measure progress toward achievement of outcomes and goals;
- Maintain records to document client progress and ensure accountability;
- Prepare and review necessary reports.

When other service providers are used as part of the CPS caseworker's overall risk-reduction strategy, it is important to establish a contract with the referral agency or individual professional. The contract should include the following:

- Results of the family assessment, including an identification of the most critical risk factors that the service provider is to address;
- Copy of the case plan with tasks, outcomes, goals, and identification of the service provider's role;
- Specification of the purpose of the referral and the expectations regarding the type, scope, and extent of services needed;
- Specification of the number, frequency, and method of reports required, as well as reasons for reports;
- Expectations for reporting on observable changes in achievement of client tasks, outcomes, and goals;
- Measures of client progress;
- Provisions for coordinating among providers and monitoring service provision.

Treatment and Intervention

Since child maltreatment is rooted in a variety of personal and environmental factors, interventions need to address as many of these contributing issues as possible. Early evaluation research on treatment effectiveness suggests that successful intervention requires a comprehensive package addressing both the interpersonal and concrete needs of all family members. This research suggests that programs relying solely on professional therapy without other supportive or remedial services to children and families offer less opportunity for maximizing client gains. In addition, the findings suggest that during the initial months of treatment agencies should invest the most intensive resources to engage the family, then begin altering behavior as close to the point of initial referral as possible.[97]

Clearly, each community should possess a broad range of services to meet the multidimensional needs of abused and neglected children and their families, but that is not always the case due to funding or other issues. Nevertheless, CPS maintains responsibility for identifying and obtaining the most appropriate services available. Selecting services in a particular case is based on:

- Assessment of the factors contributing to the risk of maltreatment and the family's strengths;
- Outcomes targeted for change;
- Treatment approaches best suited to a particular outcome;
- Resources available in the community.

Exhibit 9-2 reflects a broad selection of treatment and other intervention services for child abuse and neglect, although it is not a comprehensive guide. These services range from support for children and families to long-term treatment interventions. Some services require extensive training before implementation. Arranged alphabetically by title within categories, the exhibit summarizes the primary focus and target population for each type of service. Information regarding evaluation and research support, and related studies is included, along with references to selected manuals, curricula, guidelines for implementation, and other background material.

Exhibit 9-2. Selected Treatment and Intervention Services

Service	Focus	Population	Research	Reference Information
		Services for Children and Adolescents		
Art Therapy	To use art to help children deal with feelings of victimization, loss, and separation. Used for assessment and treatment.	Abused children	Generally supported in clinical literature and practice, yet no controlled studies of its efficacy at time of writing.	Literature review and supporting information are available.[98]
Cognitive Processing Therapy	Through cognitive restructuring, provides relief of symptoms arising from exposure to traumatic events.	Children and adolescents with post-traumatic stress disorder (PTSD) or related depression	Research indicates positive results.[99]	Treatment manual, guidelines, and supporting information are available.[100]
Early Childhood Programs	To provide children with respite from a stressful home situation by giving them clear structure and opportunities to interact with positive adult role models in a safe childcare setting.	Abused and at-risk children	When provided in conjunction with other appropriate services, research indicates positive results.[101]	Supporting information is available.
Eye Movement Desensitization and Reprocessing	To integrate a range of therapeutic approaches in combination with eye movement stimulation to affect cognitive processes and resolve therapeutic issues at a faster rate.	Traumatized children or adolescents	When provided in conjunction with other appropriate services, research indicates positive results.[102]	Guidelines, protocols, training, and supporting information are available.[103]
Family Foster Care and Kinship Care	To provide a safe, supportive environment through out-of-home placement while working toward family reunification or permanent placement.	Children and adolescents who have been abused or are at high risk for further maltreatment.	Some research indicates positive results of kinship care; while others suggest concerns about the availability of fewer services to these families.[104]	Supporting information is available.[105]
Resilient Peer Training Intervention	School-based service designed to enhance the social competencies of vulnerable children through interactions with resilient peers and supportive adults.	Abused and at-risk children	Research indicates positive results.[106]	Guidelines and supporting information are available.[107]
Sex Offender Treatment for Adolescents	To change beliefs and attributions that support sex abuse, improve reactions to negative emotions, enhance behavioral risk management, and promote pro-social behaviors.	Adolescent sex offenders	Some research suggests promising results, yet there is no clear evidence.[108]	Treatment manuals and supporting information are available.[109]

Exhibit 9-2. (Continued)

Service	Focus	Population	Research	Reference Information
Services for Children and Adolescents				
Supportive Services	To provide assistance, guidance, and positive role models. May include services provided by Big Brothers/Big Sisters, YMCA, Foster Grandparents, and faith and community based groups.	Abused and at-risk children	Generally supported in research and practice, yet empirical evidence of efficacy has varied. [110]	Supporting information is available. [111]
Trauma-focused Play Therapy	To use play to enable abused children to express overwhelming emotions and thoughts. Used for both assessment and treatment.	Abused children	Generally supported in clinical literature and practice, yet no controlled studies of its efficacy. Review of literature suggests positive results. [112]	Guidelines and supporting information are available. [113]
Treatment Foster Care	To provide therapeutic services to children within the private homes of trained families. Serves as a less restrictive, family-based alternative to residential or institutional care.	Children and adolescents with significant behavioral, emotional, and mental health problems	Research indicates positive results. [114]	Supporting information is available. [115]
Services for Parents				
Adult Child Molester Treatment	To address harmful thinking and behaviors that led offenders to sexually abuse by replacing them with appropriate thoughts and choices.	Adult sex offenders	Research indicates positive results. [116]	Supporting information is available. [117]
Focused Treatment Interventions	To increase child safety, reduce risk, identify and build family strengths, and clarify responsibility in child maltreatment cases using a multidisciplinary approach.	Families that have experienced abuse	Initial research suggests positive results. [118]	Guidelines and supporting information are available. [119]
Focus on Families	To decrease drug use and enhance parenting skills. Sessions address relapse, family management, and promoting children's success in school.	Maltreating, substance abusing parents	Research indicates positive results. [120]	Training curriculum is available. [121]
Parent-Child Education Program for Physically Abusive Parents	To establish positive parent-child interactions and child rearing methods that are responsive to situational and developmental changes.	Physically abusive parents	Research indicates positive results. [122]	Guidelines and treatment manuals are available. [123]

Exhibit 9-2. (Continued)

Service	Focus	Population	Research	Reference Information
Services for Parents				
Parents Anonymous, Inc.	To provide opportunities to strengthen parenting skills through mutual support, shared leadership, and personal growth in groups co-led by parents and trained facilitators.	At-risk and abusive parents	Generally supported in clinical literature and practice, yet no controlled studies of its efficacy. Limited research supports positive results.[124]	Guidelines, facilitation manual, and supporting information are available.[125]
Services for Parents and Children				
Attachment-Trauma Therapy	To create a secure primary attachment relationship for child and caregiver by increasing communication and building trust.	Caregivers and children	Generally supported in clinical literature and practice, yet no controlled studies of its efficacy.	Guidelines and treatment manual are available.[126]
Behavioral Parent Training Interventions for Conduct-Disordered Children	To teach parents specific skills regarding child-focused behavioral interventions to minimize coercive interactions between parent and child.	Children with conduct disorders and their families	Research indicates positive results.[127]	Guidelines and supporting information are available.[128]
Cognitive-Behavioral and Dynamic Play Therapy	To help children gain insight into their needs and behaviors, and educate parents on age-appropriate sexual behavior through behavior modification techniques.	Sexually abused children ages 6 to 12 with sexual behavior problems and their parents	Generally supported in clinical literature and practice, yet no controlled studies of its efficacy.	Guidelines, treatment manual, and supporting information are available.[129]
Family Preservation Services	To allow children to remain safely in their own homes by building on family strengths and reducing family deficits through frequent individualized services.	Families in crisis or with chronic problems	Most evaluations of family preservation services have focused on intensive family preservation services (see below).	Supporting information is available.[130]
Family Resolution Therapy	To develop long-term resolution for family relationships, which may range from full-family reunification to termination of parent-child contacts. Concerned with the latter stages of treatment process.	Families where sexual or physical abuse has occurred, and where professional intervention with family is complete	Generally supported in clinical literature and practice, yet no controlled studies of its efficacy.	Guidelines and supporting information are available.[131]
Intensive Family	To prevent out-of-home placement and reduce the risk of child maltreatment by changing	Families whose children have been	Research varies regarding the effectiveness of this intervention.[132]	Supporting information is available.[133]

Exhibit 9-2. (Continued)

Service	Focus	Population	Research	Reference Information
Services for Parents and Children				
Preservation Services	behaviors and increasing skills through intensive, time-limited, and comprehensive services.	identified at risk for placement		
Physical Abuse-focused, Cognitive-behavioral Treatment for Individual Child and Parent	To address beliefs about abuse and violence and improve skills to enhance emotional control and reduce violent behavior. Children and parents work with separate therapists for 12 to 16 sessions.	Physically abusive parents and their children	Research indicates positive results.[134]	Supporting information is available.[135]
Integrative Developmental Model for Treatment of Dissociative Symptomatology	To address dissociative behavior by teaching the child and parents alternative communication strategies and by helping the family learn new interactive patterns.	Children with dissociative symptoms and their families	Generally supported in clinical literature and practice, yet no controlled studies of its efficacy.	Guidelines, treatment manual, and supporting information are available.[136]
Multisystemic Therapy	To assess the "fit" between identified problems and broader systemic issues, and implement a tailored, action-oriented intervention.	Maltreated children and their families	Research indicates positive results.[137]	Supporting information is available.[138]
Nurturing Parenting Programs	To teach nurturing skills and discipline while reinforcing positive family values. Programs are available for different target populations based on child's age, family's culture, and special needs.	Families at risk of physical abuse or neglect	Research indicates positive results.[139]	Training manual is available.[140]
Parent-Child Interaction Therapy	To improve the quality of the parent-child relationship by decreasing child behavior problems and increasing positive parent behaviors.	Children ages 2 to 8 years and their parents	Research indicates positive results.[141]	Treatment manual and supporting information are available.[142]
Parents United: Child Sexual Abuse Treatment Program	To offer clinical and support services to individuals affected by sexual abuse through group sessions.	Victims, offenders, adults molested as children, and their support persons	Generally supported in clinical literature and practice, yet no controlled studies of its efficacy.	Guidelines, treatment manual, and supporting information are available.[143]

Exhibit 9-2. (Continued)

Service	Focus	Population	Research	Reference Information
Services for Parents and Children				
Physical Abuse-informed Family Therapy	To promote cooperation, develop shared views about the value of non-coercive interaction, and increase skills of family members.	Physically abusive parents and their children	Research indicates positive results. [144]	Guidelines and supporting information are available. [145]
Project 12-Ways	To deliver 12 services, including parent-child training, stress reduction for parents, basic skill training for children, money management training, behavior management, problem solving, and marital counseling.	Families who have experienced abuse or neglect, or are at risk	Initial research studies suggest positive results; however, potential for replication is unclear. [146]	Supporting information is available. [147]
Strengthening Families Program	To strengthen family attachment while addressing substance abuse. Interventions consist of parent training, social and life skills training for children, and family practice sessions.	Families who are at risk of substance abuse	Research indicates positive results. [148]	Supporting information is available. [149]
Strengthening Multiethnic Families and Communities	To decrease risk factors related to violence through a training program with five components: cultural or spiritual, enhancing relationships, positive discipline, rites of passage, and community involvement.	Parents of children ages 3 to 18 from diverse ethnic and cultural backgrounds	Research indicates positive results [150]	Training manual is available. [151]
Therapeutic Child Development Program	To provide children with a consistent, safe, monitored environment, while also providing parents with educational and support services.	Abused preschool children and their parents	Research indicates positive results [152]	Guidelines and supporting information are available. [153]
Trauma-focused, Cognitive-behavioral Therapy	To reduce children's negative emotional and behavioral responses and correct maladaptive beliefs related to abusive experiences. Used in individual, family, and group therapy, and in office-based and school-based settings.	Sexually abused children and individuals exposed to other traumatic events	Research indicates positive results. [154]	Guidelines, treatment manual, and supporting information are available. [155]
Trauma-focused, Integrative-eclectic Therapy	To increase safety in the home, enhance the quality of the parent-child relationship, and assist children and teenagers by addressing issues of shame and self-blame.	Abused children, their parents, or families	Generally supported in clinical literature and practice, yet no controlled studies of its efficacy.	Guidelines, treatment manual, and supporting information are available. [156]

For more information on these treatment and intervention services, please visit the *User Manual Series* Web site at www.calib.com/nccanch/pubs/usermanual.cfm or review the related literature. Inclusion in this exhibit does not reflect an endorsement of the treatment or intervention by the U.S. Department of Health and Human Services.

10. FAMILY PROGRESS

Determining the extent and nature of family progress is central to child protective services (CPS) intervention. Monitoring change should begin as soon as intervention is implemented, and should continue throughout the life of a case until the family- and program-level outcomes have been achieved. This chapter explores caseworker decisions based on the collection and analysis of information on family progress.

Collect and Organize Information on Family Progress

The process of evaluating family progress is a continual case management function. Once the case plan is established, each contact with the children and family should focus on assessing the progress being made to achieve established outcomes, goals, and tasks, and to reassess safety. Formal case evaluations should occur at regular intervals, however, specifically to measure progress and to redesign case plans if appropriate. Caseworkers should evaluate family progress at least every 3 to 6 months by following these steps:

- **Review the case plan.** Outcomes, goals, and tasks are written in measurable terms so that they can be used to determine progress toward reducing risk and treating the effects of maltreatment. Many agencies have a review form that should be used to document the change process.

- **Collect information from all service providers.** Intervention and service provision are typically a collaborative effort between CPS and other agencies or individual providers. Consequently, the evaluation of family progress must also be a collaborative venture. Referrals to service providers should clearly specify the number, frequency, and methods of reports expected. The caseworker must also clearly communicate expectations for reporting concerns, observable changes, and family progress. It is the caseworker's responsibility to ensure the submission of these reports and to request meetings with service providers, if indicated. In addition, when the court is involved, it is appropriate to obtain information from the parent's attorney, the child's attorney, and the court-appointed special advocate (CASA) or the Guardian ad Litem (GAL).

- **Engage the child and family in reviewing progress.** Using the case plan as a framework for communication, the caseworker should meet with the family to review progress jointly. Family members should be asked about their perceptions of task, goal, and outcome progress. If these have been established in measurable terms, there should be agreement about the level of progress. Any differences in the family's and caseworker's perceptions should be clarified in the written evaluation. The caseworker should then discuss any need to revise the case plan.This is also the family's opportunity to identify any barriers to participation in the case plan or any new problems or concerns to be discussed.

- **Measure family progress.** Change is measured during the evaluation of family progress on two levels. The most critical risk factors (identified during family assessment) should be assessed. Specifically, what changes have been made in the conditions and behaviors causing the risk of maltreatment? The same criteria used to assess these factors during the family assessment should be used again to understand the current level of risk. The second level of measurement evaluates the extent to which specific outcomes, goals, and tasks have been accomplished by the family, caseworker, and service provider.

- **Document family progress.** Thorough documentation allows the caseworker to measure family progress between the initial assessment and current evaluation. This documentation provides the basis for many case decisions.

Analyze and Evaluate Family Progress

Once the information has been collected, the caseworker should analyze it to help determine progress and decide on further actions. The focus of the evaluation of family progress should address the following issues:

- **Is the child safe? Have the protective factors, strengths, or safety factors changed, thereby warranting the development of a safety plan or a change in an existing safety plan?** Safety should be assessed at specific times throughout the life of the case—minimally at receipt of referral, during first contact with the family, at the conclusion of the initial assessment or investigation, during establishment of the case plan, at the case review, and at case closure. Assessing safety requires caseworkers to identify and examine the risk factors affecting the child's safety. To re-evaluate safety, the caseworker examines the factors to determine whether there have been any changes in the family situation requiring the implementation of a safety plan, the change or elimination of a safety plan, or the taking of necessary action to insure the safety of the child.

- **What changes have occurred in the factors contributing to the risk of maltreatment?** Change is measured by comparing the conditions and behaviors identified during the family assessment to the current functioning of the family and individual family members.

- **What progress has been made toward achieving case goals and outcomes?** When goals and outcomes are specific, measurable, achievable, realistic, and time-limited, they can be used to determine the level of change. Goals should indicate what specifically will be different in the family when the conditions or behaviors contributing to the risk of maltreatment have been successfully addressed.

- **How effective have the services been in achieving outcomes and goals? If ineffective, what adjustments need to be made to find effective services for children and families?** The caseworker is responsible for assessing the extent to which services are being provided as planned and for determining whether services should be altered to enhance risk reduction. Specific questions that should be considered are:
  - Have the services been provided in a timely manner?
  - Has the family participated in services as scheduled?
  - Has the service provider developed rapport with the family?
  - Is there a need to alter the plan of service based on changes in the family?

- **What is the current level of risk in the family?** Based on the changes made by family members, the caseworker must determine the current level of risk of maltreatment to the children. The factors that were used to determine the level of risk of maltreatment during the initial assessment or investigation and family assessment should be applied again.

- **Have the risk factors been reduced sufficiently so that the parents or caregivers can protect their children and meet their developmental needs, allowing the case to be closed?** One of the primary purposes of CPS intervention is to help the family change the behaviors and conditions that will likely lead to maltreatment in the future. The caseworker should also be realistic about change. While it may not be possible to help a family reach optimal levels of functioning in relation to all of the conditions and behaviors contributing to the risk of maltreatment, it may be possible to help a family change the most critical issues so that the parent is able to provide sufficient care for the child. The criteria used to determine whether to close the case should be minimal, not optimal standards. If risk is reduced sufficiently and the child is safe, then the case should be closed. Ongoing support for the family and treatment for the child by other professionals may be needed, however, even after the case has been closed by CPS.

- **Is reunification likely in the required time frame or is an alternate permanency plan needed?** Assessment of the appropriateness of reunification or other permanent placement is based on whether:
  - Current level of threats to safety have been reduced to a level that ensures that the family can protect the child in the home;
  - Protective factors or strengths have been developed to respond to future threats;
  - Social supports are available to sustain the strengths and prevent the return of threats to safety.[157]

After evaluating family progress, the caseworker must discuss with the casework supervisor the decisions made and the next steps. Chapter 13, "Supervision, Consultation, and Support," provides information on supervisory consultation.

11. CASE CLOSURE

Termination is the process of ending the caseworker's relationship with the family and providing the family with the opportunity to put closure on their relationship with the caseworker (and possibly with the agency). Depending on the nature of the relationship between the caseworker and the children and family, what was accomplished, and the nature of the closure, termination may generate a range of feelings.[158] Involuntary clients are less likely than voluntary clients to experience regret at closure. Since they did not seek contact, termination may be approached with relief that an unsought pressure will be removed. However, if the caseworker has been able to work through the resistance and engage the family in the intervention process, they may experience regret. This is a positive sign because family members will feel these feelings only if the relationship or the work has come to be valued.[159]

Types of Case Closure

For the most part, child protective services (CPS) case closures will be one of four types:

- **Termination.** If all of the outcomes have been achieved, or if the family feels unready or unwilling to work toward those outcomes, and there is sufficient reason to believe that the child is safe (even though there may still be some risk of maltreatment), then the caseworker may agree that ending the relationship with the family is appropriate. This also means that the family will not move on to work with other service providers.

- **Referral.** If the family is able or willing to continue to work with other service providers toward some or all of the outcomes that have not yet been accomplished, then the caseworker will work with the family to identify other strategies to support the work. This may include referral to other agencies or providers, or it may include the identification of such informal supports as family or friends who will encourage and guide them.

- **Transfer.** If the caseworker's time with the family is ending, but they will work with another caseworker in the agency, then the ending work with the family will, in part, focus on developing a relationship with the new caseworker. If the caseworker had developed a positive relationship with the family, it is desirable that both the current and new caseworker have at least one joint session to introduce the colleague to the client.

- **Discontinuation by family.** If the family is receiving voluntary services and makes a unilateral decision to end their relationship with the agency, this decision may be communicated behaviorally. For example, family members may gradually or suddenly stop keeping scheduled appointments and not respond to outreach attempts to reconnect. The caseworker must consult with the supervisor to examine the agency's response.[160] Discontinuation by the family is the least desirable type of case closing, but likely to happen some of the time. The family, however, cannot legally discontinue services if the court mandates the services.

Process of Case Closure

Caseworkers should take the following steps in terminating services:

- **Review risk reduction.** Talk with the family about the specific accomplishments, emphasizing the positive change in behaviors and conditions.

- **Review tasks completed.** Discuss any obstacles encountered and focus on the successes and knowledge obtained.

- **Review general steps in problem solving.** Remind families of the strides made as well as the methods they can use when future problems arise.

- **Consider any remaining needs or concerns.** Help family members plan how to maintain the changes. Discuss any potential obstacles they may encounter as well as strategies for overcoming them.[161]

Community Collaboration during Case Closure

When a family has received services from CPS and other agencies or individual providers, the evaluation of family progress must be a collaborative venture. The caseworker should determine the family's progress based on information from all service providers. In some cases, it may be appropriate to convene a team meeting to review the family's progress in relation to the assessment, case plan, and service agreement(s) prior to case closure.

When the court is involved in a case that is being closed, the court must approve case closure as well as terminate any existing court orders. Depending on the jurisdiction, this may involve written notification to the court or a hearing.

Family Involvement during Case Closure

Each child and family's experience of and response to ending the relationship will be unique. Feelings can range from relief, satisfaction, and happiness to sadness, loss, anger, powerlessness, fear, rejection, denial, and ambivalence. It is important to encourage family members to discuss their feelings. Even if it has been a difficult relationship, the caseworker should provide some positive statement of closure.[162]

Some practical steps to involve the family include:

- Meeting with the family to discuss the case closure;
- Anticipating a family-created crisis that may occur as a reaction to independence resulting from the planned closure;
- Reviewing the progress made as a result of CPS involvement;
- Referring the family to any additional resources needed;
- Leaving the door open for services should they be needed in the future, including providing appropriate contact information.

12. EFFECTIVE DOCUMENTATION

Case documentation provides accountability for both the activities and the results of the agency's work. In child protective services (CPS), case records and information systems must carefully document: (1) contact information; (2) the findings of the assessments; (3) decisions at each stage of the case process; (4) interventions provided to the family both directly and indirectly; (5) the progress toward goal achievement, including risk reduction; (6) the outcomes of intervention; and (7) the nature of partnerships with community agencies. This chapter describes the primary purposes of record- keeping, principles about the way both paper and automated records should be maintained, and content that should be documented at each step of the process. The strategies outlined here not only assure accountability to others, but also facilitate a way of thinking and a process to measure the results of the agency's work with families and children.[163]

Purposes of Child Protective Services Record-Keeping

The key purposes for keeping records are to:

- **Guide the CPS process.** Case records provide an ongoing "picture" of the nature of CPS involvement with families, the progress toward achieving outcomes, and the basis of decisions that eventually lead to case closure. The process of record-keeping itself helps to clarify and focus CPS work.

- **Provide accountability for the agency and the caseworker.** Records should describe who is and is not served (including any other household members who may not be participating in services), the kinds of services provided (or not provided due to availability or level of service issues), the basis for all decisions, the degree to which policies and procedures are implemented, and other aspects of accountability and quality control. The record provides a statement about the quality of CPS work that may decrease personal liability should legal action be taken against the agency or a caseworker.

- **Serve as a therapeutic tool for the caseworker and the family.** Case records can demonstrate the way in which the caseworker and family collaborate to define the purpose of CPS work, including the goals and outcomes that will reduce the risk of maltreatment, and serve to evaluate the progress toward them. Some CPS agencies are using instruments and tools that seek input, and, therefore, the record itself provides an illustration of this collaborative process.

- **Organize the caseworker's thinking about the work.** Structured presentation of factual information leads to more in-depth assessment and treatment planning. Sloppy recording and disorganized thinking go hand-in-hand and will likely lead to poor service delivery to clients.[164]

In addition to the primary purposes of record- keeping listed above, the case record becomes a means for supervisory review, statistical reporting and research, and interdisciplinary communication.

Content of Case Records

Case records should factually document what CPS does in terms of assessment and intervention, as well as the results of CPS-facilitated interventions and treatment, which serve the outcomes of child safety, permanence, and well-being. Family records, whether paper or automated, should include:

- Information about the nature and extent of the referral or report; identify demographic data on the child, family, and significant others; and the response of the agency to the referral.
- A record of all dates and length of contacts, including in-person and telephone interviews with all family members, collateral sources, and multidisciplinary team, as well as the location and purposes of these contacts.
- Documentation that the family has been informed of the agency's policy on the release of information from the record.
- Information about the initial assessment, including documentation of what may have already occurred (e.g., the report of alleged child maltreatment), as well as the assessment of the risk to and safety of the child.
- Information about any diagnostic procedures that may have been part of the initial assessment (e.g., medical evaluations, x-rays, or other medical tests; psychological evaluations; and alcohol or drug assessments).
- Clear documentation of initial decisions with respect to substantiation of the alleged maltreatment, risk assessment and safety evaluation, basis for any placement in out-ofhome care or court referral (if necessary), and reasons for continued agency involvement or for terminating services.
- The safety plan, if one was developed, and documentation of referrals to other programs, agencies, or persons who will participate in the implementation of the safety plan.

- A record of the family assessment (including risks and strengths) and a delineation of the treatment and intervention needs of the child, caregivers, and the family.
- A description of any criminal, juvenile, or family court involvement and the status of any pending legal action in which the client may be involved.
- The case plan with specific measurable goals, as well as a description of the process used to develop the plan.
- Specification of the intervention outcomes, which, if achieved, will reduce the risks and address the effects of maltreatment. These intervention outcomes should lead to the achievement of child safety, permanency, and child and family well-being.
- Documentation of the case activities and their outcomes, including information from all community practitioners providing intervention or treatment (written reports should be requested from all providers) and information about the family's response to intervention and treatment.
- Information about the progress toward the achievement of outcomes, completion of case plans, risk reduction process, and reunification of children with their families or other permanency options.
- Information provided to the court, if court involvement was necessary.
- Inclusion of a case-closing summary that describes:
    - Outline summarizing the original reason for referral;
    - Process of closure with the family;
    - Outcomes and goals established with the family;
    - Nature of the services provided and the activities undertaken by the various practitioners and the family;
    - Description about the level of progress accomplished with respect to outcomes and goals;
    - Summary of any new reports of maltreatment that may have occurred during intervention;
    - Assessment of risk and safety as it now exists;
    - Problems or goals that remain unresolved or unaccomplished;
    - Reasons for closing the case.[165]

Principles of Record-Keeping

The case record is a professional document and tool. As such, it should be completed in a timely and professional manner, and confidentiality should be respected at all times. This means that appropriate controls should be in place to ensure the security of paper and automated files.

Caseworkers should:

- Maintain only information that is relevant and necessary to the agency's purposes. Facts should be recorded and distinguished from opinions. When opinions are offered, their basis should be documented (e.g., Mr. Smith appeared to be intoxicated; his eyes were red; he had difficulty standing without losing his balance; his breath smelled of alcohol).

- Never record details of clients' intimate lives or their political, religious, or other personal views, unless this information is relevant to CPS purposes.
- Record as much information as possible based on direct communication with clients.
- Inform clients about the agency's authority to gather information, their right to participate (or not) in the process, the principal purpose for the use of the information that they provide, the nature and extent of the confidentiality of the information, and under what circumstances information in records may be shared with others.
- Never disclose any verbal or written information about clients to other practitioners without a signed "release of information" prior to disclosure. An exception usually exists in State child abuse-reporting laws to provide for the sharing of information between members of a multidisciplinary team. Specific State laws and policies should guide these actions.
- Retain and update records to assure accuracy, relevancy, timeliness, and completeness. Mark errors as such rather than erasing or deleting them.
- Use private dictation facilities when using dictation equipment to protect a client's right to confidentiality.
- Never include process recordings in case files. The primary purpose of a process recording is to build the practitioner's skills. As such, they do not belong in an agency record.
- Obtain the child and family's permission before audiotaping or videotaping any session and inform the client that refusal to allow taping will not affect services.
- Never remove case records from the agency, except in extraordinary circumstances and with special authorization (e.g., if the record was subpoenaed for the court).
- Never leave case records or printouts from the automated file on desks or in other open spaces where others might have access to them.
- Keep case records in locked files. Keys should be issued only to those requiring frequent access to files. There also should be a clear record of the date that the file was removed and by whom. Similar security procedures (e.g., password- protected) should be provided for automated case records.[166]

Quality record-keeping is an integral part of professional CPS practice. When the case record is used as an opportunity to organize the worker's thinking and to integrate an approach to measuring the results of CPS work, it becomes an important part of the CPS process rather than something that only documents the process.

13. SUPERVISION, CONSULTATION AND SUPPORT

Child protective services (CPS) supervisors are responsible for ensuring that the agency mission and goals are accomplished, and that positive outcomes for children and families are achieved through the delivery of competent, sensitive, and timely services. The supervisor is the link between the front-line of service delivery and the upper levels of administration. It is the supervisor who brings the resources of the organization into action at the front line—the point of client contact.[167]

The supervisor has two overarching roles: building the foundation for and maintaining unit functioning, and developing and maintaining staff capacity.[168] These roles are accomplished through the following activities:

- Communicating the agency's mission, policies, and practice guidelines to casework staff;
- Setting standards of performance for staff to assure high-quality practice;
- Assuring that all laws and policies are followed, and staying current with changing policies and procedures;
- Creating a psychological and physical climate that enables staff to feel positive, satisfied, and comfortable about the job so that clients may be better served;
- Helping staff learn what they need to know to effectively perform their jobs through orientation, mentoring, on-the-job training, and coaching;
- Monitoring workloads and unit and staff performance to assure that standards and expectations are successfully achieved;
- Keeping staff apprised of their performance and providing recognition for staff efforts and accomplishments;
- Implementing safety precautions.[169]

This chapter examines the role of the CPS supervisor, including the supervisor's involvement in decision- making, clinical consultations, monitoring, and feedback. Finally, the chapter looks at the ways in which supervisors and peers provide support to caseworkers, prevent burnout, and ensure worker safety.

Supervisory Involvement in Decision-Making

Supervisors must be involved in any casework decision that affects child safety and permanence. The supervisor and caseworker should collaborate to reach consensus on decisions regarding safety and achieving permanence for the child. Since the caseworker is the primary holder of the information, the supervisor should review the caseworker's documentation and meet with the caseworker to analyze the information. The supervisor and caseworker work together to understand and arrive at the most appropriate decision.[170] This approach requires that the supervisor respects the caseworker, works with the caseworker to gather thorough and accurate information from the family and collateral sources, analyzes the information thoughtfully, and draws reasonable conclusions (inferences and deductions). Ultimately, the supervisor is responsible for directing the activities of the worker and will share in any liability that results from the caseworker's action or failure to act.

Supervisory Involvement in Clinical Consultation

Caseworkers are not expected to have all of the answers. There are many avenues available to CPS workers for consultation on cases. Within the CPS unit, caseworkers often turn to their supervisors when they are unsure about how to handle a situation, when they need help with a particular decision, or when they need to discuss their conclusions or ideas with an objective person

---

WHEN TO CONSULT SUPERVISORS ON CASEWORK DECIS

Caseworkers must always consult their supervisors about the following decisions:

- Upon receipt of a report of child abuse or neglect, caseworkers must decide how soon to initiate contact. State laws typically dictate the time frame for initiating the investigation; however, the caseworker and supervisor must make a decision regarding which cases necessitate immediate contact with the child.
- During the first contact with the child and family, the caseworker must decide if the child will be safe while the initial assessment or investigation proceeds. Supervisors review the decision and approve or modify it.
- Upon conclusion of the initial assessment or investigation, and after the decisions regarding the validity of abuse or neglect and the risk assessment have been made, caseworkers and supervisors must determine whether the child will be safe in his or her home with or without continuing CPS intervention.
- If it is determined that the child is unsafe, the caseworker and supervisor must determine which interventions will assure the child's protection in the least intrusive manner possible.
- When the child has been placed in out-of-home care, the reunification recommendation must be made between the caseworker and supervisor.
- When the child has been placed in out-of-home care, the recommendation to change to another permanent goal other than reunification must be made between the caseworker and supervisor.
- At the point of case closure, the caseworker and supervisor must evaluate risk reduction and client progress toward assuring the child's protection and meeting the child's basic developmental needs.

CPS supervisors are responsible for assuring that children are safe, their families are empowered to protect them from harm and meet their basic needs, and effective interventions and services are provided to families. Key aspects of supervision through which this is accomplished are case consultation and supervision or clinical supervision. Case consultation and supervision focuses on the casework relationship including any direct interaction, intervention, or involvement between the caseworker and the children and families. It involves the supervisory practices of review, evaluation, feedback, guidance, direction, and coaching. Specifically, case consultation and supervision focuses on:

- Rapport or the helping relationship between the worker and the client;
- A caseworker's ability to engage the client;
- Risk and safety assessment and the associated decisions or plans;
- Comprehensive family assessment and development of the case plan;
- Essential casework activities to assist the family in changing;
- Client progress review and evaluation;

- Casework decision-making.[171]

In individual supervision, case consultation should occur on an ongoing basis. It may also occur when problems or needs arise. The following case consultation format gives shape to the consultation so it will be focused, goal driven, maximize the use of time, and encourage sharing of expertise:

- Describe briefly why the family came to the attention of CPS.
- Identify the safety issues that need to be immediately addressed.
- Outline what the family wants, what CPS wants, and how the differences can be reconciled.
- Determine the inner resiliencies, strengths, or resources in the family that will provide the foundation for change.
- Examine the success of previous contacts with the family. For example, what was accomplished? What still needs to be accomplished? What has the caseworker contributed to the results, and what has the family contributed to the results?
- Identify the purpose of the next contact with the family. Examine how it ties in with where the family is in the intervention process.
- Assess the caseworker's relationships with each family member. Define what family members need in order to assure that the family is willing and able to experience the process of change and achieve the necessary goals to assure greater permanence, safety, and well-being for the children.
- Describe the specific strategies that will help family members accomplish their goals.
- Discuss what services the family says have been most helpful.
- Determine the level of risk within the family. Identify the risks, the strengths, or protective factors within the family, and how the agency will know when the risk has been reduced.
- Establish what needs to happen in the family for the agency to return the child and what needs to happen in the family to close the case.
- Identify the signs of success for the family.[172]

Peer Consultation

In addition to receiving clinical consultation from their supervisors, caseworkers can also consult other caseworkers in the unit. Experienced and competent CPS caseworkers may have handled similar situations and be able to provide suggestions, guidance, and direction.

Also, group case staffings involving the whole unit are extremely beneficial sources of consultation. In group case staffings, caseworkers present a problematic case. The supervisor and other caseworkers in the unit share their expertise and suggest actions, services, resources, or decisions. Many CPS agencies use case staffings to help with such major case decisions as the return of children to the home and case closure within the entire unit.

Professionals in the community are another source of consultation. Depending on the relationship between the caseworker or the CPS unit and the professional community, informal consultation on cases may be possible. Formal consultation in the form of an evaluation may be necessary, such as in a drug screening or developmental evaluation.

The Child Abuse Prevention and Treatment Act (CAPTA) requires that every State establish a citizen review panel to evaluate State and local CPS agencies, their implementation of CAPTA, and their coordination of foster care and adoption services. The inclusion of community members can often bring a fresh perspective to the CPS case review process, as well as provide an opportunity for the community to better understand CPS. Citizen review of case plans in cases where the child has been placed in foster care can also be a source of information and assistance.

In addition, multidisciplinary case reviews are excellent resources for CPS staff. Not only do these case reviews provide consultation from other disciplines on a particular case, they also provide opportunities to address coordination and collaboration issues as well.

Supervisory Monitoring of Casework Practice

Since supervisors are ultimately responsible for assuring accomplishment of program outcomes and are accountable for what happens in each case, they must have systems in place to monitor practice. There are three methods that the supervisor can use to learn what caseworkers are doing with clients:

- Reviewing casework documentation
- Providing individual supervision
- Observing caseworkers with clients

Documentation is an essential part of casework practice. (See Chapter 12, "Effective Documentation," for a more detailed description of what and how to document case activities and what information to include.) Supervisors should review case documentation on a regular and systematic basis. Review of case documentation provides the supervisor with information about the frequency and content of caseworker-client contacts; the family's strengths, needs, and risks; the plan to assure safety; casework decisions; services or interventions to reduce risk; progress toward outcomes; and any changes in the child and family's situation.

As stated previously, supervisors should have scheduled weekly individual conferences with staff. Supervisors should have a monitoring system in place that assures that each case is discussed in depth on at least a monthly basis. This will enable supervisors to remain apprised of actions taken or needed in cases, progress toward change or risk reduction, and casework decisions. It also will enable the supervisor to provide consultation, guidance, direction, and coaching to caseworkers regarding casework practice.

Finally, supervisors do not truly know a caseworker's effectiveness in working with clients unless they observe caseworker-client interaction directly. Regular observation should be conducted with all caseworkers. There are many opportunities for observation, including:

- Home visits
- Office visits
- Court hearings

- Supervised family-child visits
- Case staffings and reviews
- Family group conferences or meetings

The observations can be structured in a number of ways, depending on what is negotiated between the caseworker, supervisor, and family. For example, the caseworker may feel "stuck" in a case and, with the family's permission, would like consultation from an objective observer.

Based on the review and evaluation of the caseworker's efforts with families, the supervisor recognizes the caseworker's efforts and accomplishments and provides positive feedback on the specific casework practices that he or she is doing well. Areas and skills needing improvement also are addressed, as well as ways to do so.

Caseworker Safety

Since any CPS case has the potential for unexpected confrontation, supervisors and caseworkers must work together to ensure worker safety. Difficulties may occur at any point in the CPS process, but threats and volatile situations are more likely to occur during the initial assessment or investigation, during crisis situations, and when major actions are taken (e.g., the removal of the child).

The first step in ensuring caseworker safety is to assess the risk of the situation before the initial contact. Before caseworkers conduct an initial assessment, they need to assess the risk to themselves. Questions caseworkers should consider include:

- Is there a history of domestic violence?
- Does the complaint indicate the possibility of a family member being mentally ill, using drugs, or being volatile?
- Are there firearms or other weapons noted in the report?
- Is the family's geographic location extremely isolated or dangerous?
- Is this a second or multiple complaint involving the family?
- Is the initial assessment scheduled after normal working hours?[173]

If the answers to the first four questions are "yes," law enforcement may need to be involved in the initial assessment. If the answers to the last two questions are "yes," two caseworkers may need to conduct the home visit.

Peer Support and Burnout Prevention

Providing child protective services is a complex, demanding, and emotionally draining job. Making decisions that affect the lives of children and families takes a toll on caseworkers. Because working with families experiencing abuse and neglect is difficult, it may elicit multifaceted feelings. In order to maximize performance and minimize burnout, support systems must be developed within the CPS unit to provide caseworkers with opportunities to discuss and deal with feelings that may range from frustration and helplessness to anger and incompetence. Opportunities to discuss these feelings openly in the unit are essential. However, it is important that when support groups are established they do not degenerate into "gripe sessions," where caseworkers leave feeling worse than when they came to the group. A certain amount of discussion of feelings is cathartic; a positive outcome, however, must result for caseworkers to benefit from the discussion. In addition, whenever crises occur in cases (e.g., a child is reinjured or a child must be removed from his or her family) the caseworker involved needs extra support and guidance.

Effective supervision is one of the key factors in staff retention. An effective supervisor demonstrates empathy toward the needs and feelings of CPS staff. In addition, the supervisor should facilitate the development and maintenance of a cohesive work team. Group cohesion provides emotional support to staff, as well as concrete assistance in carrying out case activities.

TAKING CARE OF YOURSELF

CPS caseworkers need support in order to find a balance between their professional and personal lives. Due to stress inherent in CPS work, it is important that workers find effective ways to unwind and relax. It is important to:

- Be aware of the potential for burnout, stress, and trauma that can occur in child welfare work;
- Identify and use social supports to prevent burnout and stress while working in the child welfare system;
- Look to supervisors, peers, and interdisciplinary teams to talk about difficult client situations, including fatalities and serious injury situations;
- Be alert to signs of vicarious trauma and take steps to seek help when these signs endure and affect the quality of practice.

Conclusion

Working with CPS is usually challenging for all involved—children and families, professional and citizen partners, and caseworkers. Children and families are often fearful of and upset by CPS involvement in their lives, particularly due to the uncertainty associated with the process. Professional and citizen partners sometimes struggle with initiating and identifying their roles in addressing child maltreatment issues. The CPS caseworker must walk a fine line between following the legal mandate to protect maltreated children and recognizing parents' rights to rear their children as they deem appropriate. Additionally, CPS caseworkers are consistently confronted with numerous and multifaceted problems that affect many of the families involved with CPS, such as substance abuse, mental illness, domestic violence, and poverty. This manual is intended to address the concerns of these various audiences, as well as to serve as a practical and user-friendly guide in addressing and effectively responding to the ever-changing demands in the child welfare field.

APPENDIX A. GLOSSARY OF TERMS

Adjudicatory Hearings — held by the juvenile and family court to determine whether a child has been maltreated or whether another legal basis exists for the State to intervene to protect the child.

Adoption and Safe Families Act (ASFA) — signed into law November 1997 and designed to improve the safety of children, to promote adoption and other permanent homes for children who need them, and to support families. The law requires CPS agencies to provide more timely and focused assessment and intervention services to the children and families that are served within the CPS system.

CASA — court-appointed special advocates (usually volunteers) who serve to ensure that the needs and interests of a child in child protection judicial proceedings are fully protected.

Case Closure — the process of ending the relationship between the CPS worker and the family that often involves a mutual assessment of progress. Optimally, cases are closed when families have achieved their goals and the risk of maltreatment has been reduced or eliminated.

Case Plan — the casework document that outlines the outcomes, goals, and tasks necessary to be achieved in order to reduce the risk of maltreatment.

Case Planning — the stage of the CPS case process where the CPS caseworker develops a case plan with the family members.

Caseworker Competency — demonstrated professional behaviors based on the knowledge, skills, personal qualities, and values a person holds.

Central Registry — a centralized database containing information on all substantiated/founded reports of child maltreatment in a selected area (typically a State).

Child Abuse Prevention and Treatment Act (CAPTA) — the law (P.L. 93-247) that provides a foundation for a national definition of child abuse and neglect. Reauthorized in October 1996 (P.L. 104-235), it was up for reauthorization at the time of publication. CAPTA defines child abuse and neglect as "at a minimum, any recent act or failure to act on the part of a parent or caretaker, which results in death, serious physical or emotional harm, sexual abuse or exploitation, or an act or failure to act which presents an imminent risk of serious harm."

Child Protective Services (CPS) — the designated social services agency (in most States) to receive reports, investigate, and provide intervention and treatment services to children and families in which child maltreatment has occurred. Frequently, this agency is located within larger public social service agencies, such as Departments of Social Services.

Concurrent Planning — identifies alternative forms of permanency by addressing both reunification or legal permanency with a new parent or caregiver if reunification efforts fail.

Cultural Competence — a set of attitudes, behaviors, and policies that integrates knowledge about groups of people into practices and standards to enhance the quality of services to all cultural groups being served.

Differential Response — an area of CPS reform that offers greater flexibility in responding to allegations of abuse and neglect. Also referred to as "dual track" or "multi-track" response, it permits CPS agencies to respond differentially to children's needs for safety, the degree of risk present, and the family's needs for services and support. See "dual track."

Dispositional Hearings — held by the juvenile and family court to determine the legal resolution of cases after adjudication, such as whether placement of the child in out-of-home care is necessary, and what services the children and family will need to reduce the risk of maltreatment and to address the effects of maltreatment.

Dual Track — term reflecting new CPS response systems that typically combine a nonadversarial service-based assessment track for cases where children are not at immediate risk with a traditional CPS investigative track for cases where children are unsafe or at greater risk for maltreatment. See "differential response."

Evaluation of Family Progress — the stage of the CPS case process where the CPS caseworker measures changes in family behaviors and conditions (risk factors), monitors risk elimination or reduction, assesses strengths, and determines case closure.

Family Assessment — the stage of the child protection process when the CPS caseworker, community treatment provider, and the family reach a mutual understanding regarding the behaviors and conditions that must change to reduce or eliminate the risk of maltreatment, the most critical treatment needs that must be addressed, and the strengths on which to build.

Family Group Conferencing — a family meeting model used by CPS agencies to optimize family strengths in the planning process. This model brings the family, extended family, and others important in the family's life (e.g., friends, clergy, neighbors) together to make decisions regarding how best to ensure safety of the family members.

Family Unity Model — a family meeting model used by CPS agencies to optimize family strengths in the planning process. This model is similar to the Family Group Conferencing model.

Full Disclosure — CPS information to the family regarding the steps in the intervention process, the requirements of CPS, the expectations of the family, the consequences if the family does not fulfill the expectations, and the rights of the parents to ensure that the family completely understands the process.

Guardian ad Litem — a lawyer or lay person who represents a child in juvenile or family court. Usually this person considers the "best interest" of the child and may perform a variety of roles, including those of independent investigator, advocate, advisor, and guardian for the child. A lay person who serves in this role is sometimes known as a court-appointed special advocate or CASA.

Home Visitation Programs — prevention programs that offer a variety of family-focused services to pregnant mothers and families with new babies. Activities frequently encompass structured visits to the family's home and may address positive parenting practices, nonviolent discipline techniques, child development, maternal and child health, available services, and advocacy.

Immunity — established in all child abuse laws to protect reporters from civil law suits and criminal prosecution resulting from filing a report of child abuse and neglect.

Initial Assessment or Investigation — the stage of the CPS case process where the CPS caseworker determines the validity of the child maltreatment report, assesses the risk of maltreatment, determines if the child is safe, develops a safety plan if needed to assure the child's protection, and determines services needed.

Intake — the stage of the CPS case process where the CPS caseworker screens and accepts reports of child maltreatment.

Interview Protocol — a structured format to ensure that all family members are seen in a planned strategy, that community providers collaborate, and that information gathering is thorough.

Juvenile and Family Courts — established in most States to resolve conflict and to otherwise intervene in the lives of families in a manner that promotes the best interest of children. These courts specialize in areas such as child maltreatment, domestic violence, juvenile delinquency, divorce, child custody, and child support.

Kinship Care — formal child placement by the juvenile court and child welfare agency in the home of a child's relative.

Liaison — the designation of a person within an organization who has responsibility for facilitating communication, collaboration, and coordination between agencies involved in the child protection system.

Mandated Reporter — people required by State statutes to report suspected child abuse and neglect to the proper authorities (usually CPS or law enforcement agencies). Mandated reporters typically include professionals such as educators and other school personnel, health care and mental health professionals, social workers, childcare providers, and law enforcement officers, but some States require all citizens to be mandated reporters.

Multidisciplinary Team — established between agencies and professionals within the child protection system to discuss cases of child abuse and neglect and to aid in decisions at various stages of the CPS case process. These terms may also be designated by different names, including child protection teams, interdisciplinary teams, or case consultation teams.

Neglect — the failure to provide for the child's basic needs. Neglect can be physical, educational, or emotional. *Physical neglect* can include not providing adequate food or clothing, appropriate medical care, supervision, or proper weather protection (heat or coats). *Educational neglect* includes failure to provide appropriate schooling, special educational needs, or allowing excessive truancies. *Psychological neglect* includes the lack of any emotional support and love, chronic inattention to the child, exposure to spouse abuse, or drug and alcohol abuse.

Out-of-Home Care — child care, foster care, or residential care provided by persons, organizations, and institutions to children who are placed outside their families, usually under the jurisdiction of juvenile or family court.

Parent or caretaker — person responsible for the care of the child.

***Parens Patriae* Doctrine** — originating in feudal England, a doctrine that vests in the State a right of guardianship of minors. This concept has gradually evolved into the principle that the community, in addition to the parent, has a strong interest in the care and nurturing of children. Schools, juvenile courts, and social service agencies all derive their authority from the State's power to ensure the protection and rights of children as a unique class.

Physical Abuse — the inflicting of a nonaccidental physical injury upon a child. This may include, burning, hitting, punching, shaking, kicking, beating, or otherwise harming a child. It may, however, have been the result of over-discipline or physical punishment that is inappropriate to the child's age.

Primary Prevention — activities geared to a sample of the general population to prevent child abuse and neglect from occurring. Also referred to as "universal prevention."

Protocol — an interagency agreement that delineates joint roles and responsibilities by establishing criteria and procedures for working together on cases of child abuse and neglect.

Protective Factors — strengths and resources that appear to mediate or serve as a "buffer" against risk factors that contribute to vulnerability to maltreatment or against the negative effects of maltreatment experiences.

Psychological Maltreatment — a pattern of caregiver behavior or extreme incidents that convey to children that they are worthless, flawed, unloved, unwanted, endangered, or only of value to meeting another's needs. This can include parents or caretakers using extreme or bizarre forms of punishment or threatening or terrorizing a child. The term "psychological maltreatment" is also known as emotional abuse or neglect, verbal abuse, or mental abuse.

Response Time — a determination made by CPS and law enforcement regarding the immediacy of the response needed to a report of child abuse or neglect.

Review Hearings — held by the juvenile and family court to review dispositions (usually every 6 months) and to determine the need to maintain placement in out-of-home care or court jurisdiction of a child.

Risk — the likelihood that a child will be maltreated in the future.

Risk Assessment — to assess and measure the likelihood that a child will be maltreated in the future, frequently through the use of checklists, matrices, scales, and other methods of measurement.

Risk Factors — behaviors and conditions present in the child, parent, or family that will likely contribute to child maltreatment occurring in the future.

Safety — absence of an imminent or immediate threat of moderate-to-serious harm to the child.

Safety Assessment — a part of the CPS case process in which available information is analyzed to identify whether a child is in immediate danger of moderate or serious harm.

Safety Plan — a casework document developed when it is determined that the child is in imminent risk of serious harm. In the safety plan, the caseworker targets the factors that are causing or contributing to the risk of imminent serious harm to the child, and identifies, along with the family, the interventions that will control the safety factors and assure the child's protection.

Secondary Prevention — activities targeted to prevent breakdowns and dysfunctions among families who have been identified as at risk for abuse and neglect.

Service Agreement — the casework document developed between the CPS caseworker and the family that outlines the tasks necessary to achieve goals and outcomes necessary for risk reduction.

Service Provision — the stage of the CPS casework process when CPS and other service providers provide specific services geared toward the reduction of risk of maltreatment.

Sexual Abuse — inappropriate adolescent or adult sexual behavior with a child. It includes fondling a child's genitals, making the child fondle the adult's genitals, intercourse, incest, rape, sodomy, exhibitionism, sexual exploitation, or exposure to pornography. To be considered child abuse, these acts have to be committed by a person responsible for the care of a child (for example a baby-sitter, a parent, or a daycare provider) or related to the child. If a stranger commits these acts, it would be considered sexual assault and handled solely be the police and criminal courts.

Substantiated — an investigation disposition concluding that the allegation of maltreatment or risk of maltreatment was supported or founded by State law or State policy. A CPS determination means that credible evidence exists that child abuse or neglect has occurred.

Tertiary Prevention — treatment efforts geared to address situations where child maltreatment has already occurred with the goals of preventing child maltreatment from occurring in the future and of avoiding the harmful effects of child maltreatment.

Treatment — the stage of the child protection case process when specific services are provided by CPS and other providers to reduce the risk of maltreatment, support families in meeting case goals, and address the effects of maltreatment.

Universal Prevention — activities and services directed at the general public with the goal of stopping the occurrence of maltreatment before it starts. Also referred to as "primary prevention."

Unsubstantiated (not substantiated) — an investigation disposition that determines that there is not sufficient evidence under State law or policy to conclude that the child has been maltreated or at risk of maltreatment. A CPS determination means that credible evidence does not exist that child abuse or neglect has occurred.

APPENDIX B. RESOURCE LISTINGS OF SELECTED NATIONAL ORGANIZATIONS CONCERNED WITH CHILD MALTREATMENT

Listed below are several representatives of the many national organizations and groups that deal with various aspects of child maltreatment. Please visit www.calib.com/nccanch to view a more comprehensive list of resources and visit www.calib.com/nccanch /database to view an organization database. Inclusion on this list is for information purposes and does not constitute an endorsement by the Office on Child Abuse and Neglect or the Children's Bureau.

Child Welfare Organizations

American Public Human Services Children's Division
address: 63 Inverness Dr., East Englewood, CO 80112-5117
phone: (800) 227-4645
               (303) 792-9900
fax: (303) 792-5333
e-mail: children@americanhumane.org
Web site: www.americanhumane.org
Conducts research, analysis, and training to help public and private agencies respond to child maltreatment.

American Public Human Services Association
address: 810 First St., NE, Suite 500 Washington, DC 20002-4267
phone: (202) 682-0100
fax: (202) 289-6555
Web site: www.aphsa.org

Addresses program and policy issues related to the administration and delivery of publicly funded human services. Professional membership organization.

American Professional Society on the Abuse of Children
address: 940 N.E. 13th St. CHO 3B-3406, Oklahoma City, OK 73104
phone: (405) 271-8202
fax: (405) 271-2931
e-mail: tricia-williams@ouhsc.edu
Web site: www.apsac.org

Provides professional education, promotes research to inform effective practice, and addresses public policy issues. Professional membership organization.

AVANCE Family Support and Education Program
address: 301 South Frio, Suite 380 San Antonio, TX 78207
phone: (210) 270-4630
fax: (210) 270-4612
Web site: www.avance.org

Operates a national training center to share and disseminate information, material, and curricula to service providers and policy-makers interested in supporting high-risk Hispanic families.

Child Welfare League of America
address: 440 First St., NW, Third Floor Washington, DC 20001-2085
phone: (202) 638-2952
fax: (202) 638-4004
Web site: www.cwla.org

Provides training, consultation, and technical assistance to child welfare professionals and agencies while also educating the public about emerging issues affecting children.

National Black Child Development Institute
address: 1023 15th St., NW, Suite 600 Washington, DC 20005
phone: (202) 387-1281
fax: (202) 234-1738
e-mail: moreinfo@nbcdi.org
Web site: www.nbcdi.org

Operates programs and sponsors a national training conference through Howard University to improve and protect the well-being of African-American children.

National Children's Advocacy Center
address: 00 Westside Sq., Suite 700 Huntsville AL 35801

phone: 256) 533-0531
fax: (256) 534-6883
e-mail: webmaster@ncac-hsv.org
Web site: www.ncac-hsv.org
Provides prevention, intervention, and treatment services to physically and sexually abused children and their families within a child-focused team approach.

National Indian Child Welfare Association
address: 5100 SW Macadam Ave., Suite 300 Portland, OR 97201
phone: (503) 222-4044
fax: (503) 222-4007
e-mail: info@nicwa.org
Web site: www.nicwa.org
Disseminates information and provides technical assistance on Indian child welfare issues. Supports community development and advocacy efforts to facilitate tribal responses to the needs of families and children.

National Resource Centers

National Resource Center on Child Maltreatment
address: Child Welfare Institute 3950 Shackleford Rd., Suite 175 Duluth, GA 30096
phone: (770) 935-8484
fax: (770) 935-0344
e-mail: tsmith@gocwi.org
Web site: www.gocwi.org/nrccm
Helps States, local agencies, and Tribes develop effective and efficient child protective services systems. Jointly operated by the Child Welfare Institute and ACTION for Child Protection, it responds to needs related to prevention, identification, intervention, and treatment of child abuse and neglect.

National Resource Center on Domestic Violence: Child Protection and Custody
address: Family Violence Department National Council of Juvenile and
              Family Court Judges P.O. Box 8970 Reno, NV 89507
phone: (800) 527-3223
fax: (775) 784-6160
e-mail: info@dvlawsearch.com
Web site: www.nationalcouncilfvd.org/res_center
Promotes improved court responses to family violence through demonstration programs, professional training, technical assistance, national conferences, and publications.

National Child Welfare Resource Center for Family-Centered Practice
address: Learning Systems Group 1150 Connecticut Ave., NW,
              Suite 1100 Washington, DC 20036
phone: (800) 628-8442

fax: (202) 628-3812
e-mail: info@cwresource.org
Web site: www.cwresource.org
Helps child welfare agencies and Tribes use family- centered practice to implement the tenets of the Adoption and Safe Families Act to ensure the safety and well-being of children while meeting the needs of families.

National Child Welfare Resource Center on Legal and Judicial Issues

address: ABA Center on Children and the Law 740 15th St., NW
                Washington, DC 20005-1019
phone: (800) 285-2221 (Service Center)
                (202) 662-1720
fax: (202) 662-1755
e-mail: ctrchildlaw@abanet.org
Web site: www.abanet.org/child
Promotes improvement of laws and policies affecting children and provides education in child- related law.

Prevention Organizations

National Alliance of Children's Trust and Prevention Funds

address: Michigan State University Department of Psychology East Lansing,
                MI 48824-1117
phone: (517) 432-5096
fax: (517) 432-2476
e-mail: millsda@msu.edu
Web site: www.ctfalliance.org
Assists State children's trust and prevention funds to strengthen families and protect children from harm.

Prevent Child Abuse America

address: 200 South Michigan Ave., 17th Floor Chicago, IL 60604-2404
phone: (800) 835-2671 (orders)
                (312) 663-3520
fax: (312) 939-8962
e-mail: mailbox@preventchildabuse.org
Web site: www.preventchildabuse.org
Conducts prevention activities such as public awareness campaigns, advocacy, networking, research, and publishing, and provides information and statistics on child abuse.

Shaken Baby Syndrome Prevention Plus

address: 649 Main St., Suite B Groveport, OH 43125
phone: (800) 858-5222
                (614) 836-8360

fax: (614) 836-8359
e-mail: sbspp@aol.com
Web site: www.sbsplus.com

Develops, studies, and disseminates information and materials designed to prevent shaken baby syndrome and other forms of child abuse and to increase positive parenting and child care.

Community Partners

The Center for Faith-Based and Community Initiatives
e-mail: CFBCI@hhs.gov
Web site: www.hhs.gov/faith

Welcomes the participation of faith-based and community-based organizations as valued and essential partners with the U.S. Department of Health and Human Services. Funding goes to faith- based organizations through Head Start, programs for refugee resettlement, runaway and homeless youth, independent living, childcare, child support enforcement, and child welfare.

Family Support America
(formerly Family Resource Coalition of America)
address: 20 N. Wacker Dr., Suite 1100 Chicago, IL 60606
phone: (312) 338-0900
fax: (312) 338-1522
e-mail: info@familysupportamerica.org
Web site: www.familysupportamerica.org

Works to strengthen and empower families and communities so that they can foster the optimal development of children, youth, and adult family members.

National Exchange Club Foundation for the Prevention of Child Abuse
address: 3050 Central Ave. Toledo, OH 43606-1700
phone: (800) 924-2643
            (419) 535-3232
fax: (419) 535-1989
e-mail: info@preventchildabuse.com
Web site: www.nationalexchangeclub.com

Conducts local campaigns in the fight against child abuse by providing education, intervention, and support to families affected by child maltreatment.

National Fatherhood Initiative
address: 101 Lake Forest Blvd., Suite 360 Gaithersburg, MD 20877
phone: (301) 948-0599
fax: (301) 948-4325
Web site: www.fatherhood

Works to improve the well-being of children by increasing the proportion of children growing up with involved, responsible, and committed fathers.

For the General Public

Childhelp USA

address: 15757 North 78th St. Scottsdale, AZ 85260
phone: (800) 4-A-CHILD
              (800) 2-A-CHILD (TDD line)
              (480) 922-8212
fax: (480) 922-7061
e-mail: help@childhelpusa.org
Web site: www.childhelpusa.org

Provides crisis counseling to adult survivors and child victims of child abuse, offenders, and parents, and operates a national hotline.

National Center for Missing and Exploited Children

address: Charles B. Wang International Children's Building 699 Prince St.
              Alexandria, VA 22314-3175
phone: (800) 843-5678
              (703) 274-3900
fax: (703) 274-2220
Web site: www.missingkids.com

Provides assistance to parents, children, law enforcement, schools, and the community in recovering missing children and raising public awareness about ways to help prevent child abduction, molestation, and sexual exploitation.

Parents Anonymous

address: 675 West Foothill Blvd., Suite 220 Claremont, CA 91711
phone: (909) 621-6184
fax: (909) 625-6304
e-mail: parentsanon@msn.com
Web site: www.parentsanonymous.org

Leads mutual support groups to help parents provide nurturing environments for their families.

For More Information

National Clearinghouse on Child Abuse and Neglect Information

address: 330 C St., SW Washington, DC 20447
phone: (800) 394-3366
              (703) 385-7565
fax: (703) 385-3206

e-mail: nccanch@calib.com
Web site: www.calib.com/nccanch

Collects, stores, catalogs, and disseminates information on all aspects of child maltreatment and child welfare to help build the capacity of professionals in the field. A service of the Children's Bureau.

APPENDIX C. STATE TOLL-FREE TELEPHONE NUMBERS FOR REPORTING CHILD ABUSE

Each State designates specific agencies to receive and investigate reports of suspected child abuse and neglect. Typically, this responsibility is carried out by child protective services (CPS) within a Department of Social Services, Department of Human Resources, or Division of Family and Children Services. In some States, police departments also may receive reports of child abuse or neglect.

Many States have an in-State toll-free telephone number, listed below, for reporting suspected abuse. The reporting party must be calling from the same State where the child is allegedly being abused for most of the following numbers to be valid.

For States not listed or when the reporting party resides in a different State than the child, please call **Childhelp, 800-4-A-Child** (800-422-4453), or your local CPS agency.

Alaska (AK)	**Kansas (KS)**	**Nebraska (NE)**
800-478-4444	800-922-5330	800-652-1999
Arizona (AZ)	**Kentucky (KY)**	**Nevada (NV)**
888-SOS-CHILD	800-752-6200	800-992-5757
(888-767-2445)		
Arkansas (AR)	**Maine (ME)**	**New Hampshire (NH)**
800-482-5964	800-452-1999	800-894-5533
		800-852-3388 (after hours)
Connecticut (CT)	**Maryland (MD)**	**New Jersey (NJ)**
800-842-2288	800-332-6347	800-792-8610
800-624-5518 (TDD)		800-835-5510 (TDD)
Delaware (DE)	**Massachusetts (MA)**	**New Mexico (NM)**
800-292-9582	800-792-5200	800-797-3260
Florida (FL)	**Michigan (MI)**	**New York (NY)**
800-96-ABUSE	800-942-4357	800-342-3720
(800-962-2873)		

Illinois (IL)	Mississippi (MS)	North Dakota (ND)
800-252-2873	800-222-8000	800-245-3736
Indiana (IN)	Missouri (MO)	Oklahoma (OK)
800-800-5556	800-392-3738	800-522-3511
Iowa (IA)	Montana (MT)	Oregon (OR)
800-362-2178	800-332-6100	800-854-3508, ext. 2402
Pennsylvania (PA)	Utah (UT)	Washington (WA)
800-932-0313	800-678-9399	866-END-HARM
		(866-363-4276)
Rhode Island (RI)	Vermont (VT)	West Virginia (WV)
800-RI-CHILD	800-649-5285	800-352-6513
(800-742-4453)		
Texas (TX)	Virginia (VA)	Wyoming (WY)
800-252-5400	800-552-7096	800-457-3659

APPENDIX D. NATIONAL ASSOCIATION OF SOCIAL WORKERS CODE OF ETHICS

The National Association of Social Workers Code of Ethics provides guidance regarding the everyday professional conduct of all social workers, including child protective services (CPS) caseworkers. The following standards are based on guidelines for professional conduct with clients:

Commitment to clients. A CPS caseworker's primary responsibility is to assure child safety, child permanence, child well-being, and family well-being.

Self-determination. CPS caseworkers respect and promote the right of clients to self-determination and help clients identify and clarify their goals. The right to self-determination may be limited when the caseworker, in their professional judgment, determines that the clients' actions or potential actions pose a serious and foreseeable, imminent risk to their children.

Informed consent. CPS caseworkers should provide services to clients only in the context of a professional relationship based, when appropriate, on valid informed consent. In instances where clients are receiving services involuntarily, CPS caseworkers should provide information about the nature and extent of services and about the extent of clients' right to refuse the services.

Competence. CPS caseworkers should provide services and represent themselves as competent only within the boundaries of their education, preservice and inservice training, license, and certification.

Cultural competence and social diversity. CPS caseworkers should understand culture and its function in human behavior, recognizing the strengths in all cultures. Caseworkers should be knowledgeable about their clients' cultures and demonstrate competence in providing services that are sensitive to the cultures and to differences among people and cultural groups.

Conflicts of interest. CPS caseworkers should be alert to and avoid any conflict of interest that may interfere with the exercise of professional discretion and impartial judgment. Caseworkers should not take any unfair advantage of a professional relationship or exploit others for personal gain.

Privacy and confidentiality. CPS caseworkers should respect the child and family's right to privacy. They should not solicit private information from clients unless it is essential to assuring safety, providing services, or achieving permanence for children. Caseworkers can disclose information with consent from the client or person legally responsible for the client's behalf. Caseworkers should discuss with clients and other interested parties the nature of the confidentiality and the limitations and rights of confidentiality. Caseworkers should protect the confidentiality of all information, except when disclosure is necessary to prevent serious, foreseeable, and imminent harm to the child.

Access to records. Caseworkers should provide clients with reasonable access to the records about them. Caseworkers should limit client access to records when there is compelling evidence that such access could cause serious harm to the child or family. When providing access to records, caseworkers must protect the confidentiality of other individuals identified in the record, such as the name of the reporter.

Sexual relationships. Caseworkers should not, under any circumstances, engage in sexual activities or sexual contact with current or former clients, client's relatives, or others with whom the client maintains a close personal relationship when there is a risk of exploitation or potential harm to the client. Caseworkers should not provide clinical services to individuals with whom they have had a prior sexual relationship.

Sexual harassment. Caseworkers should not make sexual advances or sexual solicitation, request sexual favors, or engage in other verbal or physical conduct of a sexual nature with clients.

Physical contact. Caseworkers should not engage in physical contact with children and parents when there is a possibility of psychological harm.

Derogatory language. Caseworkers should never use derogatory language in their verbal or written communication about clients. Caseworkers should use behavioral, respectful, and sensitive language in their communications to and about clients.

Clients who lack decision making capacity. When acting on behalf of clients who lack the capacity to make informed decisions, caseworkers should take reasonable steps to safeguard the interests and rights of those clients.

Termination of services. CPS caseworkers should terminate services to clients when child safety is assured or permanence has been achieved.

Source: National Association of Social Workers. (1999). *Code of ethics of the National Association of Social Workers.* Washington, DC: Author.

End Notes

[1] Child Welfare League of America. (1999). *CWLA standardsof excellence for services for abused and neglected childrenand their families* (Rev. ed.). Washington, DC: Author.
[2] Pecora, P. J., Whittaker, J. K., Maluccio, A. N., Barth, R. P., & Plotnick, R. D. (2000). *The child welfare challenge* (2nd ed.). New York, NY: Aldine de Gruyter; Zlotnick, J. (2000). What are the core competencies for practitioners in child welfare agencies? In H. Dubowitz & D. DePanfilis (Eds.), *Handbook for child protection practice*(pp. 571-576). Thousand Oaks, CA: Sage.
[3] Rauch, J. B., North, C., Rowe, C., & Risley-Curtiss, C. (1993). *Diversity competence: A learning guide.* Baltimore, MD: University of Maryland School of Social Work.
[4] Child Welfare League of America. (1999); Holder. W., & Costello, T. (1989). *Caseworker desk guide for self assessment of child protective services practice competencies.* Charlotte, NC: ACTION for Child Protection 1989; Costello, T. (1989). *Survey results–national child protective services competency-based training project: Defining and measuring critical CPS competencies.* Washington, DC: U.S. Department of Health and Human Services, Administration for Children, Youth and Families.
[5] Zlotnick, J. (2000).
[6] Abramczyk, L. (1994). Should child welfare workers have an M.S.W.? In E. Gambrill & T. Stein (Eds.), *Controversial issues in child welfare* (pp. 174-179). Needham, MA: Allyn & Bacon.
[7] National Association of Public Child Welfare Administrators. (1999). *Guidelines for a model system of protective services for abused and neglected children and their families.* Washington, DC: American Public Human Services Association; Child Welfare League of America. (1999); Rittner, B., & Wodarski, S. S. (1999). Differential uses for BSW and MSW educated social workers in child welfare services. *Children and Youth Services Review,* 21(3), 2 17-23 8.
[8] Russell, M. (1987). 1987 *National study of public child welfare job requirements.* Portland, ME: University of Southern Maine, National Resource Center for Management and Administration.
[9] Child Welfare League of America. (1990). *Florida recruitment and retention study.* Washington, DC: Author.
[10] Hess, P. M., Folaron, G., & Jefferson, A. B. (1992). Effectiveness of family reunification services: An innovative evaluative model. *Social Work,* 37, 304-311.
[11] Booz, Allen & Hamilton. (1987). *The Maryland social services job analysis and personnel qualifications study, executive summary.* Baltimore, MD: Maryland Department of Human Resources.
[12] Dhooper, S., Royse, D., & Wolfe, L. (1990). Does social work education make a difference? *Social Work,* 35(1), 57-61.
[13] Abers, E. C., Reilly, T., & Rittner, B. (1993). Children in foster care: Possible factors affecting permanency planning. *Child and Adolescent Social Work Journal,* 10(4): 329-341.
[14] Hopkins, K., & Mudrick, N. (1999). Impact of university/ agency partnerships in child welfare on organizations, workers, and work activity. *Child Welfare, 78(6),* 749-773.
[15] Rome, S. H. (1997). The child welfare choice: An analysis of social work students' career plans. *Journal of Baccalaureate Social Work,* 3(1), 31-48.
[16] DePanfilis, D. (2000a). How do I develop a helping alliance with the family? In H. Dubowitz & D. DePanfilis (Eds.), *Handbook for child protection practice* (pp. 36-40). Thousand Oaks, CA: Sage.
[17] DePanfilis, D. (2000a).
[18] Horejsi, C. (1996). *Assessment and case planning in child protection and foster care services.* Englewood, CO: American Humane Association, Children's Division.

[19] Rogers, C. (1957). The necessary and sufficient conditions of therapeutic personality change. *Journal of Consulting Psychology, 21*, 95-103; Truax, C., & Carkhuff, R. (1967). *Toward effective counseling and psychotherapy.* Chicago, IL: Aldine de Gruyter.

[20] DePanfilis, D. (2000a); Truax, C., & Carkhuff, R. (1967).

[21] Fong, R. (2001). Culturally competent social work practice: Past and present. In R. Fong & S. Furturo (Eds.), *Culturally competent practice: Skills, interventions, and evaluation* (pp. 1-9). Needham Heights, MA: Allyn and Bacon.

[22] Rogers, C. (1957); Truax, C., & Carkhuff, R. (1967).

[23] Berg, I. K., & Kelly, S. (2000). *Building solutions in child protective services.* New York, NY: W. W. Norton; DePanfilis, D. (2000a); Rooney, R. (2000). How can I use authority effectively and engage family members? In H. Dubowitz & D. DePanfilis (Eds.), *Handbook for child protection practice* (pp. 44-46). Thousand Oaks, CA: Sage.

[24] Anderson, J. (1988). *Foundations of social work practice.* New York, NY: Springer.

[25] Rooney, R. (2000).

[26] Griffin, W. V., Montsinger, J. L., & Carter, N. A. (1995). *Resource guide on personal safety for administrators and other personnel.* Durham, NC: Brendan Associates and ILR.

[27] Prochaska, J. O., & DiClemente, C. C. (1982). Transtheoretical therapy: Toward a more integrative model of change. *Psychotherapy: Theory, Research, and Practice, 19,* 276-288.

[28] National Association of Public Child Welfare Administrators. (1999).

[29] Child Welfare League of America. (1999).

[30] Child Welfare League of America. (1999).

[31] National Research Council. (1993). *Understanding child abuse and neglect.* Washington, DC: National Academy Press.

[32] Pecora, P. J., et al. (2000).

[33] Wells, S. (1997). Screening in child protective services: Do we accept a report? How do we respond? In T. Morton & W. Holder (Eds.), *Decision-making in children's protective services: Advancing the state of the art* (pp. 94-106). Atlanta, GA: Child Welfare Institute and Denver, CO: ACTION for Child Protection.

[34] Wells, S. (1997); Wells, S. (2000a). How do I decide whether to accept a report for a child protective services investigation? In H. Dubowitz & D. DePanfilis (Eds.), *Handbook for child protection practice* (pp. 3-6). Thousand Oaks, CA: Sage.

[35] Wells, S. (2000a).

[36] Child Welfare League of America. (1999).

[37] Wells, S. (1997).

[38] Wells, S. (2000b). What criteria are most critical to determine the urgency of the child protective services response? In H. Dubowitz & D. DePanfilis (Eds.), Handbook for child protection practice (pp. 7-9). Thousand Oaks, CA: Sage.

[39] Zuravin, S., & Shay, S. (1991, June). Preventing child neglect. In D. DePanfilis & T. Birch (Eds.), *Proceedings of the National Child Maltreatment Prevention Symposium.* Washington, DC: U.S. Department of Health and Human Services, National Center on Child Abuse and Neglect.

[40] Farrow, F. (1997). *Child protection: Building community partnership.* Getting from here to there. Cambridge, MA: Harvard University, John F. Kennedy School of Government; Gordon, A. L. (2000). What works in child protective services reforms. In M. P. Kluger, G. Alexander, & P. A. Curtis (Eds.), *What works in child welfare* (pp. 57-66). Washington, DC: CWLA Press; Pelton, L. H. (1998). Four commentaries: How we can better protect children from abuse and neglect. *The Future of Children: Protecting Children from Abuse and Neglect,* 8(1), 120-132; Waldfogel, J. (1998). Rethinking the paradigm for child protection. *The Future of Children: Protecting Children from Abuse and Neglect,* 8(1), 104-119; Weber, M. W. (1998). Four commentaries: How we can better protect children from abuse and neglect. *The Future of Children: Protecting Children from Abuse and Neglect,* 8(1), 120-132.

[41] Turnell, A., & Edwards, S. (1999). *Signs of safety: A solution and safety oriented approach to child protection casework.* New York, NY: W. W. Norton.

[42] Turnell, A., & Edwards, S. (1999).

[43] Drake, B. (2000). How do I decide whether to substantiate a report? In H. Dubowitz & D. DePanfilis (Eds.), *Handbook for child protection practice* (pp. 113-117). Thousand Oaks, CA: Sage.

[44] Filip, J., McDaniel, N., & Schene, P. (1992). *Helping in child protective services: A competency-based casework handbook (p. 189).* Denver, CO: American Humane Association.

[45] DePanfilis, D. (2000b). What is inadequate supervision? In H. Dubowitz & D. DePanfilis (Eds.), *Handbook for child protection practice* (pp. 134-136). Thousand Oaks, CA: Sage.

[46] DePanfilis, D. (2000b).

[47] DePanfilis, D. (2000c). How do I determine if a child is neglected? In H. Dubowitz & D. DePanfilis (Eds.), *Handbook for child protection practice* (pp. 134-136). Thousand Oaks, CA: Sage.

[48] Dubowitz, H. (2000). How do I determine whether a child has been physically abused? In H. Dubowitz & D. DePanfilis (Eds.), *Handbook for child protection practice* (pp. 134-136). Thousand Oaks, CA: Sage.

[49] Adams, J. (2000). How do I determine if a child has been sexually abused? In H. Dubowitz & D. DePanfilis (Eds.), *Handbook for child protection practice* (pp. 175-179). Thousand Oaks, CA: Sage.

[50] Hart, S., Brassard, M., & Karlson, H. (1996). Psychological maltreatment. In J. Briere, L. Berliner, J. Bulkley, C. Jenny, & T. Reid (Eds.), *The APSAC handbook on child maltreatment* (pp. 72–89). Thousand Oaks, CA: Sage.

[51] Brassard, M., & Hart, S. (2000). How do I determine whether a child has been psychologically maltreated? In H. Dubowitz & D. DePanfilis (Eds.), *Handbook for child protection practice* (pp. 215-219). Thousand Oaks, CA: Sage.

[52] Pecora, P. J. et al. (2000).

[53] Hollinshead, D., & Fluke, J. (2000) What works in safety and risk assessment for child protective services. M. Kluger, G. Alexander, & P. Curtis (Eds.), *What works in child welfare* (p. 67). Washington, DC: CWLA Press.

[54] Hollinshead, D., & Fluke, J. (2000).

[55] Holder, W., & Morton, T. (1999). *Designing a Comprehensive approach to child safety.* Atlanta, GA: Child Welfare Institute and Denver, CO: ACTION for Child Protection.

[56] Holder, W., & Morton, T. (1999).

[57] Young, N., Gardner, S., & Dennis, K. (1998). *Responding to alcohol and other drug problems in child welfare: Weaving together practice and policy* (p. 126). Washington, DC: CWLA Press.

[58] Young et al. (1998).

[59] Ganley, A., & Schechter, S. (1996). *Domestic violence: A national curriculum for child protective services.* San Francisco, CA: Family Violence Prevention Fund.

[60] Ganley, A., & Schechter, S. (1996).

[61] Pecora, P. J. et al. (2000).

[62] DePanfilis, D. (1997). Is the child safe? How do werespond to safety concerns? In T. Morton & W. Holder(Eds.), *Decision making in children's protective services:Advancing the state of the art* (pp. 121-142). Atlanta, GA:Child Welfare Institute and Denver, CO: ACTION forChild Protection.

[63] DePanfilis, D. (1997).

[64] Berg, I. K., & Kelly, S. (2000).

[65] Christian, S. M. (1997). *New directions for child protective services: Supporting children, families and communities through legislative reform.* Washington, DC: National Conference of State Legislatures.

[66] Farrow, F. (1997).

[67] Waldfogel, J. (1997). *The future of child protection: How to break the cycle of abuse and neglect.* Cambridge, MA: Harvard University Press.

[68] Pintello, D. (2000). How do I interview non-maltreating parents and caregivers? In H. Dubowitz & D. DePanfilis (Eds.), *Handbook for child protection practice* (pp. 80-84). Thousand Oaks, CA: Sage.

[69] Child Welfare League of America. (1999).

[70] Miller, W., & Rollnick, S. (1991). *Motivational interviewing: Preparing people to change addictive behavior.* New York, NY: The Guilford Press.

[71] Saywitz, K. J., & Goodman, G. S. (1996). Interviewingchildren in and out of court: Current research and practiceimplications. In J. Briere, L. Berliner, J. Bulkley, C.Jenny, & T. Reid (Eds.) *The APSAC handbook on childmaltreatment* (pp. 297-318). Thousand Oaks, CA: Sage;Kolko, D., Brown, E., & Berliner, L. (2002). Children'sperceptions of their abusive experience: Measurement andpreliminary findings. *Child Maltreatment, 7*(1), 42-55.

[72] Berliner, L., & Loftus, E. (1992). Sexual abuse accusations: Desperately seeking reconciliation. *Journal of Interpersonal Violence, 7*(4), 570-578; Saywitz, K. J., & Goodman, G. S. (1996); Kolko, D., Brown, E., & Berliner, L. (2002).

[73] Boat, B., & Everson, M. (1986). *Using anatomical dolls: Guidelines for interviewing young children in sexual abuse investigations.* Chapel Hill, NC: University of North Carolina, Department of Psychiatry.

[74] American Humane Association. (1997). *Worker safety for human services organizations.* Denver, CO: Author; Griffin, W. V. et al. (1995).

[75] American Humane Association. (1997).

[76] Holder, W. (2000).

[77] National Association of Public Child Welfare Administrators. (1999).

[78] Dunst, C. J., Trivette, C. M., & Deal, A. G. (1994). *Supporting and strengthening families: Volume 1: Methods, strategies, and practices.* Cambridge, MA: Brookline Books; Horejsi, C. (1996).

[79] Child Welfare League of America. (1999). (p. 41).

[80] Kinney, J., Strand, K., Hagerup, M., & Bruner, C. (1994). Beyond the buzzwords: *Key principles in effective frontline practice.* Falls Church, VA: National Center for Service Integration and Chicago, IL: National Resource Center for Family Support Programs.

[81] Whittaker, J., Schinke, S., & Gilchrist, L. (1986). Theecological paradigm in child, youth, and family services:Implications for policy and practice. *Social Service Review,60*, 483-503; Bronfenbrenner, U. (1979). *The ecology ofhuman development: Experiments by nature and design.*Cambridge, MA: Harvard University Press; Garbarino, J.(1982). *Children and families in the social environment.*Hawthorne, NY: Aldine de Gruyter.

[82] Hudson, J., Morris, A., Maxwell, G., & Galaway, B. (1996). *Family group conferences: Perspectives on policy and practice.* Monsey, NY: Willow Tree Press; Merkel-Holguin, L. (2000). How do I use family meetings to develop optimal service plans? In H. Dubowitz & D. DePanfilis (Eds.), *Handbook for child protection practice* (pp. 373- 378). Thousand Oaks, CA: Sage; Merkel-Holguin, L. (1998). Implementation of family group decision making in the U.S.: Policies and practices in transition. *Protecting Children, 14*(4), 4-10; Merkel-Holguin, L. (2001). Family group conferencing: An "extended family" process to safeguard children and strengthen family well-being. In E. Walton, P. Sandau-Beckler, & M. Mannes (Eds.), *Family- centered services and child well-being: Exploring issues in policy, practice, theory, and research* (pp. 197-2 18). New York, NY: Columbia University Press; U.S. Department of Health and Human Services, Administration on Children and Families, Children's Bureau. (2000). *Rethinking child welfare practice under the Adoption and Safe Families Act of 1997.* Washington, DC: Author.

[83] Compton, B., & Galaway, B. (1999). *Social work processes* (6th ed.). Pacific Grove, CA: Brooks/Cole Co.; Congress, E. P. (1994). The use of culturagrams to assess and empower culturally diverse families. *Families in Society, 75,* 531-539; Hartman, A. (1978). Diagrammatic assessment of family relationships. *Social Casework, 59,* 465-476; Hartman, A., & Laird, J. (1983). *Family-centered social work practice.* New York, NY: The Free Press; Dunst, C. J. et al. (1994); Children's Bureau of Southern California. (1997). *Family assessment form.* Washington, DC: CWLA Press; Magura, S., & Moses, B. S. (1986). *Outcome measures for child welfare services: Theory and applications.* Washington, DC: CWLA Press.

[84] Abney, V. (1996). Cultural competency in the field of child maltreatment. In J. Briere, L. Berliner, J. A. Bulkely, C. Jenny, & T. Reid (Eds.), *The APSAC handbook on child maltreatment* (pp. 409-419). Thousand Oaks, CA: Sage.

[85] Ivey, A. E., Ivey, M. B., & Simek-Downing, L. (1987). Individual and cultural empathy. *In Counseling and psychotherapy: Integrating skills, theory, and practice* (pp. 91-118). Englewood Cliffs, NJ: Prentice-Hall.

[86] Shepard R. (1987). Cultural sensitivity. In D. DePanfilis (Ed.), *Enhancing child protection service competency: Selected readings.* Charlotte, NC: ACTION for Child Protection.

[87] Merkel-Holguin, L. (2000).

[88] DePanfilis, D. (1997).

[89] Courtney, M. (2000). What outcomes are relevant for intervention? In H. Dubowitz & D. DePanfilis (Eds.), *Handbook for child protection practice* (p. 373). Thousand Oaks, CA: Sage; U.S. Department of Health and Human Services, Administration on Children and Families, Children's Bureau. (2000).

[90] Courtney, M. (2000).

[91] DePanfilis, D. (2000c). How do I match risks to client outcomes? In H. Dubowitz & D. DePanfilis (Eds.), *Handbook for child protection practice* (pp. 367-372). Thousand Oaks, CA: Sage.

[92] Lutz, L. (2000). *Concurrent planning: Tool for permanency survey of selected sites.* New York, NY: City University of New York, Hunter College School of Social Work, National Resource Center for Foster Care and Permanency Planning.

[93] Gelles, R. J. (2000). Treatment-resistant families. In R. M. Reece (Ed.), *Treatment of child abuse* (pp. 304-312). Baltimore, MD: The Johns Hopkins University Press.

[94] National Association of Public Child Welfare Administrators. (1999). Reprinted with permission.

[95] LeVine, E. S., & Sallee, A. L. (1999). *Child welfare clinical theory and practice.* Dubuque, IA: Eddie Bowers.

[96] Rose, S. M. (Ed.). (1992). *Case management and social work practice.* White Plains, NY: Longman.

[97] Cohn, A., & Daro, D. (1987). Is treatment too late? What 10 years of evaluative research tell us. *Child Abuse and Neglect, 11,* 433-442; Daro, D., & Cohn, A. (1998). Child maltreatment evaluation efforts: What have we learned? In G. T. Hotaling, D. Finkelhor, J. T. Kirkpatrick, & M. A. Straus, (Eds.), *Coping with family violence: Research and policy perspectives* (pp. 275-287). Thousand Oaks, CA: Sage; Dubowitz, H. (1990). Costs and effectiveness of interventions in child maltreatment. *Child Abuse and Neglect, 14,* 177-186.

[98] Malchiodi, C. A. (1997). *Breaking the silence: Art therapy with children from violent homes.* Bristol, PA: Brunner/ Mazel; Johnston, S. S. M. (1997). The use of art and play therapy with victims of sexual abuse: A review of the literature. *Family Therapy, 24*(2), 101-113; Riordan, R. J., & Verdel, A. C. (1991). Evidence of sexual abuse in children's art products. *The School Counselor, 39,* 116- 121; Culbertson, R. M., & Revel, A. C. (1987). Graphic characteristics on the Draw-a-Person test for identification of physical abuse. *Art Therapy: Journal of the American Art Therapy Association, 4*(2), 78-83.

[99] Resick, P. A., & Schnicke, M. K. (1992). Cognitive processing therapy for sexual assault victims. *Journal of Consulting and Clinical Psychology, 60*(5), 748-756; Ellis, L. F., Black, L. D., & Resick, P. A. (1992). Cognitive- behavioral treatment approaches for victims of crime. In P. A. Keller & S. R. Heyman (Eds.), *Innovations in clinical practice: A source book* (pp. 23-3 8). Sarasota, FL: Professional Resource Exchange.

[100] Resick, P., & Clum, G. (2001). Cognitive processing therapy (CPT). In B. E. Saunders, L. Berliner, & R. F. Hanson (Eds.), *Guidelines for the psychosocial treatment of intrafamilial child physical and sexual abuse* (pp.30-3 1). Charleston, SC: Medical University of South Carolina, National Crime Victims Research and Treatment Center; Resick, P. A., & Schnicke, M. K. (1993). *Cognitive processing therapy for rape victims: A treatment manual.* Newbury Park, CA: Sage.

[101] Roditti, M. G. (2001a). What works in child care. In M. P. Kluger, B. Alexander, & P. A. Curtis (Eds.), *What works in child welfare* (pp. 285-292). Washington, DC: CWLA Press; Roditti, M. G. (2001b). What works in center-based childcare. In M. P. Kluger, B. Alexander, & P. A. Curtis (Eds.), *What works in child welfare* (pp. 293-301). Washington, DC: CWLA Press; Roditti, M. G. (2001c). What works in child care for maltreated and at-risk children. In M. P. Kluger, B. Alexander, & P. A. Curtis (Eds.), *What works in child welfare* (pp. 311-319). Washington, DC: CWLA Press; Seitz, V., Rosenbaum, L. K., & Apfel, N. H. (1983). Effects of family support intervention: A 10-year follow-up. *Child Development, 56*, 376-39 1; Oats, R. K., Grey, J., Schweitzer, L., Kempe, R. S., & Harmon, R. J. (1995). A therapeutic preschool for abused children: The KEEPSAFE Project. *Child Abuse and Neglect, 19*, 1379-1386.

[102] Chemtob, C. M., Naksahima, J., Hamada, R., & Carlson, J. (in press). Brief treatment for elementary school children with disaster-related PTSD: A field study. *Journal of Clinical Psychology*; Puffer, M. K., Greenwald, R., & Elrod, D. E. (1998). A single session EMDR study with 20 traumatized children and adolescents. *Traumatology 3*, (2) [On-line serial]. Available: http://www.fsu.edu/ ~trauma/v3i2art6.html; Scheck, M. M., Schaeffer, J. A., & Gilette, C. S. (1998). Brief psychological intervention with traumatized young women: The efficacy of eye movement desensitization and reprocessing. *Journal of Traumatic Stress, 11*, 25-44; Soberman, G. S., Greenwald, R., & Rule, D. L. (in press). A controlled study of eye movement desensitization and reprocessing (EMDR) for boys with conduct problems. *Journal of Aggression, Maltreatment, and Trauma*.

[103] Chemtob, C. (2001). Eye movement desensitization and reprocessing (EMDR). In B. E. Saunders, L. Berliner, & R. F. Hanson (Eds.), *Guidelines for the psychosocial treatment of intrafamilial child physical and sexual abuse* (pp. 32-3 5). Charleston, SC: Medical University of South Carolina, National Crime Victims Research and Treatment Center; Greenwald, R. (1993). *Using EMDR with children*. Pacific Grove, CA: EMDR Institute; Shapiro, F. (1995). *Eye movement desensitization and reprocessing: Basic principles, protocols, and procedures*. New York, NY: The Guilford Press.

[104] Berrick, J. D. (2001). What works in kinship care. In M. P. Kluger, B. Alexander, & P. A. Curtis (Eds.), *What works in child welfare* (pp. 127-133). Washington, DC: CWLA Press; Berrick, J. D., Barth, R. P., & Needell, B. (1994). A comparison of kinship foster homes and foster family homes: Implications for kinship foster care as family preservation. *Children and Youth Services Review, 16*, 13- 63; LeProhn, N. S. (1994). The role of the kinship foster parent: A comparison of the role conceptions of relative and non-relative foster parents. *Children and Youth Services Review, 16*, 107-122; Berrick, J. D., Needell, B., Barth, R. P., & Johnson-Reid, M. (1998). *The tender years*. New York, NY: Columbia University Press; Courtney, M., & Needell, B. (1997). Outcomes of kinship care: Lessons from California. In J. D. Berrick, R. P. Barth, & N. Gilbert (Eds.), *Child Welfare Research Review 2* (pp. 130-149). New York, NY: Columbia University Press; Berrick, J. D. (2001); Berrick, J. D. et al. (1994); Dubowitz, H. (1990). *The physical and mental health and educational status of children placed with relatives: Final report*. Baltimore, MD: University of Maryland School of Medicine, Department of Pediatrics; Meyer, B. S., & Link, M. K. (1990). *Kinship foster care: The double-edged dilemma*. Rochester, NY: Task Force on Permanency Planning for Foster Children, Inc.; Zwas, M. G. (1993). Kinship foster care: A relatively permanent solution. *Fordham Urban Law Journal, 20*(2), 343-373.

[105] Berrick, J. D. (2001).

[106] Fantuzzo, J., Sutton-Smith, B., Atkins, M., & Meyers, R. (1996). Community-based resilient peer treatment of withdrawn maltreated preschool children. *Journal of Clinical and Consulting Psychology, 64*, 1377-1368.

[107] Fantuzzo, J. (2001). Resilient peer training intervention. In B. E. Saunders, L. Berliner, & R. F. Hanson (Eds.), *Guidelines for the psychosocial treatment of intrafamilial child physical and sexual abuse* (pp. 38-39). Charleston, SC: Medical University of South Carolina, National Crime Victims Research and Treatment Center; Fantuzzo, J., Weiss, A., & Coolahan, K. (1998). Community-based partnership- directed research: Actualizing community strengths to treat victims of physical abuse and neglect. In R. J. Lutzker (Ed.), *Child abuse: A handbook of theory, research, and treatment* (pp. 213-238). New York, NY: Pergamon Press.

[108] Chaffin, M. (2001). Adolescent sex offender treatment. In B. E. Saunders, L. Berliner, & R. F. Hanson (Eds.), *Guidelines for the psychosocial treatment of intrafamilial child physical and sexual abuse* (pp. 87-89). Charleston, SC: Medical University of South Carolina, National Crime Victims Research and Treatment Center; Borduin, C. M., Henggeler, S. W., Blaske, D. M., & Stein, R. J. (1990). Multisystemic treatment of adolescent sexual offenders. *International Journal of Offender Therapy and Comparative Criminology, 34*, 105-113; Alexander, M. A. (1999). Sexual offender treatment efficacy revisited. *Sexual Abuse: A Journal of Research and Treatment, 11*(2), 101- 116.

[109] Henggeler, S. W., Swenson, C. C., Kaufman, K., & Schoenwald, S. K. (1997). *MST supplementary treatment manual for juvenile sexual offenders and their families*. Charleston, SC: Medical University of South Carolina, Family Services Research Center; Kahn, T. J. (1996a). *Pathways: A guided workbook for youth beginning treatment*. Orwell, VT: Safer Society Press; Kahn, T. J. (1996b). *Pathways guide for parents of youth beginning treatment*. Orwell, VT: Safer Society Press; Marsh, L. F., Connell, P., & Olson, E. (1988). *Breaking the cycle: Adolescent sexual abuse treatment manual*. (Available from St. Mary's Home for Boys, 16535 SW Tualatin Valley Highway, Beaverton, OR 97006); O'Brien, M. J. (1994). *PHASE treatment manual*. (Available from Alpha PHASE, Inc., 1600 University Avenue West, Suite 305, St. Paul, MN 55104-3825); Steen, C. (1993). *The relapse prevention workbook for youth in treatment*. Orwell, VT: Safer Society Press;

Way, I. F., & Balthazor, T. J. (1990). *A manual for structured group treatment with adolescent sexual offenders*. Notre Dame, IN: Jalice.

[110] Tierney, J., & Grossman, J. B. (2001). What works in promoting positive youth development: Mentoring. In M. P. Kluger, B. Alexander, & P. A. Curtis (Eds.), *What works in child welfare* (pp. 323-328). Washington, DC: CWLA Press; Cave, G., & Quint, J. (1990). *Career beginning impact evaluation*. New York, NY: Manpower Demonstration and Research Corporation; Johnson, A. W. (1998). *An evaluation of the long-term impact of the Sponsor-a-Scholar (SAS) Program on student performance*. Princeton, NJ: Mathematica Policy Research; Tierney, J. P., Grossman, J., & Resch, N. L. (1995). *Making a difference: An impact study of Big Brothers/Big Sisters*. Philadelphia, PA: Public/Private Ventures.

[111] Tierney, J., & Grossman, J. B. (2001).

[112] Johnston, S. S. M. (1997). The use of art and play therapy with victims of sexual abuse: A review of the literature. *Family Therapy*, 24(2), 101-113.

[113] Gil, E. (in press). Moving mountains: Helping traumatized children through collaborative play. Rockville, MD: Launch Press; Gil, E. (1991). The healing power of play: Working with abused children. New York, NY: The Guilford Press; Gil, E. (2001). Trauma-focused play therapy. In B. E. Saunders, L. Berliner, & R. F. Hanson (Eds.), Guidelines for the psychosocial treatment of intrafamilial child physical and sexual abuse (pp. 47-48). Charleston, SC: Medical University of South Carolina, National Crime Victims Research and Treatment Center.

[114] Chamberlain, P. (2001). What works in treatment foster care? In M. P. Kluger, B. Alexander, & P. A. Curtis (Eds.), *What works in child welfare* (pp. 157-162). Washington, DC: CWLA Press; Clark, H., Boyd, L., Redditt, C., Foster-Johnson, L., Hard, D., Kuhns, J., Lee, G., & Steward, E. (1993). An individualized system of care for foster children with behavioral and emotional disturbances: Preliminary findings. In K. Kutash, C. Liberton, A. Algarin, & R. Friedman (Eds.), *Fifth Annual Research Conference Proceedings for a System of Care for Children's Mental Health* (pp. 365-3 70). Tampa, FL: University of South Florida, Research and Training Center for Children's Mental Health; Chamberlain, P., & Reid, J. (1998). Comparison of two community alternatives to incarceration for chronic juvenile offenders. *Journal of Consulting and Clinical Psychology*, 6, 624-633; Hawkins, R., Almeida, C., & Samet, M. (1989). Comparative evaluation of foster family-based treatment and five other placement choices: A preliminary report. In A. Algarin, R. Friedman, A. Duchnowski, K. Kutash, S. Silver, & M. Johnson (Eds.), *Children's mental health services and policy: Building a research base* (pp. 98-119). Tampa, FL: University of South Florida Mental Health Institute, Research and Training Center for Children's Mental Health.

[115] Meadowcroft, P., Thomlinson, B., & Chamberlain, P. (1994). Treatment foster care services: A research agenda for child welfare. *Child Welfare*, 33, 565-58 1.

[116] Adkerson, D. L. (2001). Adult child molester treatment. In B. E. Saunders, L. Berliner, & R. F. Hanson (Eds.), *Guidelines for the psychosocial treatment of intrafamilial child physical and sexual abuse* (pp. 90-92). Charleston, SC: Medical University of South Carolina, National Crime Victims Research and Treatment Center; Association for the Treatment of Sexual Abusers (ATSA). (in press). The ATSA report on the effectiveness of treatment for sexual offenders. *Sexual Abuse: A Journal of Research and Treatment*; Alexander, M. A. (1999). Sexual offender treatment efficacy revisited. *Sexual Abuse: A Journal of Research and Treatment, 11*(2), 101-116; Dwyer, S. M. (1997). Treatment outcome study: Seventeen years after sexual offender treatment. *Sexual Abuse: A Journal of Research and Treatment, 9*(2), 149-160; Hansen, R. K., Steffy, R. A., & Gauthier, R. (1992). *Long-term follow-up of child molesters: Risk prediction and treatment outcome*. Ottawa, Canada: Corrections Branch, Ministry of the Solicitor General of Canada.

[117] Association for the Treatment of Sexual Abusers (ATSA). (1997). *Ethical standards and principles for the management of sexual abusers*. Beaverton, OR: Author; Abel, G. G., Becker, J. V., Cunningham-Rathner, J., Rouleau, J. L., Kaplan, M., & Reich, J. (n.d.). *The treatment of child molesters*. Atlanta, GA: Authors; Bays, L., & Freeman-Longo, R. (1989). *Why did I do it again? Understanding my cycle of problem behaviors*. Holyoke, MA: NEARI Press; Bays, L., Freeman-Longo, R., & Hildebran, D. D. (1990). *How can I stop? Breaking my deviant cycle*. Holyoke, MA: NEARI Press; Barbaree, H. E., & Seto, M. C. (1997). Pedophilia: Assessment and treatment. In D. R. Laws & W. O'Donohue (Eds.), *Sexual deviance: Theory, assessment, and treatment* (pp. 175-193). New York, NY: The Guilford Press; Freeman-Longo, R., & Bays, L. (1988). *Who am I and why am I in treatment?* Holyoke, MA: NEARI Press; Salter, A. C. (1988). *Treating child sex offenders and victims*. Newbury Park, CA: Sage.

[118] Swenson, C. C., & Ralston, M. E. (1997).

[119] Lipovsky, J., Swenson, C. C., Ralston, M. E., & Saunders, V. E. (1998). The abuse clarification process in the treatment of intrafamilial child abuse. *Child Abuse and Neglect, 22*, 729-74 1; Ralston, M. E. (1982). *Intrafamilial sexual abuse: A community system response to a family ystem problem*. Charleston, SC: Author; Ralston, M. E. (1998). A community system of care for abused children and their families. *Family Futures, 2*(4), 11-15; Ralston, M. E., & Swenson, C. C. (1996). *The Charleston collaborative project intervention manual*. Charleston, SC: Authors; Swenson, C. C., & Ralston, M. E. (1997). *The Charleston collaborative project implementation manual*.

[120] Kumpfer, K. L. (1999). *Strengthening America's families: Exemplary parenting and family strategies for delinquency prevention*. Washington, DC: U.S. Department of Justice, Office of Juvenile Justice and Delinquency Prevention; Catalano, R., Haggerty, K., Flemming, C., & Brewer, D. (1996). *Focus on families: Scientific findings from family prevention intervention research*. Paper presented at National Institute of Drug Abuse conference: Drug Abuse Prevention Through Family Intervention, Gaithersburg, MD.

[121] Haggerty, K. P., Mills, E., & Catalano, R. F. (1991). *Focus on Families: Parent training curriculum*. Seattle, WA: Social Development Research Group.

[122] Wolfe, D. A., Sandler, J., & Kaufman, K. (1981). A competency-based parent training program for child abusers. *Journal of Consulting and Clinical Psychology, 49*, 63 3-640; Wolfe, D. A., St. Lawrence, J., Brehony, K., Bradlyn, A., & Kelly, J. A. (1982). Intensive behavioral parent training for a child abusive mother. *Behavior Therapy, 13*, 438-451; Wolfe, D. A., Edwards, B., Manion, I., & Koverola, C. (1988). Early intervention for parents at risk for child abuse and neglect: A preliminary investigation. *Journal of Consulting and Clinical Psychology, 56*, 40-47.

[123] Wolfe, D. (2001). Parent-child education program for physically abusive parents. In B. E. Saunders, L. Berliner, & R. F. Hanson (Eds.), *Guidelines for the psychosocial treatment of intrafamilial child physical and sexual abuse* (pp. 7 1-73). Charleston, SC: Medical University of South Carolina, National Crime Victims Research and Treatment Center; Wolfe, D. A. (1991). *Preventing physical and emotional abuse of children*: Treatment manuals for practitioners series. New York, NY: The Guilford Press.

[124] Kumpfer, K. L. (1999); Behavior Associates. (1976). Parents Anonymous self-help for child abusing parenting project: Evaluation report. Tuscon, AZ: Behavior Associates; Cohn, A. H. (1979). Essential elements of successful child abuse and neglect treatment. In Child Abuse and Neglect, 3, 491- 496.

[125] Hanson, R., & Rosen, S. (2001). Parents Anonymous. In B. E. Saunders, L. Berliner, & R. F. Hanson (Eds.), *Guidelines for the psychosocial treatment of intrafamilial child physical and sexual abuse* (pp. 84-85). Charleston, SC: Medical University of South Carolina, National Crime Victims Research and Treatment Center; Lieber, L., & Baker, J. M. (1977). Parents Anonymous—Self-help treatment for child abusing parents: A review and evaluation. *Child Abuse and Neglect, 1*, 133-148; Rafael, T., & Pion-Berlin, L. (1996). *Parents Anonymous program bulletin*. Claremont, CA: Authors; Rafael, T., & Pion-Berlin, L. (1999). *Parents Anonymous: Strengthening families*. Washington, DC: U.S. Department of Justice, Office of Juvenile Justice and Delinquency Prevention; Hermann, E. (1993). *Manual for group facilitators*. Los Angeles, CA: Parents Anonymous.

[126] James, B. (2001). Attachment-trauma therapy. In B. E. Saunders, L. Berliner, & R. F. Hanson (Eds.), *Guidelines for the psychosocial treatment of intrafamilial child physical and sexual abuse* (pp. 36-37). Charleston, SC: Medical University of South Carolina, National Crime Victims Research and Treatment Center; James, B. (1994). *Handbook for treating attachment-trauma problems in children*. New York, NY: Free Press/Simon & Schuster.

[127] Breston, E., & Payne, H. (2001). Behavioral parent training intervention for conduct-disordered children. In B. E. Saunders, L. Berliner, & R. F. Hanson (Eds.), *Guidelines for the psychosocial treatment of intrafamilial child physical and sexual abuse* (pp. 52-5 6). Charleston, SC: Medical University of South Carolina, National Crime Victims Research and Treatment Center; Alexander, J. R., & Parsons, B. V. (1973). Short-term behavioral intervention with delinquent families: Impact on family process and recidivism. *Journal of Abnormal Psychology, 81*, 2 19-225; Barkley, R. A., Guevremont, A. D., Anastopoulos, A. D., & Fletcher, K. E. (1992). A comparison of three family programs for treating family conflicts in adolescents with attention-deficit hyperactivity disorder. *Journal of Consulting and Clinical Psychology, 60*, 450-462; Bernel, M. E., Klinnert, M. D., & Schultz, L. A. (1980). Outcome evaluation of behavioral parent training and client centered parent counseling for children with conduct problems. *Journal of Applied Behavior Analysis, 13*, 677-691; Hughes, C., & Wilson, P. H. (1989). Behavioral parent training: Contingency management versus communication skills training with or without the participation of the child. *Child and Family Behavior Therapy, 10*, 11-23; Kazdin, A. E., Esveldt-Dawson, K., French, N. H., & Unis, A. (1987). Effects of parent management training and problem-solving skills training combined in the treatment of antisocial child behavior. *Journal of the American Academy of Child and Adolescent Psychiatry, 26*, 416-424; Kazdin, A. E., Siegel, T. C., & Bass, D. (1992). Cognitive problem solving skills training and parent management training in the treatment of antisocial behavior in children. *Journal of Consulting and Clinical Psychology, 60*, 733- 747.

[128] Breston, E., & Payne, H. (2001). Forehand, R. L., & McMahon, R. J. (1981). Helping the noncompliant child: A clinician's guide to parent training. New York, NY: The Guilford Press; Patterson, G. R. (1976). *Living with children: New methods for parents and teachers*. Champaign, IL: Research Press; Patterson, G. R., & Gillion, M. E. (1968). *Living with children: New methods for parents and teachers*. Champaign, IL: Research Press.

[129] Bonner, B. (2001). Cognitive-behavioral and dynamic play therapy for children with sexual behavior problems and their caregivers. In B. E. Saunders, L. Berliner, & R. F. Hanson (Eds.), *Guidelines for the psychosocial treatment of intrafamilial child physical and sexual abuse* (pp. 27-29). Charleston, SC: Medical University of South Carolina, National Crime Victims Research and Treatment Center; Bonner, B., Walker, C. E., & Berliner, L. (1999a). *Treatment manual for cognitive-behavioral group therapy for children with sexual behavior problems*. Norman, OK: Oklahoma University Health Sciences Center, Center on Child Abuse and

Neglect; Bonner, B., Walker, C. E., & Berliner, L. (1999b). *Treatment manual for cognitive-behavioral group treatment for parents/caregivers of children with sexual behavior problems.* Norman, OK: Oklahoma University Health Sciences Center, Center on Child Abuse and Neglect; Bonner, B., Walker, C. E., & Berliner, L. (1999c). Treatment manual for dynamic group play therapy for children with sexual behavior problems and their parents/ caregivers. Norman, OK: Oklahoma University Health Sciences Center, Center on Child Abuse and Neglect.

[130] N Nelson, K. (2000). When do family preservation services make sense, and when should other permanency plans be explored? In H. Dubowitz & D. DePanfilis (Eds.), *Handbook for child protection practice* (pp. 257-266). Thousand Oaks, CA: Sage; Walton, E., & Denby, R. (1997). Targeting families to receive intensive family preservation services: Assessing the use of imminent risks of placement as a service criterion. *Family Preservation Journal, 2,* 53-70; Barth, R. (1988). Theories guiding home-based intensive family preservation services. In J. Whittaker, J. Kinney, E. Tracey, & C. Booth (Eds.), *Improving practice technology for work with high risk families: Lessons from the Homebuilders Social Work Education Project* (pp. 91-113). Seattle, WA: Center for Social Welfare Research; Barth, R. (1990). Theories guiding home-based intensive family preservation services. In J. K. Whittaker, J. Kinney, E. M. Tracey, & C. Booth (Eds.), *Reaching high-risk families: Intensive family preservation in human services* (pp. 89- 112). Hawthorne, NY: Aldine de Gruyter; Bronfenbrenner, U. (1979); Berry, M. (1991). The assessment of imminence of risk of placement: Lessons from a family preservation program. *Children and Youth Services Review, 13,* 239-256; Berry, M. (1992). An evaluation of family preservation services: Fitting agency services to family needs. *Social Work, 37,* 314-321; Grigsby, R. K. (1993). Theories that guide intensive family preservation services: A second look. In E. S. Morton & R. K. Grigsby (Eds.), *Advancing family preservation practice* (pp. 16-27). Newbury Park, CA: Sage; Schuerman, J. R., Rzepnicki, T., & Littell, J. (1994*). Putting families first: An experiment in family preservation.* New York, NY: Aldine de Gruyter.

[131] Lipovsky, J. et al. (1998); Saunders, B. E., & Meinig, M. (2000). Immediate issues affecting long-term family resolution in cases of parent-child sexual abuse. In R. M. Reece (Ed.), *Treatment of child abuse: Common ground for mental health, medical, and legal practitioners* (pp. 36- 53). Baltimore, MD: The Johns Hopkins University Press; Saunders, B. E., & Meinig, M. (2001). Family resolution therapy (FRT). In B. E. Saunders, L. Berliner, & R. F. Hanson (Eds.), *Guidelines for the psychosocial treatment of intrafamilial child physical and sexual abuse* (pp. 62-63). Charleston, SC: Medical University of South Carolina, National Crime Victims Research and Treatment Center.

[132] Schuerman, J. R., Rzepnicki, T., & Littell, J. (1994); Jordan, K., Alvarado, J., Braley, R., & Williams, L. (2001). Family preservation through home-based family therapy: An overview. *Journal of Family Psychotherapy, 12*(3), 31-44.

[133] Booth, C. (2001). Intensive family preservation services. In B. E. Saunders, L. Berliner, & R. F. Hanson (Eds.), *Guidelines for the psychosocial treatment of intrafamilial child physical and sexual abuse* (pp. 66-67). Charleston, SC: Medical University of South Carolina, National Crime Victims Research and Treatment Center; Kinney, J. M., Haapala, D., & Booth, C. L. (1991). *Keeping families together: The Homebuilders model.* New York, NY: Aldine de Gruyter; Nelson, K. (2000).

[134] Kolko, D. (2001). Individual child and parent physical abuse-focused cognitive-behavioral treatment. In B. E. Saunders, L. Berliner, & R. F. Hanson (Eds.), *Guidelines for the psychosocial treatment of intrafamilial child physical and sexual abuse* (pp. 36-37). Charleston, SC: Medical University of South Carolina, National Crime Victims Research and Treatment Center; Swenson, C. C., & Kolko, D. J. (2000). Long-term management of the developmental consequences of child physical abuse. In R. M. Reese (Ed.), *Treatment of child abuse: Common ground for mental health, medical, and legal practitioners* (pp. 135-154). Baltimore, MD: The Johns Hopkins University Press.

[135] Kolko, D. (1996). Individual cognitive behavioral therapy and family therapy for physically abused children and their offending parents: A comparison of clinical outcomes. *Child Maltreatment, 1,* 322-342.

[136] International Society for the Study of Dissociation. (2000). Guidelines for the evaluation and treatment of dissociative symptoms in children and adolescents. *Journal of Trauma and Dissociation, 1,* 105-154; Owaga, J. R., Sroufe, L. A., Weinfield, N. S., Carlson, E. A., & Egeland, B. (1997). Development and the fragmented self: Longitudinal study of dissociative symptomatology in a nonclinical sample. *Development and Psychopathology,9,* 855-879; Putnam, F. W. (1997). *Dissociation in children and adolescents.* New York, NY: The Guilford Press; Silberg, J. (2000). Fifteen years of dissociation in maltreatment children: Where do we go from here? *Child Maltreatment, 5,* 199-136; Silberg, J. (2001). Integrative developmental model for treatment of dissociative symptomatology. In B. E. Saunders, L. Berliner, & R. F. Hanson (Eds.), *Guidelines for the psychosocial treatment of intrafamilial child physical and sexual abuse* (pp. 64-65). Charleston, SC: Medical University of South Carolina, National Crime Victims Research and Treatment Center; Silberg, J. (in press). Treating maladaptive dissociation in a young teenage girl. In H. Orvaschel, J. Faust, & M. Hersen (Eds.), *Handbook of conceptualization and treatment of child psychopathology.* Oxford, UK: Elsevier Science LTD; Wieland, S. (1998). *Techniques and issues in abuse-focused therapy.* Thousand Oaks, CA: Sage..

[137] Swenson, C. C., & Henggeler, S. (2001). Multisystem therapy (MST) for maltreated children and their families. In B. E. Saunders, L. Berliner, & R. F. Hanson (Eds.), *Guidelines for the psychosocial treatment of*

intrafamilial child physical and sexual abuse (pp. 68-70). Charleston, SC: Medical University of South Carolina, National Crime Victims Research and Treatment Center; Brunk, M., Henggeler, S. W., & Whelan, J. P. (1987). A comparison of multisystemic therapy and parent training in the brief treatment of child abuse and neglect. *Journal of Consulting and Clinical Psychology, 55*, 311-318; Kumpfer, K. L. (1999).

[138] Henggeler, S. W., Schoenwald, S. K., Borduin, C. M., Rowland, M. D., & Cunningham, P. B. (1998). *Multisystemic treatment of antisocial behavior in children and adolescents.* New York, NY: The Guilford Press.

[139] Bavolek, S. J., Comstock, C. M., & McLaughlin, J. A. (1983). *The Nurturing Program: A validated approach to reducing functional family interactions.* Rockville, MD: National Institute of Mental Health; Kumpfer, K. L. (1999).

[140] Bavoleck, S. (1983). *The Nurturing Parenting Program: Parent trainer's manual.* Eau Claire, WI: Family Development Associates, Inc.

[141] Urquiza, A. (2001). Parent-child interaction therapy (PCIT). In B. E. Saunders, L. Berliner, & R. F. Hanson (Eds.), *Guidelines for the psychosocial treatment of intrafamilial child physical and sexual abuse* (pp. 74-76). Charleston, SC: Medical University of South Carolina, National Crime Victims Research and Treatment Center; Borrego, J., & Urquiza, A. J. (1998). Importance of therapist use of social reinforcement with parents as a model for parent-child relationships: An example with parent-child interaction therapy. *Child and Family Behavior Therapy, 20*(4), 27-54; Borrego, J., Urquiza, A. J., Rasmussen, R. A., & Zebell, N. (1999). Parent-child interaction therapy with a family at high-risk for physical abuse. *Child Maltreatment, 4*, 331-342; Eyberg, S. M. (1998). Parent-child interaction therapy: Integration of traditional and behavioral concerns. *Child and Family Behavior Therapy, 10*, 33-46; Eyberg, S., & Robinson, E. A. (1982). Parent-child interaction training: Effects on family functioning. *Journal of Clinical Child Psychology, 11*, 130-137.

[142] Hembree-Kigin, T., & McNeil, C. B. (1995). *Parent-child interaction therapy.* New York, NY: Plenum; Urquiza, A. J., Zebell, N., McGrath, J., & Vargas, E. (1999). *Parent-child interaction therapy: Application to high-risk and maltreating families.* Sacramento, CA: University of California Davis Medical Center, Department of Pediatrics, Child Protection Center; Urquiza, A. J., Zebell, N., McGrath, J., & Vargas, E. (1999). *Parent-child interaction therapy: Application to high-risk and maltreating families.* Videotape series. Sacramento, CA: University of California-Davis Medical Center, Department of Pediatrics, Child Protection Center; Urquiza, A. J., & McNeil, C. B. (1996). Parent-child interaction therapy: An intensive dyadic intervention for physically abusive families. *Child Maltreatment, 1*, 132-141.

[143] Johnson, D. A. (2001). Parents United (child sexual abuse treatment program). In B. E. Saunders, L. Berliner, & R. F. Hanson (Eds.), *Guidelines for the psychosocial treatment of intrafamilial child physical and sexual abuse* (pp. 79-84). Charleston, SC: Medical University of South Carolina, National Crime Victims Research and Treatment Center; Child Sexual Abuse Treatment Services. (1994). *Treatment manual for child sexual abuse treatment services.* Modesto, CA: Author.

[144] Kolko, D. (1996).

[145] Kolko, D. (2001); Swenson, C. C., & Kolko, D. (2000).

[146] Lutzker, J. R., & Rice, J. M. (1984). Project 12-Ways: Measuring outcome of a large-scale in-home service for the treatment and prevention of child abuse and neglect. *Child Abuse and Neglect, 8*, 5 19-524; Lutzker, J. R., & Rice, J. M. (1987). Using recidivism data to evaluate Project 12-Ways: An ecobehavioral approach to the treatment and prevention of child abuse and neglect. *Journal of Family Violence, 2*, 283-290; Dachman, R. S., Halasz, M. M., Bickett, A. D., & Lutzker, J. R. (1984). A home-based ecobehavioral parent-training and generalization package with a neglectful mother. *Education and Treatment of Children, 7*, 183-202; Campbell, R. V., O'Brien, S., Bickett, A., & Lutzker, J. R. (1983). In-home parent-training, treatment of migraine headaches, and marital counseling as an ecobehavioral approach to prevent child abuse. *Journal of Behavior Therapy and Experimental Psychiatry,14*, 147-154; Tertinger, D. A., Greene, B. F., & Lutzker, J. R. (1984). Home safety: Development and validation of one component of an ecobehavioral treatment program for abused and neglected children. *Journal of Applied Behavior Analysis, 17*, 159-174; Lutzker, S. Z., Lutzker, J. R., Braunling-McMorrow, D., & Eddleman, J. (1987). Prompting to increase mother-baby stimulation with single mothers. *Journal of Child and Adolescent Psychotherapy, 4*, 3-12; Lutzker, J. R., Bigelow, K. M., Doctor, R. M., Gershater, R. M., & Greene, B. F. (1998). An ecobehavioral model for the prevention and treatment of child abuse and neglect. In J. R. Lutzker (Ed.), *Handbook of child abuse research and treatment* (pp. 239-266). New York, NY: Plenum.

[147] Lutzker, J. R., & Rice, J. M. (1984); Lutzker, J. R. et al. (1998).

[148] Kumpfer, K. L. (1998). Selective prevention interventions: The Strengthening Families program. In R. S. Ashery, E. B. Robertson, & K. L. Kumpfer (Eds.), *Drug abuse prevention through family interventions* (pp. 160-207). Rockville, MD: U.S. Department of Health and Human Services, National Institute on Drug Abuse; Kumpfer, K. L. (1999).

[149] Kumpfer, K. L. (1998); Kumpfer, K. L. (1999).

[150] Steele, M. L. (2001). *Beech Acres Family Center evaluation analyses.* Los Angeles, CA: Author; Kumpfer, K. L. (1999).

[151] Steele, M., & Marigna, M. (1999). *Workshop manual program components: Strengthening multiethnic families and communities: A violence prevention parent training program.* Los Angeles, CA: Authors.

[152] Moore, E., Armsden, G., & Gogerty, P. L. (1998). A 12-year follow-up study of maltreated and at-risk children who received early therapeutic care. *Child Maltreatment, 3,* 3-16.

[153] Sheehan, L. (2001). Therapeutic child development program. In B. E. Saunders, L. Berliner, & R. F. Hanson (Eds.), *Guidelines for the psychosocial treatment of intrafamilial child physical and sexual abuse* (pp. 40-41). Charleston, SC: Medical University of South Carolina, National Crime Victims Research and Treatment Center; Childhaven. (n.d.). *Childhaven therapeutic child development manual.* Seattle, WA: Author.

[154] Berliner, L., & Saunders, B. E. (1996). Treating fear and anxiety in sexually abused children: Results of a controlled 2-year follow-up study. *Child Maltreatment, 1*(4), 294-309; Celano, M., Hazzard, A., Webb, C., & McCall, C. (1996). Treatment of traumagenic beliefs among sexually abused girls and their mothers: An evaluation study. *Journal of Abnormal Child Psychology, 24,* 1-16; Cohen, J. A., & Mannarino, A. P. (1996). A treatment outcome study for sexually abused preschool children: Initial findings. *Journal of the American Academy of Child and Adolescent Psychiatry, 35,* 42-50; Cohen, J. A., & Mannarino, A. P. (1997). A treatment study of sexually abused preschool children: Outcome during a 1-year follow-up. *Journal of the American Academy of Child and Adolescent Psychiatry, 36,* 1228-1235; Cohen, J. A., & Mannarino, A. P. (1998). Interventions for sexually abused children: Initial treatment findings. *Child Maltreatment, 3,* 17-26; Deblinger, E., McLeer, S. V., & Henry, D. (1990). Cognitive behavioral treatment for sexually abused children suffering post-traumatic stress: Preliminary findings. *Journal of the American Academy of Children and Adolescent Psychiatry, 19,* 747-752; Deblinger, E., Lippman, J., & Steer, R. (1996). Sexually abused children suffering traumatic stress symptoms: Initial treatment outcome findings. *Child Maltreatment, 1,* 310-321; Deblinger, E., Steer, R. A., & Lippmann, J. (1999). Two-year follow-up study of cognitive behavioral therapy for sexually abused children suffering post-traumatic stress symptoms. *Child Abuse and Neglect, 23,* 1371-1378; Stauffer, L., & Deblinger, E. (1996). Cognitive behavioral groups for nonoffending mothers and their young sexually abused children: A preliminary treatment outcome study. *Child Maltreatment, 1,* 65-67.

[155] Cohen, J., & Deblinger, E. (2001). In B. E. Saunders, L. Berliner, & R. F. Hanson (Eds.), *Guidelines for the psychosocial treatment of intrafamilial child physical and sexual abuse* (pp. 42-44). Charleston, SC: Medical University of South Carolina, National Crime Victims Research and Treatment Center; Cohen, J., & Mannarino, A. P. (1993). A treatment model for sexually abused preschoolers. *Journal of Interpersonal Violence, 8,* 115- 131; Deblinger, E., & Heflin, A. H. (1996). *Treatment for sexually abused children and their non offen ding parents: A cognitive-behavioral approach.* Thousand Oaks, CA: Sage.

[156] Friedrich, W. N. (2001). Trauma-focused integrative-eclectic therapy (IET). In B. E. Saunders, L. Berliner, & R. F. Hanson (Eds.), *Guidelines for the psychosocial treatment of intrafamilial child physical and sexual abuse* (pp. 38-39). Charleston, SC: Medical University of South Carolina, National Crime Victims Research and Treatment Center; Friedrich, W. N. (1998). Treating sexual behavior problems in children: A treatment manual. (Available from the author at the Mayo Clinic, Department of Psychiatry and Psychology, Rochester, MN 55905); Friedrich, W. N. (1995). *Psychotherapy with sexually abused boys.* Thousand Oaks, CA: Sage; Friedrich, W. N., Luecke, W. J., Beilke, R. L., & Place, V. (1991). Group treatment of sexually abused boys: An agency study. *Journal of Interpersonal Violence, 7,* 396- 409.

[157] Morton, T. (2000). When can a child be safely reunited with his or her family? In H. Dubowitz & D. DePanfilis (Eds.), *Handbook for child protection practice* (pp. 522- 525). Thousand Oaks, CA: Sage.

[158] Glazer-Semmel, E. (2000). How do I prepare families for case closure? In H. Dubowitz & D. DePanfilis (Eds.), *Handbook for child protection practice* (pp. 531-534). Thousand Oaks, CA: Sage.

[159] Rooney, R. (1992). Strategies for working with involuntary clients. New York, NY: Columbia University Press.

[160] Cournoyer, B. (2000). *The social work skills workbook* (3rd ed.). Belmont, CA: Brooks/Cole.

[161] Rooney, R. (1992).

[162] Glazer-Semmel, E. (2000).

[163] DePanfilis, D. (2000d). How do I use the case record to guide intervention and provide accountability? In H. Dubowitz & D. DePanfilis (Eds.), *Handbook for child protection practice* (pp. 598-603). Thousand Oaks, CA: Sage; Child Welfare League of America. (1999); Hepworth, D. H., Rooney, R. H., & Larsen, J. (2002). *Direct social work practice* (6th ed.). Pacific Grove, CA: Brooks/Cole.

[164] DePanfilis, D. et al. (2000d).

[165] DePanfilis, D. et al. (2000d).

[166] DePanfilis, D. et al. (2000d).

[167] Morton, T., & Salus, M. (1994). Supervising child protective services caseworkers. Washington, DC: U.S. Department of Health and Human Services, National Center on Child Abuse and Neglect.

[168] Morton, T., & Salus, M. (1994).

[169] Colorado Department of Human Services, & National Child Welfare Resource Center for Management and Administration. (1994). *Standards for supervision in child welfare.* Portland, ME: University of Southern Maine, National Child Welfare Resource Center for Management and Administration.

[170] Holder, W., & Morton, T. (1999).

[171] Salus, M. (1996). *Case consultation and supervision.* Denver, CO: University of Denver, School of Social Work.

[172] Salus, M. (1999). *The educational role of the supervisor.* Baton Rouge, LA: Louisiana Department of Social Services, Office of Community Services; Berg, I. K., & Kelly, S. (2000).

[173] Griffin, W., & Bandas, J. (1985). Risk assessment—early warning program. Helena, MT: Montana Department of Social and Rehabilitative Services, Community Services Division.

In: Child Protection, the Courts and Social Workers
Editor: Terrance R. Langely

ISBN: 978-1-60741-279-3
© 2010 Nova Science Publishers, Inc.

Chapter 3

WORKING WITH THE COURTS IN CHILD PROTECTION

William G. Jones

1. PURPOSE AND OVERVIEW

The courts play a central role in making decisions regarding the protection of children who have been maltreated. Understanding this process is crucial for any professional involved in child protection. By having a thorough knowledge of this legal process and by working in partnership with the courts, child protective services (CPS) caseworkers and other professionals can work toward the safety, permanency, and well-being of children more effectively.

Child maltreatment cases are handled in a variety of courts. Thus, the rules and procedures that govern these cases may differ depending on the *type* of proceeding within which an allegation of abuse is brought, the laws governing the court involved, and the local practice in a particular court.

In recent years, a number of reforms have addressed the unique nature of child maltreatment and the special needs of its victims. Both legislative and judicial efforts have improved the ability and flexibility of the courts to respond to allegations of abuse or neglect. Courts now have more alternatives and resources with which to work when faced with a case where abuse or neglect has been established by the required burden of proof under State law.

This manual provides the basic information needed by CPS caseworkers to work successfully with the courts. It introduces concepts and terminology associated with the courts, describes the key court processes, and presents practical information to help caseworkers prepare for what can be an overwhelming experience. The manual describes:

- The general or common court system;
- The powers of the court and the rights of parents and children in child maltreatment cases;
- The interplay between child maltreatment legislation and caseworker practice;

- The juvenile court process;
- The criminal court process;
- Domestic relations and other court proceedings;
- The issues involved in going to court;
- The relationship between CPS caseworkers and the court;
- Court improvement and best practices.

Appendices to this manual include a glossary, resource listings, and guidelines for CPS caseworkers for permanency and review hearings.

Various terms are used within the field and throughout communities to describe CPS agencies and caseworkers, including:

- CPS agency:
  - Department of Social Services – Child welfare agency
  - Social services
  - Family services
- CPS caseworker:
  - Caseworker
  - Social worker
  - Social caseworker
  - Worker

In many settings, there is little or no distinction among these terms. For the sake of clarity and ease of understanding, this manual primarily uses "CPS" and "CPS caseworker."

One note of caution is necessary. On its own, this manual cannot adequately prepare any professional, legal or non legal, to practice in the area of child protection. Consultation with a skilled legal specialist is *critical*, as is comprehensive training on working with the courts, particularly with respect to unique State laws and local practices.

Information and suggestions incorporated throughout this manual do not necessarily imply endorsement by the U.S. Department of Health and Human Services or official interpretation of Federal requirements.

2. THE COURT SYSTEM AND CHILD PROTECTION

State courts, including county and municipal courts, are responsible for resolving a wide variety of issues and do so increasingly in diverse ways. In addition to going to court for child abuse and neglect cases, child protective services (CPS) caseworkers often also must be involved in court proceedings for child support, domestic violence, criminal conduct, juvenile delinquency, child custody, mental health, and directly related proceedings such as termination of parental rights (TPR) and adoption. How courts are organized and how they divide their caseloads vary widely by State and even within a State. Thus, it is important for CPS caseworkers to know which courts hear which kinds of cases in their communities.

This chapter begins with an introduction to the concept of jurisdiction. The chapter continues with an overview of the juvenile court, then provides descriptions of other specialized courts. To set the stage for the later discussion of court processes, the chapter also reviews the general powers of the court, as well as the rights accorded to parents and children in judicial proceedings.

Jurisdiction

To hear and to decide a case, a court must have jurisdiction or "authority" over that type of case, as specified by State law. The allegations of the petition initiating the case must satisfy the statutory criteria for cases of that type. The court must have jurisdiction over the parties against whom the case is brought, such as the parents of a child removed from the home. It is the judge's responsibility to decide at the outset whether the court has jurisdiction over the subject matter of the case and over the parties. Objections to jurisdiction, although infrequent in child abuse and neglect cases, can be complex and require CPS to have legal representation.

Juvenile Court

The juvenile court decides whether children have been victimized by maltreatment, as defined by State law. It then assumes responsibility for ordering services and monitors cases to ensure that its interventions are as beneficial and effective as possible.

The Focus of Juvenile Courts

The juvenile court—the earliest of the specialized courts—originated in Illinois in 1899. Initially, the juvenile court's primary focus was on delinquency (i.e., the commitment by youth of what would be crimes if they were adults) and status offenses (i.e., transgressions of children that would not be crimes if adults committed them). The emphasis was on the rehabilitation and reform of the youth who came before the court. Over time, the juvenile court concept spread rapidly to other States and expanded to include protecting children from child abuse and neglect.

The juvenile court operates according to the legal power of *parens patriae*. The *parens patriae* doctrine stipulates that the State has the legal authority to act as the guardian of children whose parents are unable to provide adequate protection or meet their needs sufficiently.

Today, juvenile court judges hear cases alleging child abuse and neglect, delinquency, and status offenses. Most also hear TPR cases and adoption matters. Some juvenile courts have responsibility for mental health commitment and admission hearings, abortion consent waivers for minors, and petitions for emancipation.

The organization and structure of juvenile courts vary widely from State to State and within States, depending on how State legislatures create their court systems and on the volume of cases in each jurisdiction. Some large communities have full-time courts dedicated to hearing just child abuse and neglect or delinquency cases, while others have one or more full-time courts that hear a mix of juvenile cases. Judges in smaller and rural communities regularly hear a variety of case types and commonly hear all the juvenile cases on the same docket with other types of cases.

How juvenile courts are different from other courts

Juvenile courts operate like other courts when deciding whether a child was abused or neglected or committed a delinquent act or a status offense. What is unique about juvenile courts is that they also make extensive use of experts, including CPS caseworkers, juvenile probation officers, psychologists, mental health professionals, physicians, domestic violence specialists, educators, child development specialists, foster parents, relative caretakers, and others. The court utilizes the expertise of these individuals to understand children and their families better, why events occurred that necessitated court intervention, and how to prevent recurrence. Juvenile courts attempt to look beyond individual and family deficits to understand the family and child as a whole. They aim to make well-informed decisions to address needs for housing, childcare, in-home services, domestic violence advocacy, mental health or substance abuse treatment, paternity establishment, child support, educational services, or employment. Also unique to the juvenile court, particularly in CPS cases, are the frequent review of parents and the assessment of agency performance.

Specialized Courts

Many communities are experimenting with "specialized" or "dedicated" courts that focus on particular areas, such as mental health, truancy, domestic violence, substance abuse, child support, and reentry. Specialized courts are designed to require treatment and services for the specific offense in addition to, or instead of, punishment, such as incarceration. These courts are more common in larger communities that have available funding. Three specialized courts that are particularly relevant to CPS cases are highlighted here.

Family courts

Several States either have or are implementing "unified" or "coordinated" family courts that hear most, if not all, of the different types of cases having to do with children and families. Family courts are characterized by:

- Case management practices that expedite the resolution of cases;
- Specialized services;
- Coordination of all cases involving the same family, often before the same judge;
- Extensive use of alternative dispute resolution methodologies;
- Reduced court appearances;
- Enhanced training for judicial officers;
- A commitment to providing participants with good customer service.

MODEL FAMILY COURTS

Currently, there are 25 model family courts located throughout all the States and the District of Columbia. The National Council of Juvenile and Family Court Judges

(NCJFCJ) has conducted extensive information dissemination, curriculum development, and training and technical assistance in support of the model courts process. Its nationally recognized Child Victims Act Model Courts Initiative works to improve juvenile and family court practices in child abuse and neglect cases nationwide.[1]

A "model court" is created when a lead judge in a juvenile court jurisdiction seeks to implement the principles of court reform. These were first formulated in the 1995 NCJFCJ publication *Resource Guidelines: Improving Court Practices in Child Abuse and Neglect Cases* (online at http://www.ncjfcj.org/images/stories/dept/ppcd/pdf/resguide.pdf). The model court teams identify impediments to the timeliness of court events and to the delivery of services for families with children in care and then design and implement court- and agency-based changes to address these barriers. Model courts receive ongoing technical assistance and training from the Permanency Planning for Children Department of NCJFCJ. For more information on model courts and this initiative, visit the "Frequently Asked Questions" page of the NCJFCJ Web site at http://www.ncjfcj.org/content/view/267/156.

Family court cases are fundamentally different from criminal cases for several reasons. First, they involve intimate, interpersonal relationships and highly charged emotions that profoundly affect how the parties approach the litigation. Commonly, the courtroom battle is an extension of unresolved personal conflicts. The adversarial process only heightens the conflict. Second, they involve multiple claims, each with a unique set of issues and timetables for court action. Third, the litigation is ongoing. Any changes in the circumstances in the lives of the parents or children, changes in the financial circumstances, or noncompliance with support or visitation provisions of an order frequently require renewed litigation.

Where family courts have been established, they typically include the juvenile court and attempt to coordinate cases that arise there with cases on other dockets involving the same family. They also provide access to a variety of services, some of which may be valuable resources in child maltreatment cases (e.g., child waiting rooms with capable caretakers when parents need to be in court).

Drug courts

Drug courts, an increasingly common specialized court, emphasize recovery from addiction, provide access to immediate treatment, and conduct frequent reviews to monitor abstinence, participation in treatment, and compliance with court orders. The reviews are a constructive and supportive group process in which each participant's performance is assessed in the drug court. While drug courts handle mostly criminal cases and require an underlying criminal conviction to mandate participation, the number of dependency, delinquency, and child custody drug courts is rising.

Drug courts, including criminal ones, are resources CPS should utilize whenever possible. Studies suggest that parental substance abuse is a contributing factor for between one-third and two-thirds of children involved with CPS.[2] Drug courts can facilitate access to treatment, which otherwise may not be available. Individuals with substance use disorders who access services through drug courts generally initiate treatment sooner, have lower rates of recidivism, and participate in treatment longer.[3]

For more on drug courts, including grants and funding information, visit the National Criminal Justice Reference Service at http://www.ncjrs.org/ drug_courts/summary.html.

Juvenile and family drug courts

Recently, a number of jurisdictions have referred to the experiences of adult drug courts to determine how juvenile courts might adapt to the increasing population of substance abusing juveniles and parents. The result is the emergence of:

- **The juvenile drug court**—a drug court that focuses on juvenile delinquency matters and status offenses that involve juveniles who are substance abusers.[4]

- **The family drug court**—a drug court that deals with cases involving parental rights in which:
  - An adult is the litigant (i.e., any party to a lawsuit, which means plaintiff , defendant, petitioner, respondent, cross-complainant or cross-defendant, but not a witness or attorney);
  - The case comes before the court through either the criminal or civil process;
  - The case arises out of the substance abuse of a parent.[5]

FAMILY DRUG COURTS

As of December 31, 2004, there were 153 family drug courts in 33 States and the District of Columbia. A family drug court, also known as a family dependency treatment court, is a juvenile or family court docket in which selected abuse, neglect, and dependency cases are identified and treatment providers collaborate to provide safe homes for children while simultaneously providing drug and alcohol treatment and other support services to the parents.[6] Family drug courts typically operate within the general court organization in their respective jurisdiction. In most family drug courts, the judge, after consultation with attorneys, CPS, and treatment providers, will decide which cases to accept into the program. Once in the program, participants are subjected to frequent drug screenings and may appear more frequently before the judge, sometimes as often as once a week, to report on their progress with treatment.[7]

Juvenile and family drug courts provide immediate intervention in the lives of children and parents using drugs or those exposed to substance abuse through family members. They also provide a structure allowing for the ongoing, active participation and oversight of a judge. Common goals of juvenile drug courts include providing children with substance abuse treatment and services, offering constructive support to aid them in resisting further criminal activity, supporting them to perform well in school and to develop positive relationships in the community, and helping them to build skills that will aid in leading productive substance- and crime- free lives. The goals of family drug courts are similar, but also include helping parents become emotionally, financially, and personally self-sufficient and develop effective parenting skills.

For more information on family drug courts, go to http://www.ncjrs.org/pdffi les1/bja/206809.pdf.

Powers of the Court

Courts and judges often are viewed as possessing enormous power and influence. The power of the courts is ever changing, and the authority of judges varies considerably from State to State. Some courts exercise the authority to dictate to CPS where children should be placed, sometimes including specific foster homes. Other States are more prescriptive in their statutory laws about placement options for children in State custody and give less discretion and authority to the courts. CPS caseworkers who recognize and know how to access the powers of the court will find them advantageous to the resolution of their cases. This section describes seven different powers held by the court:

- Power to subpoena witnesses;
- Power to subpoena documents and records;
- Power to assist CPS investigations;
- Power to make negative "reasonable efforts" determinations;
- Power to hold individuals in contempt;
- Power to order treatment;
- Inherent power of the position.

This section also highlights how these powers can benefit casework practice and court processes.

Power to subpoena witnesses

Courts have the power to subpoena witnesses. A subpoena is a court order that directs a person to appear in court. Anyone who is properly served with a subpoena and who fails to appear as directed is subject to being held in contempt.

Courts also can compel a witness to testify, unless there is a constitutional right or a privilege that protects the witness from having to do so. The U.S. Constitution's Fifth Amendment privilege against self-incrimination is a protection that applies to criminal proceedings as well as to testimony in any other forum, including child abuse and neglect courts, if the testimony might be used against the witness in a future prosecution.

There are two types of immunity that the prosecuting attorney or, in some States, the judge may grant:

- **Use immunity**—bars the use of a witness's testimony and statements from being used directly or indirectly against that person in a subsequent trial. Future prosecution must be based on evidence independent of the immunized testimony or statements.
- **Transactional immunity**—bars any subsequent court action against the immunized person, regardless of the source of the evidence against that person.

Use immunity is generally preferred because it does not prevent prosecuting the person based on independently acquired evidence. For example, both parents are allegedly the only people present when their child is killed. The prosecutor may grant use immunity to the parent believed not to have participated in the actual murder to gain that parent's testimony against the other. If subsequent evidence is uncovered from an independent source that implicates the immunized parent (e.g., an eyewitness comes forward or a videotape of the incident is discovered), he can then be prosecuted. If transaction immunity had been granted, however, even with this subsequent evidence, the parent could not be charged. If either type of immunity is granted, the witness can be compelled to testify.

Depending on State law, witnesses who are doctors, clergy, lawyers, and mental health professionals may not be compelled to divulge confidential communications made to them by or about their clients. The content of these communications is privileged and cannot be disclosed without the express, informed consent of the client. These privileges encourage those seeking professional assistance to interact freely and openly with those professionals in order to maximize the benefits of their services and to eliminate fear of repercussions. Such privileges, however, may not apply if the client reveals child maltreatment. Under those circumstances, the professional may be required to make a report to CPS and to testify in court if a court proceeding results from the report. The court ultimately determines whether any claim of privilege applies. Any witness who refuses a court directive to provide testimony can be held in contempt and incarcerated until the testimony is given.

Power to subpoena documents and records

Courts also have the power to issue a subpoena *ducestecum* (i.e., a court order requiring the release of specified documents or records). This subpoena commands a person to produce in court certain designated documents or records. For example, a court may require a hospital to provide its records on a child's care or compel a CPS caseworker to produce a case file or notes of conversations.

Power to assist CPS investigations

CPS caseworkers can face seemingly insurmountable barriers in their investigations of suspected child maltreatment. For example, parents are under no legal obligation to allow CPS to enter their homes to conduct an investigation. The Child Abuse Prevention and Treatment Act (CAPTA), as amended by the Keeping Children and Families Safe Act (P.L. 108– 36), requires a CPS worker to advise the individuals being investigated for child abuse or neglect of the complaints and allegations being made against them, but they must still protect the confidentiality rights of the person who reported the suspected abuse. (42 U.S.C. 5106a(b) (2) (A) (xviii)).

Obtaining formal documents and other information related to the alleged maltreatment, such as medical or school records, is also difficult. To assist CPS in obtaining information necessary to investigations, some States have granted courts the authority to order parents to allow CPS to examine and to interview their children and to compel others who have information relevant to a child maltreatment investigation to make that information available for CPS examination.

Power to make a negative "reasonable efforts" determination

A court can find that CPS has failed to make "reasonable efforts" to:

- Avoid a child's removal from the home;
- Secure an adoptive home or other permanent placement for a child.

A negative reasonable efforts finding can result in a court order preventing CPS from seeking reimbursement for the cost of that child's care or to report the finding to Federal and State oversight agencies.

"Reasonable" is a familiar term in the law, and determining what is reasonable is a familiar standard for judges. It is applied on a case-by-case basis to the particular needs of that child and family and the services necessary to meet those needs. (For more information on reasonable efforts, refer to the section on the Adoption and Safe Families Act (ASFA) in Chapter 3, *The Interplay Between Child Maltreatment Legislation and Caseworker Practice.*)

Power to hold individuals in contempt

There are two types of contempt, civil and criminal. Civil contempt is the willful failure to do something that a court has ordered, such as refusing to testify when the court has found that no privilege applies or refusing to pay child support when there are ample funds to do so. Civil contempt is punishable by incarceration, which, in theory, can last until the witness relents and complies. Usually, however, a compromise is negotiated or one side relents before anyone is sent to jail.

Criminal contempt can be indirect or direct. Indirect contempt is a willful violation of a court's order. Examples of indirect contempt include a CPS caseworker's refusal to arrange for a particular evaluation or a parent's refusal to submit to paternity testing. Indirect criminal contempt requires advanced notice of the specific charge and a full hearing. Direct contempt occurs in the presence of the judge and usually involves some disruptive or disrespectful behavior, such as uttering an epithet when the judge announces an unfavorable decision. Direct criminal contempt is punishable immediately. Both direct and indirect criminal contempt can be punished by incarceration for a fixed time determined by statute, a fine, or both.

Power to order treatment

Some States specifically authorize courts to order parents to participate in mental health or substance abuse treatment. Whether or not the court has that power by statute, it does have the power to determine if the child should be removed from or returned to a parent, which may be conditioned on the parent's participation in treatment.

Inherent power of the position

One of the most significant judicial powers is not found in statutes or in case law; it is the power to gain the attention of others. Most of the professionals involved with child maltreatment respect the position and authority of the court and are responsive to judicial requests or inquiries. When a judge calls a meeting to address a particular issue or invites stakeholders in a child abuse or neglect case to a meeting, they usually attend. This is the power "to get people to the table." Of course, the outcome of such a meeting depends on the judge's leadership skills and the extent to which the attendees are willing and able to communicate effectively and to collaborate in achieving system improvements. (See Chapter 9, *Court Improvement and Best Practices* for more on judicial leadership.)

> For information on any particular State's child abuse and neglect laws, visit http://www.childwelfare. gov/systemwide/laws_policies/search/index.cfm.

The Rights of Parents and Children in Child Maltreatment Cases

The court system accords both parents and children certain legal rights and entitlements, depending on the type of proceeding in which they are involved, including:

- The right to family integrity;
- The right to notice of the proceedings;
- The right to a hearing;
- The right to counsel;
- The right to a jury trial;
- The CAPTA requirement of a Guardian ad Litem or court-appointed special advocate;
- The entitlement to reasonable efforts.

Parents and children must not only be informed of their rights, but they also must understand the protections those rights afford them. Court representatives and CPS caseworkers can educate families about their rights and help them feel empowered in an otherwise intimidating process.

The right to family integrity

Public policy has long recognized a right to family integrity, and there has been ample case law defending that right. The legal framework regarding the parent-child relationship balances the rights and responsibilities among parent, child, and State, as guided by Federal statutes. It has long been recognized that parents have a fundamental liberty interest, protected by the Constitution, to raise their children as they choose. This parent-child relationship grants certain rights, duties, and obligations to both parent and child, including the responsibility of the parent to protect the child's safety and well-being. If a parent, however, is unable or unwilling to meet this responsibility, the State has the power and authority to take action to protect a child from significant harm.[8]

A series of U.S. Supreme Court cases have defined when it is constitutional for the State to intervene in family life.[9] Although the Court has given parents great latitude in the upbringing and education of their children, it has held that the rights of parenthood and the family have limits and can be regulated in the interest of the public. The Court has further concluded that the State, as *parens patriae*, may restrict the parent's control by regulating or prohibiting the child's labor, by requiring school attendance, and by intervening in other ways to promote the child's wellbeing.[10]

In a recent case, the U.S. Supreme Court reaffirmed the right to family integrity in *Troxel v. Granville* when it said that parents' interest in the "care, custody, and control of their children is perhaps the oldest of fundamental liberty interests."[11] In *Troxel v. Granville*, the U.S. Supreme Court reviewed a Washington State statute authorizing grandparent visitation. The Court decided that the statute unconstitutionally infringed on *Granville's* fundamental liberty interest in raising her children free from State interference. This fundamental interest extends to a family's right to remain together.

As discussed in the next chapter, CAPTA is one of the primary pieces of Federal legislation guiding casework (See Chapter 3, *The Interplay Between Child Maltreatment Legislation and Caseworker Practice*), and it supports the right of family integrity through community-based grants that aim to strengthen families. Of course, this right is not absolute. A compelling State interest, such as the need to protect children from significant harm, will justify infringement on the right to family integrity.

The right to notice of the proceedings

Parents or other custodians of a child have the right to "notice" of any petition filed regarding that child and to be notified of any hearing regarding that petition. The right to notice encompasses the right to be formally given the petition, which also must state what the parent has done or not done that makes court involvement necessary. The right to notice is a fundamental element of the constitutional right to due process. Due process specifies the right to be present in court, representation by an attorney, and procedures that are speedy, fair, and impartial. It applies to both parents, whether or not they are living together. Orders entered without notice are subject to being withdrawn.

Putative fathers (those identified as the biological parent, but whose paternity has not been legally established) also must be identified in the petition and be served. Their relationship to the child needs to be determined as early in the proceeding as possible by formal acknowledgment or by genetic testing. If paternity is established, these fathers or their families may become financial and placement resources for the child.

Petitions may be filed and emergency *ex parte* orders may be entered without advance notice to parents. *Ex parte* is defined as being on behalf of or involving only one party to a legal matter and in the absence of and usually without notice to the other party. For example, an emergency removal of a child from an unsafe home situation may be done through an *ex parte* order. Action must be taken, however, to serve the parents with the petition and order as quickly as possible. Foster parents and kinship care providers also must be notified of pending court hearings and be given an opportunity to be heard during these proceedings. (For more information on *ex parte* communications, see Chapter 7, *Going to Court.*)

The right to a hearing

Another fundamental element of due process is the right to a hearing on the merits of a petition, including the right to cross-examine or to question any witness called by CPS, by the other parent, or on behalf of the child, as well as the right to present evidence on one's own behalf.

The right to counsel

Most States provide court-appointed lawyers for indigent parents in child maltreatment cases, but there is no Federal constitutional right to counsel in such cases. A constitutional right to counsel (i.e., every citizen's right to an attorney) does attach in some TPR cases, but not all.[12]

The quality of this representation varies widely among lawyers and courts. With the goal of improving quality, national, as well as many State and court, standards or guidelines exist for attorneys practicing juvenile and family law. Some jurisdictions also mandate training before appointing attorneys to child abuse and neglect proceedings. In fact, the amended CAPTA requires that attorneys representing children receive training that is "appropriate to [their] role."[13]

The right to a jury trial

A few States grant parents the right to a jury trial in child maltreatment cases, but the right is usually "waived" or "voluntarily given up" by the parent. In criminal child maltreatment cases, by contrast, the U.S. Constitution gives adult defendants in every State a right to trial by jury.

The CAPTA requirement of a Guardian ad Litem or court-appointed special advocate

Children who allegedly have been maltreated are entitled to a Guardian ad Litem (GAL), who is an independent advocate for the children's best interest. States must comply with this requirement in order to satisfy CAPTA State Grant funding requirements. The GAL role may be fulfilled by the appointment of an attorney, a volunteer who is not an attorney, or both. Volunteers also may be called court-appointed special advocates (CASA). The volunteers often are professionals trained in other disciplines, such as nursing, psychology, or education. Responsibilities of the GAL or CASA include:

- Meeting the child;
- Exploring the facts of the case;
- Obtaining medical, educational, and other records;
- Determining the child's perspective and needs;
- Identifying appropriate services and resources;
- Monitoring the progress of the case;
- Promoting the child's interests.

Where both an attorney and a GAL are appointed, it is with the expectation that they will function as a team in performing those tasks and in advocating for the child, as well as in making the child's own views known to the court. These advocates can be valuable sources of knowledge and information and important allies when they and the CPS caseworker concur on how the case should be resolved.

In some States, an attorney usually is appointed as the child's GAL. Laws in some States require the GAL to advocate in the best interests of the child, even when contrary to the expressed wishes of the child. In other States, however, the GAL's advocacy may be guided more clearly by legal ethics that compel advocacy in support of a child's stated wishes.

Although legal ethics may dictate that the attorney advocate the client's position zealously, there also is consideration in ethical rules for the common situation where certain clients (e.g., very young children) are considered incapable of possessing the judgment necessary to guide an attorney's actions. These situations likely will result in the GAL advocating what is believed to be in the child's best interest.

NATIONAL COURT APPOINTED SPECIAL ADVOCATE ASSOCIATION

The National Court Appointed Special Advocate Association (NCASAA) promotes and supports volunteer advocacy in juvenile courts for children alleged to be maltreated. NCASAA provides money and technical assistance to start and expand programs, disseminates performance standards, produces training manuals and other publications, and trains program leaders and volunteers. For more information on NCASAA and GAL, go to http://www.casanet.org.

How children are represented in child maltreatment cases—whether by a lawyer, a volunteer GAL or CASA, or one of each—is a matter of State law or local practice. CPS caseworkers will want to know what model is used in their community and whether any advocates who are attorneys owe allegiance to the child's stated or best interest.

In addition to CAPTA's requirements of counsel or a GAL, minors who are parents also may be eligible, in some States, for a different type of GAL. This is nearly universal in civil cases, which include child maltreatment and TPR proceedings. The assignment is articulated in the States' Rules of Civil Procedure, most of which track the Federal rules, which state that minors are entitled to have a responsible adult function as a decision-maker for them in matters related to any litigation. The court appoints someone to fulfill this responsibility. If there is no conflict of interest between the roles of counsel for the minor parent and the GAL, the same person can be appointed to perform both functions. It is not required, however, nor is it required that the GAL be a lawyer.

The entitlement to reasonable efforts

Except in certain aggravated circumstances, parents and children are entitled under the Adoption. Assistance and Child Welfare Act (P.L. 96–272) and ASFA (P.L. 105–89) to have State agencies make reasonable efforts to keep them together, or if a child has been removed from the family, to make reasonable efforts to reunify the family. ASFA also states that children who are not going to be reunited with their families are entitled to reasonable efforts by State agencies or departments to secure a permanent placement for them.

Federal law further requires that judges decide at each critical stage of an abuse or neglect case whether the agency has complied with the reasonable efforts requirement. The obligation to make reasonable efforts applies to CPS alone, not to the parents, any other individuals, or service providers.

"Reasonable efforts" is not defined in Federal law. Some States, however, have attempted to define it, and caseworkers will need to familiarize themselves with any definition in their State's statutes. Information about the application of reasonable efforts in a State's appellate court should be provided by the CPS agency's attorney to the head of the agency for dissemination to caseworkers and other pertinent staff , along with clarification of the decision's impact on their responsibilities.

> Caseworkers are encouraged to read *Making Reasonable Efforts: A Permanent Home for Every Child*, developed by the Youth Law Center, for a comprehensive discussion on the reasonable efforts requirement and how it affects their responsibilities and those of their agency, attorneys for all parties, and the judges. It can be obtained online at http://www.emcf.org/pdf/children

3. THE INTERPLAY BETWEEN CHILD MALTREATMENT LEGISLATION AND CASEWORKER PRACTICE

Children had little legal protection from maltreatment until the early 20th century when addressing child abuse and neglect became a component of the new juvenile court movement. Court practices varied, but generally were inadequate to meet the needs of abused and neglected children and their families. The identification of battered child syndrome in 1962 heightened public interest in child maltreatment and resulted in the passage of legislation in most States to enhance protections for children.[14]

As recently as the late 1 970s, it was common that the only people in the courtroom in child maltreatment cases were the caseworker, the judge, and sometimes the parents. Children rarely participated in the process and none of the parties, including child protective services (CPS), had legal representation. Nor were there Guardians ad Litem (GALs) or court-appointed special advocates (CASAs). The court's role was limited. If it found abuse or neglect, it would place the child in the custody of CPS, and that ended its responsibility. There were no case plans, no court reports, no periodic reviews, no reasonable efforts requirement, and no permanency planning.

Since then, sweeping changes have occurred in the law, CPS practice, and the litigation of child maltreatment cases. Family dynamics and problems (e.g., AIDS, homelessness, substance abuse) have become more complex as well. These changes have increased the frequency of interaction between the courts and CPS dramatically and have transformed the nature of their relationship. Therefore, it is imperative that CPS caseworkers understand the implications of significant legislation on successful outcomes for families.

The case example in Exhibit 3-1 illustrates a family experiencing multiple issues needing intervention. Following the case example are summaries of relevant legislation, including:

- The Child Abuse Prevention and Treatment Act;
- The Individuals with Disabilities Education Act;
- The Indian Child Welfare Act;
- The Adoption Assistance and Child Welfare Act;
- The Adoption and Safe Families Act;
- The Interstate Compact on the Placement of Children.

Following each summary is a discussion of how that legislation may be applicable in the case example.

The Child Abuse Prevention and Treatment Act

The first Federal legislation to address child maltreatment became law in 1974 with the passage of the Child Abuse Prevention and Treatment Act (CAPTA) (P.L. 93–247).[15] In return for Federal funding, CAPTA required that States adopt mandatory child abuse reporting laws, ensure the confidentiality of agency records and court proceedings, and appoint a GAL for every child in maltreatment proceedings in juvenile court. CAPTA has been reauthorized periodically and amended by Congress, most recently as part of the Keeping Children and Families Safe Act of 2003 (P.L. 108–36).

EXHIBIT 3-1. CASE EXAMPLE

April Smith is a 32-year-old mother of three children, aged 16 months, 4 years, and 12 years. CPS conducted an emergency removal of the three children due to allegations of severe neglect, inappropriate supervision, the sexual abuse of the 12-year-old child, and domestic violence. A CPS investigation concluded that the allegations possessed substantial evidence warranting ongoing CPS involvement and the filing of a petition to juvenile court for foster care placement.

The CPS petition contained the following information and allegations:

- The 16-month-old and two unrelated 7-year-old children were left at home for approximately 3 days in the care of the 12-year-old child without any adult supervision;
- The 4-year-old and 12-year-old children reported witnessing violent, physical attacks against Ms. Smith;
- The 12-year-old child reported that Robert Johnson had touched her inappropriately on three occasions;
- The 12-year-old attempted suicide, is failing academically in school, is suspected of having a learning disability, and was suspended from school on two occasions for fighting with peers;
- The rental home was littered with broken glass, animal and human feces, molding food, and hazardous electrical fixtures;
- The domestic violence perpetrator, Mr. Johnson, is the biological father of Ms. Smith's 16-month-old and 4-year-old children, but Ms. Smith and Mr. Johnson are not married;
- Ms. Smith abuses alcohol and cocaine;
- Mr. Johnson also abuses alcohol and cocaine;
- Ms. Smith was employed by a cleaning service, but recently lost her job;
- Mr. Johnson is employed as a landscaper.

The initial hearing granted CPS temporary legal and physical custody of the three children. At the adjudication hearing, the court ordered that the children be placed in foster care, that CPS develop a case plan for reunification, and that Ms. Smith and Mr. Johnson cooperate with CPS in receiving services. (See Chapter 4, *The Juvenile Court Process*, for definitions of "initial hearing" and "adjudication hearing.")

The CPS caseworker assigned to the Smith family faced several issues:

- The siblings were not placed in the same foster home. While the 16-month-old and 4-year-old children were placed in the same foster home, the lack of available therapeutic foster homes or residential facilities prompted placement of the 12-year-old child in a temporary receiving shelter until approval was granted for placement into a therapeutic residential facility or home located in a neighboring State. There were no known relatives available for placement.
- The whereabouts of Eric Lequoi, the alleged biological father of the 12-year-old child, were unknown. Mr. Lequoi's last known whereabouts were with his family at a Native American reservation in Wyoming.
- Ms. Smith denied having a substance abuse problem and wanted to maintain her relationship with Mr. Johnson.
- Mr. Johnson refused to participate in substance abuse treatment, sexual off ender assessment, or a batterer intervention program and denied that he was the biological father of the 16-month-old child. Ms. Smith maintained that Mr. Johnson was the biological father of the 16-month-old and 4-year-old children.

Considerations and actions regarding this case and how existing legislation affects the provision of services are discussed throughout the remainder of this chapter.

The recent amendment to CAPTA changed the confidentiality requirements so that States now are obligated to share confidential information with any agency or individual who has a statutory duty to protect children.[16] This amendment also contains language that allows States flexibility to determine State policies that permit public access to child abuse court proceedings.

- Caseworkers follow the definitions established by CAPTA and State laws to substantiate child abuse and neglect against Ms. Smith and Mr. Johnson. The condition of the home and the act of leaving three under-aged children without adult supervision for 3 days meet the threshold for substantiating neglect.

The Individuals with Disabilities Education Act

Originally enacted in 1975, the Individuals with Disabilities Education Act (IDEA) (P.L. 94–142) entitles eligible children to education programs that meet their special needs. An Individual Education Plan (IEP) is developed for eligible children to identify their specific educational needs as well as strategies for meeting them. In its most recent reauthorization, CAPTA contains a provision that requires CPS to refer children under the age of three for evaluation of IDEA eligibility in substantiated cases of abuse or neglect.[17]

- The 12-year-old child's poor academic performance and possible learning disability are significant presenting problems. IDEA offers the CPS caseworker the opportunity to engage Ms. Smith in meeting the educational needs of her child and in coordinating services with the child's teacher and special education administrator. IDEA also provides access to individualized services that address the child's educational needs, as well as her emotional and mental difficulties. Through IDEA, CPS can demonstrate reasonable efforts to collaborate with external agencies to meet children's needs and to reunify families.

The Indian Child Welfare Act

The Indian Child Welfare Act (ICWA) (P.L. 95– 608) of 1978 requires specific protections to Native American children involved in CPS and juvenile court proceedings. If a child is affiliated with a tribal organization, the tribe has the right to intervene in proceedings or to petition to have the case transferred to tribal court.[18]

- Eric Lequoi, the alleged father of the 12-year-old child, is Native American. The CPS caseworker will need to locate Mr. Lequoi to establish paternity. If he is the child's biological father, the caseworker will need to determine whether he is a viable permanency option for the child or can provide child support and medical insurance. Once the paternity of the child is established, the caseworker will need to determine whether the child is entitled to the protections of ICWA.

The Adoption Assistance ad Child Welfare act

The Adoption Assistance and Child Welfare Act (P.L. 96–272) of 1980 requires that CPS make reasonable efforts to avoid unnecessary removals of children from their homes and to reunify foster children with their families. "Reasonable efforts" means providing a parent with useful resources that enable them to protect the child, to provide a stable home environment, and to promote the child's well-being.

If the court fi nds that reasonable efforts have not been made, CPS funding from Federal and State sources may be reduced.

- In this case example, the requirements for bypassing reunification efforts are not met, so the caseworkers should assume that the goal is to reunify the children with their biological parent, Ms. Smith. (For more information on circumstances where reunification should not be the goal, see the next section on The Adoption and Safe Families Act, as well as Exhibit 4.2, Circumstances Under Which Reunification Is Not Attempted.) In order to meet the reasonable efforts requirement, the CPS caseworker must conduct a comprehensive and thorough family assessment to identify specific services that will address the issues prompting removal of the children. The CPS caseworker, for example, may recommend that a domestic violence specialist conduct a domestic violence assessment with Ms. Smith and that Mr. Johnson participate in a batterer intervention program.
- In this case, the court also may expect that the following services will be offered to demonstrate reasonable efforts:

- A developmental or medical assessment of the children;
- A child sexual abuse assessment of the 12- year-old;
- A substance abuse assessment and treatment plan for Ms. Smith and Mr. Johnson;
- Domestic violence counseling;
- A parenting program;
- Emergency benefits for the family (e.g., temporary shelter, groceries voucher);
- Enrollment in the Temporary Assistance for Needy Families program;
- Vocational rehabilitation services;
- Parent and sibling visitation.
- Additionally, reasonable efforts require that services be available and accessible to Ms. Smith and Mr. Johnson. Thus, if transportation to substance abuse treatment or weekly urine screens is an issue, the CPS caseworker may want to provide transportation or bus tokens to them.

The Adoption and Safe Families Act

In 1997, Congress passed the Adoption and Safe Families Act (ASFA) (P.L. 105–89) in response to concerns that many children were remaining in foster care for long periods or experiencing multiple placements. The law requires timely permanency planning for children. Permanency for children involves either reunification with the biological parent, legal guardianship with a relative or caregiver, adoption, or an alternative planned permanent living arrangement. ASFA emphasizes that the child's safety is the paramount concern in any child maltreatment case.

In addition, ASFA addressed the lack of clarity regarding what constituted making "reasonable efforts" to keep families together. The legislation:

- Restricts the reasonable efforts requirement of attempting to keep families intact by permitting it to be waived under specified circumstances, such as severe or chronic maltreatment or the death of another child in the household due to maltreatment;
- Expands the reasonable efforts requirement to make it applicable to CPS efforts to secure permanent homes for children who will not be reunited with their families;
- Mandates a permanency hearing to occur no more than 12 months after a child is placed in foster care;
- Dictates, with some exceptions, that petitions for termination of parental rights need to be filed for children who have been in foster care for 15 of the previous 22 months;
- Includes several provisions to promote, to facilitate, to fund, and to support adoptive placements;
- Gives substitute care providers the right to receive notice of court hearings and the opportunity to be heard;
- Requires criminal record checks on all substitute care providers;
- Directs that compliance with these provisions and other performance standards be carefully monitored and enforced.[19]

ASFA has a significant impact on caseworker practice, guiding caseworkers through family reunification, the provision of services to the family, and alternative permanent placements, if necessary.

- Ms. Smith and Mr. Johnson abuse alcohol and cocaine, which exacerbates the incidence and severity of physical violence perpetrated by Mr. Johnson. Substance use disorder and domestic violence are commonly known to be chronic issues that typically require extensive time for successful treatment and resolution. ASFA requires that Ms. Smith and Mr. Johnson address and resolve their substance abuse and domestic violence issues in a shortened and restricted length of time. If Ms. Smith and Mr. Johnson cannot resolve their issues within 12 months, the CPS caseworker is faced with the possibility of making a recommendation at the permanency hearing that parental rights be terminated and the children be placed for adoption. The caseworker also could utilize concurrent planning, which seeks to reunify children with their birth families while, at the same time, establishing an alternative permanency plan if reunification cannot take place.[20] In either case, the CPS caseworker needs to be diligent and expeditious in engaging Ms. Smith and Mr. Johnson in services. It is equally important for the caseworker to ensure compliance with the court-ordered case plan. The caseworker also may collaborate with service providers to assist Ms. Smith and Mr. Johnson with addressing their issues in a timely manner.
- Establishing paternity is another critical piece of casework practice to prevent further delays in achieving permanency. If the permanency plan's goal is adoption, the children cannot be freed for adoption unless the parental rights of their biological parents are terminated. In this case, Mr. Johnson denies paternity of the 16-monthold child. The CPS caseworker must ascertain if Mr. Johnson's claims are true and, if so, begin proceedings to locate the biological father. Additionally, if the children remain in foster care placement, child support needs to be established and paid to the CPS agency by Ms. Smith and Mr. Johnson. If Ms. Smith and Mr. Johnson are separated, each parent will need a separate child support order. The CPS caseworker can utilize the Child Support Enforcement (CSE) office that is responsible by law for establishing and for enforcing paternity, child support, and medical insurance obligations for children in foster care. Collaboration with the CSE office is an example of the CPS caseworker's ability to demonstrate reasonable efforts to the courts and to ensure timely permanency for Ms. Smith's children.

The Interstate Compact on the Placement of Children

In addition to Federal legislation, the Interstate Compact on the Placement of Children (ICPC) also can play an important role in caseworker practice. ICPC is an agreement among all 50 States, the District of Columbia, and the U.S. Virgin Islands regarding placement (e.g., kinship care, adoption, foster care) across State lines. The placement must be approved by the ICPC offices of each of the affected States before it can occur.

- Due to the special needs of the 12-year-old consuming and can prolong the quest for child and the lack of an appropriate therapeutic permanency. Thus, the CPS caseworker will need foster care placement, an alternative foster to contact the State ICPC office immediately, care placement located in a neighboring State follow all ICPC requirements, and pursue timely was recommended. This process can be time completion of the ICPC process.

> For more information on Federal child abuse and neglect legislation, visit the Legal issues and Laws page of the Child Welfare Information Gateway website at http://www.childwelfare.gov/systemwide/laws_ policies/search/index.cfm.

4. THE JUVENILE COURT PROCESS

Other than judges or attorneys, most people fi nd court proceedings intimidating and confusing. Child protective services (CPS) caseworkers and families involved in juvenile court face the daunting task of understanding the court process, the roles of court personnel, the complex legal jargon, and the court's expectation of them. CPS caseworkers need to be competent in navigating the juvenile court process to achieve positive outcomes for children and families. This chapter discusses the juvenile court process and the responsibilities of child protection caseworkers, attorneys, and judges at each step of a family's involvement with the court. Exhibit 4-1 presents a flow chart of the juvenile court process. Because the process varies widely across jurisdictions, this flow chart illustrates one example of how a child maltreatment case might proceed.

The Petition for Removal

Cases of any type begin with the filing of an initial pleading with a court. A child protection proceeding is initiated by filing a petition. The petition usually will be captioned "In re Jane Doe," meaning it is brought regarding her. The State or county is the petitioner and the parents, caretakers, or child may be referred to as respondents. They are not "defendants" and the petition does not "charge" them with child abuse or neglect. The petition contains the essential elements of the conduct that is alleged to be child maltreatment. It does not need to contain all the facts known to the petitioner, but should include enough to establish the court's jurisdiction.

The decision to file a child maltreatment petition is made by the CPS caseworker and supervisor, often in consultation with the agency's lawyer. Most States allow only CPS to initiate child protection proceedings, but some also permit other public officials or even private citizens to do so. It is a complex and difficult decision that requires assessing the risk of harm to the child and weighing it against the distress caused by removal. The decision to file should always be based on safety considerations and not on how likely it is that the case can or cannot be won in court. As a result, child maltreatment petitions tend to concern children who are exposed to serious threats to their safety.

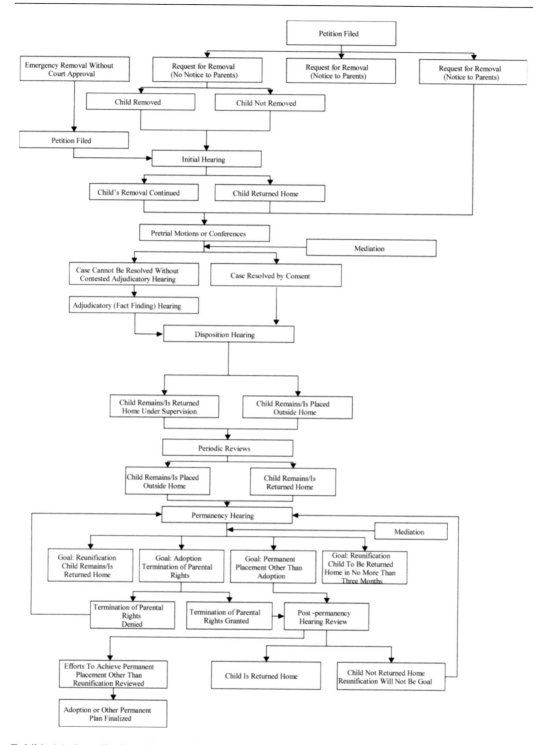

Exhibit 4-1. Juvenile Court Process Flow Chart

The requirements for reasonable efforts have resulted in more attempts to "remove the harm and not the child" by effectively addressing maltreatment without going to court. These attempts include diverting families to community-based programs and services, such as residential mental health treatment, substance abuse treatment combined with the placement of the child with a relative, housing subsidies, child care, or financial support; in-home services ranging from intensive family preservation to periodic monitoring; and ordering violent or sexually abusive adults out of the child's home.

Another important factor that CPS caseworkers and others in the court process, including service providers, must keep in mind is the importance of learning and respecting the cultural traditions and strengths of the families in which they intervene. Every effort must be made, either through written materials in the native language of the parents and child or by using certified interpreters, to ensure that CPS and the parents understand each other.

Content of petitions

Petitions, or "complaints," alleging child maltreatment should be prepared by lawyers with the information provided by CPS caseworkers. These facts need to be conveyed in a manner that clearly describes what the parent or parents did or failed to do and how it affected the child. Together, the lawyer and the caseworker should construct a real-life story by identifying the characters, by describing the setting and the events, and by relating their impact on the child or other participants.

In documenting cases, caseworkers need to be careful to state only the facts and not legal conclusions. For example, the caseworker should write, "On January 1, 2003, Joe Smith hit his son Jack Smith, age 7, on the arm with a baseball bat, breaking the boy's arm," instead of "the father physically abused his son."

Lawyers' opinions and practices vary widely regarding whether a petition should be detailed or should recite only the facts essential to establishing jurisdiction. (See Chapter 2, *The Court System and Child Protection*, regarding jurisdiction.) The length of the petition also will vary depending on the complexity of a particular case and on local practice. Long petitions may be a useful guide for gathering and presenting evidence at trial. Care must be taken not to include any allegation in a petition that cannot be proven by evidence in court. Whether short or long, the petition must contain allegations of fact to support every element of the particular claim asserted. Otherwise, the court will dismiss the petition.

Filing and serving petitions

The CPS caseworker or attorneys representing CPS typically are responsible for delivering new petitions to the clerk of the juvenile court for filing. The clerk will file the case and give it a docket number and an initial hearing date. The caseworker should request a stamped copy of the petition.

Once a petition is filed, it needs to be served on the respondents. Serving a petition generally is accomplished by personally delivering to each respondent the petition, the summons, and the notice of hearing. Typically, the sheriff or another law enforcement officer is responsible for this act. In many States, service also can be made by registered or certified mail with a return receipt. In some communities, the papers may be served by the CPS caseworker. It can be difficult to serve persons whose whereabouts are unknown, so they will need to be served by following the State's alternative processes for providing notice of the petition, such as placing an ad in a newspaper. (See the section, "Termination of Parental Rights," later in this chapter for further discussion on this topic.)

Petitions and removals

State and local practices regarding the filing of petitions, emergency removals, and prior authorization of removals by judicial officers are not governed by Federal law and vary widely between and within States. Ideally, no child should be removed from a family until after a petition is filed and the court has conducted a hearing at which the parents were present and had an opportunity to be heard. In reality, most removals are authorized by *ex parte* orders and the first hearing is conducted after the removal has occurred.

Petitions alleging maltreatment do not have to include a request that the child be removed. It sometimes may be useful to file a petition without asking for removal.

An example would be a case in which maltreatment is substantiated and removal does not appear necessary, but the parents are resistant to CPS intervention. The court may be convinced to exercise its powers of persuasion, or even coercion, to promote parental cooperation.

Where *ex parte* removal is requested, judges have the option of denying the request or of scheduling an initial hearing at which the issue of placement can be considered more fully. In making the decision whether to grant the application *ex parte*, the judge will determine the risk of harm to the child if removal is not authorized and what efforts CPS has made or could make to avoid removal or reduce the risk of harm.

When immediate removal of a child is dictated by emergency circumstances, a petition should be filed promptly and judicial approval for the removal obtained. The laws of some States set time limits for obtaining retroactive approval for the removal. Courts have procedures in place to ensure that CPS caseworkers have round-the-clock access to a judge with the expertise and authority to respond to requests for removal. If these procedures are not available or preferred by the court, a CPS caseworker needs to ensure that the timely filing of the petition occurs immediately after emergency removals.

In some jurisdictions, removals by police or CPS caseworkers are sometimes made without judicial authorization or any attempt to obtain it, even in non emergencies. This practice was condemned by the U.S. Court of Appeals for the Second Circuit, which held that "[I]t is unconstitutional for State officials to effect a child's removal on an 'emergency' basis where there is reasonable time safely to obtain judicial authorization consistent with the child's safety."[21] While this ruling may apply only to States within the Second Circuit, it reminds practitioners of the importance of obtaining judicial authorization whenever possible.

Continuances, adjournments, postponements, and delays

Continuances (postponements of a date of a trial, hearing, or other court appearance to a later date) or adjournments (temporary postponements of the proceedings of a case until a specified future time) should be avoided, if at all possible. They waste court time and inconvenience the parties, CPS caseworkers, attorneys, Guardian ad Litem (GAL) or court-appointed special advocate (CASA) volunteers, and witnesses. Typically, the impact of these delays is felt most acutely by the children and families involved. Most importantly, they delay resolution of the case and permanency for the child.

The Initial Hearing

The first event in court after the filing of a petition is the initial hearing, known also as the preliminary protective hearing, shelter care hearing, detention hearing, emergency removal hearing, or temporary custody hearing. It occurs soon after the filing of the petition or the removal of the child from the home. The precise deadline for this hearing depends on State law. Ideally, it should occur on the first day following the filing of the petition, upon removal of the child, or as soon as possible thereafter.

The initial hearing is the most critical stage in the child abuse and neglect court process. Many important decisions are made and actions taken that chart the course for the remainder of the proceeding. At this hearing, the relationships between those involved in the process also are established, and the tone is set for their ongoing interactions. Too often, these hearings are brief and perfunctory, but to the extent that sufficient time is devoted to them to address the relevant issues thoroughly, initial hearings facilitate and expedite the resolution of the case.[22] From a caseworker's perspective, being ill-prepared, having incomplete information, or having a judge unfamiliar with family court proceedings typically lead to a poor initial hearing. Having thorough documentation, service plans, and an established positive relationship with the judge frequently lead to a good initial hearing.

The main purpose of the initial hearing is to determine whether the child should be placed in substitute care or remain with or be returned to the parents pending further proceedings. The critical issue is whether in- home services or other measures can be put in place to ensure the child's safety.

> For information about the appropriate lengths for hearings in the juvenile court rocess, refer to the National Council of Juvenile and Family Court Judges' *Adoption and Permanency Guidelines: Improving Court Practice in Child Abuse and Neglect Cases*, and *Resource Guidelines: Improving Court Practice in Child Abuse and Neglect Cases* at http:// www.pppncjfcj.org/html/publications.html.

Parties to be present at initial hearings

Both parents, including any putative father, need to be notified of the hearing and be present. Extended family members who could become placement options also need to be identified as a part of this process. Issuing domestic violence protective, restraining, or similar orders directed to alleged abusers may be considered as an alternative to removing the child.

The child also should be present at the hearing unless it would be detrimental to the child's well-being. As an alternative, the judge may decide to meet with the child in chambers. Much can be learned from observing the interactions between a child and parent or other relatives, even in an artifi cial and stressful setting. In addition, the judge and others in the case who will not have ongoing contact with the child can meet, observe, and interact. This has the benefits of humanizing the process, emphasizing that the child is more than another name on another file, and underscoring that the child has real needs that require prompt resolution. Some courts welcome or even require a regularly updated photo of the child for the file.

Counsel should have been appointed for the parents at the time the petition was filed and should be present in advance of the hearing to talk with them and to prepare their presentation to the court. The GAL or CASA and any attorney for the child also should have been appointed and be prepared to proceed in advance of the initial hearing. Courts needs to have policies and procedures in place to ensure that these appointments are made and that the initial hearing is scheduled and conducted expeditiously.

Issues addressed at the initial hearing

In addition to assessing the child's safety and making a placement decision, the court must make a reasonable efforts determination. Many courts require the filing of a reasonable efforts affidavit detailing the efforts that were made. Whether it is required or not, CPS caseworkers should be prepared to inform the court, preferably in writing, of the efforts they made to avoid removal and placement of the child or to explain the difficult or unusual circumstances that precluded the need to make such efforts.[23] Guidance for reasonable efforts and safety requirements for foster care placements are laid out in the U.S. Code as part of the State plan requirements of Title IV-E of the Social Security Act (42 U.S.C. 671(a)(15)).

Other issues that need to be addressed at the initial hearing include:

- The verification of any immediate needs the child or parents may have and determination of how they can be met;
- The appointment of counsel for the parents and of a GAL, CASA, or attorney for the child, if not previously made;
- The determination of whether the Indian Child Welfare Act is applicable;
- The determination of paternity of any putative father;
- The assessment of the need for mental health, substance abuse, medical, or other diagnostic tests for the parents and the child (sometimes these assessments cannot be initiated until after there has been an adjudication of child maltreatment);
- The identification and location of any absent parent or family member who is a potential placement option or source of emotional or financial support for the child or family;
- The resolution of child support;
- The provision of relevant records including criminal, medical, educational, and substance abuse or mental health treatment for parents and the child;
- The timing of visitation with parents and siblings if the child is placed outside the home;
- The appropriateness of the case for mediation if that service is available;
- The discovery (pretrial process that allows each party to obtain information relevant to the case from the other parties);
- The determination of the next court date.

The initial hearing should establish a supportive atmosphere in which parents are treated with dignity and respect. It is a process that should focus on understanding the problems the case presents and solving them as quickly as possible so the family can be reunited safely.

The judge also should explain to the parents:

- Their rights;

- The course that the case will take, including possible outcomes ranging from dismissal to termination of parental rights (TPR);
- The roles and responsibilities of each of the other participants;
- What will happen before the next hearing;
- The court's expectations of the parents.

The judge should promote a cooperative, problem- solving approach to resolving the case and control any conflict or hostility between the parties.[24] To the extent that the initial hearing may not conform to the process outlined above, CPS caseworkers are encouraged to do what they can to fill in the gaps for parents and to incorporate these approaches in their interactions with all participants. (See Chapter 7, *Going to Court*, for a discussion of judges' expectations for CPS caseworkers and how to work effectively with others.)

Pretrial Conferences

Some courts use pretrial conferences, also known as settlement conferences, in child maltreatment cases. These conferences are opportunities for the parents, their attorneys, and the child's advocates to discuss a settlement in the form of stipulated, or agreed to, facts that would make a trial unnecessary. In courts where there are no formal pretrial conferences, these settlement negotiations often occur among attorneys by phone or at the courtroom and as late as right before the scheduled adjudication. The judge may or may not participate, depending on the jurisdiction and the nature of the case, and some judges will initiate such negotiations themselves.

Negotiated settlements can save time and money for courts, attorneys, parents, witnesses, and CPS. They also may avoid the trauma and acrimony that often result from contested adjudications. Additionally, they can expedite the development and implementation of the case plan, the terms of which are frequently included in the settlement.

MEDIATION

An increasing number of juvenile courts across the country are using mediation and other nonadversarial dispute resolution methods, such as family group conferencing, to settle child maltreatment and TPR cases. The mediation process usually is called "dependency mediation" and is similar in many ways to settlement conferences, except that there is a skilled and trained mediator facilitating the discussion. Family group conferencing also utilizes a facilitator, but tries to involve the child's extended family more fully and encourages family members to craft their own plans for the support of the child and parent.

When settlement conferences and mediation fail to produce agreement on the entire case, they nevertheless may produce agreement on some issues and at least shorten the time necessary for the adjudication.[25]

It is important, however, that provable allegations of significant child maltreatment not be negotiated away. CPS caseworkers need to participate in settlement discussions to ensure that the terms of the stipulations accurately reflect the seriousness of the maltreatment. A stipulation that the child was neglected, for example, provides no information about what actually happened. To support the development of an appropriate case plan, the critical facts of a case need to be included in the stipulations. These facts also enable participants in future proceedings to know exactly what issues necessitated court action and to measure progress.

Settlement discussions should include the child's advocates. The advocates and the CPS caseworker should ensure that the child's safety and needs are refl ected in the settlement. The court should require the recommendations of the child's GAL or CASA before it approves the agreement. Parents must not be coerced or be enticed to admit facts that they deny. Before accepting any settlement, the court must ask that the parents be certain that they have entered into the agreement freely and voluntarily and with a full understanding of the potential consequences and rights they have waived by doing so.

Discovery

Discovery is a pretrial process that allows each party to obtain information relevant to the case from the other parties. It is intended to avoid "trial by ambush," to narrow the contested issues, and to expedite settlement.

Discovery in child maltreatment cases usually involves the parents' and child's attorneys asking CPS for its records. In most States, they are entitled to those records. While details of the initial and investigative reports are revealed, the name of the reporter is not. CPS may not be able to look at certain records from other sources, such as mental health evaluations or substance abuse treatment records that carry their own confidentiality protections. Such records, however, usually can be obtained by other means. Records from a private practitioner may be obtained through a subpoena *duces tecum* (an order requiring a person to produce for the court specified documents or records). State agency records can be obtained by submitting a Freedom of Information Act request.

Other forms of discovery also are available in some States and jurisdictions. These include:

- Interrogatories or written questions that need to be answered under oath within a specified time frame;
- Requests for admissions that are deemed admitted if not denied under oath by a specific date;
- Depositions or transcribed oral examinations under oath.

The Adjudication Hearing

If the case is not settled by agreement of the parties, it will go to adjudication. Once the petition is filed, the court schedules an adjudication hearing (also known as the "fact-finding hearing" or "jurisdictional hearing"). At the adjudication hearing, the court decides whether CPS can prove the allegations in its petition. The CPS attorney will present evidence through the testimony of the CPS caseworker, law enforcement officers, or other witnesses, including any experts. Documents such as medical records or photographs also may be entered into evidence. The attorneys for the parents and the child will have the right to question or to cross-examine the witnesses and to present evidence. The parents may testify, as may other family members or neighbors who have knowledge of the facts alleged in the petition or of the care the parents provided their children.

Parent testimony

Because child maltreatment cases in juvenile court are civil as opposed to criminal, the parents do not enjoy the right against self-incrimination contained in the Fifth Amendment to the U.S. Constitution. Therefore, they can be called to testify by CPS, the other parent, or the GAL. They still can "take the Fifth," however, and refuse to testify on the grounds that their answers may incriminate them.

In a civil case, a refusal to testify can be weighed against the witness. This issue surfaces when a parent is charged with a crime arising from the same underlying facts as the child maltreatment case in juvenile court. Criminal prosecutions, particularly complex ones like child sexual abuse, usually are not resolved until after the adjudication of the child maltreatment case. Thus, a parent who is called to testify in a juvenile court maltreatment case and who is facing criminal charges may refuse to testify to avoid having her testimony used against her in the subsequent criminal prosecution. The parent's lawyer may not call her to testify for the same reason. In some courts, parents may be granted "immunity" whereby judges can order that the statements by the parents in juvenile court cannot be used against them in other court proceedings. For more on immunity, see Chapter 2, *The Court System and Child Protection*.

Burden of proof

CPS holds the burden of proof, and its attorney needs to present enough evidence to convince the judge that the maltreatment of the child alleged in the petition occurred. The burden of proof is either the greater weight (or preponderance) of the evidence or clear and convincing evidence, depending on the State. In determining whether the burden of proof has been met, the judge will take into account the quantity, quality, credibility, and convincing force of the evidence.

If the judge determines that CPS has met its burden, that determination justifies continuing CPS intervention and further court involvement. On the other hand, if the judge determines that the evidence presented by CPS fails to satisfy the burden of proof, the case will be dismissed, and CPS will have no authority to continue its involvement with the family without the family's consent.

Order

At the conclusion of an adjudication in favor of CPS (whether it is by agreement or after a contested hearing), the judge needs to enter an order finding specific facts regarding the child's maltreatment and the problems that must be resolved before the child can return home safely. Other issues to be addressed include whether CPS has made reasonable efforts to avoid placement or to achieve reunification, the child's placement, all incomplete or unresolved issues from the initial hearing, and the disposition hearing date.

The Disposition Hearing

At the disposition hearing, the court decides whether the child needs help from the court and, if so, what services will be ordered. For example, the court may enter an order that mandates counseling and rehabilitative services. The court also may enter orders providing for out-of-home placements or visitation schedules or for controlling the conduct of the parent. It also can order CPS to conduct follow-up visits with the family to ensure the child's protection. Essentially, the disposition hearing determines what will be required to resolve the problems that led to CPS intervention.

Te rules of evidence are relaxed in disposition hearings, and they are generally less formal than adjudications, although witnesses sometimes testify and are cross- examined. While the disposition hearing is sometimes held on the same day as the adjudication hearing, the National Council of Juvenile and Family Court Judges recommends that the disposition hearing be separate and follow the adjudication within 30 days.[26]

Court report

CPS must prepare a disposition court report and present it to the court, the counsel for all parties, and any GAL or CASA at least 7 calendar days prior to the hearing or by the time specified in any local court rules. The court report should:

- Outline the history of CPS involvement with the child and family including identification of the current placement as well as all prior placements;
- Specify the reasonable efforts made to avoid placement and, if the child was placed, to achieve reunification;
- Identify and evaluate placement options;
- Update the status of any unresolved issues from the initial or adjudication hearings;
- Attach the case plan and any relevant evaluations, assessments, or reports (medical, psychological, psychiatric, developmental, or educational) related to the child or parents;
- Make other appropriate recommendations for court action.

The GAL or CASA also should prepare and distribute a court report in the same manner, addressing the same issues.

The case plan

Before the disposition hearing, CPS should confer with the parents and develop with them a case plan that identifies the problems that led to CPS involvement with the family and are specified in the adjudication order.[27] The case plan will state the goal for the child's permanent placement. When the goal is reunification, which it usually is at this stage of the proceedings, the case plan will:

- Identify the actions to be taken and the behavioral improvements to be achieved by the parents;
- Specify the services to be provided by CPS to support the parents in eliminating or in alleviating the identified problems;

- Set forth the time frame for completion of each component of the case plan;
- Articulate objective, measurable criteria for determining whether the necessary improvements have been achieved;
- Identify any special needs of the child and the proposed strategies and services for addressing those needs.

If inadequacies in parenting must be addressed, the case plan should identify the specific problem behavior, spell out how the behavior must change, and suggest some way of determining whether the desired change has been accomplished. For example, if a parent disciplines a 6-month-old infant for continuing to cry after being told to stop, the desired change would be that the parent learns about developmentally appropriate behavior and can demonstrate reasonable expectations of behavior by a child of that age. The mere requirement that a parent complete a parenting course would not be sufficient because course completion does not necessarily result in improved parenting skills.

Case plans should be tailored to the facts and circumstances of each case. A template for the case plan is useful, but "boilerplate" statements of needs and services to meet those needs are not acceptable.

In some States, TPR is a dispositional option, used only in the most severe and unresolvable circumstances, such as when adoption is clearly the long-term plan for the child's placement. More commonly, a plan to pursue TPR and adoption will involve separate court proceedings.

In some States, the court must approve the case plan. In all States, the plan must be discussed and refined at the disposition hearing, and any disagreements regarding its terms must be resolved. The case plan is the blueprint for permanency.

The placement decision

Placement is the key issue at the disposition hearing. The child can be:

- Left with or returned to the parents, usually under CPS supervision;
- Kept in an existing placement;
- Moved to a new placement;
- Placed in substitute care for the first time if removal was not ordered previously.

The option that the court chooses will depend on the circumstances of the case, principally the risk of harm to the child in the home and the possibilities for reducing that risk to a safe level. The options for placement will depend on the needs of the child and include:

- Either or both parents;
- The extended family or kinship care;
- Foster care;
- A group home or institutional care.[28]

As a part of its reasonable efforts inquiry, the court needs to scrutinize carefully any CPS recommendation that the child be placed outside the home. The caseworker making that recommendation always should be prepared to discuss why the child cannot be maintained safely in the home through the provision of in-home services, a restraining order prohibiting contact by the abusive parent, close supervision, or other means. If the recommendation is foster care, the caseworker also should be prepared to say why it is preferable to placement with any available family member.

Both CPS and the court should take care to ensure that the placement is supportive of the CPS plan for reunification of the child with the family and is otherwise appropriate to the needs of the child. Where feasible, sibling groups should be placed together. Ideally, the child's ethnic heritage, cultural identity, language, religion, or special diet, if any, should be accommodated without causing any delay in the child's placement. The placement should be in close geographic proximity to the child's school, family, and any siblings who may be placed elsewhere, if possible.

Review Hearings

Review hearings are the next stage of a continuing process that begins with the initial hearing and continues through adjudication and disposition. The review hearing is an opportunity to evaluate the progress that has been made toward completing the case plan and any court orders and to revise the plan as needed. If no progress has been made, and none seems likely, it is a chance to change the goal of the plan completely. Review hearings should guide the case to permanency for the child. Unless a permanent placement is accomplished on or before the date of the permanency hearing, the court must continue to review the case periodically.

Review hearing report

CPS caseworkers must prepare a court report for each review hearing that includes or is accompanied by a reasonable efforts affidavit detailing what has been done to achieve the permanency plan. Like the disposition report, the report should be delivered to the court, the counsel for all parties, and any GAL or CASA at least 7 calendar days prior to the hearing or by the time specified in any local court rules. The GAL or CASA also needs to prepare and distribute a court report in the same manner. The court report should update the disposition hearing report and also should include:

- Whether the case plan is on target;
- Whether the child's physical, emotional, and mental health needs are being met;
- Whether progress has been made toward achieving the case plan's objectives;
- What reasonable efforts were made to achieve reunification;
- Whether the child should be returned home and, if not, why;
- What remains to be accomplished before reunification can occur;
- What timetable has been established for returning the child home;
- Whether and how the case plan should be modified.

These inquiries are the essential issues to be addressed at the review hearing. The court also should consider any lingering issues from previous hearings or orders; modify child support, visitation, and other matters as needed; and set the date for the next hearing, if one is necessary.

Timing of review hearings

Federal law, through Title IV-E of the Social Security Act (42 U.S .C. 675(5) (B)), requires that States make provision for cases to be reviewed at least every 6 months after the child is placed in substitute care. Many States' laws also require court reviews, sometimes more frequently than Federal law dictates. The review requirement of the Adoption Assistance and Child Welfare Act (P.L. 96–272) also can be satisfied by internal CPS teams or citizen review boards.

The National Council of Juvenile and Family Court Judges encourages judges to schedule reviews more frequently than the law requires.[29] They may do so to expedite resolution of the case, to address an unresolved issue, to monitor parent or agency compliance with a court directive, or to respond to a party's motion. These extra reviews can be burdensome to the CPS caseworker and other participants, but they also can aid in moving the case toward resolution more quickly. CPS caseworkers who establish a reputation for making diligent efforts to implement case plans, for supporting the parents and child, and for pursuing permanency expeditiously will earn the trust and confidence of the judge. For these caseworkers, additional reviews are less likely to be scheduled. For more information on this topic, see Appendix D, *Guidelines for Child Protective Services Caseworkers for Permanency and Review Hearings*.

The Permanency Hearing

Review hearings are intended primarily to monitor compliance with the case plan, adjust the plan as necessary, and ensure that the case is progressing toward resolution. The permanency hearing is fundamentally different as it is the point at which a definitive decision is made about the child's permanent placement. ASFA requires that the permanency hearing occur no later than 12 months from the date the child is considered to have entered foster care.[30]

The placement decision

The options for permanent placement include:

- Returning the child home;
- Returning the child home by a specific date (no more than 3 months later), provided the court finds from the evidence that the parents are making signifi cant progress toward completing the case plan;
- Terminating parental rights, if necessary, and permitting adoption by a relative, foster parent, or other nonrelative;
- Granting legal guardianship;
- Permanently placing the child with a relative, foster parent, or other nonrelative;

- Providing another specified permanent living arrangement if the court documents and finds that there is a compelling reason why it would not be in the best interests of the child to proceed with one of the other options.[31]

In making the determination about the permanent placement of the child, the court must weigh which option is in the child's best interest.[32] In some cases, concurrent planning may be pursued. Under concurrent planning, an alternative, permanent placement is developed at the same time as family reunification is attempted. With this approach, the child can be moved quickly to a stable home if reunification with the birth family cannot take place.

Permanency hearing reports

To prevent miscommunication between the agencies and the courts, CPS caseworkers should submit a detailed report to the court discussing the preferred permanent placement option, the reasons for that preference, and each of the potential alternatives. This report should be distributed at least 7 calendar days in advance of the permanency hearing and in the same manner and to the same people as the disposition and review hearing reports. The report should be accompanied by a reasonable efforts report in affidavit form to aid the court in its reasonable efforts determination.

EXHIBIT 4-2. CIRCUMSTANCES UNDER WHICH REUNIFICATION IS NOT ATTEMPTED

ASFA provides that under some circumstances reunification should not be the goal:

- A parent has aided, attempted, conspired, solicited, or committed the murder or voluntary manslaughter of another of his or her children;
- A parent has committed a felony assault resulting in serious bodily injury to the child or another of the parent's children;
- A final decision is being made regarding an involuntary TPR to a sibling;
- Other circumstances under which efforts to preserve or to reunify the family are inconsistent with the child's permanency plan, which holds the child's health and safety as paramount.[33]

Timing of permanency hearings

In some cases, the permanency hearing is the last stage of child maltreatment litigation. It determines whether the final plan will be to reunite the child and parent or to pursue an alternative, permanent home. It is a more formal hearing than reviews. If it is contested, witnesses may be called to testify and to be cross-examined. Some cases, however, may never have a permanency hearing because the children are reunited with their families after brief stays in foster care, while other cases proceed directly to the TPR hearing.

The permanency hearing usually is held after 1 year. However, if it becomes readily apparent earlier that a reunification plan will not be successful, the permanency hearing should be scheduled as soon as possible.

As presented in Exhibit 4-2, ASFA specifies circumstances under which reunification should not be the goal and in which reasonable efforts to reunify are, therefore, not necessary.

ASFA also allows States to specify additional aggravated circumstances.[34] The agency's lawyers should ensure that CPS caseworkers are aware of what those are in their respective States. Whenever the court finds aggravated circumstances, ASFA requires that a permanency hearing be held within 30 days.

Termination of Parental Rights

The 14th Amendment to the U.S. Constitution protects the fundamental liberty interest of natural parents in the care, custody, and management of their children. This protection does not disappear simply because they have not been model parents or have lost custody of a child temporarily.[35] Because the stakes are so high, TPR hearings are the most formal, longest, and frequently appealed of all child maltreatment proceedings. TPR hearings also may be called "permanent commitment," "severance," or "guardianship with the power to consent to adoption."

Grounds for termination of parental rights

The grounds for TPR are specified in the statutes of each State, and CPS caseworkers are advised to familiarize themselves with these. ASFA requires that filing for TPR must be instituted when:

- A child of any age has been in foster care for 15 of the most recent 22 months, unless exceptions apply;
- The child is an abandoned infant;
- The parent has committed, aided, or attempted the murder or voluntary manslaughter of a sibling of the child;
- The parent has committed a felony assault resulting in serious bodily injury to the child or a sibling of the child.

Most TPR proceedings arising from child abuse and neglect are initiated by CPS, but in some States, the GAL also can petition on the child's behalf for TPR. ASFA requires that if anyone other than CPS files for TPR, CPS must join in the action.[36]

Ending the legal rights and responsibilities of parents

Biological parents whose parental rights are terminated as a result of child maltreatment have no right to have contact with the child, knowledge of the child's whereabouts, pictures, or information regarding the child. In addition to losing legal rights to the child, parents whose rights have been terminated generally have no further responsibilities to the child, except to pay child support that is past due. Because of the seriousness and finality of the consequences, TPR has been called the "death penalty" of family law.

There are exceptions. Children who are old enough to remember and to know how to contact their parents may choose to do so. Some children are never adopted and remain in foster care; others are returned to foster care because of a disrupted adoption or because they were abused or neglected by an adoptive or other surrogate parent. In these situations, the original parents may be the best placement option if their circumstances have improved to the point that they pose less risk of harm to the children and if the children are older and better able to protect themselves.

Termination of parental rights petitions and service

Drafted by the CPS attorney, TPR petitions will allege facts that, if proven, would satisfy the grounds for termination in State law. In many States, TPR is a separate action from the child maltreatment case and sometimes must be filed in a different court. When it is a separate action, the complaint or petition and summons should be served on each of the parents.

Every effort should be made to locate both parents and to serve them personally. The burden of locating parents likely will fall on the CPS caseworker, which can be a difficult and time-consuming process, particularly if one or both parents has disappeared while the child maltreatment proceeding was pending or if one of the parents was never located and served at the start of that case.

Each State has a process for providing notice to the parents, or "constructive service," if a parent cannot be located after diligent efforts. Constructive service can be posting a notice in a legal newspaper or in the courthouse. Although it almost never results in actual notice, it takes time and may involve some expense. One option is to access the Federal Parent Locator Service (FPLS) of the local Federal Child Support Office.[37] (For more information on FPLS, see Chapter 6, *Domestic Relations Cases and Other Court Proceedings*.) Other sources that may yield results are State Department of Motor Vehicles records, State and local prison system records, phone directories, and various online search engines. Agencies are encouraged to develop a routine practice for completing this process, including using form affidavits to document their efforts.

Failure to make legally sufficient service can become grounds for dismissal of the termination petition or for reversal on appeal and consequently can disrupt the child's placement. In States where TPR is a dispositional alternative, service is a less complicated process, provided that each parent was served with the petition in the underlying child maltreatment action. It may be sufficient to mail the notice to the respondent's last known address. Notice of the proceeding and its time and location still should be served, but the process is less formal and technical.

Termination of parental rights trials

TPR cases rely heavily on what happened in the underlying child abuse and neglect cases. In some States, some of the findings of the court in child abuse or neglect cases may be admissible as evidence to prove aspects of the termination case.[38] Most importantly, a trial will focus on what the parents did or did not do since CPS became involved and on what CPS did to support the parents' efforts to regain custody of the child. There are appellate laws in almost every State related to TPR cases, and reversals and remands for retrial frequently are based on perceived CPS shortcomings. Caseworkers who anticipate testifying in TPR trials need to be thoroughly familiar with the history of the case, including the details of everything CPS offered to do or did for the parents and how the parents responded.

TPR cases take longer than other child maltreatment proceedings, but predicting how long is largely guesswork. Scheduling and concluding them, therefore, is a chronic problem in most courts. Frequently, they are tried piecemeal for a few hours or half days at a time. Each rescheduling of successive sessions of the trial requires finding a date and time that is satisfactory for all essential participants. Such an approach often delays conclusion of the case and permanency for the child for months. Some courts have addressed this problem by establishing "long cause" calendars for cases that do not fi t into the normal, relatively short scheduling blocks of the juvenile court. Others courts may set aside large blocks of time on future calendars in anticipation of having protracted TPR trials. CPS can urge courts to adopt these or other scheduling practices that permit termination cases to be tried from beginning to end on consecutive days.

Mediation

Mediation also can be an effective alternative to formal termination proceedings. In courts where it is an option, it often results in voluntary relinquishment of the child by the parents. Rather than focusing on parents' failures or inadequacies, mediation focuses on the child's needs and how they can best be met, and it offers parents an opportunity to make a self-sacrificing choice to give their child a safe and stable future. Most often, it is successful in States that allow "open adoptions" or "adoptions with contact" or that otherwise permits parents to receive information about their child, including letters and photographs, or even limited personal contact. Such agreements may not be enforceable depending on State law, but even where they are not, parents may choose to trust the good will of prospective adoptive parents, particularly if their identities are known, and commit to honoring a continuing contact agreement.

Burden of proof and best interest issues

TPR usually involves two issues. First, CPS must prove by "clear and convincing evidence" that one or more of the grounds for termination exist.[39] Note that this is a higher burden of proof than is required in many States to prove child abuse and neglect. The "clear and convincing evidence" is also a higher burden of proof for TPR than what existed prior to the *Santosky v. Kramer* decision upholding due process under the 14th Amendment. In this case, the Supreme Court found that a "fair preponderance of evidence" is not sufficient to terminate parental rights, and that "before a State may sever completely and irrevocably the rights of parents in their natural child, due process requires that the State support its allegations by at least clear and convincing evidence."[40]

If the court finds that CPS has met the burden of proof with respect to at least one ground for termination, it will proceed to the second issue— whether termination is in the best interest of the child. CPS can enhance the prospects for a favorable decision by preparing a report weighing the pros and cons of termination from the child's point of view and by being prepared to testify regarding the best interest issue. The prospect of a safe, stable, and permanent home is a strong selling point when contrasted with the likelihood that the child cannot return home safely within any reasonable period of time.

Some courts insist on a showing of adoptability before termination will be ordered, although the basic goal and premise of ASFA is that all children are adoptable. It obviously is more difficult to find adoptive homes for some children than for others, but if children are not "cleared for adoption," meaning that their parents' rights have not been terminated, adoption agencies may not actively pursue adoptive placements. If agencies cannot place them, they will not be adopted.

Adoptions

Children placed for adoption by CPS are entitled to a timely placement with an adoptive family. When parents' rights have been terminated, their child's involvement with juvenile court does not end at the TPR hearing. CPS caseworkers should continue to participate in post-hearing activities to ensure that CPS is complying with ASFA requirements, incorporating Federal adoption legislation into practice, and accessing a variety of adoption subsidies and post-adoption services for eligible children.

Post-termination reviews

Many post-termination reviews, or post-permanency hearings, will focus on whether CPS has made reasonable efforts to recruit an adoptive placement. The reasonable efforts inquiry might question whether the agency has an effective recruitment program for adoptive parents and whether its adoption program is adequately and expertly staff ed, knowledgeable about subsidies and interstate placements, and able to provide appropriate post-adoption services. In cases involving special needs children, CPS may be asked whether it is utilizing the specialized agencies that serve these populations. Caseworkers will want to be prepared to respond to such inquiries.

The Multi-Ethnic Placement act

Another issue that may arise at hearings to review efforts to place children available for adoption is whether the agency is complying with the Multi- Ethnic Placement Act (MEPA) of 1994, as amended by the Inter-Ethnic Adoption Provisions of 1996, laws that prohibit discrimination in foster care and adoption. These acts provide that States may not "...deny to any person the opportunity to become an adoptive or foster parent on the basis of the race, color, or national origin of the person or of the child involved; or. ..delay or deny the placement of a child for adoption or into foster care on the basis of the race, color or national origin of the adoptive or foster parent or the child involved...." [41]

MEPA primarily addresses considerations in finding out-of-home placements. During court proceedings regarding placements, the judge may ask about compliance with this and other pertinent laws, particularly if there is an aggrieved party contesting the placement. Therefore, caseworkers must be prepared to document compliance so it can be submitted in the court documents. MEPA also requires that special efforts be made to recruit minority foster and adoptive homes.

The interstate compact on adoption and medical assistance

The Interstate Compact on Adoption and Medical Assistance (ICAMA) addresses medical and other post-adoption services, as well as payment for those services, for the ongoing needs of children who are adopted across State lines. Not all States are signatories to ICAMA. T ose that are have a designated ICAMA administrator who can be an invaluable source of assistance to caseworkers in ensuring post-adoption services for children placed across State lines.

ICAMA is important since ASFA requires State child welfare plans to:

- Specify that the State will not deny or delay the placement of a child for adoption when an approved family is available outside of the court jurisdiction that has the responsibility for handling the case of the child;
- Contain assurances that the State will develop plans for the effective use of cross-jurisdictional resources to facilitate timely adoptive or permanent placements for waiting children.[42]

Interstate placements also need to comply with the Interstate Compact on the Placement of Children. (See Chapter 3, *The Interplay Between Child Maltreatment Legislation and Caseworker Practice*, for more information.) Again, the caseworker needs to provide full documentation for court records that ICAMA was adhered to before the adoption or placement is legalized; otherwise, the home State may not pay for this assistance.

Adoption assistance subsidies

Parents adopting children who are "IV-E eligible" are entitled to receive a subsidy. According to amendments to the Social Security Act, a child is IV-E eligible if the family from which the child was removed was eligible for Aid to Families with Dependent Children, as the program existed on July 16, 1996, and the child is classified as having "special needs." (See below for more information about special needs. A child classified as having special needs also is IV-E eligible if receiving Supplemental Security Income (42 U.S.C. 673(2)).[43]

Special needs are defined differently by each State and may include:

- A sibling group of two or more;
- An ethnic background that is non-Caucasian;
- Any child age 6 or older;
- A documented physical, mental, or developmental disability or disorder, or an emotional disturbance or behavior problem;
- An identified or reasonably identifiable risk of developing a physical or developmental disability, mental disability or disorder, emotional disturbance, or behavioral problem that is related to the child's history of abuse or neglect, genetic factors, or other environmental traumas;
- Psychological attachment to the foster caregiver due to placement of at least 1 year, such that placement with another family would not be in the child's best interests.

Caseworkers will need to know and be able to apply the definition of special needs to children in their States. States have discretion to determine the amount of the subsidy, but it cannot be greater than the amount that a family would have received if the child was in foster care. They can pay more if the additional amount can be supported through State or local funding. The State can make subsidy payments to a family until the adopted child is 18, but can extend assistance to age 21 for children who are disabled physically or mentally. All special needs children who are IV-E eligible, and most who are not, also are eligible for Medicaid. States are required to provide the same subsidies for special needs children who are not IV-E eligible as they provide for those who are, except that for children who are not IV-E eligible:

- Eligibility can be limited based on family income;
- All funding must be from State or local sources.

Caseworkers need to be able to inform prospective adoptive parents of the financial assistance and medical insurance to which the child will be entitled. Additionally, the courts often will ask if the caseworkers are aware of all available assistance and whether it has been provided to the adoptive parents or special needs children. Therefore, caseworkers should document all efforts to help adoptive parents secure appropriate financial assistance and insurance.

Post-adoption services

Adequate financial and health care support of children is critical to the ultimate success of an adoption. The same is true of post-adoption services, which may include providing information and referrals, parent training, education and support groups, individual and family counseling, respite care, and home- based or residential treatment services. The details of the financial support and other services adoptive parents will receive or have available to them must be put in writing, along with information about what they can do if their circumstances change or other unanticipated issues arise. The court will require documentation to ascertain that, in addition to receiving adoption assistance, provisions have been made for post-adoption services, as well as a follow- up schedule to ensure that the adoptive parents have received such services. This documentation is particularly important in cases where the adoption is disrupted. CPS caseworkers also will want to be prepared to respond to any inquiry from the court as to whether the subsidy and other post-adoption supports are sufficient to ensure reasonably that the adoption will be a permanent placement.

Appeals

Parents and CPS have the right to appeal some decisions of the juvenile court in child abuse and neglect and TPR cases. At the very least, the right to appeal attaches at the conclusion of any adjudication, disposition, or TPR trial. Some States may allow appeal from other trial court orders or decisions, but generally, only final decisions are appealed or accepted for appellate review.

Appellate courts decide cases based on the written record, or a videotape in some locations, from the trial court. They examine the record and determine whether:

- The trial judge abused his or her discretion in finding the facts;
- The facts support the judge's conclusions of the law;
- The judge correctly applied the law to the facts.

Although the child is the subject of the litigation, the child is not a "party" and, depending on the laws of that State, may not have an independent right to appeal. In States that have intermediate appellate courts, appeals most likely will be addressed to these courts. In other States, the appeal will be made directly to the State Supreme Court.

The appellate process often is extremely slow. Orders, transcripts, and appellate briefs need to be prepared, filed, and selected for submission to the appellate court. Appellate judges should confer, make a tentative decision, and identify one member to write the opinion. Negotiations over the decision can take considerable time in cases where there are significant differences of opinion. It is not uncommon for this process to take more than a year from the time of the trial court's decision until an appellate opinion is published. Meanwhile, the child, parents, and foster or adoptive parents are in limbo. Some State appellate courts have attempted to correct this problem by prioritizing the completion of cases.[44]

5. THE CRIMINAL COURT PROCESS

Conduct that rises to the level of child abuse or neglect may constitute a crime, depending on State law and the circumstances of the case; not all criminal acts, however, are prosecuted. Some prosecutors are less zealous than others, or they may believe that all but the most serious of intra-family offenses are best addressed in the juvenile court. Other reasons to forgo prosecution are that it may interfere with rehabilitating families or be traumatic for the children, particularly if they have to testify. Cases typically prosecuted include sex offenses or those that result in the death of, or serious injury to, a child.

Child protective services (CPS) caseworkers may have information about the family that is critical to the criminal court proceeding. Caseworkers always should determine whether either parent or any potential caretaker in a child abuse and neglect case has a criminal record or pending criminal charges. This information can inform a caseworker's assessment of potential risk to the child and enhance case planning and service coordination activities.

While the criminal court process may vary across jurisdictions, key stages include:

- Arrest, bail, and other conditions of release;
- Preliminary hearings;
- Discovery;
- Plea bargaining;
- Trial.

Arrest, Bail and Other Conditions of Release

Criminal prosecutions most commonly begin with an arrest. Defendants then are brought before a judicial officer (a judge, magistrate, or commissioner) who informs them of the charges against them and determines the conditions of their release pending trial.

The defendant will be notified of the conditions that must be met to be released from police custody before the trial. Defendants with stable residence and employment histories and no significant prior records often are released on their own recognizance or with a written promise to appear at subsequent court dates. For defendants who seem less reliable, a cash bond may be required. Defendants can post the full amount of the bond in cash or property or secure a bondsman for a percentage of that amount. If the defendant flees, the bondsman is obligated to pay the full amount of the bond. The judge also has the discretion to impose other conditions of release, including the defendant having no contact with the child or other parent or not returning to the residence.

CPS caseworkers can assist with protecting the child and the non-off ending parent by reporting to the prosecutor any violation of a "no contact" or "stay away" condition. In such cases, the caseworker can encourage the prosecutor to ask the criminal court judge to revoke the defendant's bond and return him to jail.

Preliminary Hearings

The purpose of a preliminary hearing is to determine whether there is probable cause to believe that the defendant committed the alleged offense and that he should be tried on that charge. If the judge finds no probable cause, the case will be dismissed. If the judge finds probable cause, the case will be transferred to the trial court for resolution.

Witnesses sometimes are called to testify and are cross-examined at preliminary hearings. The CPS caseworker or the child may be among them. As a general rule, CPS caseworkers should discourage having the child testify, except possibly in cases where there is no other way to establish probable cause. Because they may be asked to recount painful memories in a public and contentious environment, children may find testifying in court to be traumatic and uncomfortable. (See Chapter 7, *Going to Court*, for more information on children's testimony.)

In some States, evidence of criminal conduct by the defendant is presented at a preliminary hearing to a grand jury instead of a judge. The grand jury then determines whether the evidence is sufficient to constitute probable cause. If so, the grand jury will issue an indictment that also puts the case before the trial court. Only the prosecutor and State's witnesses, usually the investigating law enforcement officer, appear before the grand jury. It is unlikely that either the CPS caseworker or a child would be asked to testify. Neither the defendant nor the defense attorney has the right to be present at that proceeding.

Discovery

Discovery refers to the process of obtaining information about the charge from the opposing party and, at times, other sources. It is less accessible and less extensively used in criminal cases than in civil actions, including child abuse and neglect proceedings, due to more stringent legal requirements. Defendants in some States, however, may be entitled to access CPS records, particularly if they contain information or evidence that may be helpful to their defense. The identity of reporters of child maltreatment, however, still may be withheld.

Plea Bargaining

Plea bargaining is to the criminal process what settlements are to the juvenile court process. These negotiated resolutions conclude the majority of both types of cases. Without them, courts could not reach all the cases to be tried on a timely basis.

Plea bargaining, which results in avoiding trial, has the added benefit in child abuse and neglect cases of eliminating the need for the child to testify and of speeding the resolution of the case, both of which relieve the child's anxiety. Nevertheless, there also may be negative consequences to a plea bargain. Depending on the sentence, the child victim may feel betrayed, disbelieved, or unsafe. In addition, the public may perceive that child maltreatment is not taken as seriously as other crimes.

Trial

If no plea bargain is reached, the case goes to trial. In criminal trials, the rules of evidence are applied strictly, and the prosecutor has a greater burden of proof. In order to convict, the jurors must unanimously find "beyond a reasonable doubt" that the defendant committed the alleged offense. This is a much higher burden of proof than the "clear and convincing evidence" standard in termination of parental rights trials in some States' child abuse and neglect actions. It is higher still than the "preponderance or greater weight of the evidence" standard in civil cases generally and in child abuse and neglect cases in some States.

CPS caseworkers should know if any criminal charges were filed stemming from the facts and circumstances related to their child abuse and neglect cases. The caseworker will want to establish and to maintain contact with the prosecutor responsible for those charges to know when events in the case are scheduled, whether the child maybe called as a witness, or the terms of any plea offer. The prosecutor needs to be informed of the status of the child abuse and neglect case, the case plan, and how the prosecution can benefit from that plan. To ensure that provisions important to the child and the case plan are considered, the caseworker should ask to participate in any bond hearing or plea negotiations and in the sentencing process. However, the criminal court judge may operate independently of the juvenile court and may give little or no weight to what the caseworker requests.

The criminal court case may be concluded well after the disposition hearing in the child abuse and neglect case, and its outcome can be inconsistent with the case plan and the best resolution of the child abuse and neglect case. The opposite also can be true, and the criminal sentence can augment and enhance the case plan and the prospects for a positive outcome. In communities where the same prosecutor represents the public interest in both criminal and child abuse and neglect cases, there is greater likelihood of a coordinated approach to resolving both matters. In communities where different offices are responsible for the two types of cases, the CPS caseworker should do as much as possible to ensure that the outcome in criminal court complements and supports the case plan in the juvenile case.

The desired court outcomes might vary from case to case. For example, in a case where the mother's boyfriend has been abusive to her and the child, the caseworker may advocate that he be incarcerated for the maximum period possible. On the other hand, if he is an important figure in the child's life, has been participating successfully in a batterers' intervention program, is the principal breadwinner for the family, and the plan is reunification of all family members, then a lengthy sentence would be contrary to the case plan. A suspended sentence and probation, with conditions consistent with the case plan, could enhance prospects for the plan's success. This scenario would not impose a fine or other financial burdens that would interfere with the defendant's ability to support the family.

Frequently, a parent or other caretaker in a child abuse and neglect case will be on probation for some unrelated criminal offense (e.g., a drug charge) and be required as a condition of probation to complete a drug treatment program successfully. The threat of incarceration can be a powerful motivator for overcoming a substance abuse habit or for changing other behaviors. The caseworker will want to establish and to maintain contact with the probation officer to stay abreast of the defendant's compliance with the conditions of probation. This level of coordination of the two processes is uncommon, but positive results can be realized when the CPS caseworker establishes a good working relationship with the probation officer.

Communicating with the prosecutor and the probation officer in criminal cases involving the parents or other caretakers of children who have been maltreated is an important role for CPS caseworkers and other involved service providers. Sharing information and coordinating agency efforts with what happens in criminal court to achieve a safe, permanent home for children can produce beneficial results in a CPS case.

6. DOMESTIC RELATIONS CASES AND OTHER COURT PROCEEDINGS

Families involved with child protective services (CPS) often face multiple problems and complex challenges, some of which require court involvement. Matters involving child maltreatment or juvenile delinquency typically are resolved in juvenile court. Other issues affecting families frequently are addressed in other court venues. CPS caseworkers who work with families struggling with divorce, domestic violence, and mental health problems may fi nd these families involved in other court processes. As well as understanding the juvenile court process, CPS caseworkers also should be familiar with other court hearings that affect families and case practice.

This chapter provides an overview of three types of court hearings that may involve CPS families— custody and divorce, domestic violence, and mental health hearings. The chapter also discusses suits against CPS caseworkers and agencies and Federal class actions against agencies.

Custody and Divorce Hearings

Allegations of child abuse or neglect may arise in custody and divorce cases, which result from the separation of married partners or the estrangement of unmarried parents. These also are known in some places as matrimonial or domestic relations cases.

Actions between spouses may include claims for the division of marital property, spousal support and, when the couple has minor children, custody, visitation, and child support.

Actions between unmarried parents often are referred to as paternity cases and involve the issues of paternity, custody, and child support.

CPS Involvement in Custody Cases

Domestic relations, paternity, and domestic violence cases are civil actions, and unlike child abuse and neglect cases, they take place between private individuals. CPS may become involved, however, if allegations of child abuse or neglect are made against a parent or someone living in the parent's home. In these circumstances, CPS has the challenge of determining whether to substantiate a complaint made in the context of what often is an acrimonious battle between parents over their child. There is a temptation, therefore, to discount these complaints. CPS must be careful, however, to conduct a thorough investigation that considers the context and objectively evaluates other facts. Retaining a neutral, well-trained, experienced, and widely respected custody evaluator may be useful.[45]

If abuse or neglect is substantiated, deciding whether to try the case in the domestic relations or the juvenile court can be an issue. CPS should not file a petition alleging child abuse or neglect if the non abusive parent is committed to protecting the child and if the court adopts an access and visitation plan that will keep the child safe. However, if CPS doubts that the parent or the court will protect the child from harm, it may choose to file a petition in juvenile court. In most States, the jurisdiction of the juvenile court to determine whether a child is abused or neglected will take precedence over a custody determination by the domestic relations court. Custody and visitation issues can be relegated to domestic relations or juvenile court upon showing that circumstances have changed substantially in ways that affect the child.

Motions to change custody or visitation frequently include allegations of child abuse as a basis for the motion. CPS needs to address these allegations as if they were new cases. For example, when a father is charged with a sex offense against his child and there is a pending custody proceeding, the domestic relations court, the criminal court, or both usually will order either no visitation or supervised visitation. If the father is acquitted or the charge is dismissed in criminal court, he may come to the domestic relations court requesting unsupervised visitation on that basis. The court's decision about custody and visitation, however, is independent of the criminal process. The domestic relations court judge must hear evidence and decide whether the child was sexually abused by the father and, if so, what to do about visitation.

Caseworkers should keep in mind that the burden of proof in criminal cases is "beyond a reasonable doubt," a much higher standard than the "preponderance of or greater weight of the evidence" standard in custody cases. Criminal charges are dismissed for a variety of reasons including the age of the child, the trauma to the child testifying, or insufficient credible evidence to prove the charge. A dismissal or an acquittal on those charges is not necessarily a determination that the defendant was innocent of the charge.

In this scenario, if the domestic relations court allows visitation that, in the judgment of CPS, will result in abuse of the child, CPS can file a child abuse and neglect petition in juvenile court, which also would hear the evidence and make an independent decision as to whether the father had sexually abused the child. If it is determined that he did, the juvenile court could order either more restricted visitation or no visitation.

Family courts

The complex relationships among different courts and potentially conflicting decisions can cause confusion among practitioners and family members. These issues are some of the driving force behind the rising popularity and implementation of family courts. (See Chapter 2, *The Court System and Child Protection*, for a description of family courts.) In a model family court, the same judge would hear the domestic relations, the domestic violence, and the child abuse and neglect cases. Family courts can offer multiple benefits:

- Minimizing the potential for conflicting orders and outcomes;
- Improving coordination among the court interventions;
- Reducing the number of court appearances;
- Enhancing the judge's familiarity with the issues and the parties;
- Bringing about a more successful end result.

While most courts are not organized, equipped, or legally able to achieve the "one family-one judge model," many are moving as far as possible in that direction. For example, some courts are making beneficial services, such as those listed below, more readily available and are committed to resolving family conflicts with minimal negative impact on the children.

Case management and services

Domestic relations courts can provide essential case management and services to families appearing before them. While not the case in every State, well-resourced domestic relations courts use case managers to:

- Ensure that discovery, motions, requests for temporary relief (e.g., spousal or child support), or other pretrial issues are addressed and resolved on schedule;
- Monitor the completion of mandatory actions, such as parent education or mediation;
- Keep the case on track for a timely, final resolution;
- Identify and facilitate the delivery of services to children and parties (whether they are available through the court or elsewhere).

The following are services offered by some domestic relations courts:

- **Mediation**—a process focusing on how parents will share responsibility for their children in the future. Facilitated by a trained mediator, mediation can be effective in resolving custody disputes without a trial.

- **Custody evaluations**—evaluative services for parents and children that can be useful to the court in making custody and visitation determinations. These services sometimes are publicly funded and other times available only from private providers at the expense of the litigants.

- **Guardians ad Litem (GAL)**—lawyers appointed by some courts for the children in custody and visitation cases, particularly if there are allegations of maltreatment or domestic violence, or if the conflict between the parents is unusually high. These

GALs typically are not associated with the GAL or CASA Program in the juvenile court.

- **Parent education programs**—courses for separating parents that can help them understand how their children may be affected by the separation and what they can do to minimize adverse effects.

- **Supervised visitation and exchange services**— programs that off er safe, comfortable settings and trained professionals to protect a child's safety during parental visits. In some programs, the supervisor will coach a parent on how to engage the child or on how to interact more appropriately with the child or with the other parent. They often will involve the use of intermediaries to transfer the child between the parents.

- **Parenting coordination**—a relatively new service, typically used in high-conflict cases, that employs a mental health professional to support and to assist parents in implementing a parenting agreement or court order. A parenting coordinator can help parents settle their differences and can enable them to avoid the time, emotional trauma, and expense of returning repeatedly to court.[46]

The above services also may be beneficial in some child abuse and neglect cases. CPS caseworkers will want to know how to access them, particularly when parents or family members are vying for custody or visitation of a child in a maltreatment case.

Child support

Many children in child abuse and neglect proceedings have unmet economic needs. Most live with one or neither of their biological parents, and of those, many do not receive any child support. CPS should, therefore, place a priority on locating biological parents, establishing paternity (if necessary), and pursuing child support and medical insurance from an absent parent. In fact, reasonable efforts requirements mandate that CPS do so.

Establishment of paternity and establishment and enforcement of child support and medical insurance obligations for foster children are by law the responsibility of Child Support Enforcement (CSE).[47] Every community has access to a CSE office, and in many places, they are co-located with, and operated by, the same agency as CPS. Caseworkers who are attempting to keep a family together need to help the family access CSE services.

Some courts establish paternity during child abuse and neglect proceedings, often at the initial hearing or the adjudication, provided the putative father is willing to consent to the entry of a judgment of paternity. When a putative father denies paternity or is not willing to acknowledge it formally, the case must be referred immediately to CSE. Genetic testing will be done, and in almost all cases, the results of that testing will be conclusive. CSE can initiate paternity establishment for putative fathers living in other States when requested to do so by CPS.

FEDERAL PARENT LOCATOR SERVICE

The Federal Parent Locator Service (FPLS) is an automated information system maintained by the Federal Office of Child Support Enforcement (OCSE). FPLS is a vast database that includes Social Security numbers, names of employers, and information on income and personal assets. It is used by CSE to locate persons who may be the father of a child or a parent who has a child support obligation. The Adoption and Safe Families Act (P.L. 105–89) requires that the resources of FPLS also be available to CPS for locating parents in its cases.[48] FPLS is an invaluable resource for caseworkers who need to fi nd and serve a putative father or absent parent.

Some courts have developed working agreements or protocols with CSE and CPS to facilitate the establishment of paternity, as well as the establishment and enforcement of support obligations, and to speed access to FPLS. These strategies may include locating OCSE staff and computers near the juvenile court to serve the parent and to help identify the paternity and child support needs of the children and families in that court. Judges have to ensure that all has been done to locate the missing parent, not only for the enforcement of child support, but also for placement options or for termination of parental rights. Therefore, the courts may require documentation from the caseworker regarding utilization of this service. For more information about FPLS, visit http://www.acf.hhs.gov/programs/cse /newhire.

Support payments made by the parents reduce CPS's (or a relative's) costs for providing for the child. The amount of child support owed by an absent parent is determined in every State by the application of a child support guideline or formula. The guidelines are based on the assumption that one parent pays support to the other. Additionally, parents whose children were already receiving child support and have been placed in foster care often have difficulty regaining custody for financial reasons. They may need housing, furnishings, security and utility deposits, or other services. The amount of their child support payments should not preclude them from having the funds necessary to achieve reunification. In these circumstances, caseworkers may want to request that a reduction of the child support payments be considered. For the same reason, consideration must be given to suspending repayment of past public assistance or arrearages.

Domestic Violence Hearings

While children should not be removed unnecessarily, neither should they be left in environments that jeopardize their safety. This has been a particularly problematic issue in cases where children are exposed to domestic violence. As CPS caseworkers become increasingly aware of the high co-occurrence of domestic violence and child maltreatment and of the potential emotional impact of exposure to domestic violence on children, more communities are filing child maltreatment petitions in such cases and requesting removal of the children.[49] Research indicates that children exposed to domestic abuse are more likely to experience physical abuse or neglect than children living in nonviolent homes.[50] Studies estimate that there are adult and child victims in 30 to 60 percent of families experiencing domestic violence, and for adult victims who experience severe forms of domestic abuse, their children are in danger of suffering serious physical harm.[51]

CPS caseworkers should recognize that "[c]hildhood exposure to adult domestic violence should not automatically be defined as maltreatment...." Instead, "[w]hat's needed... are empirical and practice-based criteria for deciding whether or not a child is at a heightened risk of harm" before placing an undue burden on the victim by removing the child.[52] Once established, these criteria must be developed into effective screening and assessment instruments for use in the field. In addition, there is a dire need to develop greater expertise within child protection agencies about domestic violence, to collaborate with domestic violence programs, and to provide alternative forms of voluntary, community- based services for exposed children and their families, including specialized parenting and intervention programs for the perpetrator.[53]

The process for filing actions for protection against domestic violence is designed to accommodate persons who do not have an attorney. Complaint forms are available, no filing fee is required, and most jurisdictions afford relatively prompt access to a judicial officer at any hour of the day or night. Litigants often request, and are able to obtain immediately, an *ex parte* order granting eviction of the alleged abusers from the parties' residence or other protective relief. Additionally, in best case scenarios, the time from filing to final hearing and conclusion of the case can be brief, ranging from a few days to a few weeks at most. For these reasons, claims for protection against domestic violence usually are filed as separate actions. Exhibit 6-1 provides more information about protection orders.

EXHIBIT 6-1. DOMESTIC VIOLENCE PROTECTIVE ORDERS

Claims for protection against domestic violence sometimes are brought in conjunction with a domestic relations case, but more often they are filed separately. These are variously known as protective orders, restraining orders, or orders of protection. These orders are available in every State and may require that the abusive partner:

- Be evicted from the parties' residence, not return there, or not go to where the victim works;
- Refrain from abusing the victim;
- Have no contact with the victim;
- Participate in substance abuse treatment or a batterers' intervention program;
- Pay support.

The order also may include protection for the children and may award custody of the children and child support. Not all of these remedies are available in every State, but statutes usually authorize the court to impose any additional terms or conditions it deems necessary for the victim's protection. In most States, orders granting relief in domestic violence cases are limited in duration from 1 to 5 years.

Federal law also makes possession of a firearm illegal for anyone who is subject to an active protective order that meets specified criteria. Some States and judges go further and order defendants against whom a protective order is issued to surrender all weapons to a law enforcement agency and to not purchase or possess any firearm as long as the order remains in effect. Possessing a firearm also is illegal for any individual who has ever been convicted of certain domestic violence crimes.[54]

Domestic violence protection or restraining orders should be logged immediately into a State's central registry as well as the National Crime Information Center Protection Order File, which can be accessed by any law enforcement officer. These orders are enforceable across State lines.[55] Violation of the order is a separate criminal offense in most States and will result in immediate arrest of defendants who are caught violating it. If the defendants are not caught, but there is probable cause to believe they violated an order, a warrant for their arrests can be issued. Alternatively, violations can subject the offenders to being found in contempt of court and punished by fines or incarceration.

CPS caseworkers with cases in which family violence is a significant problem will want to consider the efficacy of a protection order. This may involve encouraging the victim to take the actions necessary to obtain the order, or in some jurisdictions, CPS may request a protective order in the child maltreatment case. A victim should not be compelled, however, to choose between obtaining or abiding by an order and having the child removed by CPS. It is important to respect the victim's opinion of what would enhance the children's safety or would place them at greater risk. Protection orders can contribute to the safety of adult and child victims of domestic violence, but they do not ensure safety. Those orders often are violated, sometimes resulting in serious injury or even the death of the parent or children. Domestic violence victims' advocates can provide CPS caseworkers with recommendations to engage adult victims in the protection and safety of themselves and their children.

> For more information on domestic violence and child maltreatment, see the *User Manual Series* publication *Child Protection in Families Affected by Domestic Violence* at http://www.childwelfare. gov/pubs/usermanuals/domesticviolence/.

Mental Health Hearings

Some children in foster care are committed involuntarily or are admitted voluntarily to mental health treatment facilities. The CPS caseworker should work with a supervisor and a mental health professional in deciding whether to pursue such a placement and likely will be the person to accompany and to admit the child to the facility. The caseworker also will need to attend the hearing and present CPS's position regarding the child's need for continued treatment. It is unlikely that a CPS lawyer will be present although there may be a prosecutor or a lawyer for the facility. The caseworker will want to communicate with facility staff to learn the child's diagnosis and recommendations for treatment and immediately begin work with staff on a discharge plan that will meet the child's needs. Every effort must be made to avoid extending confinement in the facility because of a lack of appropriate alternative placement.

Some State laws require court approval for the voluntary admission of minors to mental health treatment facilities or for the involuntary commitment of minors or adults. Whether the law applies to a particular placement usually depends on whether it is a locked facility, such as a psychiatric hospital or residential treatment program. Voluntary admissions to mental health treatment facilities are made by a parent, guardian, or CPS for a child. The court must determine whether the child is mentally ill and in need of further treatment. Some States also require that a child not be placed in such facilities if better alternatives are available. Many children object to being admitted, and, from their perspective, the admission is involuntary. While caseworkers need to respect the child's feelings and concerns, they also need to explain the reason for admittance, such as the child being a danger to herself (e.g., suicidal tendencies) or to others. Otherwise, the caseworker should continue to find the least restrictive facility that meets the child's mental health needs. Additionally, the court must decide whether the child is mentally ill or poses a danger.

Statutes governing voluntary admissions and involuntary commitments are intended to protect the liberty interests of patients. They help ensure that the decision to deprive them of their freedom is reviewed independently and objectively and that they will not be held against their will unless a court finds that there is a legally sufficient basis for doing so.

In some States, involuntary commitment and voluntary admissions are the only vehicles for forcibly placing a child in a mental health treatment facility. In others, juvenile court judges can order that children be admitted to such facilities as the disposition for a delinquent or status offense.

Confidentiality of Court Records

The Child Abuse Prevention and Treatment Act (CAPTA) of 1974 required that records of child abuse complaints and investigations be confidential and that court proceedings be closed to the public. CAPTA was reauthorized and amended by Congress, most recently as part of the Keeping Children and Families Safe Act of 2003 (P.L. 108–36). This amendment to CAPTA changed the confidentiality requirements so States now must share confidential information with any Federal, State, or local government entity or agency with a legal responsibility to protect children. In addition, States now can conduct court proceedings at which child abuse and neglect determinations are being made more open without jeopardizing eligibility for CAPTA funds.[56]

Suits against Child Protective Services Caseworkers and Agencies

If CPS negligently fails to investigate or to intervene to protect a child when there is reason to believe the child is abused or neglected, and the child is harmed as a result, the child may be able to sue for damages through a GAL or a "next friend," the legal term for an adult who files suit on the child's behalf. A suit also can be filed for maltreatment that occurs in out-of-home care through CPS negligence or willful misconduct. An example is the physical or sexual abuse of a child by a foster parent.

The defendants in suits for damages are likely to be the CPS caseworker, the caseworker's supervisor, the agency director, and the county or State. It is difficult to generalize about the liability of caseworkers because the law on liability is defined largely by appellate decisions and is State-specific. CPS caseworkers will want to know:

- What the law regarding their liability is in the State where they work;
- Whether they have any immunity from liability and, if so, the extent of that immunity;
- Whether CPS insures them for liability and the extent of that protection;
- Whether CPS or any insurance carrier will provide legal representation for a caseworker who is sued.

Caseworkers should request this information from their agency which is frequently named as co-respondent in a suit. The National Center for Field Consultation can provide guidance on coping with child welfare litigation. Additional information on child welfare litigation is available at http://www. cwla.org/consultation/litigation.htm, by e-mailing ncfc@cwla.org, or by calling (202) 942–0287.

Class Actions against Agencies

Under some circumstances, a group of individuals who are similarly situated may bring a class action against CPS for violations of Federal law or of the U.S. Constitution. These actions usually address inadequacies in agency services, staffing, or practices. Although individual claims for monetary damages may accompany the claim for class relief, the remedy usually sought is a declaratory judgment or an injunction. A declaratory judgment is a statement by the court about what the law requires of CPS. An injunction is a directive or order requiring CPS to take certain actions or forbidding it from engaging in specified actions.

EXAMPLE OF CLASS ACTION LAWSUIT

One notable example of a class action lawsuit is *Nicholson v. Williams* in New York City. Unlike most other class action suits, it went to trial, and the result was an injunction against the city's Administration for Children Services (ACS). The injunction prohibited ACS from removing "...a child from the custody of the mother without a court order solely because the mother is a victim of domestic violence except in cases where the child is in such imminent danger to life or health that he or she must be removed and there is not reasonably sufficient time to obtain a court order." The injunction also required that petitions not be filed against a mother solely because she "engaged" in domestic violence in the presence of the children or refused to accept services unless the petition alleges with specificity how the child has been harmed. Due to the lawsuit, petitions are required to describe specifically any acts of domestic violence alleged and any harm suffered by the child as a result of such acts. Additionally, ACS was required to develop new materials and training regarding cases in which domestic violence is an issue, to employ domestic violence specialists, and to conduct a safety conference within 72 hours of the removal of any child from a mother who is a victim of domestic violence and has not otherwise abused or neglected the child.[57]

A number of such lawsuits have been filed in recent years. Most have been settled by agreement of the parties, known as a "consent decree." The relief generally has involved a commitment by CPS to improve practice and service delivery in specified ways. In most cases, the court has appointed a receiver or, more commonly, a review panel to monitor and to assist implementation of the consent decree.

The type of court that hears the case determines who is affected by the decision. State court appellate decisions have the force of law only in the States in which they are issued. U.S. District Court decisions apply only in the district in which they are issued, and U.S. Court of Appeals (Circuit Courts) decisions apply only in the States of that circuit. U.S. Supreme Court decisions, however, have national reach. Appellate courts of all types often cite decisions from other State or Federal courts to support their own rulings in similar cases.

7. GOING TO COURT

Most child protective services (CPS) caseworkers are prepared to interview family members, to conduct home visits, to document cases, and to work with other social service providers. However, there is one component of casework practice that leaves some caseworkers anxious and ill-equipped—preparing for and conducting themselves in court. Simply knowing the different types of court hearings and mastering legal terminology do not demonstrate a caseworker's competence in juvenile court. Skillful courtroom presentation, well-documented court reports, and a collaborative style also are necessary to maximize constructive family, agency, and court outcomes. This chapter presents practical guidelines to help CPS caseworkers prepare themselves for going to court, to help them work with children who also may be called to testify, and to improve their working relationships with the judges.

The Rules of Evidence

The rules of evidence determine what information can be introduced in court and for what purposes. They are intended to ensure that the court's decisions are based on reliable information.

Types of evidence
Evidence takes different forms, specifically:

- **Direct evidence** is based on personal knowledge, such as the testimony of an eyewitness;

- **Demonstrative evidence** includes items such as documents, photographs, or x-rays;

- **Circumstantial evidence** is indirect evidence from which an inference can be drawn, such as a child with an oddly shaped bruise on her back.

For example, a CPS caseworker's record might contain the following types of evidence:

- The log kept by a teacher of the days the child came to school with noticeable bruises;
- Documentation that a neighbor heard the child's screams;
- The record of the physician who examined the child reporting that she had multiple bruises of different ages and severity on her back and buttocks;
- Photographs of the bruises taken by police;
- Documentation that the child told the CPS caseworker that she lives alone with her mother and that her mother hits her with a belt;
- The belt.

In court, the child's testimony would be direct evidence. The teacher's log, the photographs, and the belt would be demonstrative evidence. Living alone with her mother, coupled with the screams and the bruises, would be circumstantial evidence identifying the mother as the abuser.

All evidence must be both material and relevant to be admitted. To be material, evidence must have a logical connection to an issue in the case. To be relevant, evidence must increase the likelihood that a particular fact is true.

The more caseworkers know about the rules of evidence, the better they can prepare for a case. The burden of proof for the particular stage of the proceeding or type of case determines how much evidence is enough. The judge or jury will decide whether the credible evidence presented satisfies the burden of proof. (See Chapter 4, *The Juvenile Court Process*, for a discussion on adjudication and the burden of proof.)

The hearsay rule and exceptions

The hearsay rule excludes evidence that is unreliable. Hearsay is defined as an out-of-court statement made by someone other than the witness, which is offered for the truth of that statement. For example, the hearsay rule would prevent a caseworker from testifying that a neighbor told the caseworker that she saw the mother hit the child with a belt. For that information to be admitted, the neighbor would have to testify in court. The rule, however, does not exclude out-of-court statements that are not offered for the truth of what was said. For example, a statement by the neighbor that she heard the mother yell, "I'm going to kill you," just before the child's screams would be admitted not for the truth of the statement but to show that the mother said it. The neighbor would not be testifying as to whether the mother actually attempted to kill or to abuse the child, only that she made the statement.

There are numerous exceptions to the hearsay rule that admit evidence that otherwise would be hearsay. These exceptions are based on the existence of other indications that the statements are reliable. Exceptions that are particularly relevant to child abuse and neglect cases include:

- **Admissions**. The mother said to the CPS caseworker, "I know I hit her too hard, but I will not do it again." The caseworker would be allowed to testify to what the mother said, even though it is an out-of-court statement offered for its truth, because it was also the admission of a party. Such an admission is thought to be reliable because it was against the mother's interest to make it.

- **Excited utterances**. An out-of-court statement that is made spontaneously under extreme emotional excitement also may be admissible as an exception to the hearsay rule. An excited utterance is viewed as trustworthy because the speaker's excitement at the time it was made is thought to prevent him or her from refl ecting long enough to fabricate the statement. The length of time between the event and the statement is a critical factor in determining the admissibility of such statements.

- **Regularly kept records**. Records are hearsay because they contain second-hand information, but their contents will be considered reliable and, therefore, admissible when they are kept regularly, systematically, and routinely. The regularity of the record-keeping process by persons with a duty to supply accurate data ensures trustworthiness. The foundation for the admission of records is established by the testimony of the person who made the record or the custodian of the records. This exception may be applied to medical records, police reports, school records, and CPS files. Caseworkers must be careful to record accurately the statements of others and their own observations. The record must be as factual as possible.

There are other exceptions to the hearsay rule, but they are used less commonly in child maltreatment cases.

Expert Testimony

Expert testimony is opinion testimony about a subject that is outside the judge or jury's knowledge or experience. The witness needs to show that she is qualified to testify as an expert on a particular subject. These qualifications may be based on experience; education and training; professional accomplishments, recognition, and memberships; prior testimony as an expert; or familiarity with the relevant professional literature. After each party has the opportunity to question the witness, the judge will decide whether the witness may testify as an expert and on what specific subject. Expert witnesses are common in child maltreatment cases. Examples of expert witnesses include:

- Medical doctors who have expertise in the causes of physical injuries or conditions, such as spiral fractures, Shaken Baby Syndrome, failure to thrive, or Munchausen syndrome by proxy;
- Mental health professionals who can diagnose mental illness or can explain issues of bonding and attachment;
- Domestic violence specialists who have the expertise to explain the debilitating eff cts on a child of witnessing the physical abuse of a parent;
- Specialists in child sexual abuse or substance abuse.

To be admitted into evidence, the expert's opinion needs to be relevant, which means that it needs to increase the likelihood that a particular fact is true or that a particular condition exists. The expert's testimony also needs to have a sound scientific basis. Application of these rules can be complicated. It is the CPS attorney's responsibility to identify the need for expert testimony, to prepare the witness to testify, and to demonstrate in court that the witness is qualified and that the testimony is admissible.[58]

Court Reports

Court reports afford caseworkers some of the best opportunities to communicate information to the court and to influence its decision. If CPS or the court has a standard format for such documents, the caseworker will need to use that. Some formats may be ineffective vehicles, however, for quickly imparting critical information. Poorly organized reports frustrate judges and other participants and are less likely to be infl uential. Caseworkers should consider adding a cover page that summarizes key decisions to be made and the CPS position with respect to each of them, including references by title and page number to any attached documentation. References to documents in the court's file should be noted by the title and date of filing.

Case plans and reasonable efforts reports also are valuable for conveying information to the court. As with the court report, they should be comprehensive, concise, and written as directly and clearly as possible. If the document is an updated version of an earlier one, the new material should be highlighted. The goal is to present the material in a manner that is easily understood. In addition, it should be simple to locate any supporting documentation. Judges will appreciate receiving reports that satisfy these criteria and will be able to understand more clearly CPS positions and the reasons for them.

The content of the court report will depend on the type of hearing for which it is presented and the status of the case. (See Chapter 4, *The Juvenile Court Process*, for further information on the issues to be addressed at various hearings over the course of a child maltreatment case.)

Testifying

Speaking to the court and other participants in a case is another excellent opportunity to communicate information that may affect the court's decision.

Relatively few child maltreatment cases are adjudicated by trial, but when one is tried, the caseworker invariably will be called to testify or to give answers under oath. Caseworkers also may be called to give formal testimony at other stages of the court process, particularly the permanency hearing, and usually at any trial related to the termination of parental rights.

More commonly, caseworkers will have the opportunity to testify informally regarding case plans, the child's well-being, reasonable efforts, visitation, parental performance, and needed services at each hearing in the case. This testimony is not under oath and usually is delivered from the CPS counsel table rather than from the witness stand.

Preparation for testimony

Before every hearing, the caseworker should review the case and be prepared to answer questions about it. The nature of the hearing will determine the types of questions that may be asked. In order to prepare to testify, the caseworker should:

- Become thoroughly familiar with the facts of the case and with the case file;
- Meet with the CPS attorney to discuss the case and the particulars of the testimony, especially any troublesome aspects;
- Identify key facts or points that the attorney will want to elicit;
- Discuss with the attorney the expected cross- examination questions;
- Outline the history of the case, including important dates and events;
- Summarize the services offered, the response, and the outcomes;
- Prepare to answer questions about reasonable efforts;
- Talk with any previous caseworkers about their involvement with the family.

The caseworker also should prepare a description of his professional experience and qualifi cations.

Guidelines for testifying

During direct examination, the attorney calls the caseworker to be a witness and asks questions. Generally, the rules for direct examination require open-ended questions (e.g., "What did you see?" or "What happened next?"). Leading questions that suggest the answer or questions calling for a "yes" or "no" answer usually are not permitted (e.g., "Didn't the mother tell you that she hit the child with a belt?"). When testifying, caseworkers should:

- Be confident and self-assured;
- Listen carefully to the question and answer it directly;
- Ask that a question be repeated if it is difficult to hear or understand, but not make a habit of doing so;
- State facts, not opinions or conclusions (e.g., instead of saying that the mother was uncooperative and rude, state exactly what she said or did);
- State whether an answer is unknown or cannot be recalled;
- Speak clearly, distinctly, and loudly enough to be heard;
- Make eye contact with the questioner and the judge;
- Refer to the case file only as necessary in order to recall information.

When an attorney objects to a question or moves to strike an answer, the caseworker should wait until the judge rules on the motion before speaking. If the judge overrules the objection, then the caseworker should answer the question. If the judge sustains the objection, then the caseworker should not answer the question; the attorney will ask another one.

Cross-examination is questioning by attorneys other than the one who called the caseworker as a witness. The purpose of cross-examination is to expose weaknesses, errors, inconsistencies, biases, or other deficiencies in the testimony of the witness. The attorney also may focus on the caseworker's lack of experience or qualifications and will try to show that the caseworker did not do a thorough investigation or exercised poor judgment. Cross-examination can be unpleasant, but it is important that caseworkers not take it personally and remain outwardly calm, confident, and respectful. If a caseworker becomes hostile or defensive, the judge may discount the testimony.

Leading questions are permitted on cross-examination. Lawyers often will ask such questions, insist they be answered "yes" or "'no," and before the witness can explain, ask another question. When a "yes" or "no" requires an explanation, the witness can ask permission to explain the answer.

Ex Parte Communications

Ex parte communications are verbal or written communications addressed to the judge in a case by one party outside the presence of another party without copying the other party. They are strictly prohibited.[59] The prohibition extends to representatives of a party, including CPS caseworkers. Thus, caseworkers must never attempt to communicate privately with any judge about an open case; however, communications that are not case-specific, such as those suggested in Chapter 8, *Working with the Courts*, are not prohibited.

Children's Testimony

The courtroom can be an intimidating and traumatizing environment for most people, but especially for children, many of whom may be terrified by the prospect of testifying. They may become anxious or distraught. Some even freeze and are unable to respond to simple, preliminary questions. Younger children are more likely to have these types of reactions. Older children also are at risk of emotional trauma because they are more likely to be cross-examined aggressively by attorneys. For these reasons, children should not be called to testify, particularly against parents or relatives, unless the children's testimony is essential to proving critical allegations of the petitions or if the children want and need to testify for their own emotional well-being.

The Decision to call a child to testify
Most child abuse or neglect cases can be proved by the testimony of other witnesses or by demonstrative or documentary evidence. In some cases, however, the child's testimony may be the only evidence. This is especially true of some sexual abuse cases.

The decision to call a child to testify should be made by CPS and its attorney, in consultation with the advocates and any therapists for the child. They need to weigh carefully the potential benefits of the child's testimony against the potential harm, both to the child from testifying and to the child, other family members, and the community if the charge is not proven.

Some CPS attorneys may not be sensitive to how a child can be affected by testifying. Consequently, the CPS caseworker (perhaps with the child's advocate and therapist) should be prepared to assert any concerns when deciding whether to call the child as a witness. It is critical that children never be put in a position of giving testimony against a parent or other caretaker unless they can be safeguarded against retaliation.

Every witness needs to be competent, which means that the witness must know the diff erence between the truth and a lie; appreciate the necessity of telling the truth; and be capable of observing, remembering, and describing events about which the witness will testify. This is a component of the *voir dire* process, a preliminary examination to determine competency of a witness or absence of bias of a juror. Under Federal law and that of many States, all witnesses are presumed competent, but some States have more restrictive requirements. If the issue is raised, the lawyers and judge may question the child to determine competency.

Younger children are more likely to not be allowed to testify due to lack of competency. T us, age is a significant factor in determining whether to call a child as a witness. The reliability and credibility of children's testimony has been the subject of much research, some of it contradictory. It can be summarized by saying that younger children are able to recall events less accurately and are more susceptible to suggestion.[60] A recommended approach for assessing children's ability to tell the truth is presented in Exhibit 7-1.

Credibility of a child's testimony

Decisions about children's credibility will depend mostly on their demeanor and the convincing force of their testimony. Other factors considered include whether the child's testimony is consistent with earlier statements or with any other credible evidence. The court also will be interested to know if there is any indication that the child has been coached or that the story is the result of intentional or unintentional influence by a parent, CPS, law enforcement, medical professionals, or others.

Care must be taken by all interviewers never to ask leading questions regarding possible abuse or neglect. Leading questions are those that suggest an answer, for example, "Didn't he grab your mother by the neck with his hands and choke her?" as opposed to "What did he do?" Any indication that the child's testimony may be the result of such suggestive questioning will undermine its credibility.

Likewise, repeated questioning of the child by the same or multiple persons, including professionals, about any abuse or neglect also will undermine credibility. CPS should have specially trained interviewers for children. CPS administrators are encouraged to develop protocols with police, prosecutors, medical personnel, and mental health treatment providers that minimize the number of interviews to which a child is subjected. Ideally, there should be only one interview, and it should occur in a safe, child-friendly environment. The interview should be videotaped to reduce the likelihood of subsequent interviews and to demonstrate that the interview was conducted appropriately.

Supporting child witnesses in the courtroom

Supportive measures for young witnesses in child maltreatment proceedings might include videotaping depositions or allowing the child to speak to the judge in chambers, a common practice in child custody cases. Some States have relaxed hearsay rules for the statements of child witnesses and are more lenient in allowing leading questions of children.[61] When a child needs to testify, the CPS caseworker must decide whether utilizing one of these measures would benefit the child and facilitate the testimony. If so, the caseworker should confer with the CPS attorney in advance of the trial to file the necessary motions, to develop the required supporting evidence, and to make arrangements for whatever equipment may be required if the motion is granted.

EXHIBIT 7-1. ASSESSING YOUNGER CHILDREN'S ABILITY OR WILLINGNESS TO TELL THE TRUTH

- Begin the inquiry by establishing a rapport with the child. For example, ask about her age or favorite activity. Use this information to guide the inquiry.
- Ask the child the following:
  - What does it mean to tell the truth?
  - Why do you tell the truth? Is it important to tell the truth? Why?
  - What happens when you tell the truth?
  - What is a lie?
  - What have you told a lie about or when have you not told the truth?
  - What happens when you lie or do not tell the truth?
  - Are there times when it is OK to lie or not tell the truth? When?
- Using information provided by the child, ask questions and reframe the child's comments to assess her ability to discern the difference between a truth or a lie, as well as her willingness to tell the truth or to correct inaccurate information.
  - For example, if the child said she was 5 years old, begin the inquiry with "So, you're 7 years old?"

    Assess if the child will correct the inaccurate statement. If the child agrees, respond by saying, "Oh, I thought you told me earlier that you were 5 years old?" Frequently, children will confi rm their original answer.

    In this situation, ask the child if the statement that she is 7 years old is a lie or the truth. Explain to the child that if information is not correct, you want them to provide the truth or correct answer and that they must be sure to do this in any situation, including court testimony.
  - Another example would be, if the interviewer is wearing black shoes, to ask the child, "If I told you my shoes were yellow, would that be the truth or a lie?" Alternatively, "If I told you that my shoes were black, would that be the truth or a lie?"
- Proceed with similar questions or statements that will help with the assessment.
- Conclude the inquiry by praising the child for his participation and affirmative answers. Stress the importance of telling the truth in court.

THE NATIONAL CHILDREN'S ADVOCACY CENTER

The National Children's Advocacy Center supports a network of community-based facilities that use a multidisciplinary team approach to respond to child abuse. The center is a resource for information about how to best conduct interviews of child victims and how to establish a model program. See Appendix

B, *Resource Listings of Selected National Organizations Concerned With Child Maltreatment*, for more information on the National Children's Advocacy Center, or go to http://www.nationalcac.org.

Taking frequent breaks and making the setting less formal are other measures a court can take to make children more comfortable in the courtroom and to facilitate their testimony.

The judges can come off the bench, sit at the same level as the children and other participants, or not wear judicial robes. Some casual conversation with children can help relax them, as will excluding unnecessary participants from the courtroom. Permitting very young children to sit on the lap of a support person while testifying is another possibility. Some judges will take or authorize these measures on their own initiative, while others may need to be asked or encouraged to do so.

A child witness should not enter the courtroom until it is time to testify and should be prepared in advance for that moment and what will happen after. There will be people present in the courtroom whom the child has never seen, often including an armed bailiff. The child will be the center of attention, which may create or heighten anxiety or fear. CPS caseworkers (or the CPS agency attorney) should do what they can to prepare the child for this experience. At minimum, preparation should include visiting the courtroom when it is not in use, practicing being sworn in, sitting in the witness stand and answering questions (unrelated to the case), speaking into the microphone, and seeing the view from the bench. Tell the child who will be present, and point out where each of those individuals will sit.

The CPS caseworker or attorney should familiarize the child with the court process, including:

- Explaining that different lawyers will ask questions and giving examples;
- Describing objections and explaining how the child should wait until the judge rules on them;
- Explaining the terms "sustained" and "overruled;"
- Role playing the competency inquiry (without telling the child the answers);
- Arranging for the child to meet with the CPS attorney (if this meeting has not yet occurred) and assisting the attorney and child so that they may interact comfortably.

While it is inappropriate to remind a child what to say or otherwise attempt to infl uence the child's testimony, it may be appropriate for the caseworker and attorney to review with the child any videotaped, audiotaped, or written statement that may have been made.

The advocates are particularly helpful allies in cases where children will testify. The GAL or CASA often may have a closer personal relationship with the child than others involved in the case and be in a better position to facilitate the child's ability to testify effectively.

Standards for testifying by alternative means

Many States have passed laws regarding child witnesses in the courtroom. These laws focus primarily on protecting a child from having to testify in the presence of the alleged abuser. One protective measure is the use of closed-circuit television in which the child's testimony is broadcast into the courtroom where the judge, jury, and defendant can see and hear what the child says. The lawyers are present with the child, and the defendant's lawyers can cross-examine the child while communicating privately with their client. This approach will be deemed constitutional regarding the right to face one's accuser, provided there is sufficient evidence for the judge to find that the child would be significantly traumatized by the presence of the defendant and, thus, unable to testify.[62] Expert testimony may be necessary to establish the basis for a request to protect a child in this way.

The most significant recent development regarding the testimony of child witnesses is the adoption of the Uniform Child Witness Testimony by Alternative Methods Act, drafted by the National Conference of Commissioners on Uniform State Laws and approved and recommended for enactment in all States.[63] In 2003, the American Bar Association approved the law. At the time of this manual's publication, three States had adopted it, and two more had legislation pending.[64] The Act applies to children under 13 years of age and to both criminal (including juvenile delinquency) and non-criminal proceedings. It establishes standards for determining whether a child witness may testify by alternative means.[65]

EXHIBIT 7-2. CHILD TESTIMONY

In noncriminal proceedings, such as child maltreatment cases, standards for child testimony are less rigorous. These differences are best demonstrated by reference to Section 5 of the Uniform Child Witness Testimony by Alternative Methods Act, entitled Standards for Determining Whether Child Witness May Testify by Alternative Method, which states:

(a) In a criminal proceeding, the presiding officer may allow a child witness to testify by an alternative method only in the following situations:

1. The child may testify otherwise than in an open forum in the presence and full view of the finder of fact if the presiding officer finds by clear and convincing evidence that the child would suffer serious emotional trauma that would substantially impair the child's ability to communicate with the finder of fact if required to testify in the open forum.

2. The child may testify other than face-to-face with the defendant if the presiding officer finds by clear and convincing evidence that the child would suffer serious emotional trauma that would substantially impair the child's ability to communicate with the finder of fact if required to be confronted face-to-face by the defendant.

(b) In a noncriminal proceeding, the presiding officer may allow a child witness to testify by an alternative method if the presiding officer finds by a preponderance of the evidence that allowing the child to testify by an alternative method is necessary to serve the best interests of the child or enable the child to communicate with the finder of fact. In making this finding, the presiding officer shall consider:

1. The nature of the proceeding;
2. The age and maturity of the child;
3. The relationship of the child to the parties in the proceeding;
   a. The nature and degree of emotional trauma that the child may suffer in testifying; Any other relevant factor, such as developmental delays.[66]

The Act also prescribes the content of the court's order and requires a full and fair opportunity to cross- examine the child witness. It does not dictate the alternative methods for receiving a child's testimony, but strongly suggests that only two current practices are likely to satisfy all provisions of the Act: closed- circuit television and courtroom arrangements that avoid direct confrontation between a witness and a particular party or the finder of fact.[67] See Exhibit 7-2 for more information about the Act.

Judges' Expectations of Child Protective Services Caseworkers

Judges and CPS caseworkers generally do not have routine, direct contact with one another. Communication typically occurs in the courtroom and often is transmitted via CPS or the parents' attorneys. Judges may ask a question or make a request directly to caseworkers, but there is limited opportunity for caseworkers to become familiar with them. Many judges, however, are receptive to enhancing their relationships and to ensuring a positive experience for individuals who appear in their courtroom. CPS caseworkers can improve these relationships through improved awareness of courtroom rules, procedures, expectations, and the personalities of those involved.

Judges expect that CPS caseworkers will successfully:

- Engage clients in the court process;
- Work effectively with others;
- Arrive on time;
- Know the law and follow court rules;
- Prepare appropriate court orders.

Fulfilling these expectations, as described below, will help improve caseworkers' court experiences.

Engaging clients in the court process

The foundation for effective casework is the relationship between the caseworker and the client. Some clients are less appealing than others or are more difficult to engage. Some caseworkers' experiences or personalities equip them to perform this aspect of the work better than others. Regardless of these variables, engaging clients at the outset is one of the keys to successful outcomes and requires sincerely communicating concern for them and their children as well as a desire that the family be together. Caseworkers should be empathetic and sensitive to clients' feelings and needs and should take an approach that identifi es the specific strengths of each client and that tailors interventions to those strengths. Caseworkers also should engage parents as a means of encouraging, motivating, and inspiring them to take the necessary steps to retain or to regain custody of their children. Caseworkers who experience the most success with families are the ones who work most effectively with parents. Insightful judges recognize this quality in caseworkers and value the results it produces.

Communication with the clients must be direct, honest, and unambiguous to avoid any misunderstanding of important information, including conveying possible case outcomes. Before the hearing, an explanation of the court process will give the parents some idea of what to expect. After the hearing, the caseworker should help parents understand key decisions, reinforce the outcome and expectations, and answer questions. Parents often leave the courtroom not knowing what happened or why, what will happen next, or what is expected of them. It is easy for those who are familiar with the court hearings, the terminology, and the consequences of a judge's decisions to forget how foreign the experience may be to others.

Most States require case and service plans to be incorporated into the court records for the judge to determine if they meet requirements regarding services and reunification efforts. In fact, discussion of the agency's actions and the parents' progress toward their goals comprises the largest part of the hearings. During testimony and in the documents, caseworkers should focus on the most serious issues that must be resolved to achieve reunification. (See Chapter 4, *The Juvenile Court Process*, for more information about developing case plans.) Since the judge often will ask how the caseworker dealt with these issues, it should be documented that the caseworker:

- Made clear what the client needs to change and how;
- Identified and built on the clients' strengths and those of the extended family;
- Offered whatever services and resources were needed;
- Rewarded the clients' successes and encouraged further progress;
- Advocated for the client with CPS supervisors, service providers, and the court;
- Took care not to demand more of clients than was realistically possible due to limitations of time, transportation, resources, other responsibilities, or innate abilities.

Working effectively with others

Another critical skill for caseworkers is the ability to establish good working relationships with others, including service providers, throughout the legal process. Some communities have multidisciplinary team meetings to discuss cases, particularly complex ones, which may involve experts who have no direct involvement with the case. Other communities commonly have "staffings" at which all service providers and those involved in the court process meet to discuss a case and to strategize ways to address the needs presented.

Whether or not these structures are in place, resolving child maltreatment cases successfully almost invariably involves a team approach, with the caseworker both the coach and a key member of the team. Success often will depend on the caseworker's collaboration skills or ability to cooperate with the other team members, particularly the child's advocates and the parents' attorneys. Working effectively means:

- Treating the other team members with respect;
- Involving them in identifying the issues the case presents;
- Thinking collectively about how to resolve those issues;
- Sharing information;
- Communicating about new developments as they arise.

Establishing good working relationships within the team is more likely to result in positive case outcomes. As working relationships become more effective, conflicts will be less likely, and future interactions in other cases will be more constructive. Judges appreciate the efforts of caseworkers who facilitate constructive interactions and who achieve consensus about the course of cases.

In some cases, service providers may have to testify about the services and the families; therefore, it is important for caseworkers to establish good relationships with them. Judges may have questions for the caseworker about the service providers, so caseworkers will want to make personal contacts with them to understand what they do, whom they serve, and their criteria for providing services and to determine the quality of their work. Service providers also should be participants in team discussions about the case.

Similarly, a good relationship between CPS and the public mental health agency is important. Unfortunately, this relationship can be acrimonious in many communities. If CPS depends on the mental health agency to perform evaluations or to provide treatment or placements, including hospitalization, CPS should take the initiative to establish a good working relationship between the two agencies. Defining each agency's responsibilities, setting timelines for completion of evaluations or other tasks, and establishing lines of communication for sharing information are just a few of the issues that need to be addressed. Discussion of these issues should involve the heads of each agency and the court. Individual caseworkers, however, can contribute to this process by identifying problems that arise between the agencies in specific cases and documenting how those problems affected the child or CPS's ability to comply with timelines established by the Adoption and Safe Families Act (ASFA) (P.L. 105–89). Sharing that information with supervisors might lead to the initiation of a process to improve communication and cooperation between the agencies. In the absence of such a process, the relationship between the caseworker and a mental health counterpart can produce good results, even in a flawed system. The ability to access quality services on a timely basis distinguishes caseworkers in the eyes of judges.

Arriving on time

Some judges are habitually late, while others are always on time. All of them, however, will expect timeliness from caseworkers in the performance of their duties, including:

- Attending court hearings;
- Filing court reports;
- Following up on the requirements of court orders;
- Transferring cases between caseworkers;
- Keeping cases on track for resolution within the ASFA timelines.

Knowing the law and following court rules

Agency and court practices and procedures in child maltreatment cases must comply with Federal and State laws. It is essential, therefore, that caseworkers have good knowledge and understanding of the key principles, mandates, and purposes of these laws.

Many courts have rules governing the filing of court reports, discovery, distribution of experts' evaluations, continuances or postponements, notice of placement changes, notice of hearings, and conduct of hearings. Caseworkers will be expected to know these rules and to abide by them. They also should expect others in the process to do likewise and, when they do not, should notify the CPS attorney.

Preparing court orders

Court orders in child maltreatment cases should be prepared at the conclusion of the hearings, then distributed to the parties and other participants. They are more accurate and complete if written or dictated while the court's decisions and directives are fresh in the minds of all participants. Any disagreements or misunderstandings can be resolved immediately, and the parents can depart with a written statement of the court's expectations of them and of CPS.

Orders need to be clear and easy to understand. The use of forms is essential, and a clerk, a lawyer, or the judge can complete them. For ease of understanding and distribution of sufficient copies, it is preferable that they be prepared on a computer and printer in the courtroom. Objections to this approach are based on the time it takes to discuss and prepare the orders. Nevertheless, it will save time that often is spent debating and clarifying what the court ordered. Lack of technology may be an impediment in some courts, so this approach to order preparation is not yet common. Where it is implemented, it contributes significantly to improved understanding and outcomes. CPS can encourage courts, and perhaps assist them with necessary hardware, to implement this practice.

8. WORKING WITH THE COURTS

Just as judges have power to initiate improvements in court practice and performance, they also can be formidable roadblocks to such improvements. Some judges may be intentional in their determination to continue operating in familiar ways; others simply may be unaware of alternatives, their power to make changes, or the resources that are available to inform and to support efforts to improve court operations. The ability of child protective services (CPS) and of individual caseworkers to improve the court process depends on their understanding judges and knowing how to work with them, to support them, and to provide them with the information and tools they need to do their job better. This chapter deals with measures agencies and individual caseworkers can pursue.

Understanding Judges

Almost all judges are lawyers. Most are politicians who had to win election or were appointed through a process that was at least partly political. Judges vary widely in terms of their values, experience, intelligence, skills, knowledge, work ethic, receptivity to change, and personalities, but like other lawyers, many tend to be analytical thinkers. Judges focus on facts and look for cases that are presented, or problems addressed, in logical progression. They expect witnesses to answer questions directly, and they want people who testify or make oral presentations to "get to the point" and to express themselves succinctly. Most are practical and decisive, and nearly all are impatient to some degree, particularly with delays, poor performance, dramatic behavior, and excessive detail.

Judges' personalities are revealed over time, as are their work habits, knowledge, skills, commitment to doing the work well, and their proclivities regarding particular issues or circumstances. Caseworkers who appear regularly in the juvenile court will learn quickly which judges are the easiest and hardest to work with and which ones are most likely to be receptive to improving court practice.

In some States, judges are elected or appointed to the juvenile court bench and sit only in that court. In most States, however, the juvenile court is part of a larger court system. In these jurisdictions, judges occasionally may remain in the juvenile court assignment for extended periods of time, but the most common practice is for judges to be assigned to that court on a periodic rotation. The length of the assignment may vary from as little as 1 day to as much as a few years. Generally, 3 to 5 years is considered optimal because it takes time to learn about the laws governing the court's proceedings; the complexities and dynamics of child maltreatment; the availability and quality of the services, resources, and interventions at the court's disposal; the administrative responsibilities of the role; and the myriad professionals who appear before the court.[68]

This is particularly true for the majority of judges who had no juvenile court experience as lawyers.

Ideally, judges and judicial officers will be assigned to the juvenile court only after substantial training on the unique responsibilities of a judge in that court, the problems and needs of the court's clientele, and the human services systems on which it relies. Court improvements are less likely to occur without the leadership and the support of a knowledgeable and experienced judge. Indeed, some States have extensive training programs for both new and experienced juvenile court judges and formal certification procedures to ensure that they are well- prepared for the difficult work of that court. Much of the knowledge that juvenile court judges acquire, however, is gained by sitting in the juvenile court on a consistent basis over a significant period of time.

What Caseworkers Can Do to Effect Change in the Court

CPS caseworkers who practice in a court that has good judicial leadership are encouraged to find ways to participate in the collaborative efforts underway in the work of that court. Doing so will enhance their knowledge and enrich their work experience. Of course, some judges are friendlier and more approachable than others, and some will be more receptive to suggestions than others. Judges are more likely to respond to an individual caseworker's suggestion if the caseworker has established credibility and earned the judge's respect by the quality of her performance in individual cases. Some judges also may respond more favorably if approached by a caseworker who is accompanied by a child's advocate or a parent's attorney, so the caseworker is not suspected of seeking favored treatment.

Interacting and building positive working relationships with judges
In taking steps to build positive working relationships with judges, CPS caseworkers can:

- Introduce themselves to the judge at each court appearance or other encounter; Speak and write as clearly and plainly as possible;
- Be concise and to the point;
- Learn as much as possible about the judge's tendencies, personality, and likes and dislikes and be guided by that knowledge;

- Determine the history of the judge's interactions with CPS and how it may affect the judge's handling of particular issues or dealings with caseworkers;
- Build relationships with clerks, bailiff s, and court reporters;
- Follow local practices and protocols regarding appropriate dress for the courtroom, for addressing the court, and for approaching the bench;
- Be polite and respectful, but when the opportunity presents itself, do not hesitate to assert strongly held opinions about what the judge should order or decide in regard to a case;
- Not display emotion, especially anger or disdain, if the judge makes a decision with which CPS or the caseworker disagrees.

JUDICIAL TRAINING PROGRAMS

Numerous training programs for juvenile court judges who hear child maltreatment cases are available at various locations through the National Council of Juvenile and Family Court Judges (NCJFCJ) and other legal, judicial, and social services organizations. Judges who are interested in improving court practices and their own knowledge and skills can be referred to those organizations or to a nearby lead judge in one of the 25 NCJFCJ model court sites across the country. NCJFCJ, the National Center for State Courts, the American Bar Association's Center on Children and the Law, the National Association of Counsel for Children, and the Youth Law Center also are excellent sources of information about child maltreatment litigation. (See Appendix B, *Resource Listings of Selected National Organizations Concerned With Child Maltreatment*, for more information on these organizations.)

Effecting change in the court

Judges often are perceived as omnipotent, and the idea that CPS, much less an individual caseworker, could infl uence them to change practice may seem fanciful. Indeed, some judges are impervious to change, regardless of the source of the suggestion or the pressure to do so. Many others, however, understand that good outcomes in child maltreatment cases require the cooperative efforts of CPS, service providers, and the court. In several urban and small communities, judges meet regularly with CPS representatives to improve procedures, policies, and practices, and to enhance services. The State Court Improvement Program and the National Council of Juvenile and Family Court Judges (NCJFCJ) Model Court Project have contributed to this development. (See Chapter 9, *Court Improvement and Best Practices*, for more information on these important initiatives.)

For those child maltreatment courts that lack strong judicial leadership, the following list offers suggestions for informing and motivating promising juvenile court judges to take leadership in constructive ways:

- Provide information about particular "best practices" that could constitute significant improvement in how the court operates. Offer to help plan and implement the practice locally or to set up a meeting of stakeholders to discuss it.
- Invite the judge to make a presentation at a training for CPS caseworkers on a topic that the judge knows well. Preparing a presentation can be a good learning

experience, particularly if the judge is provided with good resource materials for that purpose.

- Recognize the judge's accomplishments in some way that does not appear to be currying favor but, instead, may be motivational. Joining with child and parent advocates for this purpose would lessen any appearance of impropriety. A Child Abuse Prevention Month event might be a good opportunity to honor a judge.
- Devise a strategy for motivating the judge to endorse the development of a mission and goals statement by a multidisciplinary group if the court has none. Do the same if the court has no rules that govern procedures or if they need to be updated.
- Suggest the development of model templates for court reports, reports on reasonable efforts, mental health assessment referrals, child support referrals, and other common forms.
- Invite a judge on a ride-along to observe the realities of being a CPS caseworker on the frontline. The judge should not be assigned to a case resulting from anyone or anything observed during the ride-along.
- Make the judge aware of caseload demands, time constraints, and resource and service deficits.
- Ask judges to support CPS's budget request in States where judges are not precluded from such activities.
- Suggest a training event and secure the judge's endorsement. Invite the judge to help plan it, and elicit the judge's suggestions for topics. Ask the judge to make a presentation, and involve a multidisciplinary group to design the training, secure presenters, and arrange for a site. NCJFCJ and the American Bar Association (ABA) Center on Children and the Law (and its National Child Welfare Resource Center on Legal and Judicial Issues at http://www.abanet.org/child/rclji/ home.html) are able to provide quality training on a variety of topics at no charge to State or local forums.
- Encourage State judicial educators to address topics of particular importance at their periodic judicial training events and then encourage a local judge to attend.
- Keep informed of local, State, and national grant opportunities. The State Court Improvement Program is perhaps the best such opportunity. Collaborating on a grant application can be a very good learning experience that promotes understanding and strengthens working relationships, even if a grant is not awarded.
- Suggest that an ad hoc, multidisciplinary committee be formed to consider implementation of some of the recommendations of:
  - *Emerging Practices in the Prevention of Child Abuse and Neglect* at http://www. childwelfare.gov/preventing/programs/ whatworks/report/index.cfm;
  - *Adoption and Permanency Guidelines: Improving Court Practice in Child Abuse and Neglect Cases* at www.ncjfcj.org or http:// www.pppncjfcj.org;
  - *Resource Guidelines: Improving Court Practice in Child Abuse and Neglect Cases* at http:// www.pppncjfcj.org/html/publications. html.
  - *About the Pew Commission on Children in Foster Care* at http://pewfostercare.org/ about.
- Promote the creation of a multidisciplinary child abuse and neglect committee that can identify problems and devise and implement solutions.

- Identify needed, but insufficient or nonexistent, services and enlist the judge's assistance in securing or developing them. Examples might be a visitation center, a program for child observers of domestic violence, or a parenting course specifically for fathers with a history of violence toward their child's mother.
- Provide the court with periodic reports on the status of its cases.

Some of these suggestions may be undertaken by individual caseworkers; others may require involvement by CPS lawyers or administrators, depending on the size of the community and the culture of the court and CPS.

CPS caseworkers also may direct judges to valuable resources. For example, they can provide the judge with literature regarding judicial training from the NCJFCJ, the ABA Center on Children and the Law, the National Center for State Courts, and the National Association of Counsel for Children.

Similarly, caseworkers may refer judges who are interested in improving court practices and enhancing their own knowledge and skills to the above-referenced organizations for publications and technical assistance. They also can be referred for technical assistance to a nearby lead judge in one of the 25 model court sites across the country or to a State Court Improvement Project judge who has effectively addressed particular issues. Other valuable sources of training, information, and technical assistance sponsored by the Children's Bureau are the eight National Resource Centers, including one on legal and judicial issues, two clearinghouses, and four Technical Assistance Support Systems. (See Appendix B, *Resource Listings of Selected National Organizations Concerned with Child Maltreatment*, for more information on these organizations.)

Working with problem judges

Unfortunately, there are judges who are verbally abusive; unreasonably demanding; habitually late starting court, preparing orders, or reading reports; biased; or incompetent. If a pattern of any of these behaviors or some other significant deficit is identified in multiple cases by more than one caseworker, the caseworker or CPS should not feel powerless. Caseworkers should request assistance from CPS administrators and attorneys when confronting challenging judges. Actions that can be taken to address such problem behaviors include:

- Asking the CPS attorney, supervisor, or administrator to speak to the judge on behalf of CPS or the caseworkers or to file a complaint with the State's Judicial Standards Commission, depending on the nature of the problem behavior;
- Speaking out in any reappointment, retention, or re-election process in which the judge must participate, as well as identifying and encouraging alternative candidates. Joining with children's advocates or parents' attorneys would make these suggested actions more credible than if they come just from CPS.[69]

There is the risk with each of these strategies, however, that nothing will change and that the judge will be vindictive toward CPS or the caseworkers. Legitimate complaints must nevertheless be voiced because it is quite common for problem judges to be reassigned or not to be retained or re-elected when well-documented grievances are made known to authorities or the public.

9. COURT IMPROVEMENT AND BEST PRACTICES

An integrated and comprehensive approach to the complex problems of families involved with child protective services (CPS) and the courts is critical to achieving safety and permanency for children. Evolving Federal child welfare legislation has prompted CPS and the courts to implement innovative policy and programmatic changes. T us, the pioneering efforts of court and child advocates have created a variety of inventive practices focused on accomplishing positive outcomes for families. This chapter provides an overview of the Child and Family Services Reviews (CFSRs) and the courts and information about best practices and model court programs existing throughout the country. It also provides information about the importance of judicial leadership in improving court practice.

Child and Family Services Reviews and the Courts

The Federal CFSR process is a results-oriented, comprehensive monitoring and review system designed to assist States in improving safety, permanency, and well-being outcomes for children and families who come into contact with the nation's public child welfare systems.[70] Fiscal sanctions may result from failure to meet the measures of the CFSRs, but it is the State's desire to improve practice and outcomes for the nation's most vulnerable children that has motivated States to work on comprehensive Program Improvement Plans (PIP) to correct the weaknesses and gaps identified in the CFSR.[71]

Although CPS and related child welfare agencies are the primary focus of the CFSR and PIP, there is a clear need for collaboration with the courts for the following reasons:

- CPS performance depends, in part, on its relationship with the courts and on court performance;
- CPS can use the legal system to learn how to overcome legal barriers that diminish its performance;
- CPS and the courts have mutual goals for achieving child welfare outcomes, especially in the area of achieving permanency;
- Court reform requires CPS and other key stakeholders' involvement;
- CPS has an interest in ensuring that the courts carry out PIP goals.[72]

The CSFRs evaluate CPS performance based partly on how well it works with the courts and other agencies to achieve child welfare outcomes, such as the time in care until adoption or reunification. CPS collaboration with the courts also may help overcome or mitigate court-related barriers to achieving CFSR outcomes. For instance, courts may provide CPS with strategies to work with Federal and State confidentiality requirements in order to obtain complete information about an abused child's family, which may result in an improved safety outcome for the child.[73] The roles of CPS and the courts and their methods for achieving these mutual goals are most efficient and productive when a uniform, long-range plan and a cooperative relationship are established.[74]

Additionally, each State's Court Improvement Program (CIP) (discussed later in the chapter) is expected to help achieve PIP goals.[75] The juvenile and family courts cannot effectively perform their child welfare responsibilities in isolation; CPS participation is an essential part of court reform. Specific improvements, such as strengthening case management and information systems for recording a child's court and placement history, require collaboration.[76]

Using the CFSRs as a catalyst, CPS can either initiate or improve upon an already existing collaborative relationship with the State juvenile and family courts in several ways, including:

- Research other States' CFSR processes, including how they collaborate with their legal system to improve their CFSR performance;
- Consider all legal and judicial issues suggested by the CFSR performance indicators, which can be prepared with the aid of the State's legal system;
- Invite the juvenile and family court judges and legal professionals to participate in meetings to plan and to organize the State's CFSR process;
- Explain the importance of the CFSR to juvenile and family court judges and legal professionals and persuade them to participate in the CFSR process;
- Include juvenile and family court judges and legal professionals in PIP development;
- Explain to the court, legislature, and caseworkers what resources are required for successful development and implementation of the PIP.[77]

Once CPS and the courts begin working together, they can tackle systemic problems affecting child safety, well-being, and permanency more efficiently. The agency can suggest improvements that may help courts make better decisions for children, such as:

- Improving agency court reports and testimony;
- Upgrading legal representation of the agency;
- Assisting judges to implement the Adoption and Safe Families Act (ASFA) and its regulations;
- Helping courts obtain better performance data or providing them with helpful data;
- Getting caseworkers to attend court hearings more consistently;
- Working together to improve court resources;
- Improving State law to ensure better and timelier services for families, thereby making it easier for judges to deliver timely decisions.[78]

These changes could help eliminate barriers the courts face, such as insufficient information, the length of time needed to resolve permanency issues, slow progress in cases, and obstacles to timely termination of parental rights. Their implementation can aid both the courts and the agencies in achieving better outcomes for children and families.[79] For more on how and why agencies should work with the courts, see Appendix E, *Legal and Judicial Issues Suggested By The Child And Family Services Review Performance Indicators*.

PEW COMMISSION ON CHILDREN IN FOSTER CARE

The Pew Commission on Children in Foster Care was established to develop recommendations to improve outcomes for children in the foster care system. Of primary importance are expediting the movement of children from foster care into safe, permanent, and nurturing families and preventing unnecessary placements in foster care.[80] The Commission recognized that while dependency courts and child welfare agencies both work to protect children, too often they work in isolation. To address these problems, the Commission released a set of recommendations focused on reforming Federal fi nancing and court oversight of foster care, including court and agency collaboration.[81]

Several key recommendations highlighted the need for effective collaboration to promote the protection and well-being of children:

- The U.S. Department of Health and Human Services (HHS) should require that the State IV-E plans, PIPs, and CIPs demonstrate effective collaboration;
- HHS should require States to establish commissions on children in foster care, ideally co-directed by the State's child welfare agency director and Chief Justice;
- Congress should appropriate $10 million to train court personnel, a portion of which should be used for joint training of child welfare agency staff and court personnel;
- Local and State courts and agencies should collaborate and plan for the collection and sharing of all relevant data and information that can aid in making better decisions and creating better outcomes for children.[82]

The Commission's report states, "Collaboration should recognize that the children and families involved with the child welfare system are often simultaneously engaged with other community agencies and services—schools, health care, mental health, child care, and others. Children and families are better served when these multiple community partners come together on their behalf." [83] Following their release, a number of national and State child welfare organizations and judicial entities issued resolutions supporting the recommendations. These organizations and entities included the National Council of Juvenile and Family Court Judges (NCJFCJ), the Conference of Chief Justices and Conference of State Court Administrators, the North American Council on Adoptable Children, the Judicial Council of California, and the Texas Supreme Court Task Force on Foster Care.[84]

For additional information about CFSRs, go to the Children's Bureau website at http://www.acf.hhs.gov/ programs/cb/cwrp/index.htm. For more information about CPS and court collaboration related to CFSRs, visit the National Child Welfare Resource Center on Legal and Judicial Issues at http://www.abanet.org/ child/courtimp.html and http://www.abanet.org/child/rclji/online

Best Practices

Legislative changes and CPS and judicial efforts are actualized through the daily practices of court personnel and CPS caseworkers. These practices need to incorporate proven methods that are responsive to the individual and multiple needs of families who are linked to different and complex systems. Many judges and others in the courts recognize the importance of collaborating with other systems to implement creative approaches that best serve families. The following are initiatives and legislation designed to promote the use of best practices in this area.

The State CIP

The State CIP provides grants to State courts "...to conduct assessments of their foster care and adoption laws and judicial processes and to develop and implement a plan for system improvement."[85] The CIP was first authorized as part of the Omnibus Budget Reconciliation Act of 1993 (P.L. 103–66, sections 13711–13712) and was first reauthorized by ASFA (P.L. 105–89) of 1997 without substantial programmatic changes. The CIP is a Federal grant program designed to improve the quality of court proceedings in handling child abuse and neglect cases. Federal funding goes to the highest court of each State, which administers the funds and directs the project. Each State has wide discretion on how to use CIP funds, but they must be used to improve the litigation process for abused and neglected children. The program was reauthorized again in 2002 by the Promoting Safe and Stable Families Amendments of 2001 (P.L. 107–133). This reauthorization expanded the program's scope to include the implementation of a PIP, as necessary, in response to findings identified in a CFSR. Through CIP, all State court systems are required to participate in the implementation of a CFSR PIP when a State court system is involved.[86]

NEW CIP GRANTS[87]

In the Deficit Reduction Act of 2005 (DRA), Congress expanded the CIP to authorize two new grants. The new grants include:

- A data collection and analysis grant to help ensure that foster children's needs for safety, permanency, and well-being are met in a timely and complete manner;
- A grant for training judges, attorneys, and other legal personnel in child welfare cases and conducting cross-training with child welfare agency staff and contractors.

These new grants are authorized for $10 million each for five years.

The DRA also establishes the following important new collaboration requirements for both State courts and child welfare agencies:

- The law requires State court applicants to include in their applications for all three CIP grants a demonstration of meaningful and ongoing collaboration among the courts in the State, the State child welfare agency (or any other agency with which the State contracts to administer Titles IV-B or IV-E), and, where applicable, Indian Tribes.

- The law adds a Title IV-B State plan requirement for the State or Tribal child welfare agency to demonstrate substantial, ongoing, and meaningful collaboration with State courts in the development and implementation of its State plans under Titles IV-B and IV-E, as well as PIPs developed as a result of the Child and Family Services and IV-E Foster Care Eligibility Reviews.

The Model Courts Project

The Permanency Planning for Children Department (PPCD) of NCJFCJ established the Child Victims Act Model Court Project in 1992 with funding from the Office of Juvenile Justice and Delinquency Prevention.[88] There are 25 model courts across the country, including those in New York, Los Angeles, and Chicago, as well as smaller communities such as Zuni, New Mexico, the site of a Tribal court. These courts and their community partners, including CPS, work with PPCD and each other to improve court practice in child abuse and neglect cases. They identify barriers to permanency and other successful outcomes for children in their court and social services systems and develop and implement strategies for overcoming those barriers. Annual status reports outlining the goals and accomplishments of each of these communities are available from PPCD at http:// www.ncjfcj.org/content/view/81/145/ and are an excellent starting point for identifying successful resolutions of problems encountered by judges and CPS personnel.

TRIBAL COURTS

Prior to the passage of the Indian Child Welfare Act (ICWA) of 1978, private, State, and Federal agencies typically removed abused and neglected Indian children from their families and Tribal communities. Often, these children were placed without considering the cultural and other effects this would have on them.[89] State courts often ignored the sovereign authority of Tribal courts with regard to these children.

With ICWA, child welfare proceedings involving Indian children are treated differently from other child welfare cases. If the child lives on a reservation, the case must be decided by the Tribal courts of the child's Tribe instead of by State courts. Many cases involving Indian children who do not live on a reservation can be transferred to Tribal courts. These children, however, must be enrolled as a member of an Indian Tribe or be eligible for membership and have a biological parent who is a Tribe member.

When foster care placements or termination of parental rights proceedings for Indian children are brought before the State courts, those children, their Native American custodians, and their Tribes have the right to become involved, enabling the cases to be transferred to Indian Tribal courts. The children's parents, Indian custodians, and the Tribes also are entitled to a notice of the State court action, so they can appear and respond to the charges or intervene and request a transfer, if appropriate.

In 1990, Congress enacted the Indian Child Protection and Family Violence Act (P.L. 101–630). Among other things, it authorizes Federal funds to be used by the Bureau of Indian Affairs for a variety of purposes, including to help Tribes establish CPS programs and develop multidisciplinary child abuse investigation and prosecution teams.[90]

The Strengthening Abuse and Neglect Courts Act

In FY200 1, Congress enacted the Strengthening Abuse and Neglect Courts Act (SANCA) (P.L. 106–314) and funded it for the first time in FY 2002. The purpose of SANCA is to award grants to State and local courts to enable them to develop and to implement automated data collection and case-tracking systems so that they can eventually use such systems to evaluate court performance. To date, grants have been made to six States (Colorado, Florida, Georgia, Idaho, New Jersey, and Oregon) to pilot the implementation of suggested performance measures developed by the American Bar Association, NCJFCJ, and the National Center for State Courts. (See http://www.ncsconline.org/ WC/Publications/KIS_ Fam JusSANCAProject.pdf for an overview.) The Act makes financial resources available to qualifying courts "... for the purpose of developing, implementing and maintaining automated information systems that enable the nation's abuse and neglect courts to effectively and efficiently meet the intended goals of the Adoption and Safe Families Act." Courts that apply must have "...a demonstrated history of collaborative planning and court improvement..." and "must have full support from [their] collaborative partners," including CPS.[91]

The Toolkit Project

In FY 2003, the Children's Bureau funded a project to help courts develop a viable approach to engaging in continuous quality improvement with regard to the handling of dependency cases. The American Bar Association, the National Center for State Courts, and the NCJFCJ are working together to help courts improve their performance by addressing the two most critical and challenging areas of court reform: court performance measurement and judicial workload. Utilizing a guide and toolkit recently developed by these organizations under a grant from the David and Lucile Packard Foundation, the groups are providing targeted technical assistance to help six project courts achieve increased accountability and better performance. The final products of this project will be an updated guidebook and toolkit that will provide revised instrumentation and procedures based on lessons learned during the implementation study, as well as a report on the implementation of a time-study and workload assessment at the local court level.

Judicial Leadership

Strong judicial leadership is essential to successful implementation of reforms and improvements in how CPS and the courts process child maltreatment cases. Communities that have embraced ASFA and accomplished timely permanency for abused and neglected children have, without exception, benefited from judicial leadership. While judges alone cannot initiate change, their support and leadership are critical to reforming court practice.

Many communities across the country are fortunate to have judicial leaders in juvenile court who are committed to optimizing the ability of CPS and the courts to address effectively the needs of abused and neglected children and their families. Communities with model courts and strong State CIPs are good examples.

Like all effective leaders, judges must have a vision for what can and should be accomplished. For child abuse and neglect cases, that vision will include the timely achievement of safe, permanent homes for the children. The vision and how it is communicated by the words and actions of the judge and others who share it can motivate juvenile court practitioners and can provide meaning and value to their work. Areas in which judges' leadership can be exercised include court operations, interactions with other stakeholders, and advocacy for abused and neglected children.

EXAMPLES OF COURT REFORM PROJECTS

For examples of successful projects, see NCJFCJs' *Technical Assistance Bulletin, State Court Improvement Projects "Bragging Rights"* at http://www.ncjfcj.org/images and the National Court Improvement Progress Report and Catalog maintained by the National Child Welfare Resource Center on Legal and Judicial Issues at http://www.abanet.org/child/cipcatalog/home. html.

Court operations

Through the hearing and management of cases, judges set a standard for court operations, which includes the judges':

- Knowledge and skill in hearing, monitoring, and resolving individual cases;
- Commitment to timely proceedings and decisions;
- Enforcement of rules;
- Participation in training opportunities;
- Style of interacting with families and professionals.

This is important because good administrative leadership of court operations ensures that:

- The court has rules of procedure to guide practitioners;
- Petitions and other pleadings and documents are maintained in an orderly and accessible way;
- Cases are scheduled and decided on a timely basis, before the same judge, and at intervals that minimize waiting and inconvenience to participants;
- Continuances are rare;
- Decisions and orders are entered and distributed promptly.

Interactions with other stakeholders

Judicial leaders "...must encourage and promote collaboration and mutual respect among all participants in the child welfare system...," and "...should regularly convene representatives from [it] to improve operations of the system."[92] All effective juvenile courts are characterized by successful partnerships with CPS and with other community and system stakeholders. Judges meet regularly with these partners and work cooperatively with them to identify and resolve systemic problems, to plan training events, to strategize about new services to fulfi ll unmet needs, to address resource and funding issues, to improve service delivery and court processes, and to share their successes. These collaborative efforts create "...a synergy in which the contributions of the various partners enhance and magnify their individual effects."[93]

Advocacy for abused and neglected children

Judicial leaders from the juvenile court should take an active role in educating policymakers and the public about the needs of child maltreatment victims. This includes new or expanded resources and services that are necessary to meet those needs, the importance of the work being done in the juvenile court, and the statutory changes necessary to enhance that work. Because of their position within the child welfare community, judges experienced in child maltreatment cases can be particularly effective in bringing about useful changes.

COURT MANAGEMENT INFORMATION SYSTEMS

Effective administrative leadership includes maintaining an information system that tracks individual and aggregate case data. For more information about the need for courts to have good management information systems for child abuse and neglect cases, as well as suggestions for improving existing capabilities and developing and implementing new systems, see:

- *Information Management: A Critical Component of Good Practice in Child Abuse and Neglect Cases;*
- *Model Court Approaches to Information Technology: A Dependency Court Data System Implementation Guide.*

Both are published by the PPCD of the NCJFCJ and are available at http://www.pppncjfcj.org.

Conclusion

Navigating the juvenile court process in child abuse and neglect cases can be an overwhelming experience for CPS caseworkers and the families they serve. However, a solid understanding of applicable child maltreatment legislation, various court proceedings, and court expectations will help CPS caseworkers enhance their case practice and outcomes. Furthermore, juvenile and family courts throughout the country are increasingly aware that innovative court practices and partnerships with CPS and community service providers are instrumental to achieving safety, permanency, and well-being for children and families.

APPENDIX A. GLOSSARY OF TERMS

Adjournment – the suspension of business or sessions, either for a fixed time, indefinitely, or until the opening of another term.

Adjudicatory Hearings – held by the juvenile and family court to determine whether a child has been maltreated or whether another legal basis exists for the State to intervene to protect the child.

Adoption and Safe Families Act (ASFA) – signed into law November 1997 and designed to improve the safety of children, to promote adoption and other permanent homes for children who need them, and to support families. The law requires CPS agencies to provide more timely and focused assessment and intervention services to the children and families that are served within the CPS system.

CASA – court-appointed special advocates (usually volunteers) who serve to ensure that the needs and interests of a child in child protection judicial proceedings are fully protected.

Case Closure – the process of ending the relationship between the CPS worker and the family that often involves a mutual assessment of progress. Optimally, cases are closed when families have achieved their goals and the risk of maltreatment has been reduced or eliminated.

Case Plan – the casework document that outlines the outcomes, goals, and tasks necessary to be achieved in order to reduce the risk of maltreatment.

Case Planning – the stage of the CPS case process where the CPS caseworker develops a case plan with the family members.

Caseworker Competency – demonstrated professional behaviors based on the knowledge, skills, personal qualities, and values a person holds.

Central Registry – a centralized database containing information on all substantiated/founded reports of child maltreatment in a selected area (typically a State).

Child Abuse Prevention and Treatment Act (CAPTA) – see Keeping Children and Families Safe Act.

Child Protective Services (CPS) – the designated social services agency (in most States) to receive reports, investigate, and provide intervention and treatment services to children and families in which child maltreatment has occurred. Frequently, this agency is located within larger public social service agencies, such as Departments of Social Services.

Civil Contempt – the willful failure to do something that a court has ordered, such as refusing to testify when the court has found that no privilege applies or refusing to pay child support when there are ample funds to do so. The usual sanction is incarceration for a term that lasts until the person in contempt complies with the court order.

Concurrent Planning – identifies alternative plans for permanent placement of a child by addressing both reunification and legal permanency with a new parent or caregiver if reunification efforts fail.

Consent Decree – a decree entered by a court that is determined by the parties' agreement; a settlement between the parties that is subject to judicial approval and supervision.

Continuance – an adjournment of a case from one day to another or to a later hour of the same day.

Criminal Contempt – an act that obstructs justice or attacks the integrity of the court that is punishable by fine or imprisonment or both. Criminal contempt may be indirect or direct. Indirect contempt is contempt occurring outside the courtroom, such as a willful violation of a court's order. Direct contempt is disruptive or disrespectful behavior that occurs in the presence of the judge, such as uttering an epithet when the judge announces an unfavorable decision.

Cross-examination – questioning of a witness by attorneys other than the one who called the person as a witness.

Cultural Competence – a set of attitudes, behaviors, and policies that integrates knowledge about groups of people into practices and standards to enhance the quality of services to all cultural groups being served.

Declaratory Judgment – a court decision which simply declares the rights of the parties or expresses the opinion of the court on a question of law without ordering anything to be done.

Delinquency – the commitment of an offense by a youth of what would be a crime if he or she were an adult.

Dependent Child – as used in statues providing for the care of dependent, neglected, and delinquent children, the term means dependent upon the public support; any child under the age of 18 who is destitute, or whose home by reason of neglect by the parents is an unfit place for such child, or whose father, mother, guardian, or custodian does not properly provide for such a child.

Differential Response – an area of CPS reform that offers greater flexibility in responding to allegations of abuse and neglect. Also referred to as "dual track" or "multi-track" response, it permits CPS agencies to respond differentially to children's needs for safety, the degree of risk present, and the family's needs for services and support. See "dual track."

Discovery – pretrial process that allows each party to obtain information relevant to the case from the other parties.

Depositions – transcribed oral examinations under oath.

Dispositional Hearings – held by the juvenile and family court to determine the legal resolution of cases after adjudication, such as whether placement of the child in out-of-home care is necessary, and what services the children and family will need to reduce the risk and to address the effects of maltreatment.

Dual Track – term reflecting new CPS response systems that typically combine a non adversarial service-based assessment track for cases where children are not at immediate risk with a traditional CPS investigative track for cases where children are unsafe or at greater risk for maltreatment. See "differential response."

Duces Tecum – a type of subpoena or court order that requires a person to produce for the court specified documents or records.

Due Process – The principle that every person has the protection of a day in court, representation by an attorney, and the benefit of procedures that are speedy, fair, and impartial.

Evaluation of Family Progress – the stage of the CPS case process where the CPS caseworker measures changes in family behaviors and conditions (risk factors), monitors risk elimination or reduction, assesses strengths, and determines case closure.

Exculpatory – evidence or testimony that exonerates or clears the defendant.

Ex Parte – on behalf of or involving only one party to a legal matter and in the absence of and usually without notice to the other party.

Expert Testimony – opinion testimony about a subject that is outside the judge's or jury's knowledge or experience, provided by a witness with established expertise on that subject.

Family Assessment – the stage of the child protection process when the CPS caseworker, community treatment provider, and the family reach a mutual understanding regarding the behaviors and conditions that must change to reduce or eliminate the risk of maltreatment, the most critical treatment needs that must be addressed, and the strengths on which to build.

Family Drug Court – a drug court that deals with cases involving parental rights in which an adult is the litigant (i.e., any party to a lawsuit, which means plaintiff, defendant, petitioner, respondent, cross- complainant and cross-defendant, but not a witness or attorney); the case comes before the court through either a criminal or civil proceeding; and the case arises out of the substance abuse of a parent.

Family Group Conferencing – a family meeting model used by CPS agencies to optimize family strengths in the planning process. This model brings the family, extended family, and others important in the family's life (e.g., friends, clergy, neighbors) together to make decisions regarding how best to ensure safety of the family members.

Family Unity Model – a family meeting model used by CPS agencies to optimize family strengths in the planning process. This model is similar to the Family Group Conferencing model.

Full Disclosure – information provided to the family regarding the steps in the CPS intervention process, the requirements of CPS, the expectations of the family, the consequences if the family does not fulfill the expectations, and the rights of the parents to ensure that the family completely understands the process.

Guardian ad Litem – a lawyer or layperson who represents a child in juvenile or family court. Usually this person considers the "best interest" of the child and may perform a variety of roles, including those of independent investigator, advocate, advisor, and guardian for the child. A layperson who serves in this role is sometimes known as a court-appointed special advocate or CASA.

Hearsay – an out-of-court statement made by someone other than the witness that is offered for the truth of that statement.

Home Visitation Programs – prevention programs that offer a variety of family-focused services to pregnant mothers and families with new babies. Activities frequently encompass structured visits to the family's home and may address positive parenting practices, nonviolent discipline techniques, child development, maternal and child health, available services, and advocacy.

Immunity – established in all child abuse laws to protect reporters from civil law suits and criminal prosecution resulting from filing a report of child abuse and neglect.

Initial Assessment or Investigation – the stage of the CPS case process where the CPS caseworker determines the validity of the child maltreatment report, assesses the risk of maltreatment, determines if the child is safe, develops a safety plan if needed to assure the child's protection, and determines services needed.

Injunction – an equitable remedy in the form of a court order compelling a party to do or refrain from doing a specified act.

Intake – the stage of the CPS case process where the CPS caseworker screens and accepts reports of child maltreatment.

Interview Protocol – a structured format to ensure that all family members are seen in a planned strategy, that community providers collaborate, and that information gathering is thorough.

Jurisdiction – the power or right to exercise authority.

Juvenile and Family Courts – established in most States to resolve conflict and to otherwise intervene in the lives of families in a manner that promotes the best interest of children. These courts specialize in areas such as child maltreatment, domestic violence, juvenile delinquency, divorce, child custody, and child support.

Juvenile Drug Court – a drug court that focuses on juvenile delinquency matters and status offenses that involve juveniles who are substance abusers.

Keeping Children and Families Safe Act – The Keeping Children and Families Safe Act of 2003 (P.L. 108–36) included the reauthorization of the Child Abuse Prevention and Treatment Act (CAPTA) in its Title I, Sec. 111. CAPTA provides minimum standards for defining child physical abuse and neglect and sexual abuse that States must incorporate into their statutory definitions in order to receive Federal funds. CAPTA defines child abuse and neglect as "at a minimum, any recent act or failure to act on the part of a parent or caretaker, which results in death, serious physical or emotional harm, sexual abuse or exploitation, or an act or failure to act which presents an imminent risk of serious harm."

Kinship Care – formal child placement by the juvenile court and child welfare agency in the home of a child's relative.

Liaison – the designation of a person within an organization who has responsibility for facilitating communication, collaboration, and coordination between agencies involved in the child protection system.

Litigant – a party to a lawsuit.

Mandated Reporter – individuals required by State statutes to report suspected child abuse and neglect to the proper authorities (usually CPS or law enforcement agencies). Mandated reporters typically include professionals, such as educators and other school personnel, health care and mental health professionals, social workers, childcare providers, and law enforcement officers. Some States identify all citizens as mandated reporters.

Multidisciplinary Team – established between agencies and professionals within the child protection system to discuss cases of child abuse and neglect and to aid in decisions at various stages of the CPS case process. These teams also may be designated by different names, including child protection teams, interdisciplinary teams, or case consultation teams.

Neglect – the failure to provide for a child's basic needs. Neglect can be physical, educational, or emotional. *Physical neglect* can include not providing adequate food or clothing, appropriate medical care, supervision, or proper weather protection (heat or coats). *Educational neglect* includes failure to provide appropriate schooling, special educational needs, or allowing excessive truancies. *Psychological neglect* includes the lack of any emotional support and love, chronic inattention to the child, exposure to spouse abuse, or drug and alcohol abuse.

Out-of-Home Care – childcare, foster care, or residential care provided by persons, organizations, and institutions to children who are placed outside their families, usually under the jurisdiction of juvenile or family court.

Overrule – to set aside the authority of a former decision; the act of court in rejecting a motion or objection made by a party to a lawsuit.

***Parens Patriae* Doctrine** – originating in feudal England, a doctrine that vests in the State a right of guardianship of minors. This concept has gradually evolved into the principle that the community, in addition to the parent, has a strong interest in the care and nurturing of children. Schools, juvenile courts, and social service agencies all derive their authority from the State's power to protect children who are unable to protect themselves.

Parent or Caretaker – person responsible for the care of the child.

Petitions – a document containing allegations of child abuse or neglect that is typically filed by the CPS attorney in juvenile court.

Physical Abuse – the inflicting of a non-accidental physical injury upon a child. This may include, burning, hitting, punching, shaking, kicking, beating, or otherwise harming a child. It may, however, have been the result of over-discipline or physical punishment that is inappropriate to the child's age.

Preponderance of the Evidence – the burden of proof for civil cases in most States, including child maltreatment proceedings. The attorney for CPS or other petitioner must show by a preponderance of evidence that the abuse or neglect happened. This standard means that the evidence is more credible than the evidence presented by the defendant party.

Primary Prevention – activities geared to a sample of the general population to prevent child abuse and neglect from occurring. Also referred to as "universal prevention."

Protective Factors – strengths and resources that appear to mediate or serve as a "buffer" against risk factors that contribute to vulnerability to maltreatment or against the negative effects of maltreatment experiences.

Protocol – an interagency agreement that delineates joint roles and responsibilities by establishing criteria and procedures for working together on cases of child abuse and neglect.

Psychological Maltreatment – a pattern of caregiver behavior or extreme incidents that convey to children that they are worthless, fl awed, unloved, unwanted, endangered, or only of value to meeting another's needs. This can include parents or caretakers using extreme or bizarre forms of punishment or threatening or terrorizing a child. The term "psychological maltreatment" is also known as emotional abuse or neglect, verbal abuse, or mental abuse.

Putative Father – the alleged or supposed male parent; the person alleged to have fathered a child whose parentage is at issue.

Respondent – an answering party in a proceeding in juvenile or family court.

Response Time – a determination made by CPS and law enforcement regarding the immediacy of the response needed to a report of child abuse or neglect.

Review Hearings – held by the juvenile and family court to review dispositions (usually every 6 months) and to determine the need to maintain placement in out-of-home care or court jurisdiction of a child.

Risk – the likelihood that a child will be maltreated in the future.

Risk Assessment – to assess and measure the likelihood that a child will be maltreated in the future, frequently through the use of checklists, matrices, scales, and other methods of measurement.

Risk Factors – behaviors and conditions present in the child, parent, or family that likely will contribute to child maltreatment occurring in the future.

Safety – absence of an imminent or immediate threat of moderate-to-serious harm to the child.

Safety Assessment – a part of the CPS case process in which available information is analyzed to identify whether a child is in immediate danger of moderate or serious harm.

Safety Plan – a casework document developed when it is determined that the child is in imminent or potential risk of serious harm. In the safety plan, the caseworker targets the factors that are causing or contributing to the risk of imminent serious harm to the child, and identifies, along with the family, the interventions that will control the safety factors and ensure the child's protection.

Secondary Prevention – activities targeted to prevent breakdowns and dysfunctions among families who have been identified as at risk for abuse and neglect.

Service or Constructive Service – the act of delivering to, or informing someone of, a writ, summons, or other notice as prescribed by law.

Service Agreement – the casework document developed between the CPS caseworker and the family that outlines the tasks necessary to achieve goals and outcomes necessary for risk reduction.

Service Provision – the stage of the CPS casework process when CPS and other service providers deliver specific services geared toward the reduction of risk of maltreatment.

Sexual Abuse – inappropriate adolescent or adult sexual behavior with a child. It includes fondling a child's genitals, making the child fondle the adult's genitals, intercourse, incest, rape, sodomy, exhibitionism, sexual exploitation, or exposure to pornography. To be considered child abuse, these acts have to be committed by a person responsible for the care of a child (for example a baby-sitter, a parent, or a daycare provider) or related to the child. If a stranger commits these acts, it would be considered sexual assault and handled solely by the police and criminal courts.

Status Offender – a juvenile under the jurisdiction of the court because of acts that would not be criminal if committed by an adult, but that indicate that the child is beyond parental control.

Status Offenses – transgressions of children that would not be crimes if they were legal age; primarily involve running away and truancy. The age for bringing such charges varies from State to State.

Substantiated – an investigation disposition concluding that the allegation of maltreatment or risk of maltreatment was supported or founded, as defined by State law or State policy. A CPS determination means that credible evidence exists that child abuse or neglect has occurred.

Suspended Sentence – a sentence that the defendant will not have to serve if he or she complies with the conditions of probation.

Sustain – to allow or uphold as valid.

Termination of Parental Rights Hearing – a legal proceeding to free a child from a parent's legal custody so that others can adopt the child. The legal basis for termination of parental rights differs from State to State, but most States consider the failure of the parent to support or communicate with the child for a specified period, parental failure to improve home conditions, extreme or repeated neglect or abuse, parental incapacity to care for the child, and/or extreme deterioration of the parent-child relationship. In making this finding, the court is determining that the parents will not be able to provide adequate care for the child in the future by using a standard of clear and convincing evidence. This burden of proof is higher than preponderance of the evidence, which is used in civil abuse or neglect cases where termination is not sought.

Tertiary Prevention – treatment efforts geared to address situations where child maltreatment has already occurred, with the goals of preventing child maltreatment from occurring in the future and of avoiding the harmful effects of child maltreatment.

Transactional Immunity – a broader form of use immunity that bars prosecution of a witness for any event or transaction described in the witness's compelled testimony, regardless of the source of the evidence against that person.

Treatment – the stage of the child protection case process when specific services are provided by CPS and other providers to reduce the risk of maltreatment, support families in meeting case goals, and address the effects of maltreatment.

Universal Prevention – activities and services directed at the general public with the goal of stopping the occurrence of maltreatment before it starts. Also referred to as "primary prevention."

Unsubstantiated (not substantiated) – an investigation disposition that determines that there is not sufficient evidence under State law or policy to conclude that the child has been maltreated or is at risk of maltreatment. A CPS determination means that credible evidence does not exist that child abuse or neglect has occurred.

Use Immunity – bars the use of a witness's compelled testimony and statements from being used directly or indirectly against that person in a subsequent trial.

Voir Dire – the inquiry of prospective jurors to determine if the jurors are fit for jury duty in a given case.

APPENDIX B. RESOURCE LISTINGS OF SELECTED NATIONAL ORGANIZATIONS CONCERNED WITH CHILD MALTREATMENT

Listed below are several of the many national organizations and groups dealing with various aspects of child maltreatment. Visit http://childwelfare. gov/pubs/usermanual.cfm to view a more comprehensive list of resources and visit http://www. childwelfare.gov/ organizations/index.cfm to view an organization database. Inclusion on this list is for information purposes only and does not constitute an endorsement by the Office on Child Abuse and Neglect or the Children's Bureau.

Child Welfare Organizations

American Humane Association Children's Division
    address: 63 Inverness Dr., East Englewood, CO 80112-5117
    phone: (800) 227-4645
              (303) 792-9900
    fax: (303) 792-5333
    e-mail: children
    Web site: http://www.americanhumane.org
Conducts research, analysis, and training to help public and private agencies respond to child maltreatment.

American Professional Society on the Abuse of Children
    address: P.O. Box 30669 Charleston, SC 29417
    phone: (843) 764-2905
              877) 40A-PSAC
    fax: (803) 753-9823
    e-mail: tricia-williams@ouhsc.edu
    Web site: www.apsac.org
Provides professional education, promotes research to inform effective practice, and addresses public policy issues. Professional membership organization.

American Public Human Services Association
    address: 810 First St., NE, Suite 500 Washington, DC 20002-4267

phone: (202) 682-0100
fax: (202) 289-6555
Web site: http://www.aphsa.org

Addresses program and policy issues related to the administration and delivery of publicly funded human services. Professional membership organization.

AVANCE Family Support and Education Program
address: 118 N. Medina San Antonio, TX 78207
phone: (210) 270-4630
fax: (210) 270-4612
Web site: www.avance.org

Operates a national training center to share and disseminate information, material, and curricula to service providers and policy-makers interested in supporting high-risk Hispanic families.

Child Welfare League of America
address: 440 First St., NW, Third Floor Washington, DC 20001-2085
phone: (202) 638-2952
fax: (202) 638-4004
Web site: http://www.cwla.org

Provides training, consultation, and technical assistance to child welfare professionals and agencies while also educating the public about emerging issues affecting children.

National Association of Counsel for Children
Address: 1825 Marion Street, Suite 242 Denver, CO 80218
phone: (888) 828-NACC
e-mail: advocate@NACCchildlaw.org
Web site: http://www.naccchildlaw.org

Provides training and technical assistance to child advocates and works to improve the child welfare, juvenile justice and private custody systems.

National Black Child Development Institute
address: 1101 15th St., NW, Suite 900 Washington, DC 20005
phone: (202) 833-2220
fax: (202) 833-8222
e-mail: moreinfo@nbcdi.org
Web site: www.nbcdi.org

Operates programs and sponsors a national training conference through Howard University to improve and protect the well-being of African-American children.

National Center for State Courts
address: 300 Newport Ave.Williamsburg, VA 23185-4147
phone: (800) 616-6164
fax: (757) 564-2022
Web site: http://www.ncsconline.org

Enhances court operations with the latest technology, collects and interprets the latest data on court operations nationwide, and provides information on proven "best practices" for improving court operations.

National Children's Advocacy Center
address: 210 Pratt Ave Huntsville AL 35801
phone: (256) 533-KIDS
fax: (256) 534-6883
Web site: http://www.nationalcac.org

Provides prevention, intervention, and treatment services to physically and sexually abused children and their families within a child-focused team approach.

National Council of Juvenile and Family Court Judges
address: NCJFCJ – Permanency Planning for Children Department
              1041 North Virginia St. P.O. Box 8970
              Reno, NV 89507
phone: (775) 784-6012
fax: (775) 784-6628
email: admin@ncjfcj.org
Web site: http://www.pppncjfcj.org

Serves the Nation's children and families by improving the courts of juvenile and family jurisdictions. Its mission is to better the justice system through education and applied research and improve the standards, practices, and effectiveness of the juvenile court system. NCJFCJ strives to increase awareness and sensitivity to children's issues and focuses on providing meaningful assistance to the judges, court administrators, and related professionals in whose care the concerns of children and their families have been entrusted.

National Court Appointed Special Advocate Association
address: North Tower, 100 West Harrison St., Suite 500
              Seattle, WA 98119-4123
phone: (800) 628-3233
fax: (206) 270-0078
email: inquiry@nationalcasa.org
Web site: http://www.nationalcasa.org

Promotes and supports volunteer advocacy in juvenile courts for children alleged to be maltreated. It receives Federal and private funding, provides money and technical assistance to start and expand programs, promulgates performance standards, produces training manuals and other publications, and trains program leaders and volunteers.

National Indian Child Welfare Association
address: 5100 SW Macadam Ave., Suite 300 Portland, OR 97239
phone: (503) 222-4044
fax: (503) 222-4007
e-mail: info@nicwa.org
Web site: http://www.nicwa.org

Disseminates information and provides technical assistance on Indian child welfare issues. Supports community development and advocacy efforts to facilitate tribal responses to the needs of families and children.

Youth Law Center

address: Children's Legal Protection Center 1010 Vermont Ave., NW,
Suite 310 Washington, DC 20005-4902
phone: (202) 637-0377
fax: (202) 379-1600
e-mail: info@youthlawcenter.com
Web site: http://www.youthlawcenter.com

Works to ensure that vulnerable children are provided with the conditions and services they need, particularly focusing on children living apart from their families in child welfare and juvenile justice systems.

National Resource Centers

National Child Welfare Resource Center on Legal and Judicial Issues

address: ABA Center on Children and the Law 740 15th St., NW
Washington, DC 20005-10 19
phone: (800) 285-2221 (Service Center)
(202) 662-1720
fax: (202) 662-1755
e-mail: ctrchildlaw@abanet.org
Web site: http://www.abanet.org/child/rclji/home. html

Provides technical assistance, training and consultation to State, local and Tribal agencies and courts to strengthen their knowledge of legal and judicial issues related to child welfare and juvenile and family courts. Its expertise on a wide variety of subjects includes court improvement, agency and court collaboration, termination of parental rights, non-adversarial case resolution, reasonable efforts requirements, legal representation of children, permanent guardianship, confidentiality, and other emerging child welfare issues.

National Resource Center for Adoption

address: 16250 Northland Drive, Suite 120 Southfi eld, MI 48075
phone: (248) 443-0306
fax: (248) 443-7099
e-mail: nrc@nrcadoption.org
Web site: http://www.nrcadoption.org

Develops and distributes training curricula, publications, and videos and sponsors three national conferences to improve the effectiveness and quality of adoption and post-adoption services. The center also provides training on current practices, policies, and issues in special needs adoption; permanency planning; post-adoption services; and cultural competence.

National Resource Center for Child Protective Services

address: 925 #4 Sixth Street NW Albuquerque, New Mexico 87102

phone: (505) 345-2444

fax: (505) 345-2626

e-mail: theresa.costello@actionchildprotection.org

Web site: http://www.nrccps.org

Focuses on building State, local, and Tribal capacity through training and technical assistance in CPS, includingmeeting Federal requirements, strengthening programs, eligibility for the CAPTA grant, support to State Liaison Officers, and collaboration with other NRCs.

National Resource Center on Domestic Violence: Child Protection and Custody

address: Family Violence Department National Council of Juvenile
            and Family Court Judges
            P.O. Box 8970 Reno, NV 89507

phone: (800) 527-3223

fax: (775) 784-6160

e-mail: fvdinfo@ncjfcj.org

Web site: http://www.ncjfcj.org/dept/fvd/res_center

Promotes improved court responses to family violence through demonstration programs, professional training, technical assistance, national conferences, and publications.

National Resource Center for Family-Centered Practice and Permanency Planning

address: National Resource Center for Family- Centered Practice and Permanency
            Planning Hunter College School of Social Work 129 East 79th Street
            New York, NY 10021

phone: (212) 452-7053

fax: (212) 452-7475

Web site: http://www.hunter.cuny.edu/socwork/ nrcfcpp/

Provides training and technical assistance and information services to help States through all stages of the CFSRs, emphasizing family-centered principles and practices and helping States build knowledge of foster care issues. Partners with the Child Welfare League of America and the National Indian Child Welfare Association to provide training, technical assistance, and information services.

Technical Assistance Support System Organizations

Interstate Compact on Adoption and Medical Assistance

address: Association of Administrators of the Interstate Compact on Adoption
            and Medical Assistance
            810 First St., NE, Suite 500
            Washington, DC 20002

phone: (202) 682-0100

fax: (202) 289-6555

Web site: http://aaicama.aphsa.org/index.html

Provides technical and legal assistance, education and training, and materials on practice and policy issues to facilitate the administration of the Interstate Compact on Adoption and Medical Assistance.

Interstate Compact on the Placement of Children

address:	Association of Administrators of the Interstate Compact on the Placement of Children American Public Human Services Association 810 First St., NE, Suite 500 Washington, DC 20002-4267
phone:	(202) 682-0100
fax:	(202) 289-6555
e-mail:	ICPCinbox@aphsa.org
Web site:	http://icpc.aphsa.org

Provides ongoing administrative, legal, and technical assistance to individual States that administer the Interstate Compact on the Placement of Children, which is a uniform State law that establishes a contract among party States to ensure that children placed across State lines receive adequate protection and services.

Prevention Organizations

National Alliance of Children's Trust and Prevention Funds

address:	5712 30th Ave. NE Seattle, WA 98105
phone:	206-526-1221
fax:	206-526-0220
e-mail:	trafael@juno.com
Web site:	www.ctfalliance.org

Assists State children's trust and prevention funds to strengthen families and protect children from harm.

Prevent Child Abuse America

address:	200 South Michigan Ave., 17th Floor Chicago, IL 60604-2404
phone:	(800) 835-2671 (orders)
	(312) 663-3520
fax:	(312) 939-8962
e-mail:	mailbox@preventchildabuse.org
Web site:	http://www.preventchildabuse.org

Conducts prevention activities such as public awareness campaigns, advocacy, networking, research, and publishing, and provides information and statistics on child abuse.

Shaken Baby Syndrome Prevention Plus

address:	649 Main St., Suite B Groveport, OH 43125
phone:	(800) 858-5222
	(614) 836-8360
fax:	(614) 836-8359

e-mail: sbspp@aol.com
Web site: http://www.sbsplus.com

Develops, studies, and disseminates information and materials designed to prevent shaken baby syndrome and other forms of child abuse and to increase positive parenting and child care.

Community Partners

The Center for Faith-Based and Community Initiatives

address: U. S. Department of Health and Human Services
             200 Independence Ave., SW.
             Washington, DC 20201
phone: 1-877-696-6775
e-mail: cfbci@hhs.gov
Web site: http://www.hhs.gov/faith

Welcomes the participation of faith-based and community-based organizations as valued and essential partners with the U.S. Department of Health and Human Services. Funding goes to faith- based organizations through Head Start, programs for refugee resettlement, runaway and homeless youth, independent living, childcare, child support enforcement, and child welfare.

Family Support America
(formerly Family Resource Coalition of America)

address: 205 West Randolph Street, Suite 2222 Chicago, IL 60606
phone: (312) 338-0900
fax: (312) 338-1522
e-mail: info@familysupportamerica.org
Web site: www.familysupportamerica.org

Works to strengthen and empower families and communities so that they can foster the optimal development of children, youth, and adult family members.

National Exchange Club Foundation for the Prevention of Child Abuse

address: 3050 Central Ave. Toledo, OH 43606-1700
phone: (800) 924-2643
             (419) 535-3232
fax: (419) 535-1989
e-mail: info@preventchildabuse.com
Web site: http://www.nationalexchangeclub.com

Conducts local campaigns in the fi ght against child abuse by providing education, intervention, and support to families affected by child maltreatment.

National Fatherhood Initiative

address: 101 Lake Forest Blvd., Suite 360 Gaithersburg, MD 20877
phone: (301) 948-0599

fax: (301) 948-4325
Web site: http://www.fatherhood

Works to improve the well-being of children by increasing the proportion of children growing up with involved, responsible, and committed fathers.

For the General Public

Childhelp USA
address: 15757 North 78th St.Scottsdale, AZ 85260
phone: (800) 4-A-CHILD
              (800) 2-A-CHILD (TDD line)
              (480) 922-8212
fax: (480) 922-7061
e-mail: help@childhelpusa.org
Web site: http://www.childhelpusa.org

Provides crisis counseling to adult survivors and child victims of child abuse, off enders, and parents, and operates a national hotline.

National Center for Missing and Exploited Children
address: Charles B. Wang International Children's Building
              699 Prince St.
              Alexandria, VA 22314-3175
phone: (800) 843-5678
              (703) 274-3900
fax: (703) 274-2220
Web site: http://www.missingkids.com

Provides assistance to parents, children, law enforcement, schools, and the community in recovering missing children and raising public awareness about ways to help prevent child abduction, molestation, and sexual exploitation.

Parents Anonymous
address: 675 West Foothill Blvd., Suite 220 Claremont, CA 91711
phone: (909) 621-6184
fax: (909) 625-6304
e-mail: Parentsanonymous@parentsanonymous.org
Web site: www.parentsanonymous.org

Leads mutual support groups to help parents provide nurturing environments for their families.

For More Information

Child Welfare Information Gateway
address: 1250 Maryland Avenue, SW Eighth Floor Washington, DC 20024

phone: (800) 394-3366
              (703) 385-7565
fax: (703) 385-3206
e-mail: info@childwelfare.gov
Web site: http://www.childwelfare.gov/

Collects, stores, catalogs, and disseminates information on all aspects of child maltreatment, child welfare, and adoption to help build the capacity of professionals in the field. A service of the Children's Bureau.

APPENDIX C. STATE TELEPHONE NUMBERS FOR REPORTING CHILD ABUSE

Each State designates specific agencies to receive and investigate reports of suspected child abuse and neglect. Typically, this responsibility is carried out by child protective services (CPS) within a Department of Social Services, Department of Human Resources, or Division of Family and Children Services. In some States, police departments also may receive reports of child abuse or neglect.

Many States have local or toll-free telephone numbers, listed below, for reporting suspected abuse. **The reporting party must be calling from the same State where the child is allegedly being abused for most of the following numbers to be valid.**

For States not listed, or when the reporting party resides in a different State from the child, please call Childhelp, 800-4-A-Child (800-422-4453), or your local CPS agency. States may occasionally change the telephone numbers listed below. To view the most current contact information, including State Web addresses, visit

Alabama (AL)
334-242-9500

Alaska (AK)
800-478-4444

Arizona (AZ)
888-SOS-CHILD
(888-767-2445)

Arkansas (AR)
800-482-5964

Colorado (CO)
303-866-5932

Connecticut (CT)
800-842-2288
800-624-5518 (TDD)

Hawaii (HI)
808-832-5300

Idaho (ID)
800-926-2588

Illinois (IL)
800-252-2873
217-524-2606

Indiana (IN)
800-800-5556

Iowa (IA)
800-362-2178

Kansas (KS)
800-922-5330

Mississippi (MS)
800-222-8000
601-359-4991

Missouri (MO)
800-392-3738
573-751-3448

Montana (MT)
866-820-KIDS (5437)

Nebraska (NE)
800-652-1999

Nevada (NV)
800-992-5757
775-684-4400

Delaware (DE)
800-292-9582

District of Columbia (DC)
202-671-SAFE (7233)

Florida (FL)
800-96-ABUSE
(800-962-2873)

New York (NY)
800-342-3720
518-474-8740
800-369-2437 (TDD)

Oklahoma (OK)
800-522-3511

Pennsylvania (PA)
800-932-0313

Puerto Rico (PR)
800-981-8333
787-749-1333

Rhode Island (RI)
800-RI-CHILD
(800-742-4453)

Kentucky (KY)
800-752-6200

Maine (ME)
800-452-1999
800-963-9490 (TTY)

Massachusetts (MA)
800-792-5200

South Carolina (SC)
803-898-7318

South Dakota (SD)
605-773-3227

Tennessee (TN)
877-237-0004

Texas (TX)
800-252-5400
512-834-3784

Utah (UT)
800-678-9399

Vermont (VT)
800-649-5285
(after hours)

New Hampshire (NH)
800-894-5533
603-271-6556

New Jersey (NJ)
877-652-2873
800-835-5510(TDD/ TTY))

New Mexico (NM)
800-797-3260
505-841-6100

Virginia (VA)
800-552-7096
804-786-8536

Washington (WA)
866-END-HARM
(866-363-4276)
800-562-5624(after hours)
800-624-6186 (TTY)

West Virginia (WV)
800-352-6513

APPENDIX D. GUIDELINES FOR CHILD PROTECTIVE SERVICES CASEWORKERS FOR PERMANENCY AND REVIEW HEARINGS

Individuals Who Should Be Present at Both Permanency and Review Hearings

- The judge who has monitored the case from the first hearing;
- The child, unless inappropriate for a specific reason;
- The parent whose rights have not been relinquished or terminated;
- The attorney for the parent;
- The assigned social services caseworker;
- The prosecuting or agency attorney;
- For Indian children, a representative from the child's tribe and tribal attorney, if any;

- The guardian ad litem for the child, whether attorney, social worker, or other paid nonattorney, volunteer, or Court-Appointed Special Advocate;
- The attorney for the child, if applicable;
- The foster parent, legal-risk foster parent, or adoptive parent;
- Relatives, other interested persons, and witnesses;
- The court reporter or suitable recording technology;
- The court security and other court staff .

Questions for All Cases: What Are the Child's Special Needs?

- What is the child's health and education status?
- What is being offered to address the child's cultural needs, if applicable?
- What is the child's current placement adjustment?
- What services are being provided to the child, what progress has the child made, and what issues still need to be addressed?

For the Permanency Hearing

If Reunification Is Recommended:

- How have the conditions or circumstances leading to the removal of the child been corrected?
- Why is this plan in the best interests of the child?
- How often is visitation occurring and what is the impact on the child?
- What is the date and detailed plan for the child's safe return home and follow-up supervision after family reunification?
- What are the plans to continue any necessary services to the child?
- What are the plans to continue any necessary services to the family?
- If a change of school will occur, what will be done to prepare for the transition?

If Termination of Parental Rights and Adoption Are Recommended:

- What are the facts and circumstances supporting the grounds for termination?
- What reasonable efforts were made to reunify?
- Why is this plan in the best interests of the child?
- Has the petition been filed and, if not, what is the date it will be filed?
- Are there relatives who will adopt the child if termination of parental rights is granted? If so, is the child living with the relative? If not, why not? If there are no relatives willing and able to adopt, why not?
- If relative adoption is not the plan, is adoption by the foster parents the plan? If not, why not?
- If an adoptive home must be recruited, what efforts are being made to identify potential adoptive homes both locally and in other jurisdictions? Are there adults

with whom the child has a positive relationship and are they potential adopting families?

Will Adoption With Contact Be Recommended and Why or Why Not?

- What counseling will occur to assist the child to deal with this change of plan?
- If the child is an Indian child, have Indian Child Welfare Act requirements been met?

If Permanent Guardianship or Permanent Custody is Recommended:

- Why is this option preferable to termination of parental rights and adoption? Why is it in the best interests of the child?
- What reasonable efforts were made to reunify?
- What are the facts and circumstances demonstrating the appropriateness of the individual or couple to serve as permanent family to the child? Is there another person who spends significant time in the home, and if so, has that individual been interviewed for appropriateness?
- Has there been full disclosure to the family of the child's circumstances and special needs?
- What is the plan to ensure that this will be a permanent home for the child?
- What contact will occur between the child and parents, siblings, and other family members?
- What financial support will be provided by the biological parents?
- What are the plans to continue any necessary services to the child? How will these services be funded after guardianship or custody has been granted?
- If the child is not already placed in this home, why not and:
  - How often is visitation occurring and what is the impact on the child?
  - What is the date and detailed plan for the child's placement in this home and follow-up supervision after placement?
  - If a change of school will occur, what will be done to prepare for the transition?

If Another Plan Is Being Recommended:

- What are the compelling reasons not to proceed with reunification, termination of parental rights, permanent guardianship, or permanent custody? What is the plan, and why is this plan in the child's best interests?
- What reasonable efforts were made to reunify the child with the parent?
- How will this plan provide stability and permanency for the child?
- What contact will occur between child and parents, siblings, and other family members?
- What are the plans to continue any necessary services to the child?
- If the child is a teenager, what is the plan to prepare the child for independent living?
- If the child is not already placed in this home, why not and:
  - How often is visitation occurring and what is the impact on the child?

- What is the detailed plan for the child's placement in this home and follow-up supervision after placement?
- If a change of school will occur, what will be done to ease the transition?

Findings and Conclusions:

- Record the persons present and whether absent parties were provided with appropriate notice; verification that reports offered into evidence have been provided to all parties in advance of the hearing.
- A finding as to what reasonable efforts the agency has made to reunify the family and to finalize a permanent plan. A well-designed, appropriate case plan and meaningful case reviews should prevent unexpected findings of "no reasonable efforts" at this stage of a case. Should it be found that additional remedial steps are necessary, specific expectations should be set out in a detailed order, with a short time frame (e.g., 30 days) for holding the follow-up permanency hearing. A copy of the order should be forwarded to the head of the social services agency.
- A statement addressing special factors or conditions of the child that are identifi ed as special needs, what services are to be provided to address these needs, and who is responsible for providing the services.
- The court's determination of the permanent plan for the child and why the plan is in the best interests of the child. The order should state the steps to be taken and time lines for accomplishing the permanent goal. If the plan is reunification, the date for reunification should be stated.
- If the plan is termination of parental rights and the petition has not yet been filed, the order should state expected time frame for filing a petition for termination of parental rights that must be within 30 days. If the petition has been filed, the court should schedule pretrials, mediation, and trial dates.
- If the plan is termination of parental rights, and a parent wishes to relinquish parental rights at the permanency hearing, the court should be prepared to accept the relinquishment and include the relinquishment in the order.
- For any plan, next hearing date and purpose, unless all court and agency involvement is terminated (i.e., permanent guardianship, permanent custody, or reunification without protective supervision).

For Review Hearings that Follow Permanency Hearings or Termination of Parental Rights Hearings

If Reunification Is the Permanent Plan:

- What progress has been made on each of the issues that prevented implementation of this plan at the permanency hearing?
- How often is visitation occurring and what is the impact on the child and family?
- What is the date and detailed plan for the child's safe return home and follow-up supervision after family reunification?

- What are the plans to continue any necessary services to the child?
- What are the plans to continue any necessary services to the family?
- If a change of school will occur, what will be done to prepare for the transition?
- If the family has not made adequate progress to enable a safe return home, what alternate permanent plan is recommended and what are the steps and time frames for its implementation?

If Permanent Guardianship or Permanent Custody Is the Permanent Plan:

- What progress has been made on each of the issues that prevented implementation of this plan at the permanency hearing?
- What contact is occurring between the child and parents, siblings, other family members and tribal and clan members, if applicable, and is this contact working well for the child and all involved individuals?
- Has there been full disclosure regarding the child's background history and current or potential disabilities?
- What are the plans to continue any necessary services to the child? How will these services be funded after guardianship or custody has been granted?
- What is the plan for financial support from the biological parents?
- Is there any reason that permanent guardianship or permanent custody should not be granted today?
- If sufficient progress has not been made to enable the granting of permanent guardianship or permanent custody at this hearing, what alternate permanent plan is recommended and what are the steps and time frames for its implementation?

If Relative or Foster Home Adoption Is the Permanent Plan:

- What progress in approving the relative or foster home as the adoptive home has been made since the termination of parental rights hearing? If it is not yet approved, why not, what remains to be done, and when will it be approved?
- Has there been full disclosure regarding the child's history, and current or potential disabilities?
- If adoption with contact has been agreed upon, what contact is occurring between the child and parents, siblings, other family members, or tribal and clan members, if relevant, and is this contact working well for the child and all involved individuals?
- How soon can the adoption be finalized? What specific steps must occur and what is the time frame for each of the steps?
- Has the adoption assistance agreement been negotiated? If not, why not? Have all appropriate subsidies been identified and has all paperwork been completed with regard to these subsidies? Will services follow the family if they move out of State? Is the adopting family aware of the details of all appropriate subsidy issues?
- Has the relative or foster parent been made aware of ways to access needed services after the adoption is finalized? Has the relative or foster parent been given contacts for support groups or other adopting families who can serve as mentors and supports?

If an Adoptive Home Has Been Recruited Since the Last Hearing but the Child Has Not Yet Been Placed in the Home:

- A detailed description of the family and the neighborhood in which the family lives. Is there another person who spends significant time in the home, and if so, has this individual been interviewed for appropriateness?
- If the child is an Indian child, does the home meet the placement preferences listed in the Indian Child Welfare Act, and if not, why not? What efforts has the agency made to identify a placement under Indian Child Welfare Act?
- Has there been full disclosure to the adopting family of the child's circumstances, history, special needs, and potential disabilities?
- Have all available subsidies been identified and discussed with the adopting family?
- Is the adopting family aware of any adoption with contact agreement and are they accepting of the agreement?
- What is the visitation and placement plan and its time frame? If visits have begun, how are the child and the adopting family adjusting?
- If the home is out of State, have all regulations regarding the Interstate Compact for the Placement of Children and the Interstate Compact on Adoption and Medical Assistance been followed? Are there any known or anticipated issues relative to these compacts that may cause delays and if so, what is being done to resolve or avoid the delays?
- Has there been full disclosure regarding the child's history and current or potential disabilities?
- What are the plans to continue any necessary services to the child? How will these services be funded after guardianship or custody has been granted?
- What is the plan for financial support from the biological parents?
- Is there any reason that permanent guardianship or permanent custody should not be granted today?
- If sufficient progress has not been made to enable the granting of permanent guardianship or permanent custody at this hearing, what alternate permanent plan is recommended and what are the steps and time frames for its implementation?

If the Child Has Been in the Adoptive Home Since the Last Hearing:

- What progress has been made since the last hearing toward finalization? When will finalization occur? What specific steps must occur and what are the time frames for each step?
- Have any new problems or issues occurred since the last hearing? What is the plan to address the problems or issues?
- If full disclosure regarding the child's history and current or potential disabilities had not yet occurred at the last hearing, has it now occurred?
- If adoption with contact has been agreed upon, what contact is occurring between the child and parents, siblings or other family members, and is this contact working well for the child and all involved individuals?

- Has the adoption assistance agreement been negotiated? If not, why not? Have all appropriate subsidies been identified and has all paperwork been completed with regard to these subsidies? Will services follow the family if they move out of state? Is the adopting family aware of the details of all appropriate subsidy issues?
- Has the adopting family been made aware of ways to access needed services after the adoption is finalized? Has the adopting family been given contacts for support groups or other adopting families who can serve as mentors and supports?

If the Agency Is Recruiting an Adoptive Home:

- What efforts have been made since the termination of parental rights hearing or last review hearing to identify potential adoptive homes both locally and in other jurisdictions?
- If the child is an Indian child, what efforts are being made to identify potential adoptive homes in the child's tribal community?
- What is the status of investigating adults with whom the child has or has had a positive relationship with regard to their potential to become adopting families?
- On what adoption exchanges and Internet sites is the child listed?
- How many potential families have expressed interest in the child and what is the status of investigating each family?
- What efforts are being made by the agency to comply with Indian Child Welfare Act placement preferences, if applicable?

If Another Plan Is the Permanent Plan:

- What progress has been made since the permanency hearing and is the existing permanent plan still in the child's best interests?
- Do the compelling reasons not to proceed with reunification, termination of parental rights, permanent guardianship, or permanent custody that existed at the permanency hearing still apply?
- If they do not, what is the new permanent plan and how is it in the child's best interests? What are the steps and time frames that have occurred, or still need to occur to fully implement this new plan?
- What is the frequency and duration of contact that is occurring between the child and parents, siblings, other family members, tribal or clan members, or other signifi cant adults? Is this contact working well for the child and all involved individuals?
- What is the plan to prepare the child for independent living?
- If a change of placement is planned:
  - Why is this change necessary and in the best interests of the child?
  - What is the plan for pre-placement visits? Have they begun and how is the child responding? What is the detailed plan for the child's placement in this home and follow-up supervision after placement?
  - If a change of school or service providers will occur, what will be done to ease the transition?

Findings and Conclusions:

- Who is present at the hearing and whether absent parties were provided with appropriate notice. If the child is an Indian child, the court should verify whether the child's tribe received notice and was offered an opportunity to participate. It should be verified that reports provided to the court were made available to all parties prior to the hearing.
- A finding as to whether the agency has made reasonable efforts to finalize a permanent home with detail to support the finding. If the child is in an adoptive home, the finding should indicate whether the agency is doing everything possible, as quickly as possible, to approve the home, complete all aspects of the adoption assistance agreement including subsidies and services, and move toward finalization. If an adoptive home must be recruited, the finding should indicate whether the agency is doing everything possible, as quickly as possible, to list the child on all appropriate exchanges, Internet sites, and with all appropriate private agencies, and to promptly screen and complete home studies on prospective adopting parents.
- If the child is an Indian child, a finding as to whether the agency has complied with the placement preferences within the Indian Child Welfare Act, and if not, the efforts made to comply.
- If there are any changes or adjustments to the permanent plan, a description with time lines for implementation and the reasons that these adjustments or changes are in the best interests of the child.
- If visitation issues, including agreements for adoption with contact apply, are the terms and schedules of visitation being complied with and are they effective.
- A statement addressing special factors or conditions of the child that are identified as special needs, what services are being provided to address the needs and how the child is progressing.
- Any specific orders that are to be implemented.
- Unless the permanent plan is finalized at the hearing, the date and time for the next review or the finalization hearing.

Source: National Council of Juvenile and Family Court Judges. (2000). *Adoptions and permanency guidelines: Improving court practice in child abuse and neglect cases.* Reno, NV: Author.

APPENDIX E. LEGAL AND JUDICIAL ISSUES SUGGESTED BY THE CHILD AND FAMILY SERVICES REVIEW PERFORMANCE INDICATORS

To help States consider the legal dimensions of the seven safety, permanency, and well-being outcomes and the seven systemic factors (including the 45 related specific performance indicators identifi ed by the Federal government), this appendix annotates the 45 performance indicators addressed in the fi rst round of reviews. That is, the 45 Federal performance indicators are listed verbatim and boldface below, while legal and judicial aspects of each performance area are provided as bullets. *Note*: These bullets are meant to illustrate the kinds of legal practice and policy issues that may require attention to comply with each performance area.

I. Safety

1. **Timeliness in initiating child abuse and neglect investigations.**
    *   Effective legal help is available to overcome barriers to investigations.
    *   Legal advice is provided to the agency that supports the filing of actions in dependency court whenever abused and neglected children need State intervention.
    *   Legislation and court rules provide legal remedies allowing agencies to complete investigations when family members or other people familiar with the child refuse to cooperate.
    *   Statutes, regulations, and procedures provide clear and appropriate guidance for investigators and caseworkers to obtain otherwise confidential information from substance abuse treatment providers, criminal justice agencies, schools, mental health providers, doctors, and other professionals.

2. **Recurrence of abuse or neglect by parents.**
    *   Courts remove children from home and enforce comprehensive judicial protective supervision.
    *   Courts carefully consider safety factors when deciding whether to return a child home.
    *   Courts exercise caution when deciding whether to terminate court jurisdiction (dismiss case).
    *   Judges and attorneys take time to carefully review documents and ask challenging questions concerning safety issues in the home.
    *   Adequate evidence demonstrating danger to the child is offered in court proceedings.
    *   Judges carefully consider evidence about the child and caretakers to ensure the child will be safe.
    *   Domestic violence policies are well defined.

3. **Services to protect children at home and prevent removal.**
    *   In appropriate circumstances judges order parents to participate in services to protect the child instead of ordering the child removed from home.
    *   Adequate evidence demonstrating whether services will alleviate danger to the child is offered in court proceedings.
    *   Laws and regulations define an array of services for abused and neglected children and their families, to be delivered immediately in emergencies.
    *   Domestic violence policies are well defined.

4. **Risk of harm to child including abuse or neglect of child while in foster care.**
   - Courts order removal of children from their foster homes when the agency appropriately requests it to avoid potential abuse or neglect. (Note that courts do not have the power in all States to block removal of a child from a foster home.)
   - Courts monitor foster placements by insisting caseworkers and children's legal representatives visit and evaluate the foster home.
   - Safety clearances are done on every adult in the foster parents' or adoptive parents' homes.

Note: Many organizational problems may affect the factors listed below. Important examples are excessive workloads, insufficient training, poor hiring practices and management, and weak case management skills. These are common problems facing caseworkers, attorneys, foster parents, child advocates, judges, and court staff and can weaken the legal system.

II. Permanency

5. **Foster care reentry.**
   - Adequate time and resources are allocated for meaningful case review before sending the child home.
   - Courts require evidence that the home is safe before authorizing the child's return home.
   - When courts allow children to remain home following adjudication of child abuse or neglect, they require that the case be brought back to court if the agency decides to place the child in foster care. Due process protections regarding subsequent removal of the child are in place.
   - Courts order specific services and refer parents to community supports to make the return successful and require that parents and children complete the services.
   - Courts gather enough information about the parent and child before return.
   - Courts ensure visitation plans are designed to foster healthy parent-child relationships and work toward successful reunification to avoid foster care reentry (e.g., efforts are made to ensure visits are meaningful, progressively longer visits are imposed).
   - Courts and agencies closely monitor cases.
   - Courts carefully and thoroughly consider the evidence when deciding whether to return children home.

6. **Stability of foster placement – too many moves of foster children into different foster homes.**
   - Judges monitor moves while children are in foster care.
   - Laws, regulations, and State policies discourage moving children between foster homes.
   - Policies and practices support training for foster parents of special needs children.
   - Judges understand bonding and attachment issues and factor them into decision-making.

- Courts thoroughly review children's needs.
- Children's counsel effectively represents children by:
  Reviewing case plans;
  Participating in case planning;
  Preserving placements;
  Advocating for reunification services;
  Advocating for independent living services;
  Visiting and interacting with the child to independently assess whether moves are necessary.

7. Permanency goal for child.

- Attorneys, judges, and court personnel are adequately trained in permanency planning practices.
- Permanency hearings are conducted in a timely manner and sufficient time is allotted for hearings.
- Judges and attorneys understand concurrent planning and support it when appropriate.
- State laws provide appropriate grounds for legal guardianship, clear and efficient procedures for establishing legal guardianships, and adequate legal protections and financial supports for legal guardians.
- State laws provide appropriate grounds for termination of parental rights (TPR) and clear and efficient procedures for TPR.
- State laws and policies provide appropriate exceptions for mandatory petitions for TPR, based on Federal requirements.
- State laws and policies provide workable procedures for determining whether to file or join petitions for the TPR.

8. Reunification, guardianship, or permanent placement with relatives.

- Courts consistently follow or enforce time limits for hearings and judicial decisions. Courts have a comprehensive system of time limits governing all stages of the court process.
- Adequate judicial case tracking systems are in place.
- Judges fully explore all possible placement resources.
- Judges routinely establish or approve specific permanency plans for foster children.
- Courts minimize delays by notifying appropriate parties, denying adjournments, ensuring diligent efforts to locate missing parents at start of case, determining paternity early in case, and addressing other procedural problems.
- Multi-court involvement in different stages of child protection cases is discouraged to avoid delays, loss of information, and other inefficiencies.
- Court practices are efficient to minimize time to achieve reunification.
- Clear, efficient procedures exist to indefinitely transfer custody to a non-custodial parent or relative in child protection proceedings.
- State laws provide appropriate grounds for legal guardianship, clear and efficient procedures for establishing legal guardianships, and adequate legal protections and financial supports for legal guardians.

- Courts consistently and thoroughly review reasonable efforts to achieve a new permanent home for the child.

9. Achievement of adoption.
- Courts adequately track case progress toward adoption.
- Courts thoroughly consider the appropriateness of prospective adoptive caretakers.
- Judges fully explore all possible placement resources.
- Courts understand when TPR petitions are required and the exceptions to such requirements.
- Courts take steps to encourage or require TPR petitions, when appropriate.
- State laws provide appropriate grounds for TPR and clear and efficient procedures for TPR.
- Sufficient resources and court time are available to promote timely TPRs.
- The appellate process is streamlined to avoid TPR delays.
- Courts and attorneys inform agencies of available steps to speed appeals.
- Courts actively oversee cases between TPR and finalization of adoption
- Courts minimize scheduling delays and prioritize cases when needed.
- Courts minimize delays by notifying appropriate parties, denying adjournments, ensuring diligent efforts to locate missing parents at start of case, determining paternity early in case, and addressing other procedural problems.
- Multi-court involvement in different stages of child protection cases is discouraged to avoid delays, loss of information, and other inefficiencies.

10. Permanency goal of other planned permanent living arrangement.
- "Another planned permanent living arrangement" is clearly defined to avoid misapplication.
- Courts carefully use this permanency option, ensuring compelling reasons exist and giving thought to long-term permanency planning.
- Courts order or recommend services that might allow the child to move into a more permanent placement.
- Courts review case plans to determine agency compliance with services and visitation for other planned permanent living arrangements.
- Courts operate with the understanding that independent living (foster children "aging out") is not a permanency plan, but foster children are entitled to independent living services.
- Courts are familiar with available independent living services for children in the community and refer children to appropriate services.
- Courts are familiar with Federal legislation supporting independent living services.
- Courts ask about independent living services in most cases involving older teens in foster care.
- State laws authorize extending court jurisdiction for children who have turned 18 and specify appropriately.

11. **Proximity of foster care placement.**
    - Courts request information about the proximity of the foster care placement.
    - Courts do not order children placed outside their communities or counties if appropriate placement resources are located in close proximity.
    - Courts routinely request information based on agency visits with children placed out of State.
    - Statutes, court rules, and policies provide appropriate guidance concerning the proximity of foster care placement.

12. **Placement with siblings.**
    - Courts consistently ask agencies to present specific reasons for failing to place siblings together.
    - State statutes, court rules, and polices address the priority of placement with siblings.
    - Attorneys and judges are adequately trained on the importance of maintaining sibling ties as well as on reasons why this might not be appropriate.

13. **Visits with parents and siblings.**
    - Courts request information about the nature and quality of foster children's visits, contacts, and relationships with parents and siblings.
    - Courts address visiting, when appropriate, in court orders.
    - Attorneys request evaluations of the quality of visits with parents and siblings.
    - Statutes, court rules, and policies provide clear guidance regarding visitation.
    - Attorneys and judges are adequately trained on visitation issues.

14. **Preserving connections.**
    - Attorneys request evaluations of relatives.
    - Statutes, court rules, and policies provide clear guidance regarding maintaining relative ties.
    - Attorneys are adequately trained on the importance and pitfalls of maintaining relative ties.
    - Courts ask whether children are Native American and, if so, whether tribes have been notified.
    - Courts support collaboration with tribal courts on transfers of cases of Native American children where appropriate.
    - Courts enforce placement preferences for Native American children under ICWA, including placement with the child's extended family and with tribes.

15. **Relative placement.**
    - Courts ask about possible placement with maternal and paternal relatives early and often.
    - Courts ask agencies to present specific reasons for not placing children with relatives.
    - Attorneys and judges are adequately trained on relative placement issues.

16. **Relationship of child in care with parents.**
   - Courts consistently ask about child's relationship with parents while in care, including nature and quality of visits and other contact.
   - Courts monitor visiting arrangements and their frequency where specified in court orders.
   - Attorneys are adequately trained regarding maintaining parent-child relationships during foster placements.

III. Child and Family Well-Being

17. **Needs and services of child, parents, foster parents.**
   - Courts ensure that agencies conduct thorough assessments and provide services to meet the needs of the child, parents, and foster parents.
   - Courts review case plans submitted to the courts by the child protection agency to see if needs are being met through the provision of services.
   - Courts address barriers to service provision and delivery.
   - Attorneys and advocates identify and address their clients' needs and advocate appropriate services.
   - Attorneys, advocates, and judges have sufficient training, experience, and resources to advocate effectively for children's service needs (e.g., special education, medical, and mental health needs).
   - Judges and attorneys are sufficiently knowledgeable about confidentiality laws to help ensure that information on children's and family's needs is available to the court and agency.

18. **Child and family involvement in case planning.**
   - Attorneys and advocates participate in and encourage child and family involvement in case planning.
   - Statutes, court rules, and policies provide appropriate guidance to encourage child and family involvement in case planning.

19. **Worker visits with the child.**
   - Statutes, court rules, and policies provide appropriate guidance on worker visits with parents and children.
   - Attorneys and advocates request information about and, when appropriate, advocate for worker visits with the child.

20. **Worker visits with parents.**
   - Courts consistently review and note worker visits with parents and children.
   - Statutes, court rules and policies provide appropriate guidance on and, when appropriate, advocate for worker visits with parents.

21. **Educational needs of the child.**

- Courts request information about foster children's education from teachers, guidance counselors, caseworkers, and others.
- Court forms request education information including school records addressing the child's academic performance, behavior and adjustment to school, and special educational needs.
- Judges, attorneys, and advocates consistently determine whether foster children's education needs are being met.
- Policies offer guidance on minimizing disruptions in foster children's education due to frequent moves.
- State laws appropriately address confidentiality issues surrounding access to education records of foster children and children under protective supervision.
- Judges, attorneys, and advocates have sufficient knowledge about the education system to intervene effectively to ensure a good education for foster children.

22. Physical health of the child.
- Courts obtain information about foster children's medical needs.
- Court forms request physical health information, including any known medical problems, needed treatments, medication, and physical symptoms of abuse or neglect.
- Judges, attorneys and advocates consistently determine whether foster children's physical health needs are being met.
- Courts are aware of State requirements regarding foster children's physical health, such as those concerning medical examinations and immunizations.
- Courts inquire, when appropriate, whether health records have been reviewed, updated, and supplied to the foster care provider.
- State laws appropriately address confidentiality issues governing access to medical information about abused and neglected children.

23. Mental health of the child.
- Judges, attorneys, and advocates request information from children's therapists about foster children's mental health issues.
- Court forms request mental health information.
- Courts are aware of State requirements for diagnosis and treatment regarding foster children's mental health.
- Judges, attorneys, and advocates consistently determine whether foster children's mental health needs are being met.
- State laws appropriately address confidentiality issues governing access to mental health information.

IV. Statewide Information System

24. State operates information system that readily can identify the status, demographic characteristics, location, and goals for the placement of every child who is (or within the preceding year was) in foster care.

- Courts have created a statewide information system or good local information systems.
- Case tracking responsibilities are clearly assigned to appropriate court staff .
- Courts and agencies have automated systems that use computers and tickler systems to manage cases.
- Computer data is used to measure judicial performance.
- Agency information systems include information about critical court events to help evaluate judicial performance in child protection cases.
- Data are shared between judicial and agency computers.
- Sophisticated procedures exist to collect and report data.

V. Case Review System

25. Written case plan developed jointly with parents.
- Parents' attorneys participate in the case planning process.
- Parents' attorneys are trained on non-adversarial models for resolving conflict (i.e., Family Group Conferencing and mediation).
- Parents' attorneys advocate for meaningful case planning for their clients.
- Judges ask about parental involvement in case planning.

26. Process for periodic review at least once every six months, by court or by administrative review.
- Court procedures and forms ask hard questions and ensure thoroughness.
- Courts and/or agencies schedule 6-month reviews in a timely manner.
- Reviews thoroughly consider whether reasonable efforts have been made to achieve permanency, especially after the case goal is no longer reunification.
- Courts set aside enough time to hold review hearings that thoroughly consider the individual circumstances of each child and family and that address each issue specified by State and Federal law.
- If administrative reviews are held in lieu of judicial reviews, the courts take time to examine the reports from the reviews and address them in court proceedings.

27. Permanency hearings within 12 months after a child is considered to have entered foster care and at least once every 12 months thereafter.
- Adequate scheduling procedures for reviews are in place.
- Courts devote enough time to conduct thorough permanency hearings that address each issue specified in State and Federal statutes and to determine an appropriate permanency plan for each child.
- State laws, court rules, court forms, and court procedures create a structure for permanency hearings that encourages timely decisions by the court and agency, even in challenging cases.
- Permanency hearings thoroughly consider whether reasonable efforts have been made to achieve permanency, especially after the case goal no longer is reunification.

28. **Process for termination of parental rights proceedings in accordance with ASFA.**
    - Attorneys and judges are aware of State and Federal statutory requirements to file petitions for TPR and of the exceptions.
    - Courts routinely review agency documentation of exceptions to State and Federal requirements to file petitions for TPR.
    - Procedures for TPR fully protect parents' rights without being needlessly inefficient.
    - State laws do not require parties to reprove facts established in earlier stages of the court process in order to terminate parental rights.
    - Grounds for TPR are complete, focused, and consistent.
    - Agency procedures and policies for deciding whether to file are timely and balanced.

29. **Process for foster parents, pre-adoptive parents, and relative caregivers of children in foster care to be notified of, and have an opportunity to be heard in, any review or hearing held with respect to the child.**
    - Courts consistently encourage active participation of foster parents, preadoptive parents, and relative caregivers in court proceedings.
    - Foster parents, preadoptive parents, and relative caregivers consistently receive notice of court proceedings.
    - The wording of notice forms encourages the attendance of foster parents, preadoptive parents, and relative caregivers in court.
    - State laws and procedures specify an effective notification method for foster parents, preadoptive parents, and relative caregivers and define what is meant by "opportunity to be heard."
    - Courts have forms and procedures for review and permanency hearings that call for statements by and questioning of foster parents, preadoptive parents, and relative caregivers.
    - State laws and procedures clearly define an effective notification method for foster parents, preadoptive parents, and relative caregivers and define what is meant by "opportunity to be heard."
    - State laws, court rules, and policies clarify and reinforce the role of foster parents, preadoptive parents, and relative caretakers in court.

VI. Quality Assurance System

30. **Implementation of standards for services to children in foster care, to protect their health and safety.**
    - The agency has comprehensive standards for services to children in child protection cases and courts are aware of these standards.
    - Agencies and courts work together to exchange information on services to children.

31. **Quality assurance system in place to evaluate the quality of services, identify strengths and needs of service delivery system, provide relevant reports, and evaluate implementation of program improvement measures.**
    - Agencies enlist courts to help evaluate caseworkers' performance in court.
    - Courts have systematic quality assurance systems to evaluate their own performance.

VII. Training

32. **Staff development and training program for all staff, including training on objectives of Title IV-B plan and services under Title IV-B and IV-E. To include initial training for all staff.**
    - The State agency provides copies of its Title IV-B and IV-E plans to all judges.
    - The State agency provides to all judges and attorneys copies of lists of the services provided under Titles IV-B and IV-E.
    - Training is provided for all new judges and attorneys concerning Title IV-B and IV-E and participation is mandatory.
    - Comprehensive training is provided for all new judges and attorneys concerning child welfare law and basic social work principles and participation is mandatory.

33. **Staff development and training to address ongoing skills needed to implement Title IV-B plan.**
    - Periodic training on child protection cases is provided for experienced judges and attorneys and participation is mandatory.
    - Judicial and attorney training requirements for child protection cases are rigorous.
    - Training on permanency planning concepts and procedures is provided to ensure timely permanence.
    - Courts and agencies use appropriate cross training—addressing issues of mutual concern—and avoid inappropriate use of cross training in lieu of training in core legal skills and knowledge.

34. **Training for prospective foster parents, adoptive parents, and staff of facilities with children receiving foster care or adoption assistance under Title IV-E.**
    - Prospective foster parents receive training on the legal aspects of permanency planning, including t4e stages and purposes of the legal process.
    - Foster parents receive training and materials on their rights and responsibilities in child welfare proceedings, including the right to be heard and to participate in the case.
    - Prospective adoptive parents receive training concerning their legal responsibilities and about the legal process of adoption.

- Foster parents, prospective adoptive parents and agency staff receive training concerning legal protections (e.g., procedural rights, entitlements, contractual rights) regarding adoption assistance.

VIII. Service Array:

35. **State has array of services. The array of services assesses strengths and needs of children and families, determines other service needs, addresses needs of individual children and of families to create a safe home environment, enables children to remain at home when reasonable, and helps children in foster and adoptive placements achieve permanency.**
    - Child protection agencies inform courts of available services, who is eligible for different services, and usual waiting periods for services.
    - State laws, regulations, and budgets provide for a core of services that are consistently available to abused and neglected children and their families.

36. **The services in the array (listed in response to the above item) are accessible to families and children in all political jurisdictions covered in the State's Title IV-E plan.**
    - Contracts for services are well written and ensure availability of needed services.
    - Agencies have master plans for contracts to ensure consistent availability of key services.
    - State laws require other agencies to give priority to and ensure availability of services to clients served by the child protection agency and under court jurisdiction.

37. **The services in the array can be individualized to meet the unique needs of children and families served by the agency.**
    - State laws and policies budget for child protection services based on documented need for such services.
    - Agencies' contracts for services provide flexible services to meet material and special needs of children and families.

IX. Agency Responsiveness to the Community:

38. **Ongoing consultation with tribal representatives, consumers, service providers, foster care providers, the juvenile courts, and other public and private child and family serving agencies and includes the major concerns of these representatives in the goals and objectives of the Title IV-B plan.**
    - Courts regularly meet with the agency and meet with all of the child protection professionals listed above to work on mutual problems and improve working relationships.

- Judicial ethics clarify and encourage judicial outreach to the agency and community regarding child protection cases.

39. **The agency develops, in consultation with these representatives, annual reports of progress and services delivered under the Title IV-B plan.**
    - The agency consults with legal system representatives concerning its annual reports, including allowing them to review draft reports in advance. Among other things, the agency asks for comments concerning service delivery.

40. **The State's services under the Title IV-B plan are coordinated with services or benefits of other Federal or federally assisted programs serving the same population.**
    - The agency consults with legal system representatives specifically concerning the delivery of federally assisted services provided by agencies and entities not funded by the child protection agency.

XI. Foster and Adoptive Parent Licensing, Recruitment, and Retention:

41. **Implementation of standards for foster family homes and child care institutions, reasonably in accord with national standards.**
    - Courts have information about standards for foster and adoptive parents and concerning child care institutions.

42. **Standards applied to all foster family homes and child caring institutions receiving title IV-E or IV-B funds.**
    - Courts are informed when foster family homes and child caring institutions no longer meet agency standards.

43. **State complies with Federal requirements for criminal background checks and has a case planning process that addresses the safety of foster and adoptive placements.**
    - State law requires criminal record checks of parents found to have abused or neglected their children and of other people living in the households of abused and neglected children.
    - State law requires criminal record checks of all adults in foster and adoptive homes.
    - Courts or court forms ask about the criminal record of parents found to have abused or neglected their children and of other people living in the households of abused and neglected children.
    - Attorneys and judges are aware of State and Federal statutory restrictions concerning the licensing of specific categories of convicted criminals as foster and adoptive parents.

44. **State has process for diligent recruitment of potential foster and adoptive families that refl ect the ethnic and racial diversity of children in the State for whom foster and adoptive homes are needed.**

    • Courts and attorneys are well informed about the process of recruiting, matching, screening and evaluating foster and adoptive families.

    • In case reviews in which the permanency plan is adoption and the child is not yet placed in a preadoptive home, judges and advocates ask about State efforts to recruit and arrange such a home.

    • When evaluating whether the State made reasonable efforts to fi nalize a child's permanency plan, judges and advocates consider, if relevant, the State's efforts to recruit, evaluate, and select adoptive parents for the child.

45. **State has a process for effective use of cross-jurisdictional resources to facilitate timely adoptive or permanent placements for waiting children.**

    • Courts receive technical assistance, materials, and training on interstate placements (and overcoming barriers to such placements), including implementation of the ICPC.

    • Judges and attorneys are familiar with the ICPC, interstate adoption assistance benefits, ICAMA, and other interstate placement benefits and requirements.

    • Judges, attorneys, and advocates consistently ask informed and penetrating questions when interstate placement or services are being considered.

Source: Hardin, M. (2002). *How and why to involve the courts in your Child and Family Services Review (CFSR): Suggestions for agency administrators* [On-line]. Available: http://www.abanet.org/child/courtimp.html.

End Notes

[1] National Council of Juvenile and Family Court Judges. (2003, October). *Child Victims Act Model Court Initiative* [On-line]. Available: http://www. pppncjfcj.org/html/childvic.html.

[2] U.S. Department of Health and Human Services, Administration for Children and Families (ACF). (1999). Blending perspectives and building common ground. A report to Congress on substance abuse and child protection [On-line]. Available: http://aspe.hhs. gov/sp/subabuse99/subabuse.htm.

[3] Harrell, A., & Goodman, A. (1999). *Review of specialized family drug courts: Key issues handling child abuse and neglect cases* [On-line]. Available: http:// www.ncjrs.org/pdffi les1/nij/grants/179281.pdf.

[4] U. S. Department of Justice, Office of Justice Programs (OJP). (1998). *Juvenile and family drug courts: An overview* (p. 3). Washington, DC: Author.

[5] U. S. Department of Justice, OJP. (1998).

[6] Huddleston, C. W, Freeman-Wilson, K., & Boone, D. L. (2004). *Painting the current picture: A national report card on drug courts and other problem solving courts in the United States* [On-line]. Available: http:// www.ndci.org/publications/paintingcurrentpicture. pdf.

[7] Cooper, C., & Bartlett, S. (1998). *Juvenile and family drug courts: Profile of program characteristics and implementation issues* [On-line]. Available: http:// www.ncjrs.org/html/bja/familydrug/welcome.html.

[8] Goldman, J., & Salus, M. K. (2003). *A coordinated response to child abuse and neglect: The foundation for practice* [On-line]. Available: http://www.childwelfare. gov/pubs/usermanuals/foundation/index.cfm.

[9] *Meyer v. Nebraska*, 262 U.S. 390 (1923); *Pierce v. Society of Sisters*, 268 U.S. 510 (1925); *Prince v. Massachusetts*, 321 U.S. 158 (1944).

[10] *Prince*, 321 U.S. at 166.

[11] *Troxel v. Granville,* 530 U.S. 57, 62 (2000); *Quilloin v. Walcott,* 434 U.S. 246, 255 (1978); *Smith v. Organization of Foster Families,* 431 U.S. 816, 862– 63 (1977).

[12] *Lassiter v. Department of Social Services,* 452 U.S. 18, 26–32 (1981).

[13] Keeping Children and Families Safe Act of 2003, Pub. L. No. 108–36, Title I, Section 114(b) (2003).

[14] Kempe, C. H., Silverman, F., Steele, B., Droegmuller, W., & Silver, H. (1962). The battered-child syndrome. *Journal of the American Medical Association, 181,* 107–112.

[15] Child Abuse Prevention and Treatment Act of 1974, Pub. L. No. 93–247, 42 U.S.C. 5101, *et seq.* (1998).

[16] Keeping Children and Families Safe Act of 2003, Pub. L. No. 108–36, Title I, Section 114(b) (2003).

[17] Keeping Children and Families Safe Act of 2003, Pub. L. No. 108–36, Title I, Section 114(b) (2003).

[18] National Council of Juvenile and Family Court Judges. (2003a). *Indian Child Welfare Act checklists for juvenile and family court judges.* Reno, NV: Author; National Council of Juvenile and Family Court Judges. (2003b). Native American resource directory for juvenile and family court judges. *Technical Assistance Bulletin, 7*(4), 5.

[19] National Council of Juvenile and Family Court Judges. (2000a). Permanency planning and the permanency hearing. In *Adoptions and permanency guidelines: Improving court practice in child abuse and neglect cases* (pp. 9–22). Reno, NV: Author.

[20] DePanfi lis, D., & Salus, M. K. (2003). *Child protective services: A guide for caseworkers* [On-line]. Available: http://www.childwelfare.gov/pubs/ usermanuals/cps/index.cfm.

[21] *Tenenbaum v. Williams,* 193 F.3d 581, 596 (2nd Cir. 1999); *Nicholson v. Williams,* 181 F. Supp. 2d 182 (E.D.N.Y. 2002).

[22] Hardin, M. (1992). *Judicial implementation of permanency planning reform: One court that works.* Washington, DC: American Bar Association, Center on Children and the Law; Hardin, M., Rubin, H. T., & Ratterman-Baker, D. (1995). *A second court that works: Judicial implementation of permanency planning reforms.* Washington, DC: American Bar Association, Center on Children and the Law; National Council of Juvenile and Family Court Judges. (1995). *Resource guidelines: Improving court practice in child abuse and neglect cases.* Reno, NV: Author.

[23] 42 U.S.C. 671(a)(15) (1999).

[24] National Council of Juvenile and Family Court Judges. (1995).

[25] Chandler, S., & Giovannucci, M. (2004). Family group conferencing: Transforming traditional child welfare policy and practice. *Family Court Review, 42*(2), 216–231.

[26] National Council of Juvenile and Family Court Judges. (1995).

[27] Adoption and Safe Families Act of 1997, Pub. L. No. 105–89, § 101 (1997).

[28] Adoption and Safe Families Act of 1997, Pub. L. No. 105–89, § 107 (1997).

[29] National Council of Juvenile and Family Court Judges. (1995).

[30] Adoption and Safe Families Act of 1997, Pub. L. No. 105–89, § 103 (1997).

[31] Adoption and Safe Families Act of 1997, Pub. L. No. 105–89, § 302 (1997).

[32] Child Welfare Information Gateway. (2003). *Determining the best interests of the child: Summary of state laws* [On-line]. Available: http://www. childwelfare.gov/systemwide/laws best_interestall.pdf.

[33] Adoption and Safe Families Act of 1997, Pub. L. No. 105–89, § 101 (1997).

[34] Adoption and Safe Families Act of 1997, Pub. L. No. 105–89, § 101 (1997).

[35] FindLaw. (n.d.). *U.S. Supreme Court, Santosky v. Kramer,* 455 U.S. 745 (1982) [On-line]. Available: http://caselaw.lp.fi ndlaw.com/scripts =US&vol=455&invol=745.

[36] Adoption and Safe Families Act of 1997, Pub. L. No. 105–89, § 103 (1997); 42 U.S.C. § 675(5)(3) (1997).

[37] Adoption and Safe Families Act of 1997, Pub. L. No. 105–89, § 105 (1997).

[38] National Council of Juvenile and Family Court Judges. (1995).

[39] Child Welfare Information Gateway. (2004). *Grounds for involuntary termination of parental rights* [On-line]. Available: http://www.childwelfare.gov/ systemwide/laws_policies/statutes/groundterminall. pdf.

[40] *Santosky v. Kramer,* 455 U.S. 745 (1982).

[41] The Multi-Ethnic Placement Act of 1994, Pub. L. No. 103–382, 42 U.S.C. § 5115a (1994); The Inter- Ethnic Adoption Provisions of 1996, Pub. L. No. 104–188 (1996).

[42] Adoption and Safe Families Act of 1997, Pub. L. No. 105–89, § 202 (1997).

[43] U.S. House of Representatives, Committee on Ways and Means. (2004). *2004 Green Book* [Online]. Available: http://waysandmeans.house.gov/ Documents.asp?section=8 13.

[44] Keith, A. L., & Flango, C. R. (2002). *Iowa Court Rules, Appeals in Termination Cases, Rules 6.5–6.154.* Retrieved July 1, 2003, from LexisNexis database.

[45] Kuehnle, K. (1996). *Assessing allegations of child sexual abuse.* Sarasota, FL: Professional Resources Press; Gould, J. W., & Martindale, D. A. (in press). *Child maltreatment and child custody.* New York, NY: Guildford Press; Bow, J. N., Quinell, F. A., Saroff , M., & Assemany, A. (2002). Assessment of sexual abuse allegations in child custody cases. *Professional Psychology: Research & Practice, 33*(6), 566–575.

[46] Garrity C. B., & Baris, M. (1994). *Caught in the middle: Protecting the children of high-conflict divorce.* New York, NY: Lexington Press.

[47] The Social Security Act of 1935, 42 U.S.C. Ch. 7, (1996).

[48] National Conference of Commissioners on Uniform State Laws. (2002). *Uniform Child Witness Testimony by Alternative Methods Act* [On-line]. Available: http://www.i-lawpublishing.net/news/ucwtbama.pdf.

[49] Baker, L. L., Jaff e, P. G., Berkowitz, S. J., & Berkman, M. (2002). *Children exposed to domestic violence: A handbook for police trainers to increase understanding and improve community responses* [On-line]. Available: http://www.lfcc.on.ca/police-us.PDF.

[50] Appel, A. E., & Holden, G. W. (1998a). The co- occurrence of spouse and physical child abuse: A review and appraisal. *Journal of Family Psychology*, 12(4), 578–599; Edleson, J. L. (1999). The overlap between child maltreatment and woman battering. *Violence Against Women*, 5(2), 134–154.

[51] Appel, A. E., & Holden, G. W. (1998a); Appel, A. E., & Holden, G. W. (1998b). Co-occurring spouse and child abuse: Implications for CPS practice. *APSAC Advisor*, 11(1), 11–14; Barnett, O. W., Miller-Perrin, C. L., & Perrin, R. D. (1997). *Family violence across the lifespan: An introduction*. Thousand Oaks, CA: Sage; Edleson, J. L. (1999); Hughes, H. M., Parkinson, D., & Vargo, M. (1989). Witnessing spouse abuse and experiencing physical abuse: A "double whammy"? *Journal of Family Violence*, 4(2), 197–209.

[52] Edleson, J. L. (2000). *Should childhood exposure to adult domestic violence be defined as child maltreatment under the law?* [On-line]. Available: http://www. mincava.umn.edu/link/documents/shouldch/ shouldch.shtml.

[53] Edleson, J. L. (2003). Should childhood exposure to adult domestic violence be defined as child maltreatment under the law? *Juvenile and Family Justice Today*, 12(2), 12–14; Baker, L. L., Jaff e, P. G., Berkowitz, S. J., & Berkman, M. (2002); Goodmark, L. (2002). Assessing and treating child victims of domestic violence. *Child Law Practice, 21*(10), 149– 153.

[54] Gun Control Act of 1968, Pub. L. No. 90–618 (1968); 18 U.S.C. § 921 et seq. (2003); Mitchell, D., & Carbon, S. B. (2002). Firearms and domestic violence: A primer for judges. *Journal of the American Judges Association, 39*(2), 32–43.

[55] The Violence Against Women Act of 1994, 18 U.S.C. § 2265 (1994).

[56] Keeping Children and Families Safe Act of 2003, Pub. L. No. 108–36, Title I, Section 114(b) (2003).

[57] *In re Nicholson, et al.* 181 F. Supp. 2d 182, 188 (2002).

[58] *Daubert v. Merrell Dow Pharmaceuticals, Inc.*, 509 U.S. 579 (1993); *Kumho Tire Co. v. Carmichael*, 526 U.S. 137 (1999); *General Electric Co. v. Joiner*, 522 U.S. 136 (1997).

[59] American Bar Association. (1999a). *ABA Model Code of Judicial Conduct*, Canon 3B(7). Chicago, IL: Author.

[60] Sagatun, I. J., & Edwards, L. P. (Eds.). (1995). Expert witnesses in child abuse cases. In *Child abuse and the legal system* (pp. 209–228). Chicago, IL: Nelson-Hall; Ceci, S., & Bruck, M. (1995). *Jeopardy in the courtroom*. Washington, DC: American Psychological Association; Poole, D., & Lamb, M. (1999). *Investigative interviews of children*. Washington, DC: American Psychological Association; Walker, A. G. (1999). *Questioning of children: A linguistic perspective*. Washington, DC: American Bar Association; Ceci, S. J., & Bruck, M. (2000). Why judges must insist on electronically preserved recordings of child interviews. *Court Review, 2*, 10–12; Crossman, A. M., Powell, M. B., Principe, G. F., & Ceci, S. J. (2002). Child testimony in custody cases: A review. *Journal of Forensic Psychology Practice, 2*(1), 1–31.

[61] *Idaho v. Wright*, 497 U.S. 805 (1990).

[62] *Iowa v. Coy*, 487 U.S. 1012 (1988); *Maryland v. Craig*, 497 U.S. 836 (1990).

[63] National Conference of Commissioners on Uniform State Laws. (2002).

[64] National Conference of Commissioners on Uniform State Laws. (2005). *Child Witness Testimony by Alternative Methods Act* [On-line]. Available: http:// www.nccusl.org/Update/ActSearchResults.aspx.

[65] *Iowa v. Coy*, 487 U.S. 1012 (1988); *Maryland v. Craig*, 497 U.S. 836 (1990).

[66] National Conference of Commissioners on Uniform State Laws. (2002).

[67] National Conference of Commissioners on Uniform State Laws. (2002).

[68] Edwards, L. P. (1992). The juvenile court and the role of the juvenile court judge. *Juvenile and Family Court Journal, 42*(2), 30–32.

[69] American Bar Association. (1999b). *ABA Model Code of Judicial Conduct*, Canon 3B(4), 3B(5) and Commentary, 3B(6). Chicago, IL: Author.

[70] U.S. Department of Health and Human Services, ACF. (2004) *General fi ndings from the Federal Child and Family Services Review* [On-line]. Available: http://www.acf.hhs.gov/programs/cb/cwrp/results/ statefi ndings/genfi ndings04/genfi ndings04.pdf.

[71] Hardin, M. (2002a*). Child and Family Services Reviews (CFSRs): How judges, court administrators, and attorneys should be involved* [On-line]. Available: http://www.abanet.org/child/courtimp.html.

[72] Hardin, M. (2002b). *How and why to involve the courts in your Child and Family Services Review (CFSR): Suggestions for agency administrators* [Online]. Available: http://www.abanet.org/child/ courtimp.html.

[73] Atwood, T. C., & Ravenel, V. R. (2005). Performance measures for courts: The next step in foster care reform. *Adoption Advocate* [On-line]. Available: http://www.adoptioncouncil.org/documents/ Adoption_Advocate_Vol_No_1_06_05.pdf.

[74] Fiermonte, C., & Sidote Salyers, N. (2005). *Improving outcomes together* [On-line]. Available: http:// jeritt.msu.edu/Documents/ABA_ Collaboration_Final_06-21 -05.pdf.

[75] Hardin, M. (2002b).

[76] Atwood, T. C., & Ravenel, V. R. (2005).

[77] Hardin, M. (2002a); National Child Welfare Resource Center on Legal and Judicial Issues. (2005). *Top ten ways legal professionals can help with CFSRs* [On-line]. Available: http://www.abanet.org/child/ courtimp.html.

[78] Hardin, M. (2002b).

[79] Hardin, M. (2002b).

[80] Pew Commission on Children in Foster Care. (2005). *About the Pew Commission on Children in Foster Care* [On-line]. Available: http://pewfostercare. org/about.

[81] Fiermonte, C., & Sidote Salyers, N. (2005).

[82] Fiermonte, C., & Sidote Salyers, N. (2005).

[83] Fiermonte, C., & Sidote Salyers, N. (2005).

[84] Fiermonte, C., & Sidote Salyers, N. (2005).

[85] U. S. Department of Health and Human Services, ACF. (2003). *Instructions for States applying for court improvement program funds for fi scal years 2003–2006* [On-line]. Available: http://www.acf.dhhs.gov/programs/cb/laws/pi/pi0304.htm.

[86] U. S. Department of Health and Human Services, ACF. (2005). *Court involvement in the Child and Family Services Review* [On-line]. http://www.acf.hhs. gov/programs/cb/laws. pdf.

[87] The Social Security Act of 1935, 42 U.S.C. 629*h*; The Defi cit Reduction Act of 2005, Pub. L. No. 109-171, Title VII, Section 7401 (2005); The Social Security Act of 1935, 42 U.S.C. Title IV-E and Title IV-B; U.S. Department of Health and Human Services, ACF. (2006). *Instructions for state courts applying for new Court Improvement Program funds for fi scal years (FYs) 2006-2010* (ACYF-CB-PI-0605). Washington, DC: Author; Ohl, J. E. (2006). *Testimony on reauthorization of three Programs: The Mentoring of Children of Prisoners Program, the Promoting Safe and Stable Families Program, and the Court Improvement Program* [On-line]. Available: http://www.hhs.gov/asl/ testify/t0605 1 0.html.

[88] Mentaberry, M. (1999, January). Model courts serve abused and neglected children. *OJJDP Fact Sheet.* Washington, DC: U.S. Department of Justice, OJP, Office of Juvenile Justice and Delinquency Prevention (OJJDP).

[89] Goldsmith, D. J. (2002). In the best interest of an Indian child: The Indian Child Welfare Act. *Juvenile and Family Court Journal, 53*(4), 9–17.

[90] Feller, J. N., Davidson, H. A., Hardin, M., & Horowitz, R. M. (1992). *Working With the courts in child protection* [On-line]. Available: http://www. childwelfare.gov/pubs/usermanuals/courts/index.cfm.

[91] U. S. Department of Justice, OJP, OJJDP. (2003). *Notice of solicitation for the Strengthening Abuse and Neglect Courts in America: Management Information Systems Project, 68 Fed. Reg. 14699–14705* [On-line]. Available: http://www.ojp.usdoj.gov/docs/SANCA. txt.

[92] National Council of Juvenile and Family Court Judges. (1999, October). Key principles for permanency planning for children. *Technical Assistance Brief* [On-line]. Available: http:// www.ncjfcj.org/images/stories/dept/ppcd/pdf/ tabriefkeyprinciples.pdf.

[93] Rottman, D. B., Casey, P., & Efkeman, H. (1998, February). *Court and community collaboration: Ends and means: A discussion paper* [On-line]. Available: http://www.courtinfo.ca.gov/programs/community/endsmeansfoot.htm.

CHAPTER SOURCES

The following chapters have been previously published:

Chapter 1 – This is an edited, excerpted and augmented edition of a United States Department of Health and Human Services, Administration for Children and Families, Administration for Children, Youth and Families Bureau, Office on Child Abuse and Negelct, User Manuel Series, dated 2003.

Chapter 2 – This is an edited, excerpted and augmented edition of a United States Department of Health and Human Services, Administration for Children and Families, Administration for Children, Youth and Families Bureau, Office on Child Abuse and Negelct, User Manuel Series, dated 2003.

Chapter 3 – This is an edited, excerpted and augmented edition of a United States Department of Health and Human Services, Administration for Children and Families, Administration for Children, Youth and Families Bureau, Office on Child Abuse and Negelct, User Manuel Series, dated 2006.

INDEX

American Indian, 14
American Psychological Association, 325
anger, 102, 105, 154, 173, 183, 275
animals, 142
antecedents, 83
antisocial behavior, 11, 17, 204, 206
anxiety, 17, 20, 26, 105, 119, 137, 142, 207, 250, 268
appellate courts, 247, 248
appellate review, 247
appendix, 310
application, 221, 231, 255, 276
applied research, 296
argument, 136
Arizona, 82, 195, 302
Arkansas, 82, 195, 302
arrest, 12, 27, 53, 248, 257
Asian, 8, 14
assault, 7, 10, 44, 75, 126, 188, 201, 241, 242, 292
assessment tools, 146
assets, 255
assignment, 69, 221, 274
atmosphere, 67, 233
ATSA, 203
attachment, 3, 21, 35, 88, 96, 166, 168, 204, 246, 262, 312
attachment theory, 88
attacks, 105, 223, 287
attitudes, 18, 19, 21, 23, 71, 102, 145, 152, 153, 185, 287
authority, x, 38, 42, 43, 44, 55, 68, 74, 91, 92, 102, 103, 104, 113, 144, 153, 177, 187, 199, 211, 215, 216, 217, 218, 231, 236, 282, 289, 290, 291
autonomy, 42
availability, 27, 52, 130, 159, 164, 174, 274, 321
awareness, 29, 30, 31, 32, 45, 51, 77, 79, 101, 106, 136, 192, 194, 270, 296, 299, 301

B

babies, 72, 186, 289
back, 40, 57, 102, 106, 116, 136, 150, 158, 260, 261, 312
bail, 248
banks, 35
bargaining, 248, 250
barriers, 67, 68, 93, 170, 213, 216, 278, 279, 282, 311, 316, 323
basic needs, 2, 4, 9, 11, 39, 65, 73, 93, 105, 115, 120, 156, 157, 179, 187, 290
battery, 7, 44
beating, 74, 111, 187, 291
behavior modification, 166

behavioral problems, 26, 28
beliefs, 4, 9, 21, 93, 102, 134, 146, 152, 153, 157, 164, 167, 168, 207
benchmark, 57, 154
benefits, 64, 68, 106, 155, 162, 216, 226, 232, 253, 265, 322, 323
Best Practice, 218, 275, 278, 281
bias, 265
biological parents, 19, 20, 227, 254, 305, 307, 308
birth, 19, 21, 22, 23, 34, 42, 57, 64, 65, 97, 111, 127, 142, 152, 159, 227, 241
blame, 142, 168
blaming, 106, 136
bleeding, 25
blindness, 25
blocks, 244
bodily injury, 241, 242
body language, 140
body size, 139
bonding, 21, 96, 262, 312
boys, 14, 20, 202, 207
brain, 24, 25, 87, 126
brain damage, 24, 126
brain development, 25, 87
breakdown, 37, 86
breakfast, 158
broad spectrum, 29
brothers, 126, 158
buffer, 27, 74, 187, 291
burn, 122
burning, 74, 111, 187, 291
burnout, 178, 182, 183
burns, 8, 24, 111, 122
buttocks, 8, 116, 158, 261

C

campaigns, 30, 31, 45, 78, 79, 192, 193, 299, 300
Canada, 203
cancer, 26
candidates, 277
caregivers, 3, 4, 5, 15, 17, 22, 27, 33, 46, 54, 56, 57, 58, 59, 64, 111, 120, 121, 122, 128, 130, 134, 140, 141, 143, 145, 155, 156, 157, 171, 176, 200, 204, 319
caregiving, 34, 37
caretaker, 5, 6, 9, 71, 74, 102, 103, 121, 133, 184, 187, 248, 251, 265, 290
carrier, 259
case law, 6, 64, 217, 218
cell, 105, 144
Centers for Disease Control, 42
cerebral palsy, 25

I

M